Beyond The Bar

Sailing Ventures from a Suffolk River

Richard Roberts

Foreword by John McCarthy

Cover: *Premuda*
Artwork by C. Riley

2020 First Edition

Printed by
Leiston Press
Unit 1 -1b Masterlord Ind Est
Leiston
Suffolk
IP16 4JD
01728 833003
www.leistonpress.com

ISBN: 978-1-911311-60-7

© Richard Roberts

All rights reserved. No part of this book may be reproduced, stored in a retrieval system, or transmitted in any form or by any means electronic, mechanical, photocopying, recording or otherwise, without the prior permission of the author.

Reproduction photography by Jonathan Cheney

Dedication

This is for Wendy who gave me the Freedom of the Seas, and for our sons Jamie, Ralph and Don, who shared it with me.

Quantz at anchor 2019   Sean MacBride-Stuart

Contents

	Page
Acknowledgements and Apologies	9
Editorial Policy	11
Foreword	12
Introduction	14
Chapter 1 *Fore-runners* (Earliest records)	17
Chapter 2 *Trail-blazers* (early 1950s)	23
Chapter 3 *Round Holland, Round Britain* (later 1950s to early 60s)	29
Chapter 4 *Cockleshell Heroes* (1959 to early 1970s)	40
Chapter 5 *Departure and Landfall* (1967-72)	59
Chapter 6 *Coast to Coast* (late 1970s)	72
Chapter 7 *Four Ventures and a Rescue* (1981-82)	83
Chapter 8 *Ditch-crawlers and other cruises* (1983-86)	103
Chapter 9 *Maxis in the Med* (1986-89)	116
Chapter 10 *Round Brittany and Britain with Babaji* (1990-93)	138
Chapter 11 *Water music and war* (1990-92)	154
Chapter 12 *Orford to the Indies, and less far* (1996)	167
Chapter 13 *Routes into Russia* (1994-98)	178
Chapter 14 *Crossing Thresholds* (1999-2000)	191

Chapter 15 *Into the Baltic* (2001)   204

Chapter 16 *Canals and Castles* (2002)   227

Chapter 17 *To the World's End and Back* (2003-04)   240

Chapter 18 *Brazil and Back* (2003-04)   257

Chapter 19 *The Generation Game* (1992 to the present)   280

Chapter 20 *Katrina to St Petersburg* (2014)   291

Chapter 21 *Dinghy cruising (1996-2016)*   307

Chapter 22 *Pearly Miss to Westerly Typhoon* (1961- 2019)   319

Chapter 23 *Time Past and Time Future* (2010- 2019)   331

Last Word *From Hebe to Tahira* (1970- 2019)   339

Dates listed above are approximate and tend to overlap.

N.B. All locations approximate

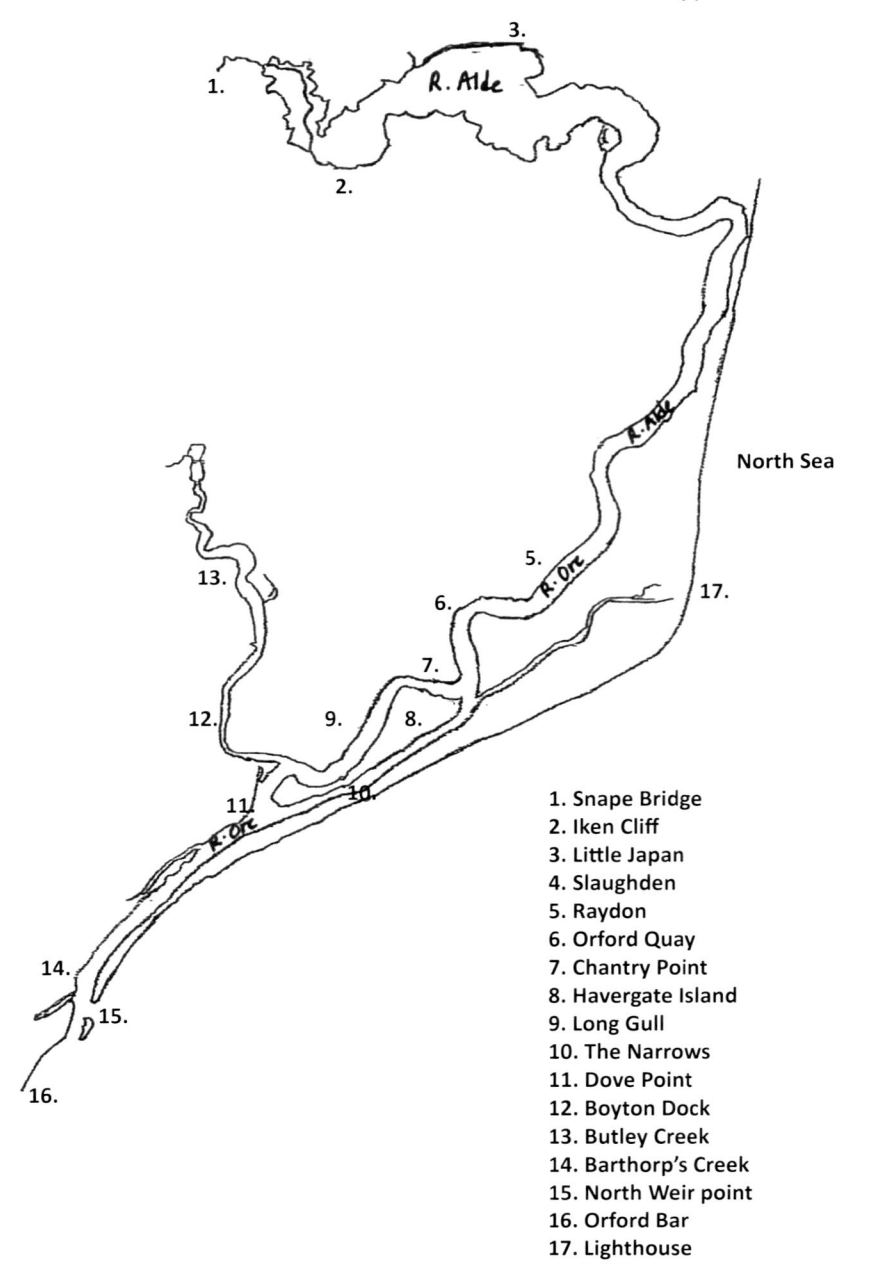

1. Snape Bridge
2. Iken Cliff
3. Little Japan
4. Slaughden
5. Raydon
6. Orford Quay
7. Chantry Point
8. Havergate Island
9. Long Gull
10. The Narrows
11. Dove Point
12. Boyton Dock
13. Butley Creek
14. Barthorp's Creek
15. North Weir point
16. Orford Bar
17. Lighthouse

N.B. All locations approximate

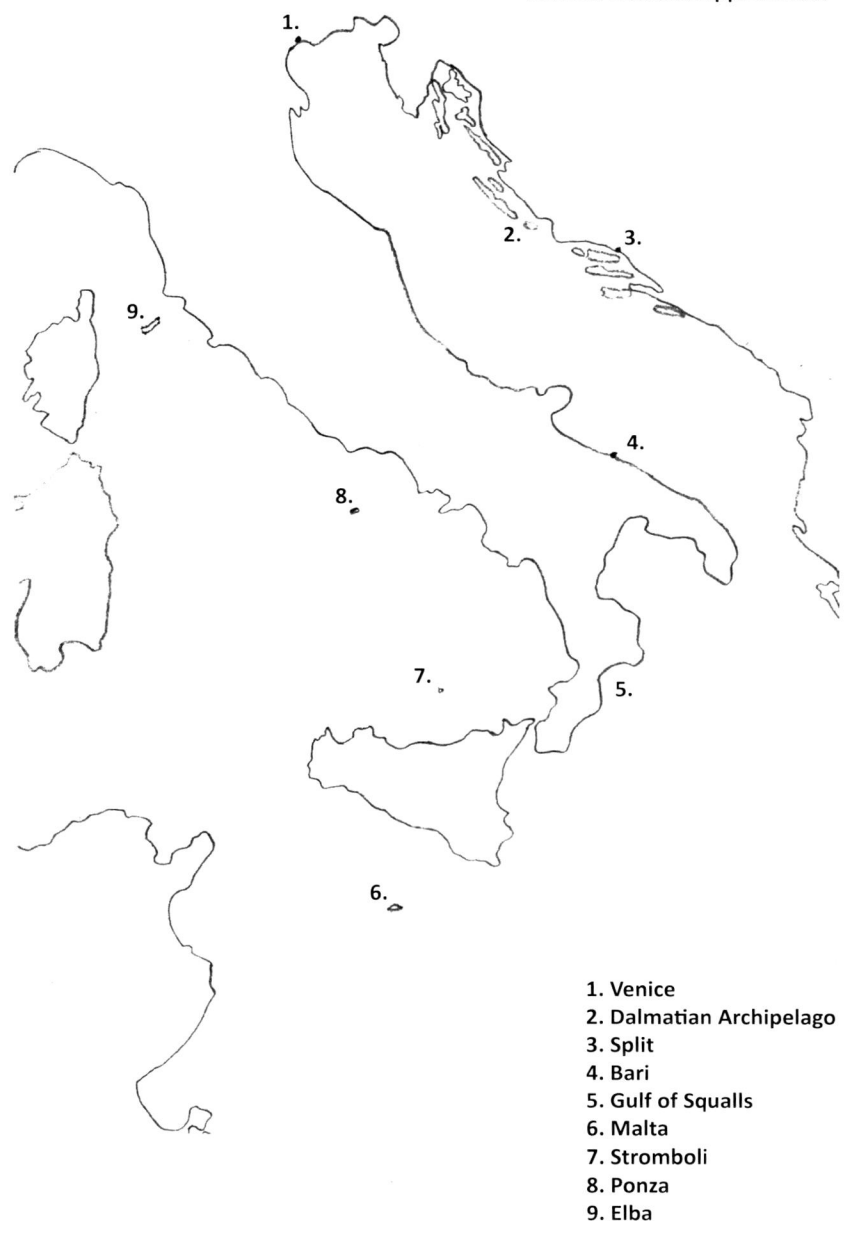

1. Venice
2. Dalmatian Archipelago
3. Split
4. Bari
5. Gulf of Squalls
6. Malta
7. Stromboli
8. Ponza
9. Elba

Acknowledgements and Apologies

I wish I could find the words to thank John McCarthy properly for his agreement to write the Foreword to this book, for finding the time to do so and for capturing the spirit and intention of it so well. I am equally grateful to James Robinson whose friendship with John brought this about.

I owe a particular debt to Charles Iliff, who encouraged the project from the outset and patiently read and corrected my errors throughout the process. He also undertook the onerous task of preparing the Index of Yachts. Monica Iliff often solved problems which my limited expertise on the keyword had failed to manage, as did Daisy Roberts in addition to her thorough scrutiny of the draft text and work on maps. This was reinforced by the scrupulous attention to syntax, punctuation and style provided, in red ink, by Ian Rowley, (a role reversal which both of us enjoyed). Even so, Jan Harber's proof-reading was indispensable and I most grateful to her.

The readiness of Derek Bingham to give advice in general and make valuable suggestions at key stages has been a great help. So too has been the involvement of Jonathan Cheney in the handling and presentation of illustrations. The early historical background of sailing in Orford owed much to the records originally compiled by the late Ray Maunder. Frank Craig and his sister Margaret Young provided all the material on the many voyages undertaken by their parents and the Craig family in the post-war era.

The whole book, of course, would have been impossible without many individual contributions, log extracts and memories. For these I am immensely grateful to Simon Baker, Florence and Sheena Barrow, Colin Barry, Chris Best, John Colvin, Susie Cooper, Fiona Cox, Liz Feibusch, Mike Finney and David 'Doc' Foreman, who not only allowed me to use extracts from his own book *Tuesday 'n Me* but was generous with time and discussion of important points. He also alerted me to the exploits of John Seymour in *Willynilly* and lent me the book.

Chris Gill and Caroline were major contributors, not only with regard to their own voyages but those of her parents. It would be impossible to do justice to the extraordinary cruising record of Ray Glaister and Margo without access to his logs of circumnavigations and Baltic voyaging provided by Malcolm Glaister and his sister Alison Ward. Sadly, only brief reference is available regarding the Millennium voyage in 2000 culminating, we believe, in returning via Archangel, the North Cape and the Arctic Circle.

Mary Goldin passed on important early memories of *Gudgeon* and Tom Griffin provided details of *Aimée* which I was glad to have. In addition to all the help offered by Charles Iliff, his accounts of significant voyages in his own boats and the influence which he had on the whole development of cruising activity based in Orford are central to this book. It is entirely appropriate that the picture of *Premuda* which hangs in Rosehill, should appear on the cover. This is also the point at which the willingness of the Royal Cruising Club to permit use of extracts from *Roving Commissions*, their annual publication, should be gratefully acknowledged.

It was a privilege to include reference to the voyages of David and Candy Masters in *Endeavor*. Sailing is never without risk and Howard Nash's account of *Wombat's* stormy North Sea crossing and the assistance of Aldeburgh lifeboat is a vivid reminder of this fact. Johnny Oakes witnessed this saga and shared his enjoyable memories of his Swedish trip with Nick Oglethorpe. The sailing experiences of the Pearce family range across the decades as well as round the coast and across the sea. Mike Redmond's account of *Martiena's* recent circumnavigation added value to a distinguished OSC list.

I am grateful to Jamie, Ralph and Don Roberts for countless happy times and for accompanying me on many a sea passage to ensure that this Duffer would not drown (Ransome readers will recognise the allusion). I am not only grateful to their mother for entrusting them to me at sea, and a lot more besides, but for tolerating the time I have spent on this book and not on other domestic or family obligations which she has undertaken instead. James Robinson's role as mentor and pilot is mentioned and highly valued by many contributors; modest accounts of a few of his own voyages only partially reflect his achievements. Dan Spinney well represents the influence of OSC through the generations and his company was one of the best features of my own Baltic summers.

Richard Waite's name occurs often; but the full extent of his development as a cruising yachtsman from boyhood to the present only becomes clear in the contribution which I deliberately held back to stand as a summary and epilogue. So too the Webb family, Jamie and his mother's reminiscences of *Melody* and his uncle Ken's of *Gudgeon* take us back and also forward through the years.

Finally I wish to thank Annie Lambert at the Leiston Press and the team responsible for producing *Beyond the Bar* with such helpful proficiency. If there are errors of fact or other faults, they are entirely mine. I also plead guilty to self-indulgence in re-living my sailing life in the course of these pages with a plea of defence that otherwise they would not have been written. I am sure there are other stories I ought to have sought out or followed up, other boats and sailors who deserved mention. That would require another volume and a year or two extra, which, perhaps, I might not have to spare.

Editorial Policy

To minimise inconsistency in the format of contributions from different sources the following policy has been implemented so far as possible.

'Changes from the main narrative to contributions by individual sailors are indicated (as in this paragraph) by the use of single quotation marks. Longer, continuous passages from such sources are separated (as here) by an extra line space from the previous narrative and similarly when it resumes.'

Double quotation marks are used for direct speech or official notices when quoted. Boat names are in italics; also book and magazine titles.

All times are given as 1125, 2215 etc. Dates are as August 6th 1979.

Numerals below 10 are normally in words e.g. five knots, except before abbreviations 5mph, 6ft or when two numerals are used close together in the same context as in 5 to 15 knots. Any number involving decimal points should be 4.5 etc.

Wind speeds and directions follow Met Office usage: winds in lower case, speeds as numerals, e.g. south-west force 4 or 5. Points of compass are usually in lower case except for major geographical areas like West Coast of Scotland or when wind directions are abbreviated e.g. NE or WSW.

The use of – is usually preferred to … but the latter is used to indicate that words or a continuous passage have been left out within a quotation.

The following abbreviations often occur. VHF for Very High Frequency, RDF for Radio Direction Finder, GPS for Global Positioning System and AIS for Automatic Identification System, NM for nautical miles. CEVNI stands for the Certificate required for Navigation on European Inland Waters etc.

Despite this statement I cannot guarantee that it has been followed without a single deviation.

Foreword

Reading these cruising tales from Orford sailors takes me right back to the delights of the Ore, Deben and other East Coast rivers and creeks I explored when I belonged to the OSC.

Orford is such a special place and for me, even just sitting on the boat at her mooring was a joy. I have a photo on the wall of my London home. It's of me in the dinghy in Butley River. My wife, Anna, took it from our yacht *Elan's* cockpit as we lay at anchor. We were the only boat there. Ten minutes earlier rain had been hammering down on the saloon roof in what sounded like a tropical storm. Emerging afterwards, the high and wide East Anglian sky suddenly cleared and, it being low tide, we were surrounded by acres and acres of mud. I had an extraordinary feeling of being somewhere utterly wild and remote, on a tributary of some vast exotic waterway, the Amazon, Mekong or Zambezi perhaps.

There were many other times afloat filled with the same magical sense of escape and freedom. And often they were shared with other members of the OSC. Sailing in the company of, rafting up with friends like Peter Norris and James Robinson on *Petronella*, 'Doc' David Foreman on *Tuesday*, ships and crews who feature in several of the stories that Richard Roberts has brought together in *Beyond the Bar*. The camaraderie and support offered me by OSC sailors was truly special.

I only started sailing in my late thirties and through wonderful luck it was at Orford that I did my day skipper course with Philippe Taylor. I was equally fortunate to get my own yacht and have a mooring at Orford.

Philippe gave me a great start and although my sailing skills improved over the years, I often reflected that I'd have managed my ship much better if I'd been lucky enough to have been at Orford in my youth and learned to sail dinghies there. Richard rightly pays tribute to those who have instructed and advised so many Orford sailors over the years.

James Robinson is mentioned a fair few times for the advice and support he offers fellow sailors and certainly he was my great mentor as a proud, but inexperienced yacht owner. On one of our first outings together on *Elan*, he kept a watchful, reassuring eye on me as I tacked down river from the quay through the moored boats. All was going well until I put in a tack just beside my own mooring. Suddenly we lurched to an abrupt stop. And I found myself looking about in panic a confusion as *Elan* sat there, sails full, but moving not an inch. I looked at James in utter alarm.

"Well", he said calmly, "that's a novel way of picking up the mooring – with your rudder!"

I started jumping about, thinking I must dive over the side and cut us free. James gently put a hand on my shoulder and with a twinkle in his eye, said,

"You're not hurt, I'm not hurt, and *Elan* seems fine and certainly isn't going anywhere. Why don't you get the sails down and stowed while I put the kettle on? Then we can make a cunning plan to get out of this intriguing predicament."

It was a fantastic lesson from a very wise sailor and lovely man. Captain Cock Up had come aboard, but no damage had been done (except to my pride) and we'd got an unexpected challenge to work out together.

The cruise logs included here bring out not only the excitement of sailing and cruising, but are also evidence of the fact that, even with expertise (far greater than mine), things can go awry. But rather than mistakes being rewarded with criticism or disdain, they are acknowledged as bound to happen and instead of being judged failures, are seen as opportunities for learning and for honing skills.

Those attitudes, coupled with a very relaxed and friendly attitude all round, are what I remember of the atmosphere and ethos which flowed through the OSC and all its members. Richard has captured all that brilliantly in this book.

Many years ago, when I was kept in bleak underground cells as a hostage in Lebanon, I used to fantasize about escaping, making my way to the Mediterranean coast, stealing a boat and sailing to freedom. Of course, back then I had no idea how to actually sail, but the dream of being out on the water, free and relying only on myself and the power of nature was a powerful antidote to the reality of being confined and subject to the power of men with guns.

Sailing at Orford brought those dreams to life and while I can't claim to have crossed the North Sea, cruised to and from the Med – let alone covered the Atlantic solo, as David Foreman did, I do have many happy memories of my adventures sailing from Orford.

It's good to know that should I ever be caught up somewhere unpleasant again, or even just in life's dull moments, I will always be able to escape the current tedium or difficulty by conjuring recollections of Butley River, Pyefleet Creek, the Walton Backwaters and the times spent with fellow sailors from the OSC.

And now, thanks to *Beyond the Bar*, I also have the stories of other ships, their crews and voyages to daydream about. Thank you, Richard, for this history of a great sailing club!

John McCarthy

Introduction. The *Dulcibella* Effect

This book is a companion and follow-up to *Ten Footers and All That* published in 2017. It continues and extends the story of sailing in Orford and across the seas. It should also have wider interest for those who enjoy cruising in relatively small yachts whether they belong to Orford or not.

During my sailing life, which began on the Ore in 1945, the number of sea-going craft moored here has increased steadily, from one or two, which rarely left the river, to over 50. Some are content with short coastal trips; many have made frequent North Sea or Channel crossings; others have ranged significantly further, across the Atlantic, into the Mediterranean, through inland Europe, or into the Arctic, across the Baltic to Russia or round Britain.

I am not suggesting that this development is exceptional; every east coast river and most clubs have seen an increase in moored craft or marina berths, although the Ore and Alde estuary has avoided the latter. Demographic and social trends have played their part; post-war generations have enjoyed peace and relative prosperity; life-spans have increased and many have benefited from generous pensions and years of active retirement. Nevertheless the history of cruising from Orford has several unusual features.

Orford Sailing Club or the Orford Dabchick Sailing Club, as it was known for the first 50 years of its existence, has never been a large, fashionable institution, with a bar, carpeted floors and its own boatman. Our yacht skippers often sail single-handed, or with minimal crews. Their boats tend to be of modest size, 30 feet perhaps, or less on the waterline. This has not prevented a high number of significant and ambitious voyages beyond the ordinary range of East Coast sailing. This is perhaps reflected in the proportion of members elected to the Royal Cruising Club which currently matches or exceeds that of several older, larger and smarter clubs that fly blue ensigns.

So my primary purpose is to tell the story of this development with accounts of representative voyages, some long, some short, with their highs and lows. In the process I shall explore the motivation and often differing temperaments of the skippers and crews involved. As the Acknowledgements show I have depended to a great extent on their individual reminiscences and contributions. Limitations of space have sadly forced me to leave out some stories or fail to mention boats and owners worthy of mention. The stories told here should be regarded as representative of the rest.

Interwoven with their varied experiences, I shall be re-living some of my own sailing odyssey, with a very small 'o'. This is in gratitude to the intense satisfaction that I have enjoyed from fifty years of sailing two small yachts, 21 and 25 feet in length overall respectively, both with the simplest Bermudan sloop rig and rather basic equipment. These pleasures have been accompanied, heightened even, by discomfort, terror, a queasy stomach and the determination 'never to do this again'; emotions always swiftly forgotten as soon as calm waters and a safe haven had been reached. I shall not hold it against any reader who prefers to skip these passages and move on.

For me this all began in my early teens. It would have been earlier if wartime restrictions on the river Ore had not prevented any leisure sailing. I believe the seeds had already been sown in my earliest years by steamship voyages across the world as a colonial child, from and to the Pacific and across to East Africa before I was seven.

Then, soon after my 13th birthday, my father gave me Erskine Childers' *The Riddle of the Sands*. I still have that battered copy and I have lost count of the times I have read it since. Fifty years later the book accompanied me on the first of several explorations of the Friesian Islands and a little later, in the wake of Childers himself and the *Dulcibella,* a converted lifeboat in which his fictional hero sailed through the Kiel Canal into Danish waters and beyond.

No doubt I shared this inspiration with hundreds of other yachtsmen, some may also have nursed a boyhood ambition, like mine, to become a naval officer. Fortunately for the Royal Navy, and probably for me, this was thwarted in December 1944. I somehow contrived to pass the entrance examination and even to satisfy the fearsome collection of admirals, captains and headmasters at the Interview Board, held that last winter of the war in the land-locked grandeur of Worcester College Oxford. Then a medical examination predicted, correctly, that I would need glasses before I was 15, which put paid to a naval career. It is possible that I have been compensating for this disappointment ever since, in command of the dinghies and other vessels which I have owned ever since my first ten footer *Ariel* was launched in 1946.

Those who, like me, started sailing in childhood or early youth, owed a great debt to their mentors, parents or to qualified instructors, although there are also notable instances of much later induction among cruising sailors. So it is my further aim to show how early training in Orford, whether structured or informal, has influenced the lives, sometimes the careers, marriages and families of successive generations of boys and girls. Several younger club members have crossed the Atlantic under sail, others have manned Tall Ships or had other noteworthy sailing adventures. This has especially been the case since regular annual courses began in the 1970s led by Ray Maunder, then by Liz Feibusch and her successors up to the present. Earlier still, junior racing in ten foot dinghies under the guidance of Elizabeth Russell, Tony Lingard and others, watched over by the Brinkleys with a critical yet benevolent eye, had laid important foundations.

In those post-war years the Orford Dabchick Sailing Club was essentially concerned with sailing and racing dinghies or half-decked boats up to 18 feet in length. The classic 'Bombay Tomtits', of which there were three or four on the water each summer, were the pride of the club, but there were other similar craft like Dr Craig's Victory class *Sandpiper* and Gus Hacon's *Lady Sarah*. These and several 14ft dinghies, notably Joyce and Stephen Johnston's thoroughbred International 14 *Plain Jane* formed a small core fleet which had also sailed before the war. Racing took place regularly on Saturday afternoons in summer based on an arbitrary and idiosyncratic handicap system. This did not detract from keen rivalry.

For me, and I believe for a good many others, it was not just the racing, but the general sailing experience that mattered. We explored the river from Iken, or even Snape, down to the sea and as far up Butley Creek as we could go. Our dinghies, at least in our imagination, cruised far and wide across longitudes and centuries. Nosing into shallow waters or along twisting channels marked by errant withies was the stuff of adventure. Decades later, navigating the approaches to St. Valery sur Somme, following the meanders of the channel to Schiermonikoog or crossing the inland tidal thresholds south of Norderney, I felt surprisingly at home.

I believe one explanation for the enthusiasm and success of cruising based in Orford is to be found in the varied shape and shoreline of our estuary itself. Shingle banks give way to river walls, fronted by saltings. Gradually low hills, woods and sandy cliffs appear. Turning inland, the upper reaches take on a more homely character. Or is it the location of Orford itself? The river mouth lies only five miles south, and the beckoning sea is visible from most upstairs windows, less than a mile distant as the gull flies, beyond Orfordness. Sadly the lighthouse beam no longer swings inland and far out to sea. But the sturdy tower, banded red and white, still stands defiant on our eastern shore.

All these influences probably combine. Even more significant, however, will be the individual characters of the men and women who have headed out beyond the Orford Haven buoy over the last half century or more. Their stories are the heart and soul of this book.

1. Forerunners

Imagine Orford Regatta sponsored by Royalty and ships full of spectators from Ipswich coming to watch the racing. This is not a fantasy. I cannot produce evidence of cruising activity based on this river before the 1920s but it is well established that yacht racing was indeed a feature of the Orford Regatta held yearly from 1876 until 1913.

According to newspaper reports, quoted by Ray Maunder in his invaluable file of the Orford Sailing Club History, the first Orford Regatta took place in 1876 and did involve yacht racing. It was typical of many such events up and down the coast, quite a grand affair, supported by patronage from the local gentry and aristocracy. The Subscribers in 1881 included HRH the Prince of Wales, who was friendly with Sir Richard Wallace of Sudbourne Hall. Our own Wallace Cup was presented to the Regatta by Lady Wallace. A full page advertisement for the 1888 Regatta gives the flavour of the occasion with a 'Band, Concert and Fireworks'. Although billed as a one-day event, yacht racing sometimes extended over two days or more, involving races to or from Lowestoft and in Hollesley Bay. Other reports even mention paddle-steamers bringing spectators from Ipswich.

In the 1888 advertisement the 'Sailing Match for Yachts' is limited to those 'not to exceed 5 tons' which is not to say that these or larger craft did not undertake coastal or more distant cruises as many Corinthian sailors, like Erskine Childers or E.F. Knight, did in the Victorian and Edwardian eras. The History File also contains an interesting report from the *East Anglian Daily Times* dated August 18th 1921, under the heading 'Orford Regatta A Fine Day's Sport'.

In addition to all the races for sailing and rowing dinghies, as well as swimming for different age groups of men and boys (but no women or girls), the first two races listed in this newspaper account were Handicap Races for Yachts. One was for '7 tons and under TM' (Thames measurement) with a single entry *Dona*, which 'sailed over', the other for '5 tonsTM and under', which attracted six starters. Both courses were 'Twice Round Havergate Island'. The latter race, for the Frazer Cup, is described in some detail quoting handicaps and owners' names.

'At the start *Andrum* ,1 min, (T. Glover) was right on the line, with *Paulina,* 6 mins, (P.M. Faraday). *Andrum* kept her lead and gradually drew away, finally by nearly five minutes on the actual time, and securing the cup, but losing on handicap to *Narcissus,* 14 mins, (Dr A. Travers Kevern). After the race *Paulina* entered a protest against *Andrum* on the ground that she dropped her dinghy after, instead of before the five minute gun.'

Sadly, the outcome of the protest is not revealed, nor an explanation of why the cup could be won by *Andrum* when *Narcissus* beat her on handicap. The other starters listed were *Gemma,* scratch, (B. de Quincey); *Dewdrop,* 5 secs, (Sir Ernest Rowney) and *Scylla,* 4 mins 30 secs, (Mr Rowney). At least two of these names, de Quincey and Rowney, albeit spelt Roney, I remember myself, from a whole generation later, as belonging to prominent Aldeburgh yachtsmen in the late 1940s. This reinforces my suspicion that yachts, as opposed to dinghies, were more often located upriver than at Orford in that era.

Interestingly, there was a separate Handicap Race over the same course for 'Fishing Boats not exceeding 15 tons TM', which I guess would have been a fine sight even with only three starters 'with a nice strong breeze from the south-east.' This proved to be a runaway win for the scratch boat *Wenonah* (G. Stoker) which in the report's words 'would have proved a worthy opponent for some of the yachts racing'. The other owners mentioned; G. Brinkley, sailing *Mary,* 12 mins, and Smy (no initial) in *Anne Marie,* 18 mins, were plainly Orford men, and we know that Charles Stoker would become first Commodore of Orford Dabchick Sailing Club three years later. I suspect 'C' not 'G' Stoker was the right initial in this case.

Again, if my memory can be relied upon, in the decade after the end of World War II not many keel yachts with cabins and cruising capacity were moored in Orford. Indeed the only one which I can still visualise in 1945 or '46 was *Siwash,* belonging to Mr Eve. Thomas Eve was a Maldon man who had come to Orford in the 1920s to run the original Butley Creek oyster fishery for Macfisheries. Like Charlie Stoker, who had brought his smack round from Mersea to help with the oysters, he was a founding member of the Orford Dabchick Sailing Club. The Eve family lived in Rosehill, tucked away between Market Hill and Broad Street. *Siwash* and the Eves form a link between the earliest days of ODSC and the post-war era. Rosehill, now owned by the Iliff family, has enjoyed a pivotal role as a nursery for Orford cruising as will be revealed later.

Thomas Eve had been a notable sailor in his time, aboard the famous *Jolie Brise;* in his own yacht *Ultra* he had cruised from Brest to the Baltic. *Ultra* was replaced in Orford by *Hind,* then finally by *Siwash,* which was actually his very first boat, re-discovered, bought back and given a cabin top for his latter years. He was also an early member of The Royal Cruising Club. Perhaps for that reason visiting yachtsmen would find their way to Rosehill for a bath, often enjoying a meal and a night ashore and always plenty of sailing talk. According to his son Martin's reminiscences, cruising days were past; he recalls just once, his only 'cruise' with his father, when he was six, sailing down the Gulls and up Butley Creek, where he climbed into one of the woollen sleeping-bags while they spent the night at anchor.

There is, however, a mysterious reference in the *History of the Royal Cruising Club* to 'one of the club's younger members living in Orford' – mysterious because the date is 1930, when Martin was only six but his father probably over 40. Did this still put him in the younger age-group or was there another Orford RCC member, identity unknown? Whoever it was, this source tells us:

'Being determined to attend the Meet (on the Helford River in Cornwall) he left his home in Orford, Suffolk, to travel the 450 miles in a small motor car. He had procured two old wheels from a disused aeroplane and attached them to a cradle specially constructed to carry the boat which he towed behind the car, sleeping at night by the roadside. No mishaps were recorded and his log was not entered for the competition, perhaps because his entire cruise was, as it were, under power.'

This very early example of trailer-sailing does sound like an Eve exploit. The aeroplane wheels presumably came from Orfordness – with or without permission.

In 1941, still under 18, Martin falsified his age and joined up straight from Bryanston School as an Ordinary Seaman, serving on a corvette in the Atlantic and Mediterranean until he was commissioned in 1943. He became a navigating officer on the Hunt class destroyer HMS *Talybont*, notably on D Day in support of the American landings, dangerously close inshore off Omaha Beach. A fellow officer described him as an excellent seaman, 'unusually for an RNVR officer – his father having taught him all that a small-boat sailor needed to know'.

When peace came, Martin studied at Cambridge, where he was active in left-wing politics and read history. He worked in publishing and before long had set up his own Merlin Press, again with a strong left-leaning tendency. Later he also established Seafarer Books, reflecting his sea-going and sailing experience. In 1965 this received fresh, practical expression by the acquisition and restoration of *Privateer*, a traditional gaff-rigged sailing smack, hailing from Boston. Although Martin never lived in Orford after leaving Cambridge, *Privateer* quite often returned to the river with Martin, his family or friends. He told her story in his own publication *An Old Gaffer's Tale* from Seafarer Books. Although no longer a member of ODSC or OSC, he can be fairly counted among the forerunners of Orford's cruising history by virtue of his heritage and early training.

Siwash, as I remember her, was about 20 feet overall, with a rounded coach roof and cut away bow. She was painted black, which, together with her lines, gave her a piratical look, adding to the thrill when Victor Brinkley, who looked after her, sent me aboard to pump her out once or twice. The cabin smelt alluringly of salt water and old rope. I seem to recall bare bunk boards, she was furnished at best as a day-boat; I do not remember seeing her under sail, although Martin mentions sailing her with his father until he was 84, which would have been in this post-war period.

Even a year or two later, when our friends, the Davidsons, launched their brand-new *Merlin* at Whistocks in Woodbridge and brought her to Orford, I do not believe she was used for coastal cruises, still less across the North Sea. This did not detract from the excitement of sleeping aboard her, as I did for a night or two in 1950, conjuring in my imagination future voyages, even, perhaps in a boat of my own. Such dreams may have been stimulated by another present, at Christmas 1947, like *The Riddle of the Sands* a present from my father and still lurking among my books.

This was *Let's go Cruising* by Eric Hiscock, then editor of *The Yachting Year*, previously of the *Yachtsman*, and owner at that stage of *Wanderer II* a gaff-rigged cutter of four and a half tons. I have since discovered how distinguished his cruising history became. With his wife, Susan, whose keen eyesight was essential to compensate for his own poor vision, he ranged widely across the oceans doing several circumnavigations in the somewhat larger *Wanderers III* and *IV*. He also wrote a succession of books about cruising.

His 1947 book was intended to offer practical help to anyone keen to start cruising with little previous experience. He deals with choice of boat, seamanship and heavy weather sailing, pilotage and navigation, and choice of cruising grounds. The latter assume the limitations of a month at the most in summer. He ranges along the South Coast, across to Brittany and the Channel Islands, north to South-west Ireland and up to the West of Scotland as far as Skye. He also describes what he regards as the rather different delights and challenges of the East Coast, shoals and swash-ways, muddy rivers and creeks, but with, I felt, less enthusiasm and direct experience.

For me, at the age of 16, all this could only be a distant dream. I wonder, now, if my father was compensating for some of his own. As a boy he had sailed a good deal under the tutelage of his older brother, a naval cadet and then officer, on summer holidays in Pembrokeshire. Later life in the Colonial Service only offered occasional opportunities in tropical waters. Once, outside the reef off Zanzibar with my 18 year-old sister as crew, their borrowed dinghy capsized in a sudden squall. By great good fortune the moment was spotted and they were rescued, after dark, by a searching launch, luckily before the sharks found them, taking turns on the inverted hull. Now retired, with my education still a drain on finances, anything bigger than my ten footer, or the flat-bottomed rowing dinghy he built for himself, was beyond reach.

Ten years later, however, when we were living at Waldringfield, he did manage to buy the middle-aged *Esmeralda* for a few hundred pounds. She was about 20 feet in length, gaff-rigged, with a small cabin and a rusty but serviceable petrol engine. For the last four years of my father's life he was happy to tinker with her where she lay in a mud berth, approached by a crooked tidal channel through saltings below our house. It was our own private harbour, but only accessible for two hours or so either side of High Water. Perhaps a dozen times a year, usually when I was at home to help, *Esmeralda* was manoeuvred out into the Deben proper and sailed upstream towards Woodbridge or down to Ramsholt and back. We may have ventured within sight of Felixstowe Ferry, but never out to sea.

Esmeralda had to be sold soon after my father died in 1961, but by a happy chance I mentioned her to the late Geoffrey Ingram-Smith a few years ago. "Well," he said, "I remember her well. She was built before the war for my father, and what's more I've still got a tiller that belonged to her. You must have it." So I now possess this heavy iron tiller, which I have lovingly repainted to hang over the door to my shed in the garden.

At this point in my life visits to Orford were infrequent and brief; I was out of touch with the sailing scene on the Ore. Once, in 1955, I was thrilled to sail with the Webb family aboard *Gudgeon*, their graceful 42 foot Bermudan-rigged yawl, from the Deben round to Orford. We already admired *Gudgeon* from her occasional visits to Orford under the previous ownership of the Culmers, a Woodbridge family whom we knew slightly. She was everything of which I, or my father, could ever dream. But it would be nearly 20 years before I sailed my own boat, half that size, into the Ore.

Ralph Webb had begun to visit Orford soon after the war because of his naval service and friendship with Dr Craig, who regularly spent holidays with his family in the Yacht House (now known as the Pavilion). This RNVR background was a common factor among their generation and the relatively few yacht owners on the Suffolk rivers in that era. It was evident in Waldringfield, where Jack Jones designed yachts, living and working near the Quay, opposite the Maybush. On the disastrous Dieppe Raid he had been severely wounded, when commanding a Rescue Launch, but steered her home strapped to the wheel. For this he was awarded the DSO. Nearly all the yachtsmen I recall meeting about that time had similar war experience, although I never heard them talk about it.

George Arnott, historian of the Suffolk estuaries, was older. His beautiful pilot cutter *Atlanta* lay on a mooring in the reach known as The Rocks, downriver towards Ramsholt; she was another object of my envy and admiration. I was invited aboard once, but never when she was under sail. It is, however, no coincidence that he, as a prominent local estate agent, and men like Dan Craig and Ralph Webb, all had established careers and were able to acquire and maintain boats of a certain size. I could only hope and dream that I might follow their example.

2. Trail-blazers

Until 1953 the Craig family, based every summer at the Yacht House, which we now call the Pavilion, were content to sail Dr Craig's Victory class *Sandpiper*, their Alde 15 footer *Dido* and the ten foot dinghy *Puffin*, no 8. By 1953, the year of the Coronation, they were feeling the urge to venture further, and *Chaperone* was bought. She had been converted from a sailing lifeboat designed for beach-launching, built in Yorkshire over 60 years before. During the conversion the centreboard had been removed in the interest of greater space below; combined with her gaff ketch rig and large propeller this resulted in very poor windward performance until the fitting of a folding propeller made for improvement. On the plus side, she was a good sea boat.

In view of her historic role some further details deserve quotation from the description sent to me by Dr Craig's son, Captain Frank Craig RN retd:

'She had a very heavy wooden mast in a tabernacle and both main and mizen mast could be lowered using rope tackles. She carried a jib on the bowsprit, a staysail at the stem head; gaff main and gaff mizen sheeted to a bumpkin. Originally fitted with a tiller, which had a kink in it to accommodate the mizen mast, my father converted her to wheel steering. The wheel was mounted on the mizen tabernacle driving a drum with wire ropes to a yoke on the top of the rudder. Below, she had a Baby Blake toilet and a pipe cot in the forepeak, two good berths in the fore cabin and two settee berths in the saloon. The galley with a two-burner gas cooker (not gimballed) was just inside the companion way. She was fitted with a Morris Commodore (converted lorry) engine, housed under the cockpit sole, which was at times very temperamental due to damp and oiled up plugs, in later years this was changed to a diesel engine and a larger fuel tank.'

It does not seem that Dr Craig waited long before his first serious voyage. Nor did he undertake a shorter coastal shakedown cruise either. Frank has provided this account:

'*Chaperone's* first outing in father's ownership was in spring 1954 crewed by my father, Dan Craig, mother, Phyllis, and Ralph Webb. Peggy Webb joined them in Hook of Holland having crossed by the ferry. Dan and Ralph were great friends having both served as RNVR officers in HMS *Dido* during the war. Setting out for Holland on May22nd, they had little or no wind and had to motor most of the way, entering the New Waterway at the Hook of Holland 26 hours after leaving Orford Quay. Compared to today, navigation equipment was rather rudimentary, chart (black and white and depths in fathoms), compass, towed Walker log, lead line and a Beme-Loop Radio DF set. Having cleared customs and had a good night's sleep, they made their way up the New Waterway to Rotterdam.

Next day they were up early for the passage through the canals to Delft; initially this involved a lock into the Rijn-Ship canal and five bridges in quick succession. At some bridges a wooden shoe was slung out on the end of a fishing line for the toll – 1.5 cents or 3c per ton (12 or 14c for *Chaperone)*! One railway bridge caused some delay as it was difficult to get the times of opening in advance. They found Delft a beautiful and friendly city. A visit to the church, where it was possible to climb two thirds of the way up the tower gave a magnificent view over the flat countryside. Passage round Delft passed many well-kept gardens stretching right down to the canal, the road bridges opened promptly as did the first railway bridge, probably because three large barges were also waiting for it. Not so lucky at the next one, where they had to wait two hours, finally mooring at a small boatyard at Leidschendam.'

Their inland voyage continued for five days through Leiden and Haarlem, to reach Amsterdam on May 27th. But after turning into the North Sea Canal between Ijmuiden and Amsterdam they met a new challenge.

'The railway bridge had a stated clearance of 36ft 3ins and showed no signs of opening for a small yacht; *Chaperone's* mast was calculated as between 35ft 6ins and 35ft 9ins. Waiting for the wash of a police launch to clear and dipping the burgee stick, a very slow approach was made and the bridge was cleared by some 4 inches!

About an hour later they moored at the Jacht Haven in Amsterdam where they were made most welcome and the Union Flag was hoisted by the Yacht Club in their honour. Once again, they met friends of the Webbs who took them on a tour of the canals in a motor launch and out to dinner.

Up to this stage the weather had been perfect but on Saturday the heavens opened and it poured with rain. The morning was spent with the Craigs preparing for sea and the Webbs doing last minute shopping. After lunch Peggy left to return by ferry and *Chaperone* set off down the canal for Ijmuiden. The railway bridge was not so friendly this time and a slight swell caused the truck to touch one of the beams, fortunately with no damage. They were fortunate too at Ijmuiden, arriving at the sea lock with a small German coaster.

Having cleared customs, they were heading out to sea by 1930. There was a very light wind dead ahead, so it was under engine in an uncomfortable oily calm, lumpy sea. The course was 260° and the Outer Gabbard Lightship radio beacon showed she was right on their track. Light headwinds all the way and at 1800 on Sunday they passed within 50 yards of the lightship – the crew came on deck and waved. There was a heavy swell but no wind, particularly crossing the Shipwash shoal. At 2100 they passed the East Shipwash buoy, at 2140 they identified the SW Whiting buoy and with some trepidation set course for the Orford Haven Bar. There was a heavy swell at the seaward end of the South Bank and then they picked up the outer buoy, crossing the Bar at 2235 and turned into the river. At 2240 on Sunday May 30th they finally ran out of petrol and anchored.

In the morning, with a fresh NW wind they weighed and proceeded up the river to be met shortly by George Brinkley in his motor boat *Sunray*, Peggy Webb and the customs officer. They finally reached their mooring at Orford at 1200.'

Many features of this first Dutch venture will be recognised by Orford sailors who have followed in the wake of *Chaperone* since then. I well remember encountering clogs suspended from rods for the payment of tolls on Friesian canals, the frustration of waiting for a bridge to open, and sometimes unpredicted, obstinate closures. On other inland waterways I have calculated with similar anxiety the masthead clearance under a higher bridge, which never looks sufficient as we approach. Equally familiar is the trepidation heading towards the Orford Haven Bar, especially in fading light and, perhaps, low on fuel. I am full of admiration for the accuracy of Dan Craig's navigation with the relatively basic aids available. The narrative of this first voyage might almost still serve as sailing directions for a direct crossing from Ijmuiden, although new obstacles like wind farms or gas platforms might now intervene. There are other nostalgic touches – clearing Customs, and my own childish pleasure at flying the yellow duster to proclaim return from foreign parts, which suggest a past era, but one which, I suppose, may yet return.

Three months later, in August 1954, the Craigs were off to Holland again with an all family crew and two weeks to spare.

'August 7th to 21[st..] Dan Craig, Margaret (18) Frank (16) Barbara (14). Later joined by Phyllis, (Ian (11) and Robert (9). Rough crossing, Hook of Holland, Rotterdam, Delft, Leidschendam, Den Haag, Leiden, De Kaag, Veerpont, Amsterdam, Harlem – visited Zandvoort by train – Oude Wettering, Groeneweg, Leeuwensluis, Rotterdam, train trip to Den Haag and Scheveningen, Berghaven.
August 20th 0530 set sail for home, light winds or calm, periods of rain,

thunder and lightning, entered the river at 1330 on 21st. Orford Quay at 1415 to await Customs.'

Margaret Craig, Frank's sister, wrote her own account of this voyage, her first North Sea crossing, for her school magazine in her last year at Bedford High. Her description of the actual conditions merely noted above as 'rough crossing' gives a lively and realistic account of the experience. There are moments reminiscent of Ransome's *We Didn't Mean to Go to Sea*, except that the Craigs' intentions were only in doubt for a few bad minutes.

'Crossing the North Sea

Last summer four of us sailed our yacht *Chaperone* across the North Sea from Shingle Street to the Hook of Holland. We left our moorings at 1100 but the weather was so bad that we anchored at the mouth of the river to wait.

At two o'clock the wind appeared to have decreased slightly, and an improvement was forecast, so we put out to sea, with only a heavily-reefed mainsail. Outside the shelter of the harbour we met the full force of the wind which was really blowing very hard. However, it was coming from the south-west, the most comfortable direction from the sailing point of view, as we were heading due east.

We reached the Shipwash Lightship, seven miles out, at about four o'clock and had a hasty conference to decide whether to go on or turn back as the wind was obviously increasing. As the discomfort at turning back into the wind would have been considerable, we decided to go on.

To begin with we took it in turns to steer, by no means an easy task, as the sea was very rough and the waves very big and steep. *Chaperone* is inclined to roll considerably at the slightest provocation, and at times her portholes, which are normally three feet above the water, were quite submerged. The worst part though, was the knowledge that when she rolled she had to go back again, and would probably go over as far the other way.

Everything below had been carefully stowed away, but the things seemed to be continually all at queer angles, and every now and then the mattresses would partially slide off the bunks. After five hours of this perpetual buffeting my sister and I were rather seasick, and the men had to carry on through the night alone.

The wind was still increasing, indeed it had been gale force most of the time, although the BBC continually forecast improvement. As darkness fell, my father would not let my brother go forward to fix up the lights in case he should be washed overboard, although we all had substantial lifelines. We thus had to cross the main shipping lines in the dark without any lights – a dangerous procedure at any time. One big ship picked us up on radar and, thinking we were wreckage, circled round dangerously close with a searchlight. In desperation we shone a torch onto the sail, and after a while she went away.

The wind by this time had shifted to the west so that it was dead behind. There were several bad squalls and one dreadful moment when an enormous wave came up behind and broke right over us. However, practically no water came into the cockpit, which was well protected by the mizen mast, and none at all into the cabin. In one very bad gust we had an unintentional gybe (when the wind gets behind the sail suddenly and pushes it right over with tremendous force) which could have ended in disaster. Hundreds of boats have their masts torn out each season by lighter gybes than this, but she carried on. We were prepared for the next ones, none of which was so bad.

Throughout the night our helmsmen made themselves toast and soup as best they could in the swaying galley. We had a marvellous little kettle which seemed to stay on the stove in all weathers, but the saucepans were not so good. The helmsmen snatched a little sleep on an old sail on the floor of the main cabin, but by morning they were very weary.

With the coming of the dawn the wind dropped slightly. As we neared Holland we joined several big steamers from London and Harwich, and by this time my sister and I had quite recovered. Once land came in sight we approached it quickly for, being so flat, it cannot be seen far off shore. We entered the Nieuwe Waterweg, which leads up to Rotterdam, at 11am and went into Berghaven at the Hook. By this time it had begun to rain hard and everything looked rather grim. However, we had a good meal and a rest, after which we felt much brighter, and went on up to Rotterdam for the night in high spirits, all set to enjoy the rest of the holiday.

The return trip also had its bad moments, but we loved it all, and are quite ready to go again next year. Margaret Craig, VI a.'

Perhaps it was Ralph Webb's trip with the Craigs, earlier that year, which inspired or reinforced his decision to buy *Gudgeon*. Built at Poole in 1920, she was first named *La Belle Poule*, possibly a play on her port of origin. At some stage the name was changed to something less Gallic and more clearly nautical. During the following winter she underwent a major refit at Whisstocks Yard in Woodbridge. This included re-decking and a new coach-house roof. Ralph and Peggy Webb's daughter Mary, the youngest of the family, has a clear and happy memory of Easter 1955 with *Gudgeon* moored at Ramsholt and the family going ashore to walk up to Ramsholt Church for the Easter Sunday service. Only a handful of moorings were then in regular use.

Mary and her brother Ken agree that during the ten years of the family's ownership *Gudgeon's* cruising range was limited to the East Coast, north to Lowestoft and south to the Colne. Despite her graceful lines she was not easy to handle in rougher seas. In light winds, however, and with a favourable tide, she performed happily under foresail and mizen. Although they made frequent trips to the Orwell, Stour and Deben, Peggy Webb was resistant to the idea of North Sea crossings. This reluctance may have been strengthened by an incident in the entrance to the Colne, which Ken Webb places in August 1955. George Brinkley was at the helm approaching Brightlingsea, when the bolt securing the centreboard to the keel gave way and they were suddenly brought to a halt, firmly aground. It would be another two days before the tide rose enough for *Gudgeon* float again. After one night aboard, the ship's company returned to Orford. George went back two days later, enlisting the help of locals to get her off.

In addition to her coastal cruises and days spent up and down the Ore and Alde or Butley Creek, every year during Aldeburgh Regatta *Gudgeon* towed a small flotilla of dinghies up to Slaughden before anchoring upstream in Westrow Reach as a floating grandstand. Mary also recalls being at anchor there on another occasion, in very breezy conditions, so that it was necessary to keep the engine running to avoid swinging up against other moored boats. Her mother was happy to accept a lift ashore from the Yacht Club launch and took her daughter with her, much to Mary's chagrin as she was enjoying the excitement. She was also prohibited from trips at sea before she reached the age of ten, another disappointing consequence of being younger than her brothers.

Gudgeon returned to Whisstocks to lay up at the end of every season. For several years Ralph Webb employed Hector Burrell, one of a well-known family of Aldeburgh boatmen, to look after her from April to September. Every morning Hector rowed across the river at Slaughden with his bicycle in the dinghy. Then he negotiated the path along the river wall to Orford Quay before rowing out to *Gudgeon's* mooring near Raydon Point, repeating the manoeuvre in the evening. It seems likely that this was the last yacht on our river to have a paid hand or skipper.

Gudgeon retains a strong hold on the memory and affection of the Webb family, and even for me from just a few hours aboard. Some ten years ago, when I was looking for a berth in West Mersea, I spotted her distinctive hull and then the name, on one of the moorings. Since then she has returned to Suffolk and is based in the Yacht Harbour at Levington. In 2020 she will reach her centenary. How far she has ranged over the last half century we do not know, but among the Webbs she cast a spell, which has left its mark, and inspired other voyages in other generations right up to the present.

3. Round Holland, Round Britain

After two seasons in which the Craigs had used every opportunity to explore Dutch waterways the pattern continued into the 1960s, varied occasionally by shorter coastal trips and forays into the estuaries and Broads of Essex, Suffolk and Norfolk. Dan and Phyllis were able to recruit crews not only from their own children but other family members. The log narratives supplied by Frank Craig speak for themselves and allow us to imagine and share their adventures, also admiring how much they fitted into the time available. Apart from the busy life of his medical practice Dr Craig was serving as Commodore of ODSC from 1953 to 1957. This did not prevent two foreign cruises in 1955, the first, for nine days in June, mainly to Belgium; the second, in August, was not only longer but involved the Pavillon d'Or, a major canal cruise in company for motor and auxiliary yachts.

'June 18th to 27th 1955. Dan and Phyllis Craig, Maisie (Mary) Craig, Helen Garrett.
New innovation – a feathering propeller which improved sailing to windward a little! Departed Orford Quay at 1300, crossed the bar at 1340 with a fresh ENE breeze and heavy swell, set course for Hook of Holland. Sunday 19th at 12 noon, heading winds, *Chaperone's* poor performance to windward and engine problems led to altering course to Ostend; at 1745, having confirmed position, altered course for Zeebrugge. Wind now very light, started engine. 2100 rounded Zeebrugge Mole and secured to a barge about a third of the way along just as the fuel ran out.'

They visited Bruges, Lovendegem, Gent, Terneuzen and Flushing and made a bus trip to Middelburg before leaving for home on June 25th. Their return was dogged by light winds and some poor visibility. By mid afternoon on June 26th the Outer Gabbard was in sight and at 2345 they anchored in 5 fathoms ¾ of a mile south of Orfordness Lighthouse. The end of this crossing reads thus in the log: '0300 got underway and entered the river, very short of fuel then drifted up in very light airs. Anchored at the mouth of Butley Creek at 0445. 1200 sailed to the top of Havergate Island and then used last of fuel to get to the mooring at Orford at 1300.'

Only a month later they were off again.

'Wednesday July 27th to August 16th 1955. Dan and Phyllis Craig, Margaret, Frank, Barbara – joined by Ian and Robert in Holland.
'July 27th – departed Orford Quay at 2030 having embarked fuel and

stores. At 2100 anchored below Havergate Island about one mile from the bar. 28th – under way at 0720, once clear of the bar set course for the Hook of Holland stopped engine and feathered propeller. 1400 northerly wind increasing, 2300 wind freshening, stowed mizen, 0130 (29th) arrived one mile off the entrance to the New Waterway. Tacked and turned west till 0300 and then turned back for the New Waterway. Strong adverse winds made progress very slow. At 0600 about one mile off the rudder yoke line parted in a heavy sea. We managed to tack seawards and hove to while reeving a spare cable. On completion we had drifted into rather shallow water with heavy breaking seas. Underway again at 0645 we reached the New Waterway at 0745 and made our way to Rotterdam.'

There is an element of understatement in this factual narrative which does not prevent my admiration of the challenges offered by this landfall, and the calm seamanship and practical efficiency with which they were met. I know myself that the Dutch coast is not always friendly. They will have been ready for a rest in Rotterdam but there may not have been much scope for it. After a Saturday morning reception given by the Burgomeister at the Stadthuis, the cruise began in earnest on the Monday.

'The fleet began to get underway at 0700 led by a police launch and the Royal Navy guard ship MTB5514. First stop Gouda – reception at the Town Hall and then a concert in the square given by the King's Own Hussars. Tuesday. Frank spent the day on the MTB – next stop was Harlem. The journey there was rather a triumphal procession with the banks lined with children cheering and waving flags.

Thursday – on to Amsterdam – quite difficult to keep up with the fleet but a combination of sail and engine was reasonably successful.

Saturday August 6th to 15th through the Orangesluis and into the Ijsselmeer – Marken Island, Hoorn, Enkhuizen, locked out of the Ijsselmeer at Den Oeven – Den Helder, entered the North Holland Canal – Alkmaar, visited the open air cheese market – Uitguest –Zaandam – Ijmuiden.'

The Pavillon d'Or sounds a rather grander affair than a somewhat similar Dutch rally, which several OSC boats, including mine, joined in 1999. We certainly had no naval or military involvement, nor was Evening Dress required. I think some of us did manage blazers and club ties.

In 1956 Dan and Phyllis with Maisie Craig crossed to Texel in mid June and explored the inland waters of Friesland, through Leeuwarden and the Snnekermeer, reaching Stavoren on June 20th. In the second week of this cruise they retraced a previous route through the Ijsselmmeer to Amsterdam and Ijmuiden. Clearing harbour at 0545 on 26th they were back in Orford at 1400 on 27th.

Their August cruise that year was shorter and limited to home waters. Dan and Phyllis with Frank, Barbara and Ian left Orford on August 19th towing *Puffin* their ten foot dinghy. They reached Lowestoft some ten hours after clearing the river entrance and spent the night in the yacht basin.

During the next five days they made their way inland through the Broads and rivers as far as Norwich and back to Great Yarmouth. Fleet Dyke and Rockland Broad were noted as both 'very shallow'. Perhaps they made use of *Puffin* for some of sailing on the Broads. On August 25th they sailed from Yarmouth to Southwold and returned home the next day leaving harbour at 0650 and reaching Orford at 1310.

1957 also included a shorter coastal voyage, during the last week of June, when Dan and Phyllis, on their own, went south to Burnham-on-Crouch, back to Brightlingsea, then up the Blackwater to Heybridge Basin and home, with nights in the Walton Backwaters and at Pin Mill, all in the space of seven days.

In August that year they were able to make a three week cruise accompanied by their three sons. This time they towed *Puffin* across to Holland and safely back despite a couple of problem moments. After crossing to the Hook they sailed up the coast to Ijmuiden and via Amsterdam into the Ijsselmeer for a week or so. Approaching Stavoren '*Puffin* misbehaved, ran up on the steering yoke and holed her bows (patched next day with a tingle).' But she was able to be sailed independently on the Sneekermeer. Frank, now 19, then left by train to prepare to fly to Singapore to join his ship. They had been experiencing engine vibration which turned out to be a loose gearbox and bent propeller shaft. For once they had recourse to outside help with repairs by the Van de Stadt boatyard near Amsterdam before heading south via the canal route to Rotterdam and the Hook of Holland for the return crossing. They set course for Orford at 0600 on August 27th 'under power into a headwind and uncomfortable sea. 0830 set sail heading SW. 1245 dinghy towline fouled the propeller, took an hour to clear it.' The narrative does not reveal how this was managed nor what may have been said in the process but continues: '1345 underway again, eventually entered the river at 1100 on August 28th and reached Orford at 1200.'

In the spring of 1958 Dr Craig had handed over as Commodore to Sir Claude Pelly but not before agreement had been achieved and arrangements made for the move of the former Polo Pavilion at Chillesford and its re-erection on the foreshore where it would serve as ODSC's first clubhouse.

With this greater freedom from responsibility a three week cruise was possible in July of that year. In the account which follows I am particularly struck by the trust and confidence with which they felt able to leave a dinghy beached on the shore opposite Shingle Street for collection on their return. It is also something of a relief to learn that they were capable of running aground, like most of us. Otherwise it is again impressive to read how far they went and the many ports of call in that time frame. Early starts and some long days were frequent. Although I have navigated many Dutch waterways they covered many more.

'July 4th to 29th 1958. Dan and Phyllis Craig, Margaret, Barbara and Stewart Young.
0700 left Orford – left dinghy ashore at North Weir Point, crossed the bar and set course for Ijmuiden arriving at 1000 on July 5th.'

During the fortnight that followed they made their way inland as far as Arnhem then south and west to Dordrecht, Willemstad and Goes, into the Veersemeer and down to Flushing. Returning to their log narrative, it continues:

'July 18th Terneuzen. 19th – Haansweer. 20th ran aground shortly after leaving harbour and spent nine hours before the tide had risen sufficiently to get off! Eventually arrived at Terneuzen at 1900. 21st spent a very wet and windy day there. 22nd sailed to Flushing. 24th to Zeebrugge, spent five hours waiting for wind to moderate then set sail for Harwich at 1830. Light winds overnight arriving at 1120 on 25th. Cleared Customs and then set sail for Orford recovering the dinghy from the shingle bank and arriving at 1855.'

It is interesting to compare this factual account with Margaret Craig's impressions in an unfinished article, the typescript of which I was glad to see. Several passages add a personal dimension, while the opening paragraphs are especially successful in conveying the essence of a North Sea trip, and what makes us go to sea in small boats. Other features which struck me include her father's practical competence and the thoroughness with which he immersed himself in the life and language of the Netherlands to make the most of his visits.

'This July *Chaperone* crossed the North Sea for the 13th time. Luckily this did not occur to any of us until after we had reached terra firma again, after a particularly uneventful and uninspiring crossing. By this I mean that it did not blow a full gale as it has done on once or twice on other occasions; nor did the engine break down for unaccountable reasons more than once, when it was very ably mended by the skipper.
  We left Orford Quay at 0700 on July 7th and at 0815 sailed out of the mouth

of the river with the wind variable and light from the north-east – dead foul, since we wanted to set course for Ijmuiden. We sailed for two hours before putting on the engine and less than an hour later it had its first and only breakdown. When it had been mended we set course for Ijmuiden, started it again and went straight across, leaving the Shipwash light-ship to starboard at 1600 and sighting Ijmuiden 108 miles away at 0815 the following morning

Although we were quite pleased to see the chimneys of the port on the horizon, especially since our navigation had proved so accurate, and we had not once used the direction finding set in the cabin, there is something rather magnificent about the North Sea – there must be or we would not go through the discomfort year after year. One feels that life is a mighty precious thing when one is tossing about in a small boat, and even *Chaperone* provides in some measure that feeling of complete harmony with nature, of submission to the waves and some sort of heavenly power, that must be felt so much more during the solitary trips that men make in small boats sailing round the world. We thought we were small, but imagine our surprise when, on the day before leaving for home, we saw a really small boat in Flushing harbour, flying the red ensign. It was about 14 foot long, with a little mast, a pair of sails, a tiny engine and a cabin about the same size consisting of the forepeak and a bit of bright canvas. On her stern was the name of a town a few miles down the East Coast from our own home port. Two boys had sailed her across the Channel and up the Belgian Coast and were about to sail her home again. We thought about her during the stormy weather which beset our own return journey, and were heartily thankful to find her at her moorings on a visit to the town about a week after our return.

On our arrival at Ijmuiden we were greeted by some unusually strict customs officers. They even wanted to know how much tea and coffee we had on board, and being told that there were only 11 cigarettes, they obligingly helped us to finish them off.

There is no doubt that in order to see the best of a foreign country, one must see it in part through the eyes of nationals of that country. Strangers, particularly if they do not speak the language, almost invariably get a quite mistaken view. After all, how can they find out what the natives eat, how they spend their leisure, what they think about, what they talk about, unless they live with them? From the moment my father, the skipper, made up his mind to take *Chaperone* to Holland, he spent long winter evenings learning Dutch. And how it has paid off! On our second visit he made friends with a Dutchman who was admiring our boat, and who had a similar one himself. They have been friends ever since and through him and his family we have learned about and seen more of Holland and the wonderful Dutch people.'

One later extract is admirable for its description of the character of the harbours round the Ijsselmeer and further on evokes the challenge of traversing the deeper locks one may encounter on any inland Dutch voyage.

'As we sailed up to Amsterdam we were overtaken by two British minesweepers, who acknowledged our salutes. We filled up with fuel and water, and after exchanging a few words with the crew of one or two British yachts moored in the Sixhaven, little thinking that we would not see another for nearly a fortnight, we proceeded to the Oranjesluis and, after a short delay, were let through into the Ijsselmeer.

We set sail, and with a fair wind, although not too much of it, we spent a lazy afternoon crossing this heaven for yachtsmen, with its delightful harbours, such as Hoorn and Enkhuisen. Marken is rather spoilt being within easy reach of the tripper boats from Amsterdam, but what can be more lovely than to go a little further, to Urk for instance, where we spent the night, and where people wear the old costumes they have worn for centuries, not to impress tourists but because they prefer to. The children seem fascinated by strangers and stood around gazing and giggling. They had no fear and the next morning we were awakened by two or three small boys who were hanging on to the rigging for dear life and rocking the boat from side to side.

At Dieren we joined up with our friends from Zaandam again, and were taken to Vorden where we ate more than a chicken each for dinner. It was deliciously cooked and beautifully served. At Dieren the Apeldoomse Canal leads into the Rhine, or rather the Ijssel. After breakfast on Friday July 8th we lowered the mast and got under way. We had inspected the lock through which we had to pass the night before, and knew it would be exciting. It was. *Chaperone* must have felt like we do when going down in a lift. Luckily she left no more than her metaphorical stomach behind; the man on each side took care of that. The level of the water drops about 21 feet, and so quickly that you are not allowed to tie up in case anything gets caught. The water is discharged through the bottom and runs out without any swirl. It certainly was an almost incredible performance. Once in the Ijssel we moved with the 2.5 knot current at amazing speed and reached the beautiful town of Arnhem at 1300.'

At this historic place, and far inland, Margaret's original document ends, but as we know, *Chaperone* made her way home and there were other voyages to come. In 1959 *Chaperone* made two cruises, a shorter one at the end of May and a much longer one lasting from the first of August well into September, but with two crews, as Dr Craig was able to hand over to Frank, now very much the naval officer as some of the log phrasing suggests. The make up of different crews also indicates developing family links. As the routes often cover Dutch territory which was by now familiar, both accounts have been somewhat condensed.

'May 25th to June 23rd 1959. Dan and Phyllis Craig, Maisie and Barbara, and Jean Connolly.
This was the first time Jean (who was to marry Frank two years later) had ever been in anything other than a rowing boat! She and Barbara were both training at the Middlesex Hospital where Maisie (officially Mary) Dr Craig's younger sister, was a very senior nursing Sister.'

Perhaps fortunately for Jean, the crossing to Flushing was uneventful. By the evening of 26th they were in Middelburg. After a day for sightseeing in Veere they set sail for Sas van Goes. Due to repairs of the lock gate the mast (fortunately in a tabernacle) had to be partially lowered to get under the repair apparatus. Next day they sailed or motored along the canal and moored in the delightful yacht harbour, possibly one of the first Orford yachts to do so. In their words 'an interesting old town with a very large church and an excellent, welcoming yacht club' – as many would later also testify.

    Returning via the canal they navigated the same obstacle at the lock, rewarded by a present of oysters from the friendly lock keeper and proceeded to Zierikzee. After repairs to the exhaust system with asbestos rope, due to charring, they entered the South Beveland Canal at Wemeldingen and locked out at Hausweert mooring for the night alongside a large French motor yacht resembling an ex-MTB. This craft had not allowed for tidal rise or fall and at 0340 her bow line parted. Fortunately *Chaperone's* held, and disaster was averted. Reaching Terneuzen the next day they enjoyed an evening walk round the town, where everyone including *Chaperone's* crew was in their 'Sunday best.'

    Monday June 1st was Dan and Phyllis's 24th anniversary. Not every couple would have been happy to celebrate it sailing towards Breskens with the wind dead ahead, force 5, and a short steep sea lifting the screw out of the water. Undeterred, after a short stop in Breskens harbour, where they reefed the main and changed to a small jib, they left for Harwich at 1640. After an uncomfortable start the sea state improved and they were able to shake out the reef before nightfall. Eventually the wind died, and they proceeded under engine to Harwich, entered at 1400 to clear Customs and were off again an hour later to spend the night in the Deben at Ramsholt. At 0920 on Wednesday June 3rd they set sail down river and were back in Orford at 1245. Yet another relatively short but busy voyage had been recorded.

Chaperone's much longer cruise in 1959 began on Friday July 31st.

'1st crew. Dan and Phyllis Craig, Frank and Robert, July 31st to August 21st'9
2nd crew. Frank, Margaret, her future husband Stewart Young, Christopher Brain (school friend of Frank) and Vivian Woolley (university friend of Margaret) August 22nd to September 9th.
  Stored ship, Ian joined for one night. August 1st towed Ian's Lapwing *Sandpiper* to Aldeburgh, landed Ian and watched him race. 1200 set off back to Orford and picked up Frank from Quay. Cast off 2045, light WNW wind and rain. Sailed slowly down river to anchor off SW end of Havergate Island. Stowed ready for sea.
  Sunday August 2nd 0340 motored out to sea and picked a light breeze near NE Whiting buoy at 0410 and set all sail for Den Helder. By 0900 the wind was freshening to force 6 or 7. Hove to, reefed the main and lowered mizen, easing the ship without any reduction in speed now averaging 6 knots. 1645 wind force 7, sea very rough but wind starting to moderate. 0330 wind now very light and started to motor-sail. At 0850 on August 2nd arrived at Den Helder after an at times very rough passage. Owing to the speed of passage with tides not cancelling out and the strong northerly producing surface drift, landfall was about 15 miles south of the intended position. At times the waves were about four metres high and 15 to 20 metres crest to crest. We were made very welcome at a yacht harbour reserved for the Naval Yacht Club.'

After a crossing whose log narrative reads like one of the rougher ones of the Craigs' experience, the cruise continued more calmly inland. They may well have been glad of a rare non-sailing day sightseeing and swimming in the sea from a sandy beach before it continued over the next few days with visits to the Friesian islands of Vlieland and Terschelling.
  For a further two weeks they made their way through the canals of Friesland and south across the Ijsselmeer re-visiting many of the historic harbours which line their shores, already well-known to Dan and Phyllis from earlier trips, Stavoren, Sneek, Lemmer, Enkhuizen, Hoorn, to mention just a few, and Muiden, where the Dutch Royal Yacht moored just ahead of them and they dined at the Royal Netherlands Yacht Club. On August 18th Dr Craig spent the day visiting a hospital near Harlem, leaving Frank to take *Chaperone* to Amsterdam. Unfortunately, in the Oranjesluis, they were rammed by a barge as it followed them into the lock, damaging the sternpost and bumpkin. Having re-fuelled and picked up Dr Craig at Sixhaven in Amsterdam they berthed for the night at the Van de Stadt yard in Zaandam. Van de Stadt rose to the occasion and the necessary repairs were done next day, enabling them to continue south to Delft with an overnight berth in Harlem. On Friday

August 21st Dan, Phyllis and Robert left by train for the ferry to England. The rest of that day was spent 'cleaning ship' in preparation for the new crew who arrived on the 22nd.

During the next week, under Frank's command, *Chaperone* and her younger crew headed further south through Rotterdam, Zierikzee, up the canal to Goes, and on to Middelburg. They enjoyed a spell of warm weather and the log entry 'hands to bathe' occurs more than once. Whether this was an order all had to obey and whether the skipper joined in is not disclosed. On August 28th as they waited near the bridge in Middelburg another encounter with a barge took place. In Frank Craig's words:

'At 1000 the bridge failed to open for a 1276 ton barge, fortunately 'in ballast', and he had to make an emergency stop alongside the quay using us as a fender. Fortunately due to *Chaperone's* ancestry, damage was slight and restricted to the brass-capped rubbing-strake. However, the incident gave us quite a fright; it is the only time I have seen a barge skipper run! Had we been a lightly-built yacht we would have been flattened and those below seriously injured or worse.'

On this part of the cruise, continuing down the Belgian coast with overnight stages at Flushing, Terneuzen and Zeebrugge, there are several references to 'sightseeing' and even 'relaxation', unusual for the Craigs, as well as routine engine maintenance. On Tuesday September 1st they reached Dunkirk and allowed themselves more sightseeing the next day and supper ashore before setting off at 1945 on the 2nd for *Chaperone's* first Channel crossing. Frank's narrative will strike a chord for those who have had a similar experience in the same waters.

'Met a heavy sea and strong tide leaving Dunkirk and a force 4-5 head wind – very unpleasant. Once clear hoisted the reefed mainsail and left by the western approach to Dunkirk heading for Sheerness. An eventful passage across the busy channel and Thames estuary followed. Progressively, Stewart, Vivian and finally Chris became seasick and retired below leaving the ship handling to Margaret and me. Picked up the Sandette and North Goodwin Lightships and at 0430 the North Foreland Lighthouse. Plenty of shipping around – gave a wide berth to some unidentified very bright lights. 0500 altered course for Margate and sighted the coast 20 minutes later. Once in calmer water the crew recovered and eventually entered the Medway at 1115 on September 3rd. Secured to a fleet buoy at Sheerness to await Customs who came at 1210, in a hurry as the yacht behind us was flying an Australian ensign. We dropped the Customs officers with them and berthed at a mooring at Stangate.'

After three days while Ian and a friend sailed in a naval dinghy championship on the Medway, the remaining crew left Sheerness well before dawn, bound for Harwich. Light winds and poor visibility forced them to anchor for a time and ring a bell. It was a slow voyage and a long day. At last, half an hour before midnight, they dropped anchor in Harwich Harbour. *Chaperone* finally reached her Orford mooring at 1230 on September 9th after this extended cruise involving many family and friends.

In 1965 Dr Craig replaced *Chaperone* with *Killean*, originally called *Bouldogue Trois;* little else is known of her previous history. The change was motivated by his impending retirement in 1967 and his ambition to circumnavigate England and Southern Scotland without having to rely on additional crew. *Killean* was a typical 1930s-style motor cruiser. About 35 feet in length, 8 to 9 feet beam and draft 3ft 6 inches. She had two double-tier bunks forward and the galley, steps up to the wheelhouse, and steps down to a large cabin with double bunk and an open aft cockpit. When bought she was powered by a beautiful, quiet 5 cylinder Gardiner diesel with an auxiliary petrol engine driving a wing shaft; she also had a gas-powered refrigerator. The auxiliary engine was rapidly removed, as Dan did not like petrol on board, and also the refrigerator with its continuous burning pilot light. Instead of the extra engine he fitted a large headsail; together with the steadying sail on the mast he reckoned on getting out of trouble in the unlikely event of the Gardiner engine failing.

Sadly the full log of her voyages has not survived. However, the planned circumnavigation duly took place in 1967. Dan and Phyllis set off from Orford in May or June, heading south, first to the Channel Islands, then on round Land's End, stopping at various places en route. Next they headed for southern Ireland, certainly stopping at Waterford. Then they travelled up the Irish Sea and into the Clyde. Frank Craig's wife, Jean and their sons Peter and Richard joined them at Faslane, Frank himself at Rothesay on the Isle of Bute. They went up Loch Fyne to Lochgilphead before transiting the Crinan Canal. They then made their way north through the Sound of Mull to Tobermory, with sundry stops on the way before returning to Loch Linnhe and Fort William, where they entered the Caledonian Canal. Frank vividly remembers his two young boys seeing a monk on the bank at Fort Augustus and thinking he was a ghost! At the same mooring Richard (aged three) lost his small Koala bear and was teased that the Loch Ness Monster had got him through the porthole. Fortunately he had only fallen down the back of his bunk. On through Loch Ness and the Canal to Inverness; out into the Moray Firth and round the coast to Arbroath, where Jean and the boys left them and Ian Craig joined. With this full naval complement they went on down the coast eventually arriving off Spurn Head in a rising gale. With the choice of either heading three miles out to the deep water channel or risking the inner channel, they chose the latter, following a large fishing boat which they were fairly sure drew more water than *Killean.* Safety was reached, but not until they had passed six lines of breaking seas in rather shallow water.

Frank left *Killean* in Goole while Ian accompanied his parents the rest of the way down the coast to Orford. Frank is certain that on another cruise they took *Killean* into the Baltic through the Kiel Canal, visiting Denmark and Sweden. While neither he, nor his sister, Margaret, retain any details, Frank did inherit the courtesy flags of the three countries.

In 1970 Dr Craig replaced *Killean* with *La Cucuracha,* No 1 of the Roach Class built in Essex. She was ten years old when he bought her early that year, 26 feet long, draught about 3 feet with a centreboard; she was sloop-rigged with a sturdy Saab inboard diesel engine, the only one in a class of ten to have a centreboard as opposed to a fixed keel. On their first cruise in July 1970, Dan and Phyllis took her up to Great Yarmouth and spent a fortnight pottering round the Broads getting to know the boat. Heavy weather helm was countered by fitting a bowsprit rigged with jib and staysail, giving much better balance to windward. A tabernacle was fitted later so that the mast could easily be lowered for bridges in Holland. In 1971 they cruised in Holland and again the year after with Margaret and Stewart Young. In 1974 Dan and Phyllis cruised Essex rivers while in August Frank, Jean, Peter and Richard spent a week visiting the Walton Backwaters, Stour and Orwell. In the next two years Dan and Phyllis stayed in local waters or down the Essex coast; while Frank and Jean, Margaret and Stewart and their families also used her for similar cruises.

In 1977 Dan Craig, Frank, Margaret and Stewart took *La Cucuracha* to Portsmouth for the Fleet Review celebrating the Queen's Silver Jubilee, then across to Sark and Cherbourg. Phyllis joined them and the boat stayed on a mooring in Fareham Creek enabling various members of the family to cruise in the Solent. In July, Frank, with his wife Jean and their three sons, crossed the Channel to visit Alderney, Guernsey, Sark, Cherbourg, Honfleur, Dover and back to Orford. Then in 1978 Dan and Phyllis sailed from Orford to Portsmouth where ownership was transferred to Frank, shared with his brothers, sisters and Stewart Young, his brother-in-law. *La Cucuracha* was berthed and cruised from Hornet Sailing Club until 1981 when she was sold.

Thus for just over a quarter of a century three generations of the Craig family, with three different boats, inspired by the example of Dan and Phyllis, had set admirable standards for other Orford sailors to follow. Only now have I become aware of how much they had achieved.

4. Cockleshell Heroes and other Ventures

While the Craigs were busy ploughing their own course across the North Sea, round Britain and into many inland continental waters, others whose sailing had also begun in Orford were starting to feel the itch to venture further in something larger than a dinghy. Ben Johnston's first memorable voyage was in August 1959 when he was invited, or perhaps conscripted, to sail with John Sherwill, the owner of a Victory Class half-decker, from Guernsey to Orford.

John was an ex RNVR officer, at that time working as Sales Manager at Botwoods for Ernest Birkett, a much respected Orford resident and flag officer of ODSC, who had similar wartime experience. John's problem was to get his boat across from the Channel Islands and up to the East Coast without inordinate freight charges and the risk of damage, as he put it, 'to an elderly lady'. Having decided to sail her over he needed a crew, and Ben, a cadet at RAF Cranwell with plenty of dinghy sailing experience, was 'volunteered' by Ernest.

Under the title 'The Cockleshell Heroes' John wrote the story of this seven day, open boat venture covering 325 sea miles:

The Cockleshell – a Bermudan sloop with a waterline length of 17ft 6ins, a beam of 5ft 6ins and a draft of 3ft 6ins – has no engine and no cabin accommodation, being designed for day sailing. Our journey during a normal summer would be a somewhat rigorous and dangerous undertaking, but the weather made it delightful and devoid of any major worry and no shipwreck!

My crew, a senior cadet from Cranwell, helped me to rig the boat as she was launched only two or three days before our departure and we fitted a little plywood cabin top cum spray hood over the forward part of the cockpit.

Sailing from St. Peter Port on August 1st, we passed up between Alderney and Cap de la Hague, reaching Cherbourg after dark in the same evening. The next day we sailed on to St Vaast, a lovely little fishing port on the eastern coast of the Cherbourg peninsula, and had a very gay evening helping the inhabitants to celebrate their Saint's Day. The following day we decided to sail east across the Baie de la Seine well out to sea, and reached Fécamp late that night. Early the following morning we left for Dieppe, then passed on to the little holiday resort of Le Tréport. From there we set out on a north easterly course, but the tide and lack of breeze were against us and we did not arrive at Boulogne until late that night. Next morning we crossed to Dover where we spent a restful night alongside a motor cruiser from Windsor. Two of their crew, a bull terrier and a friendly cat, climbed aboard our boat to say "Hello!"

The next 24 hours were spent on passage to Orford, passing up the East Coast outside all the Thames Estuary sandbanks, heading in for the Harwich coast in the vicinity of the Kentish Knock Light Vessel. In darkness we had a restless night with too much steamer traffic for comfort, and a tide that tried hard to push us out onto the sandbanks south of us. However, just at the critical moment the wind piped up during the night and helped us on our way.

We entered the river and arrived at Orford a little before 1100 on Saturday August 8th, after a voyage of 325 miles. We had slept aboard every night, and had cooked our meals on a butane gas primus with great success. A very wonderful holiday that will be remembered for years to come.'

This somewhat understated account of the 'rigours', which John Sherwill mentions, will resonate with anyone familiar with those waters or those who have tried to sleep in very cramped quarters.

At this distance in time Ben Johnston's own recollections of the trip are limited. He remembers flying to Guernsey from Southampton Airport in a Dragon Rapide biplane with a female pilot. Although the weather was kind, on reflection, he considers it was a significant voyage by today's standards for a day sailer with no engine, radio, GPS etc. even if the Vikings did more a millennium or so before! Crossing the Baie de la Seine, which at times was flat calm, he was impressed when John produced a scull which he used effectively for hours at a stretch. Beating out of Le Tréport, or perhaps Fécamp, between the high harbour walls, he remembers Frenchmen fishing from both walls making an exit impossible without fouling their lines – there was little Entente Cordiale!

Crossing the Thames Estuary at night was also memorable, with a lot of traffic and no navigation lights and very little wind. John's knowledge of the waters from wartime experience on motor torpedo boats was reassuring, and he did a great job shining a torch on the sails, which might have been seen! It was nearly half a century later when Ben next crossed the Estuary with me in *Quantz,* working out for my benefit how to use a new hand-held Garmin, as we headed for the Swale and returned via Queenborough. Not long before that he had been an invaluable crew for me among the Danish islands and across to southern Norway.

There was at least one other open boat voyage from Orford about this time which should be mentioned although I doubt if the skipper of *Willynilly* was a member of ODSC. John Seymour was a maverick individualist, later well-known as an environmentalist and self-sufficiency guru. During the 1960s he lived in a cottage hidden in the woods to the north of the track beyond Newton Broadway on the edge of Orford. The cottage is still there, but if you go to find it, you are probably guilty of trespass. He published his account of the voyage *Willynilly to the Baltic* in 1965, so his extraordinary cruise, from Brightlingsea to Copenhagen, through Holland, the Friesian Islands and the Kiel Canal, probably took place a year or two earlier. If you can find a copy he tells the story better than any summary by me could ever do.

John Seymour's boat was akin to the Yorkshire cobles, but actually built for him at Amble, Northumberland. He then sailed her down to Orford. She is described as 'built of larch planking, with l.o.a. 21ft, l.w.l. 18ft, max beam 6ft, draft 1ft 5 ins, with rudder 2ft 8in, single lugsail and no engine.' John was accompanied by a tough 18-year-old, referred to only as 'Mogador' or 'the Oarbreaker' and, occasionally, 'Hardarse'. As this implies, they resorted to oars for auxiliary propulsion. The whole voyage, one July, took three weeks as far as Kiel, where he had arranged to meet his wife and seven year old daughter. They slept under a primitive boat tent, an old sail slung over the boom, and crossed to Flushing in a gale, or at least force 7, and were often soaked to the skin.

These open boat voyages foreshadow by a decade or more the first foreign cruises of at least two other young Orford sailors who had started in ten footers and graduated through other dinghies until they could not resist the lure of the North Sea and the continental shores beyond, even if their boats were still small, with no auxiliary propulsion except an oar. David Foreman, of whom much more later, was one.

'My first keel-boat was the Hunter 19 *Akathisia* (medical term for a pathological inability to sit still), headroom 3 ft. max, no engine, one oar for sculling, hank-on foresails, 1 metre draft, displacing half a ton. The Hunter was fast for its size and a superb sea-boat in severe conditions, but very wet indeed, fast enough to sail straight THROUGH big waves – oilskins required above force 2.

In late October 1971, I set off single-handed, first to Harwich to clear outbound Customs in Felixstowe Dock. Then with a north-east force 5 there was a long, cold, wet beat against the flood tide, in case I decided to bottle it and run for home. But by evening we were beyond the Shipwash Light Vessel, close-hauled, still force 5, wet, cold, tired, very seasick, unable to eat, but obstinately heading for the Hook of Holland. (I had sailed there several times before on other people's boats).

Beating on throughout the night, with no sleep, I was still being sick. By daylight, confused by dehydration I kept mentally adjusting for the tide by heading further NE. Late afternoon came with no land in sight, although we had easily run the distance. They call it 'uncertain of one's position', but the reality is the ghastly feeling of being, actually, 'lost'. Belatedly I realised we could only be well to the North, and on the Seafix, just, faintly, heard the aero-beacon at the Hook, at least 50 miles away to the South. So I turned southwards; over-canvassed and badly frightened in the afternoon gusts, I found myself, apparently, ten feet above the situation calmly looking down on my little boat with me in it, and thinking: "well, he ought to dump that sail off her first." So I did, and control returned.

After darkness returned on my second night at sea, seriously fuddled by now, I glimpsed a flashing light, which turned out to be a lighthouse; but I wasn't able to find it on my charts. So I balanced wind and tide and slowly sniffed my way in blindly. It took ages.

About 0100 I felt my way into a strange anonymous harbour behind a breakwater. We sailed into a fish harbour, but it was a blind alley so I had to sail/scull out again in the rain and dark. Then, in the distance, a man appeared and beckoned me into another part of the port. Sails down, tied up, then, with no preamble came the command. "Come with me to my office, now!"

Standing there swaying, now 43 hours without sleep, then propped against the wall, I suddenly noticed a third person in the room, an old man wearing oilskins, with sunken red-rimmed eyes, sallow skin, and obviously very unwell. With shock and horror the realisation came that it was ME reflected in a mirror – a truly frightening moment. "Welcome to Sch... something or other". The name meant nothing to me but sounded, well, Dutch-like. "You WILL stay here tied to this fishing- boat under my window tonight." The tone of voice prevented any argument. (I later realised that he recognised that I was in the late stages of dehydration and exhaustion, and a very real danger to myself if I carried on. He was a very wise and experienced man).

Suffering from excess adrenalin I slept little, unsure what was real and what was a dream, the noise of creaking warps and fenders all around and the heavy stink of fish and diesel oil. The next day I offered my many, embarrassed, but sincere thanks. He was the harbourmaster of Scheveningen and it was thus only a few miles' sunny sail south to The Hook, where in the afternoon I sailed into the Berghaven and tied up to a tug overnight.

By contrast it was a 36 hours sail home in variable winds of force 2 to 4, eventually a dead accurate landfall at the Shipwash by dead reckoning only, onwards into Felixstowe dock to clear Customs Inspection, then anchored off Shotley, to sleep for 14 hours with no memory of stirring at all.

For another week I headed south-west exploring the rivers further into the Thames Estuary before I managed to strand myself under Walton Naze for ten hours. My 'echo-sounder' was a lead weight at the end of a length of marked string, but not easy to handle while sailing alone. We came off in the moonlight after completely drying out on our ear, on fenders. Luckily there was no damage except to the very tip of the wooden rudder as she pitched.

I returned home weighing a lot less, and very much wiser; at last I began to realise that I had pushed the boundaries just that little bit too far. "Won't do THAT again", said I – but little did I know!'

Charles Iliff might have said very much the same about a bold, perhaps not wholly planned exploit about six months later, early in the 1972 season. In the years that followed Charles would do a great deal to encourage me and others to extend their cruising range.

'Impetuous 20 year old youth that I was, I experimented with cruising in the (shared) family Squib *Gracedew* in 1972. With my old school and Cambridge friend, Jamie Wilson (who joined us sailing to St Petersburg – in a rather larger boat – 42 years later) we set off from Orford to the Walton Backwaters – no engine of course and accommodation limited to the large and relatively comfortable space under the foredeck. There was also room to sleep in the forward part of the cockpit if the mainsail was rigged to keep off the rain. We also had a tiny inflatable and a compass. The Squib has built in buoyancy, 80% decking, a bilge pump, 55% ballast ratio, a modest sail area and takes the waves like a duck. The Hunter 19 was the cabin version.

The first night Jamie elected to sleep ashore and pitched a tent on Stone Point. He gave that up in the middle of the night – he had pitched the tent below the high water mark. Next to Brightlingsea, which I remember as being, in 1972, severely derelict and dilapidated. The following day we took the flood towards the Kent coast and the subsequent ebb delivered us neatly to Ramsgate at low water. We refreshed ourselves at the Royal Temple Yacht Club; a lovely harbour, Ramsgate has always been a favourite.

With a light south-westerly, France beckoned, and we landed in Dunkirk. No passports but no-one seemed very interested. Then Nieuwpoort, where an astounded Aldeburgh cruiser recognised the Squib. He took a photo, which has since disappeared. After that Blankenburg and then Flushing; a kind motor cruiser gave us a tow up the canal to Middelburg and passed us the best coffee I have ever tasted. The canal area that now houses the yacht harbour was empty and undeveloped but there were one or two cruisers where the 'Winkelship' now is, and we made ourselves at home. Jamie went off on a day trip to the Rijksmuseum in Amsterdam.

A northerly wind; we used our last guilders to have breakfast in the characteristic art deco railway station cafe and sailed down the canal and out to sea. We made good progress heading towards Harwich; I am uncertain as to our course over the last 20 miles, navigating at night and with little wind, which had dropped away. We made landfall just south of Clacton with the dawn but I do not think that we went over the Gunfleet -- simply that having rounded it we drifted in the light wind and were carried south-west on the flood. Certainly we went well sailing back to Shingle Street on the ebb.

My father had tried to get additional insurance to cover the trip but was astounded to hear that it was covered by the standard terms anyway. Returning to Orford we had some explaining to do. Sending a telegram – 'We didn't mean to go to sea' – to my parents – helped, but only a bit. Some people were very supportive, particularly Ralph Webb.

My father died suddenly a few months later, just weeks before I took my Final Tripos exams at Cambridge. He was very proud of the trip and that was the most important thing to me.'

Later the same year David Foreman was off again but, this time, with a female crew.

'In 1972 Fin and I sailed across to Holland in the Hunter 19, and into the Ijsselmeer, via Amsterdam, and out through the top via Den Oever and the Friesians. Back then the Ijssjelmeer was still only partly enclosed, there were no dams, nor locks, nor any barrier off Enkhuizen; from the middle you could see no land at all. Without an engine, and with only a single sculling oar, we had to SAIL along the canals and into locks, but were small enough to tack through, or in and out, without too much difficulty. The Dutch were all amazed to see that Fin was living aboard such a tiny boat, let alone crossing the North Sea. "You wouldn't get any Dutch girl willing to do that!" said the harbourmaster at Enkhuizen.

A big stationary anticyclone over the North Sea complicated the return trip, which took nearly a full three days (0700 Monday to 0300 Thursday). There was blazing sunshine but no wind by day, and cold, dense fog with absolutely no wind all night. We got blisters from sometimes trying to scull the boat along. Whoever cooked was unable to eat from feeling seasick, so we each had one hot meal every other day.

I remember flashing morse "UU": "YOU are standing into danger!" – in other words: "You're the one with the problem mate, not me!" by sighting along a powerful torch on two occasions, when ships suddenly appeared out of the evening mist, fog or murk, on collision course with us. There was no possible way for us to avoid them, even though we could hear them coming from miles away. So, with distress rockets ready to fire in hand, we watched anxiously as, to our great relief, their masthead lights heeled markedly as they turned firmly to starboard each time. I remain firmly embarrassed by this even today, but without this direct action we would have been trampled underfoot on both occasions – just a 19ft boat with no engine and only a very small radar reflector, in very poor visibility and no VHF transceivers for small yachts in those days either.

On the third day I used an Ebco sextant for real for the first time, to determine our latitude after 72 hours of dead reckoning; the result was very helpful and reassuring. Landfall was just to the north of Orford Lighthouse (no radio masts nor Sizewell B to aim for then) but with no wind we had six hours of north-flowing ebb yet to run. Anchored there off Aldeburgh Napes we rolled from gunwale to gunwale, despite my rigging 'flopper-stoppers' each side with buckets on the booms. In the utter misery of sea-sickness we clung to each other in the very middle of the boat while listening to the evening play on the Home Service.

After getting an unhappy Customs Officer in Felixstowe Dock out of bed at 0300 (but 'rules were rules' then) we anchored off Shotley as dawn broke. After that horrible voyage we were still speaking to each other (well, sort of), so we decided to get married in due course.'

David has other stories of 'voyages from hell', which will come later, for somehow, like most such experiences the rawness rubs off and 'there we go again'.

Just a few years before this there was also a generation of sailors in Orford in their early 20s or younger, among which the young Webbs and their friends were typical. There is a photograph taken in 1966 aboard *Xara* a 22ft Kestrel owned by Robin More Ede, sailing into the Ore, which typifies their shared enjoyment (see page 50).

Standing in the cockpit is Roddy Webb, just in front of helmsman Robin. Roddy's sister Mary is sitting to his left. The two other girls are Anna Trollope and Linda Brady. Anna stands in the cabin hatchway with Linda lower and just behind her. But it is the identity of the photographer, who must be on the foredeck, which completes the circle and has future significance.

Michael Pearce had only recently been introduced to Orford. His home was near Wroxham on the Norfolk Broads, where he sailed an Enterprise. At a local dance he had met Linda Brady, whose mother lived in Ferry Road, Orford. Mrs Trollope, Linda's and also Anna's grandmother, lived next door. Michael had followed up an invitation to visit. Since the Bradys and the Trollopes were friendly with the Webbs it is not surprising that Michael Pearce and Roddy also became firm friends. Such groups have been a feature of every Orford generation enjoying the river each summer. David Foreman, slightly younger than most of this particular crew, recalls an evening picnic downriver on *Xara* with 19 young people somehow crammed aboard, not far off one per foot overall length.

Just two years later Roddy Webb and Michael Pearce embarked together on the first of a series of three shared ownerships with the purchase of *Tarka*, a Hurley 22. Their choice of boat is also significant. This was one of the most successful and popular of the smaller glass-fibre yachts which were now being produced – second-hand, but only two years old, she would be within the combined budget of two young men towards the start of their careers and ideal for a cruising apprenticeship, which was initially restricted to the East Coast and its rivers. The pretty lines of the Hurley were much admired – often described as looking like 'a proper yacht' she was also capable of use for racing. Michael's connections with a haulage firm enabled *Tarka's* delivery by a convenient lorry from Hamble to Slaughden. She was then sailed up to the Broads to be hauled out for the winter at Wroxham.

There was another Norfolk sailing family, already acquainted with Orford, who would play an even more important part in Michael Pearce's life, to say nothing of the development of Orford Sailing Club and his own cruising experience in years to come. It was probably in 1962 that Gilbert Aikens first sailed into Orford in his recently acquired yacht *Vale*. He and his wife must have been impressed, because in 1963 they bought 'Corner Cottage', situated at the junction of Daphne Road and Quay Street, their Orford base for many years. It also meant that *Vale* could be based in Orford, possibly to avoid any further awkward moments such as the Newcombe Sands incident off Lowestoft with a lifeboat in attendance (see page 51).

Then in 1968 *Vale* was anchored near Slaughden during Aldeburgh Regatta as a floating grandstand. Michael was racing an Enterprise with Mary Webb, and the Webbs knew the Aikens well, so after the race they went aboard. This time Suki, the Aikens' daughter was also there. Michael and Suki were married the following year.

In 1970 Michael and Roddy moved on from *Tarka I* to *Tarka II*, a Halcyon 27 which they found at Walton. In addition to river and coastal sailing they raced her in the Haven Series from the Orwell. Just two years later she was succeeded by *Melody of Suffolk* owned jointly until 1979 and ever since, most happily, by Roddy and his family until his sad early death, notably now by his son Jamie with his wife and young children.

Melody may rightly claim to be the symbol of continuity in the Orford cruising fleet. She is a Contest 31, masthead sloop, just over 31ft overall, with good accommodation and plenty of power whether under sail or using her 25hp Volvo Penta engine, Dutch-designed and built in the 1970s she was, and remains, ideal for cruising across the North Sea and into shallow coastal or inland waters with her draft of under five feet. The purchase was arranged at Medemblik on the Ijsselmeer and she was brought over by the Woodbridge-based Small Craft Deliveries. Michael recalls that her first sail in home waters began inauspiciously when the steering jammed, due to a dinghy oar stowed under the cockpit tangling with the steering gear.

In 1973 Michael and Roddy with Suki Pearce, Mary Webb and another crew member, John Harkness, set off for Ijmuiden. To be sure of knowing whether to turn to port or starboard for harbour after a landfall they followed the fisherman's tip of aiming five degrees off course – in this case to starboard – so Ijmuiden should lie to port. With land in sight they confidently headed north. But there was no sign of any harbour. Eventually Suki, impatient, or lacking conviction as to their navigational judgement, hailed a passing windsurfer, who pointed firmly south; evidently tidal currents or some other factor had already carried them the wrong side of their destination. This was, of course, before the era of GPS, and I, for one, will admit to similar experiences.

In 1979 Roddy Webb took over the independent ownership of *Melody* while the Pearces embarked on a series of different boats including *Quintet*, a Sadler 32, for the next six years and, later, *Alruna II*, a Rival 38. With these they cruised regularly to Holland and France as well as closer to home, enjoying many family holidays afloat.

Orford Regatta, late 19th or early 20th century. (OSC archive)

Chaperone at anchor (Craig family)

Chaperone under sail (Craig Family)

Robin More Ede at helm of *Xara* with young crew (Michael Pearce)

Lifeboat attends *Vale* Newcombe Sands (Michael Pearce)

Vale on Orford Quay (Michael Pearce)

Quintet racing off Harwich
(Michael Pearce)

Melody of Suffolk in Holland at the time of purchase (Michael Pearce)

Pearce family on holiday in Veerse Meer (Michael Pearce)

Alruna II under sail (Michael Pearce)

Suki in command, Roddy and Mary Webb and crew member (Michael Pearce)

Roberts boys busy on the beach, Shell Bay, Studland 1969 (Wendy Roberts)

Patience of Orford (Michael Pearce)

Gilbert Aikens at the helm (Michael Pearce)

Quantz enters Cherbourg (Wendy Roberts)

Mobile shore party on moped (Roberts Family)

Briefing at OSC for North Sea 'Race/rally' 1982 (Wendy Roberts)

Quantz and Kehaar, Veerse Meer 1982 (believed Richard Waite)

Sea Swallow and Wombat at Flushing, 1982 (believed David Foreman)

Quantz and fleet on Goes Canal 1982 (Wendy Roberts)

5. Departure and Landfall

My own transition from dinghy sailing to small cruisers had begun in April 1967 only a week after the birth of our third son, Don. Gerald Lynch, whom I had known since school days, had invited me to spend the last week of the Easter holidays aboard *Nantucket* sailing on the South Coast. I had crewed for Gerald and his father, her owner, one week-end the previous summer, but only from Chichester Harbour to Weymouth. Now the plan was for Gerald to recruit a crew and leave *Nantucket* somewhere in Devon, ready for the Lynch family's summer cruise.

She was, so far as I remember, 45 ft or more overall, a centre-board ketch, built to a thoroughbred design by Sparkman and Stephens with a clipper bow and classic lines. My freedom to join this voyage depended entirely upon Don's punctuality and my wife's permission. Fortunately both co-operated. So, as soon as Wendy was out of hospital making good progress at home with her mother, I went off to join *Nantucket* waiting in Birdham Pool with Gerald, my colleague Neil Scott and a dentist friend, Alan Bradley. We made our way from Chichester Harbour inside the Isle of Wight to Yarmouth and dined at 'The George'. Perhaps our start the next morning was later than planned, because we missed the fair tide past Portland and spent a very awkward hour on the edge of the Race before heading into Weymouth to recover The compensation was a fine sparkling day crossing Lyme Bay to reach Dartmouth in time for dinner in the 'Royal Castle' – *Nantucket's* galley was somewhat under-used that week. Another warm sunny morning and a quiet afternoon took us into the Yealm and up to Newton Ferrers. But it was the quality of the next two days' sailing which left an indelible mark on my memory.

The early mist lifted as we left the Yealm, so the gorse and the spring grass on the hills which screen that very secret estuary from seaward, were brilliant in the sun. The wind was north-easterly, varying from force 4 to light, and back again. We set course for the Eddystone Light under main and spinnaker, carrying these sails on a splendid run all the way to the stump of rock, which we rounded, before sailing back close-hauled to Salcombe. Our final day, the return to Dartmouth, was the best of all – *Nantucket* under all plain sail was alive to the beauty of the morning. She lifted and crunched through the slight seas foaming along her lee-side while we took short turns at the wheel. Each time I was impatient for my next chance to feel that life and exhilaration through the spokes.

It may be unwise to expect or try to repeat such experiences since the precise conditions never recur; the combination of wind, weather and mood is irreplaceable, but the knowledge that this quality exists is the impulse of faith and hope behind every departure from quay or mooring, at least for me, and has been ever since. Some time that afternoon we moored in Dartmouth and returned to Kent by train. The rest of that year was busy with a move to Gloucestershire and the transition to a headmaster's life for me and for the family. But the experience of those last two days had taken hold.

A year later, in 1968, we visited friends near Poole, where our host, John Sherwell-Rogers, took us out for an afternoon in the Harbour aboard his Four 21 *Sea Swallow*. He mentioned several times that he was thinking of changing her for a larger boat, a lure that I resisted for a time. But, that winter, when he offered me first refusal before he advertised, the temptation was too great. *Sea Swallow* became mine in the spring of 1969, and I sailed her as often as I could for 11 happy seasons, based first in Poole Harbour, where we retained John's mooring off Sandbanks, and then at Orford from 1972 onwards.

The firm of Robert Ives in Christchurch, which built about 100 of the Four-21 class to a design by John Powell, was among the casualties of the recession in small boat fibre-glass construction of the next few years. I also suspect that the quality of workmanship, related to cost, was too high for sustained profitability. For a small cruising yacht, with just sufficient room within the overall length to accommodate the four berths which gave the class its defining name, the interior finish and lay-out was better, and less cramped, than many counterparts. She was bilge-keeled and carried an outboard engine, but with space for an inboard fitting, useful for extra stowage. The twin keels might not enhance windward performance but they suited the mooring where she dried out at low water springs; they were also ideal for shallow anchorages such as Shell Bay, just outside the Harbour, our favourite destination for picnics while the crew were young and small. In deeper waters she proved herself an excellent sea-boat, drier and easier in her motion than many a larger craft.

We did not venture far that first summer when Don was only two, Ralph nearly five and Jamie just eight. Poole Harbour itself and the shores of Studland Bay offered enough scope for most days; the enjoyment of going ashore is important for children, and not only for them. Longer voyages, which may seem interminable or wet, cold and frightening, are the best ways of ensuring that a family do not share one's own pleasures in the years ahead.

The sandy crescent beyond the Chain Ferry linking Sandbanks and the Studland shore was popular on sunny days. In the dunes behind the beach we played our own versions of stalking games and paddled in and out of the shallow water. When evening came we would sail round to Goathorn, in the more deserted channel which winds to the west of Brownsea Island, where only a handful of boats might moor, to be woken by the gulls and waders in the morning. Longer trips beyond the Training Bank or past Old Harry into

Swanage Bay took place occasionally, but were more common on the free days which I stole from school two or three times in a summer term, driving south through Wiltshire and Dorset in the freshness of morning and back through the late twilight, drowsy with salt air and the exertions of handling *Sea Swallow* on my own. These were not excessive in the light weather, which I managed to choose.

Looking at the chart, and remembering the further coastline towards Weymouth from my trips in *Nantucket*, I felt an increasing urge to take *Sea Swallow* into Lulworth Cove. This became my primary objective for a first night stop away from Poole, but its achievement almost forfeited future family participation. There was the obstacle of the Gunnery Ranges, extending well out to sea beyond St Alban's Head; only a long detour and a resulting period of adverse tide would avoid them, but the notices posted at Poole Quay showed that there was always some pause in firing at midday which, I persuaded myself, ought to allow a direct route across the Range area further inshore.

The chosen day was fine, but very calm with a hint of haze. The strong tide carried us well past Swanage to round St Alban's Head soon after noon. Red flags were flying on the cliff top but we had heard no gunfire and the sea ahead was dotted with sails. Further out was the grey shape of a naval patrol boat which, as advertised, would shepherd boats out of the area in case of danger. I pressed on. Half an hour later the tide was slackening and the wind had died away so I consulted the Regulation booklet once again. "Vessels may pass through the Areas but passage must be made as quickly as possible and anchorage, fishing or stopping are prohibited". It was time to start the engine.

Only as I lifted the fuel can out of the stern locker did its lightness alert me to a stupid lack of forethought – we were very short of fuel. Not wishing to alarm Wendy, I set the throttle at the most economic speed and said nothing. Twenty minutes later we were off Chapman's Pool and progress was far too slow. Time was running out, but if I increased speed the petrol would also run out before we could enter Lulworth where, according to the Pilot Book: 'there are rocks on both sides of the entrance – and the wind is fluky and often baffling when entering under sail'. Besides, there was no wind. It was just then that we saw the patrol boat come roaring in from seaward. She ranged up half a cable distant and used a loud hailer.

"You are in the danger zone! Firing will commence shortly! Make all possible speed!" I waved acknowledgement but there was little I could do to comply. Other yachts, similarly instructed, gathered speed and drew ahead. Five minutes later the shepherd was back, the Hail more urgent and fiercely imperative.

"I can't go any faster – short of fuel!", I shouted back, risking not only his probable angry response but the more immediate and no less serious wrath of my wife. There was a short pause; then a decisive reaction. "Stand By – I am taking you in tow!" Almost at once he was alongside and the tow-line thrown across. Fortunately I had the sense to take a turn round the mast step, otherwise the strain on the warp would have torn any ordinary cleat out of the deck. Even so, *Sea Swallow's* bow rose like a speed-boat's; with a jerk we surged forward and the wake foamed astern with the dinghy bouncing wildly on its painter.

Ten minutes later we were beyond the ranges and were cast off with a cheerful, forgiving wave, to motor sedately between the cliffs into the silent calm of the Cove. I had learned a useful lesson on forward planning at the cost of some embarrassment. Lulworth, however, was all that I had hoped for; we swam in clear, limpid water, and slept soundly; having filled the tank from a garage ashore, I made certain we would have enough, this time, to motor all the way back to Poole if the need arose.

Indeed this was almost the case. Our return was on a Sunday, and there was no danger signal hoisted nor any naval presence out at sea; but it was a misty morning. We would have a foul tide till midday so were in no hurry to leave; also the clear green water of the Cove and the stony beaches under the chalk cliffs were casting their spell on the family. About noon we did set off and had to use the engine most of the way. Gradually the haze thickened so that, soon after rounding St Alban's Head, the coast disappeared and quite soon visibility was down to a few yards.

This was a first test for the credibility of my navigation, all the more crucial after the previous day's event. There was a genuine risk that we might run into Peveril Ledge, or find the cliffs looming suddenly out of the fog; nor it would it do to head too far offshore with less prospect of locating the Poole Bar Buoy and the way into harbour. I laid off a course to pass close to a buoy off Anvil Point which, I estimated, we should reach in 30 minutes. Despite my professed confidence it seemed more likely that it would slip by out of sight. The tidal stream, however, should not carry us far off course and there was no wind to cause leeway. Suddenly, to my relief, the buoy emerged, dead ahead within two minutes of its scheduled appearance. It might have been a fluke, but that first minor navigational success not only raised my nautical prestige from the trough of the day before, but boosted my own faith in the value of chart and compass. We repeated the exercise to clear Old Harry safely before the late afternoon sunshine broke through to show us the way home.

A second visit to Lulworth took place just over a year later, in September. There was a fine spell of late summer, coinciding with the chance of a free day early in the new school term. I decided to drive to Poole the previous evening and to sleep aboard ready for an early start. It was such a fine night, with a soft breeze and starlight, that the temptation to set sail and to anchor, perhaps in Studland Bay, was too strong. An hour later it seemed a pity to stop before Swanage, and by the time I had passed Old Harry the idea of a night sail to Lulworth was irresistible. Wind and tide were favourable; there was no gunnery at night; the only problem might be finding the actual opening in the cliffs. The weather was calm and I was positive that the petrol tank was full. Soon after midnight the moon appeared and with its help the pattern of the shoreline with the entrance to the Cove was easy to discern. The satisfaction of gliding into that sheltered, almost secret inlet, at two in the morning, remains another of those sensations which are unrepeatable, but for which those who sail boats, large or small, are always grateful.

My confidence in handling a small cruising yacht on coastal passages, whether alone or with a family crew, was growing. So was the urge to extend the range of our voyages. The coastline between Lulworth and the Solent, the creeks of Poole Harbour, and Christchurch, the Beaulieu River and the Solent were now familiar to us. In our second summer with *Sea Swallow* I was determined to sail further west in the wake of *Nantucket*, at least to Dartmouth and Salcombe. Don was still too young for a 12 hour crossing of Lyme Bay and it was agreed that Wendy would drive the family to meet me at Torquay. Jamie was my intended crew from Weymouth, where *Sea Swallow* was already waiting, but he was in hospital, recovering from a mysterious virus. I was impatient and took the train back to Weymouth, reckoning to manage on my own as far as Torbay.

It was a fine evening and the prospect of setting sail, as always, made me reluctant to delay. Having checked the boat and the tide-table, there seemed less and less merit in lying awake till morning. If the midnight forecast was reassuring I would leave then; and it was. Not risking the inshore passage round Portland Bill in the dark, my course was set well south of the Race, where even *Nantucket* had struggled. Heading out, my only worry was the presence of unlighted buoys on the chart off Portland. The tide was running strongly and there was no moon. Would there be time to see and to avoid a heavy obstacle? One of the buoys did, indeed, come foaming into view, not quite on a collision course, although the speed of its passing only confirmed my fears. But soon we were in clearer water with the Shambles Light ahead, abeam, and finally astern. It was a new and vivid experience, not so much of loneliness but of the world shrunk to the little circle visible from the cockpit and the glow of navigation lights, a radius enclosing its own centre of power and control, and a new freedom. Emily Dickinson once called it 'the divine intoxication of the first league from the land', although I am not aware she was a sailor.

This somewhat subjective account, written from memory, may be compared with the very rudimentary notes for planning the voyage and an equally sketchy log pencilled into an old exercise book at the time.

'154° seven miles to Shambles i.e. one and a half to two hours. Shambles Gp Fl (2) every ½ min.
230° or 280° (Teignmouth).

NE wind blew up about 2230 Sailed at midnight after encouraging coastal forecast, Course 154° to Shambles but (a) set course wrong and steered for Portland until puzzled by lights and (b) nearly rammed unlit buoy off Portland MORAL CHECK CHART CAREFULLY. Breeze good for ¾ hour then fell light and fluky, motored out to Shambles, rounded at 0145 (HW Dover). Course 230° till 0300 approx 5/6 miles S of Portland Bill light which showed up well. Wind still light and variable till 0300 when changed course to 270-275°. Nice NE breeze so stopped engine.

Passed steamer eastbound at 0330. Signs of light at 0415 Full light at 0445, nothing in sight, still making good speed Soup at 0300, excellent and sausage roll etc at 0500, Yacht crossed course southbound at 0430 approx. Wind held well till 0900 but started engine then to counter adverse tide. Nothing in sight, some anxiety as to landfall. At 0930 sighted island rock. Torbay or Dartmouth? Turned out to be S end of Torbay, entered harbour soon after 1000.

Contacted harbourmaster – moored at pier to start with but then on mooring off pier £3 for week! But arrangements good. Very satisfactory voyage. Cleaned ship etc. Rang Wendy. Jamie out of hospital. Eureka! Walked to station. Train at 1520. Very tired but happy.'

I still cannot make up my mind whether the excitement, and apprehension, of leaving harbour is excelled by the satisfaction of making port. The latter may be dulled by fatigue or compounded by relief from the difficulties or hazards, which loom in the imagination during the hours of darkness, and do not entirely fade in the morning as the land obstinately refuses to appear. Certainly the dawn came very slowly that morning. I was drowsy and alone, far from confident that I had maintained the right course. Low rolling banks of mist curtained off the landward view and I had to fight against the temptation to edge northward from the compass course closer to the shore. In my imagination these misty shape took on the outline of the Devon cliffs, which must surely lie that way.

Even when the light strengthened the horizon was limited to a mile, and still empty. Eventually a darker shadow over the starboard bow began to define itself and emerged as one of the Mew Stones, rocky islets, which I remembered seeing on that coast before. Suddenly the haze lifted, there were houses on the cliffs behind, fishing boats and a small port with a tanker lying off the entrance. I could only be looking at Brixham and the sweep of Torbay beyond. So the compass had told the truth after all, and the last half hour into the yacht harbour at Torquay was warmed, not just by sunshine, but by the intense satisfaction which cancels out all the tedium, impatience and lack of sleep. Many thousands of yachtsmen and, increasingly women too, have felt the same; and many of them have accomplished far more significant and serious voyages than any of mine, not least a good number from Orford; but the quality of that exhilaration, especially for the first time, is common to us all.

Quite soon we returned to Torbay as a family, minus Don, aged three, who was parked with his grandmother. I sailed round to Dartmouth and then on to Salcombe, where we lived on a mooring for nearly a week and anchored every morning off the beach on the eastern side of the estuary opposite the town, where a happy time was spent damming the little streams that flowed across the sand. The return voyage was made in stages at the end of August, first to Dartmouth and then from there with Jamie, aged nine, as my crew on a long day across Lyme Bay We must have made an early start because the rough log note reads.

'0630, 3.5 miles from Torbay (A fix which I must have made from cross bearings).
Tide N 0-1 knots. 0730, estimate eight miles made good Course 100°. Passed yacht from Poole at 0700. He asked his position! 0830, 11 miles, cargo ship passed on parallel course. Wind NE 2.   0930, 14 miles (plot 4) wind NE 2 or less. No sightings.
   1030, 17 miles, wind v. light & backing – engine for last hour.
1130, 20 miles? Wind backed to SW but still v. light, so continuing engine. Nothing in sight.'

The log entries in my exercise book cease at this point but the Passage Plan Notes, such as they were, aimed at an ETA Portland, inside the Race, at 1630, assuming an average speed of four knots. Since we actually left early, but went slower, we probably got there about that time and were in Weymouth at perhaps 1800. I suspect this was a very long boring day for Jamie, once any initial excitement had worn off. This was of course before the days of GPS. I never invested in a Radio Direction Finder, trusting basic pilotage and direct reckoning more than my ability to interpret a radio fix safely, let alone the use of a sextant. I may have been lucky, but these limited skills got me everywhere I wanted to go for the next 25 years until my first GPS, though never across any ocean.

In 1971 our summer holiday was split between a land-based period in Scotland and an August family cruise with *Sea Swallow* from Poole to Chichester Harbour. There were several grey and rainy days when it was not so easy to keep the crew entertained as it had been in Salcombe the year before. On the first of these we were sitting in a marina berth on the Hamble when I noticed in a local newspaper that the Royal Yacht *Britannia* was due to sail from Southampton that afternoon after embarking the Queen and the Duke for their annual cruise to the west coast of Scotland. The rain had stopped although it was still overcast and breezy "Let's pop out into Southampton Water and salute the Queen", I suggested. This was met with scepticism, but when we emerged from the Hamble River there she was, steaming down from the docks with the Royal Standard at the masthead. We were almost the only other vessel under way.

"Lower the ensign", I said, "hold it down for a bit and put it up again. Then she'll respond".

"Of course she won't We're much too small".

"Go on!", I insisted.

Our tiny red ensign dipped – and we waited. For a minute or two nothing happened. We were just abreast of *Britannia* and not far away, when a sailor was seen sprinting to the stern and her huge white ensign was duly dipped and raised again. It was a proud moment for *Sea Swallow* and made our afternoon.

Gordon Turner, married to a cousin of Wendy, crewed me back to Poole from Lymington, a voyage memorable mainly for our lunch at 'The George', which delayed our departure and best use of tide, and recalled the noteworthy visit to the same inn aboard *Nantucket* four years earlier. This was *Sea Swallow's* last full season on the south coast. In 1972 it was decided to sail her round to Orford by stages; and ever since then Smithy Cottage has been our shore base, first for holidays and, since 1985, as a permanent home.

The voyage began on July 28th after a last nostalgic day spent at Shell Bay and a night at anchor off the SW corner of Brownsea Island. The first stage was from Poole to Buckler's Hard on the Beaulieu River, and I still have the narrative log which I wrote up each evening.

'Rose at 0500, breakfasted and ready for off at 0630 only to find that we were aground on exceptional low spring tide. Afloat by 0700 and dropped Cook and Ship's Boy (Wendy and Don) near ferry (so Jamie and Ralph were with me) setting out to sea against flood. Wind NW but v. light, engine all the way to Warden Point, wind variable between ENE and N. Off Needles at

1000 (very good tide with us). Hurst Castle 1045, wind freshened here and angle of heel caused some consternation to crew; changed headsails (twice) and entered Beaulieu River and reached Buckler's Hard at 1300 to find rest of family crew waiting. Picnic lunch ashore, then to Brockenhurst and tea in Forest. Children early to sleep, drink etc at 'Master Builders' Arms'. A still evening moored on piles, shattered only by floating discotheque of incredible vulgarity.

Failed to record moment of drama at start of voyage when struck underwater object – unidentified – came off astern and sustained, apparently, no damage other than shock?

Good day but tired. What of the weather for tomorrow?

P. S Lost hat overboard at Narrows; saw *Britannia* at anchor off Cowes.'

Over the years I must have lost half a dozen hats. These details only hint at Wendy's essential support and contribution to our ventures. On the eve of departure, which happened to be my birthday, she somehow produced birthday cake, my traditional favourite summer pudding and smoked salmon. *Sea Swallow's* four berths meant that Don, now aged five, slept on the floor between us. The cabin did not have standing room, the galley was primitive, sanitation non-existent. In retrospect the designation of 'cook' seems dangerously sexist and out of date. But the shore party was always there waiting patiently at the next port of call. Now we all headed for Chichester Harbour.

'With Jamie and Ralph as crew, sailed at 0645. Foggy off Cowes but sufficient visibility to salute and be answered (again) by HM Yacht. Fog closed in but picked up N Sturbridge buoy successfully – then on compass bearing with v. poor visibility but improved as we approached Chichester Bar so landfall was not difficult – wind very light and variable throughout so under engine until Bar when hoisted sail – reached Itchenor at 1100 – moored alongside barge. Picnic tea at East Head, football etc. Evening entertainment offered by Ancient Mariner and later excitement when large lady fell into river and was rescued by intrepid skipper, stripped to the waist for washing, and so to bed – not with large lady!

July 30th we went on from Chichester to Littlehampton with Ralph as crew, a full sail day with a good breeze after the first hour, so that, leaving at 0815 with a favourable tide from 1015, we were at the entrance to Littlehampton by 1345, and after sweeping in with a strong tide under us – a bit hair-raising – moored against the wharf.'

My written note concludes: 'cook tidied boat – for umpteenth time, besides serving usual delicious meal. Weather looks less settled – hope not!'

My fears about the weather for the next leg to Newhaven were unnecessary although there was a fresh south-westerly wind. Jamie took over from Ralph as crew.

'Sailed at 1145. Engine failed at harbour entrance but sailed out successfully against early flood. Fine sail with wind on starboard quarter, lunch near Shoreham, slower later when tide turned past Brighton, moderate sea but nasty swell and chop off Newhaven breakwater – dinghy survived – just. Engine still recalcitrant so sailed into Marina, docking at 1645. Met by shore party. Changed plugs and engine ran well. Cleaned ship awaiting arrival of Capt. Nalder's daughter to join ship, which she duly did at 2030. Dinner on board, drinks in pub. Bed at 2330. Heavy rain in night.'

Sally Nalder, a school friend of Wendy, was the daughter of a retired naval officer, who lived up to the traditions of the service by re-coiling, very beautifully, every rope aboard, either that evening or on the next stage to Folkestone, for which she had volunteered. I am a bit mystified as to how we accommodated an extra adult that night, perhaps Sally slept ashore.

'August 1st, Newhaven to Folkestone. Arose at 0645 after forecast – SW 3-4 veering NW 5-7 (??). Don immersed from dock at 0730 approx but without mishap, useful warning. Breakfasted well. Sailed at 0830 Wind light SW, cloudy, moderate to poor visibility. Shook out reef to encourage wind at 0945 off Seven Sisters – still using engine to counteract west-going tide. Rounded Beachy Head at 1100. Changed to big jib, still very little wind but tide helping well. Off Fairlight Head at 1400, Dungeness at 1700 having used engine in light variable winds from SW to N except for two periods of about half an hour each! Petrol getting very low as we approached Folkestone, so, after hailing a fishing boat to ascertain that they had no spare petrol, only diesel, and that harbour would still be possible for entry – in we went. Just got in alongside hulk by jetty when we grounded at 2000 approx. After mooring up, and a drink, skipper went in search of petrol – a desperate affair, garages closed etc, eventually succeeded with help of taxi-driver. Returned on board to welcome supper at 2230. Pilot book's comment: 'Folkestone not ideal for yachtsmen' fully justified by this experience, but slept well apart from interruption by noisy fishermen mooring astern at 0200 and heavy rain with thunder, later or perhaps earlier.'

It was a short trip to Ramsgate starting early the next morning with a fresh

SW astern. We were off Deal by 0900 and despite some difficulty identifying the Ramsgate Channel, for this, the first of many entrances, we were safely into harbour at 1015 and 'comfortably secured alongside to W Wall'. This comment is a reminder that marinas and pontoons were still comparatively rare on the South Coast in those years. Now I was poised for my first crossing of the Thames Estuary and a return to shallower waters, hence the need for an echo sounder.

'Put boys on train, bought Seafarer echo sounder and fitted bracket for same, not without damage to my breastbone, moved into inner harbour at 1800 and caught train later back to Chartham, soft beds and a hot bath.'

Chartham, near Canterbury, was my mother-in law's home and I was glad of two nights and a day in greater comfort before attempting this further experience. I was also short of someone older than my sons to go with me. On Saturday August 5th I spent the day back in Ramsgate 'on make and mend, cleaning etc. still windy but bright'.

Alan Bradley, who had sailed with me on *Nantucket,* also lived in Chartham, and as the next day was a Sunday, when he would be free from his dental surgery, I thought he might enjoy a day's sail out of Ramsgate, an invitation which he innocently accepted. Whether I consciously planned on going further I am honestly no longer sure. I would like to think I am not quite so devious as the account of that day might sound.

'Ramsgate to Brightlingsea   August 6th. First things first – our wedding anniversary, presents exchanged. Picked up Alan at 0800 and drove to Ramsgate 'for a sail'. Sailed at about 0930 after leaving inner harbour Moderate south-westerly about force 4 took us rapidly up to Margate, where we set course for the Tongue Light Vessel. We were making such excellent progress that the idea of a passage across the Estuary made more and more sense – at least to me. We made the decision at the Tongue at about 1155 and set course via South Edinburgh Channel. Some choppy water here in freshening wind but picked up Mid Barrow quite quickly. Some uncertainty in going through between East and West Barrow where we touched bottom but veered off safely. Thence South Swin, NE Maplin, Hook Middle and Spin Spitway. Wind fell light at about 1600 so we changed to No1 jib but it soon freshened up again and we had a spanking final sail up to Colne Bar and thence up channel to Brightlingsea. Moored on piles at 1840 and Alan went ashore to seek taxi and train almost immediately, having had a much longer voyage than he can have expected! Tidied ship and went ashore to phone Wendy. Chicken and chips very welcome, also bath at hospitable yacht club.

Slept moderately well – without pyjamas. An unusual wedding anniversary but a good day's sailing which set *Sea Swallow* well ahead on her voyage.'

I do not remember when or whether I checked on Alan's return home. Probably I asked Wendy to let his wife know he was on his way. Over the years I do not sense he held a grudge, but neither have we ever sailed together since. Perhaps it is just as well I had ceased to be his patient in the dentist's chair some time before. The frequent reference to buoys as sea-marks on this passage emphasises how much I relied upon basic pilotage and reasonable visibility at that stage in my navigational experience. Not that it ever evolved to real expertise.

'August 7th Brightlingsea to – ORFORD. After breakfast and going ashore for provisions, shaving tackle, shave in yacht club etc. – left mooring at 1030, motored out to Mersea Point where I anchored and got up sail. Wind southerly 3-4. Put in two rolls of reef and No. 2 jib; sailed at 1100 – for Harwich! Good beat out to Bar with first of ebb – almost the first beat of the whole voyage except a few tacks off Yarmouth (IOW). Off Clacton by 1300, Walton 1400 and the Medusa Channel at 1430; wind had fallen lighter but was picking up again. Now the idea came – why not go on to Orford – especially with a poor forecast, gales etc. for tomorrow? By 1530, off Felixstowe, the die was cast, wind still freshening so reduced to mainsail at 1600 – off N Cutler at 1700, saw another ship heading in to Orford Bar (*Patience of Orford* as it turned out). We came in together, *Sea Swallow* leading, although I would much have preferred to follow – some anxiety in heavy seas breaking on bar, entered at 1730; I was late in seeing leading marks and should have been nearer to Bar Buoy but lacked confidence in breaking water. However, all was well.

Inside river the ebb was still running – lovely sail up to Orford , which took me back many years. Anchored W of Quay at 1830. Went ashore to phone Wendy, then for a drink in 'Jolly Sailor' where I encountered owner of *Patience,* recently built and on a maiden voyage from Christchurch to Orford. They had come from Ramsgate that morning. Offered mooring by their son-in-law and invited to their house for a drink, then rather late to bed, but enjoyed and felt I had earned my ravioli and some of Alan's wine, donated to the ship's cellar. Rising wind – even full gale.'

I suspect a touch of exaggeration in the reference to a full gale, even if it was a windy night, but I certainly slept well in the knowledge we were in good shelter and belonged where we lay. Gilbert Aiken's son-in-law must have been none other than Michael Pearce, and his mooring probably that normally occupied by *Melody of Suffolk.* If so I was doubly privileged, and even more at home than I believed. *Sea Swallow* would spend another very happy decade in Orford before *Quantz* assumed her role. Of all my landfalls to date perhaps none was better than this.

6. Coast to Coast

Following the arrival of *Sea Swallow* in Orford we spent the rest of that 1972 summer holiday in number 24 High Street, which belonged my Aunt, Nancy Roberts. She still lived at Smithy Cottage but, aged 77, she was finding the house and its large garden hard to manage and soon moved to No 24, while we took over Smithy Cottage. About that time I must have rejoined ODSC as a family member.

This was now a different club to the 'Orford Dabchicks' of my youth. As the Commodore, Tony Pool put it with blunt frankness at the 1973 AGM: "we are in the midst of a social revolution which enables many more people to come sailing or spend their leisure on the coasts....Whether we like it or not the Club has ceased to be a village sailing club." Reading the Minutes of that time it is clear that they saw themselves primarily as a dinghy sailing club. Meetings were much concerned with the possibility of building a new clubhouse to replace the former Chillesford Polo Ground pavilion which had stood on the foreshore since 1958. Picturesque though it was, the facilities were basic and the building was often flooded by high tides, three times in the autumn of 1973. Linked with this project was the vexed question of the club's name. Despite some vigorous opposition the resolution to omit the word 'Dabchick' from the title and to replace the 'D' on the burgee by the outline of the Castle was passed at the 1973 AGM. Grant-funding problems and the risk that a separate club might claim the Orford name carried the day. I was interested to read that Dr Craig, a past Commodore and, as we know, a pioneer cruising yachtsman, had suggested going a step further and adopting the name 'Orford Yacht Club'. He foresaw that 'in the future more members will want to cruise abroad, as a few do now. He finds the greatest difficulty in getting authorities abroad to recognise the Orford Dabchick Sailing Club as an organisation, which causes him both difficulty and embarrassment.'

Until about 1980 this is the only significant reference to cruising activity that appears in these Minutes. On the other hand the Commodores's Report on the 1972 season refers to a new emphasis on class racing. '68 races were sailed of which 29 were handicap and 39 class races, Squibs, Wayfarers and Mirrors. The Squib Class eventually numbered six starters. The Wayfarer Class, whilst never exceeding seven starters, was joined by three new owners. The Mirrors numbered 22 boats and on occasions turned out 11 to 12 strong.' These numbers suggest a level of activity, from a smaller membership (310 in 1971), which compares favourably with the present day except at the height of our August holiday period. The Squib owners were mostly from the age group who tend to sail cruising yachts nowadays.

For the next four or five years our own family focus was on our boys learning to sail and race their Mirror dinghies. First came *Catspaw,* bought from Major Collett at Richmond Farm, where she had been lying in a barn for a year or two. Originally built by him from a kit, but little used, she suffered from a persistent leak in a bow compartment. Jamie, her first racing helmsman, often established early leading positions, only to be gradually overtaken as the leak and the race progressed. Judith Shallow, then Judith Hodge, sailing with her brother in their Mirror *Avocet,* vividly recalls watching *Catspaw* 'sail under' near the Raydon mark while her crew defiantly shouted "Starboard", despite being, according to Judith, on the port tack. Jamie contests her version of the event.

In 1977 *Catspaw* was succeeded by *Pussyfoot*, bought direct from Mirror Dinghies as a bare hull, which we painted and fitted out ourselves using *Catspaw's* sails, spars and sail number. Ralph and then Don benefited greatly from a leak-free hull, as their trophy records showed, including the Mirror Class event at Aldeburgh Regatta. Meanwhile until 1978 *Sea Swallow* was mainly used for day sailing, the odd night at Iken, in Butley Creek, or short trips to the Deben, Orwell and Walton Backwaters. On several occasions, however, we did sail in company with Charles Iliff in his Hunter Sonata *Kehaar,* named after the seagull in *Watership Down.* I believe it was his example and our sons' increasing independence and confidence afloat that encouraged me to think more adventurously.

Early in August 1978 I spent a night or two on my own in the Deben, setting out soon after breakfast on the return trip. It was a fine morning when I cleared the entrance, with a pleasant breeze on my port bow, for a long tack out to sea, and plenty of time in hand before I needed to enter the Ore. I sailed on past the Cutler, then over the tail of the Bawdsey Bank and well across the Shipwash Channel before I thought of heading back. Again, as I remember it, I could just fetch far enough north to counteract the south going tide and reach Orford Haven before the ebb began to flow out of the river. Everything conspired to make it an excellent and easy day's sailing. Back in Orford that evening I calculated I had covered over 40 nautical miles, getting on for half the distance across to the nearest point on the Dutch or Belgian coast. It was of course an optimistic calculation based on a day of unusually favourable conditions but it strengthened my resolve to make our first sea crossing. I also remembered sailing solo from Weymouth to Brixham overnight which was at least twice the distance I had just covered. This time I would at least have two boys to share watches.

Sea Swallow left her mooring at 0610 on Friday August 18th 1978 under engine with a light easterly breeze. Ralph and Don were with me, Jamie being reluctant to abandon *Pussyfoot* or other Orford attractions. Ralph was not quite 14, Don 11 and a half. I have often marvelled at the confidence with which their mother entrusted them to me. An hour later we passed the Haven Buoy and by 0945 we had crossed the Shipwash with a gentle south-easterly over the starboard bow. Her log continues:

'1045 Wind light, started engine, no land in sight or shipping. 1215 Re-trimmed sails. Wind SE 2 or 3. Engine off. 1230 skipper below. 1300 Lunch. 1400 Crossed Outer Gabbard. Sighted Lightship to North. Overfalls. 1420 Changed course to 120°. Engine on. Wind S 1-2.

1900 Crossing Shipping Lanes; visited by bird (wren?). 2000 Sighted unknown light to southward, altered course towards it. Engine off. 2130 Identified light as Nord Hinder. Changed course to 155°. 2300 Force 3 good breeze. Coffee and brandy taken at intervals to ensure wakefulness.

August 19th. 0200 wind veered; tacked onto 100°. 0330 spotted light, later identified as Thornton Bank. 0430 dawn approaching; tacked onto 180°, skipper below for a while.

0630 wind light, engine on, steered 95°. 1000 Scheur no 4 Buoy, wind still SE light, so engine maintained. Steered up Scheur Channel under engine and sails, strong contrary tide, slow progress.

1130 approx, sighted Zeebrugge coastline. 1300 good sailing breeze from East and tide turning favourable, beat up to Flushing, entered harbour 1600 approx and Yacht Harbour 1630 (1730 local time).

Note: use of engine 13 hours approx out of 34.
Crew for voyage: Skipper RDH Roberts; 1st Mate & Navigating Officer RMH Roberts; 2nd Mate, Bosun and Deckhand DEH Roberts.'

In retrospect this was an easy introduction to North Sea conditions, perhaps just as well. Clearly I relied on dead reckoning and the identification of occasional navigational marks to fix our position. The engine, now a newer more reliable model, was still an outboard, fine in relatively calm seas. We had no VHF or RDF; if we had been in trouble we would have relied on flares to summon help, fortunately never needed.

Over the next four days we proceeded up the canal to Middelburg, then on to Veere, where the village, the Veerse Meer and its islands cast their powerful spell over us, as they have done for so many East Coast yachtsmen and women. By the morning of August 23rd we were back in Flushing, leaving the Yacht Harbour at 0735 to share the lock, according to my log, with *Pity Me Too* 'bound for the Swale via Nieuwpoort'. With rather more wind, mostly from north-north-west or north, although never more than force 3 or 4, it was a faster return passage despite a rather southerly landfall. Log extracts include:

'0835 Left Flushing. Hoisted all plain sail, close-hauled through Deurloo Channel. 0930 changed to No 2 jib in choppier sea between banks. 1130 Passed Deurloo Buoy wind northerly 3, good sailing.

1430 Changed back to No 1 Jib, nice force 3 from north, reaching along well on 288º.

1700 approx first signs of shipping lanes. No sight of Nord Hinder, various slight alterations of course either side of 300º; during this period under observation by naval vessel. 2000 clear of shipping lanes. 2100 sighted Galloper and steered south towards it. Crew below. 2130 Reached Galloper, set course for Sunk. 2300-2400 Flares visible ahead. Brightly lit vessel near Sunk later identified as dredger. Coffee, brandy and Radio 2 welcome.

0200 some difficulty approaching Sunk against tide, past Trinity Buoy with nearby small dredger. Mate on deck very welcome, set course for Cork 310º using engine as wind light or nil from N or NE. 0300 Felixstowe Dock lights clear to west, plenty of shipping to dodge but no problems.

0600 South Whiting. 0635 Haven Buoy, entered under engine against early ebb, slow progress – steak for breakfast! 0800 Orford Quay. Customs by courtesy of *Vulcan*.

Note. Crew as before. Engine used 6 hours 1 and ½ gals in 6 hours at higher speeds. '

Vulcan must refer to another yacht already at the quay and flying the 'Q' flag requesting clearance. More often than not we did not bother with the formality and rarely, if at all, in Holland either.

Again, looking back, this was an encouraging and enjoyable experience compared with some later sea-crossings; and for a 21 foot yacht a shade under 24 hours was a respectable time, made possible by favourable conditions and good visibility helping to check my rudimentary navigation.

We repeated the exercise with the same crew a year later, accompanied, at least at the beginning and end of both crossings, and in Holland, by Charles Iliff and members of his family and friends aboard *Kehaar*. This time we left Orford Quay at 1930, under engine with a light NE, but encountered rather rougher conditions than before.

'2030 Haven Buoy. Iliffs in sight and in company for next hour. Course 120º, all plain sail.

2100 Skipper below wind N 3. 2200 skipper on helm, 2nd Mate below. 2300 1st Mate below, passed trawler, Galloper astern Outer Gabbard lights abeam. 0100 1st Mate joined skipper, changed to no 2 jib, wind force 4, pleasant night sailing. 0230 Mate below, N Hinder loom in sight.

0500 Mate on deck, crossing shipping lanes wind NW 4-5, larger, steeper seas. N Hinder in sight. two rolls down. 0630 passed N Hinder, quartering swell not v. comfortable for tummies. Skipper below till 0730 approx. Empty Quarter. 0830 more used to motion, quite big following seas.

1100 buoy in sight, NE Akkaert, shook out reefs. 1130 Scheur buoys. 1200 off Zeebrugge, wind freshening; reefed, increasingly close-hauled, shorter, steeper, wetter seas. 1430 Flushing in sight, close reach in choppy fresh conditions, 5-6? 1615 passed breakwater. 1700 moored in Yacht Harbour. Phoned Aunt Nan. Chips, Bed.'

It seems we had knocked two or three hours off our crossing time and proved that we and *Sea Swallow* could handle moderate to fresh conditions. The next morning Wendy joined us from the ferry to share the delights of South Holland which we had described after our first voyage. We reached Middelburg for lunch, and spent the rest of the day viewing the town and shopping. It was that evening, August 27th, when, we were peacefully enjoying drinks in the Jachthaven, that we heard the news of the assassination of Lord Mountbatten and others by the IRA, one of those moments when you will always remember where you were. I have no actual record of the rest of that trip nor of our return voyage. Charles Iliff has a photograph showing both boats in the canal leading up to Goes while I have a pencilled note headed August 30th which just says: '1800 set sail and under motor down canal from Zierikzee wind SE 2.'

This tends to confirm Charles' belief that we left via the Osterchelde sluice and did not return to Flushing, and his memory of very light winds all the way back to England. He was short of fuel and recalls that we, despite plenty of petrol, had engine problems. Somehow nevertheless, after a day and most of two nights with long drifting periods, we both arrived off the river entrance more or less together. I know I was passing through London on my way back to work on September 5th, the day of Mountbatten's funeral. I stood among a huge, silent crowd in Parliament Square. The singing of for 'Those in Peril on the Sea' was relayed, unforgettably, from the Abbey; then we watched his cortège emerge and drive away, before dispersing, still silently, to our own lives.

During these first years based back in Orford I was scarcely aware of other cruising activity apart from that of *Kehaar*. As mentioned in an earlier chapter *Melody of Suffolk*, jointly owned by Roddy Webb and Michael Pearce, was crossing the North Sea in the early 1970s. Hilary Grogono, who married Roddy in 1977, has happy memories of her first foreign voyage the year before. It was a very hot, often windless trip down to St Malo with long days of easy sailing and sun-bathing. *Melody* was moored in Wolverstone Marina at that time. Hilary also remembers day-sailing from there when the Pearce children were very small and Roddy revealed his talent for entertaining them by making up stories. Liz and Nick Pearce duly served as bridesmaid and pageboy for Hilary and Roddy's wedding.

After that, in Hilary's words, 'the wind blew!' Twice, when they were trying to leave Ramsgate, they had to turn back. On the third attempt work schedules forced departure whatever the weather.

A girl friend who was on board that day found it so scary that she said she would never again complain of boredom when having tea in the garden with her parents. By the time Jamie Webb was born the ownership had passed to Roddy and Hilary, when the Pearces acquired their own boat for a growing family. Jamie's carrycot was lashed to the mast when he was four months old and it was not long before *Melody* was towing a Mirror with an Optimist stowed on the foredeck. Their early trips with Jamie and Lucy were mainly on the East Coast rivers and between the Ore, the Deben and the Walton Backwaters – 'so much exploring among the islands, just the mud to get in the way!' Ramsholt, where they still have an alternative mooring, also holds cherished memories of pottering up and down the river under the watchful eye of the harbourmaster, George Collins, or anchoring at The Rocks for the night.

Later in the 1980s there were summer trips to Holland. Roddy and two or three friends would do the overnight crossings while Hilary and the children came by ferry with the Mirror on top of the car. These were very memorable happy holidays exploring the safe confines of the Issjelmeer or beyond on *Melody,* sailing in company with the Pearces on *Alruna,* their Rival 38. Roddy is remembered as 'a wonderfully assured skipper' who over the years was so good at passing on his skills and fount of knowledge to Jamie and Lucy so that they quickly gained the same passion for sailing. After his very sad death in 1998 they took over the running of *Melody.*

However, this is running ahead of the Orford scene. Although I did not know it 1980 was my last summer season with *Sea Swallow*. A change of jobs and consequent move from Gloucestershire to Surrey meant less time in Orford that year and we did not manage any foreign ventures. I christened a new log book with a birthday sail to Iken in company with *Kehaar* and *Pussyfoot,* notable for Wendy's presence all the way. Early in August we spent a night on the Deben, anchored off The Rocks, where we held our traditional fir cone rolling races down the sandy cliff. As we entered the river we passed a very trim boat surging out, some 25 feet overall, I guessed, bearing the emblem of a gull's wing on her mainsail. I noticed several apparent sister ships moored on the Deben and soon identified them as 'Wing 25s', built by Robertsons yard at Woodbridge. Much as we loved our 'Four 21', as our sons grew up her cabin space and headroom, if more than three of us were aboard, was becoming awkwardly congested. I was already imagining a successor offering more room, the appearance of faster lines, a fin keel, without much extra draught and an inboard engine with more power and thrust in rougher water or strong tides. I had the opportunity of going aboard a 'Wing' at Orford a little later and was at once convinced that this was as near my ideal as I could hope to come.

I still had a short four-day single-handed coastal cruise to enjoy that August. On the 13th I spent the night in Butley Creek 'quiet with lovely stars and phosphorescence.' In the morning I was up early and motoring out of the river with little wind, led 'an armada of 13 boats' over the Bar. Visibility remained hazy, but with clearing cloud and more breeze, I set the sails off Harwich and had a fine sail down the Essex coast. Landmarks in the Blackwater entrance were not easy to identify and there was obviously a lot of racing going on off West Mersea, where I thought mooring might be difficult. Accordingly I opted for Tollesbury Marina, where I was able to enjoy a swim in the Club pool and a shower as well as a drink. Early in the morning I left Tollesbury and breakfasted on a mooring in the Mersea Quarters. Then I sailed out to the Bench Head buoy and round into the Colne, taking the tide up to Wivenhoe, where I moored off the quay for a pub lunch ashore and shopped for stores. Later that afternoon I motored back to Pyefleet and anchored near the entrance to the creek to enjoy 'a leisurely supper in a peaceful setting with barque and barquentine astern.' The sun set with red reflections in the water and I was reminded of similar evenings in Poole Harbour ten years before.

On the last morning I was awake at dawn and under way by 0415 motor-sailing with mainsail and engine, marmalade sandwiches to sustain me. There was a fine sunrise off Jaywick where I dispensed with the engine and set the genoa. Off Walton the wind dropped and headed us so I motored to Orford Haven against the last of the tide, entering the river at 1045. The wind veered back to SE and enabled a final reach to my mooring just after noon. I summed this up as 'a very worthwhile little voyage – Colne preferable to the Blackwater' (not sure I would still endorse this) 'but W. Mersea looks pleasant' (as later visits confirmed). 'Pyefleet Creek good anchorage to remember; not so tired as I expected.' Re-reading those comments 38 years later I am envious of the energy and stamina my younger self could then boast.

That same month Charles Iliff took *Kehaar* across to Amsterdam and the Ijsselmeer. Bad weather forced him to leave her in Ijmuiden and early in September also thwarted another attempt to bring her back. In late September, with time beginning to run out, he persuaded Howard Nash and Richard Waite to help him try again, the first of many times and many miles Charles has sailed with each since then. The story of this crossing might be entitled,

'Season of Mists... and Short Rations'.

They set off on a Saturday afternoon with the prospect of light winds, a disintegrating high pressure system and a 12 hour night. In the evening a tiny bird fluttered round the masthead light. In the end, exhausted, it took its chances in the cockpit and then found a locker in the cabin as a place to rest. At dawn it reappeared in the companionway, sang a piercing song, and then flew off.

Dawn also brought restricted visibility and light winds from all directions, except ahead, and mainly from the east. In the rush to leave, as Howard and Richard often remind him, Charles had severely under-provisioned – the only bread on board was a small sliced loaf for diet consumption. Besides the thread on the replacement gas bottle was rusted up. Howard spent many hours determined to clear it. Richard still remembers the taste of cheese and slivers of ham spread wafer thin.

They sailed with a spinnaker up for several hours but the wind got lighter still. Eventually the faithful Tomos outboard was started up with visibility even worse, down to two or three hundred yards. By 1700 the light was beginning to fade. Charles had no reason to doubt his course; he had bought a new radio direction finder, a DDF, this being before Decca on yachts, let alone GPS, but it was untested. It was worth a try to get some sort of correlation of their position although he was unfamiliar with its use. The position it gave was somewhere on the Ness between the Lighthouse and the jetty opposite the Quay.

At this moment Howard, on the helm, shouted: "land ahead"! There in front of them, looming out of the mist, was Orford lighthouse! The tide was flooding south and they had about an hour of light left. They headed south-west and parallel to the Ness shore, keeping it about 50 yards off and just in sight, towards North Weir Point. Then south-east in the gathering gloom to find the Haven Buoy, after which due north over the Bar—the mouth was much more open then. In the last of the light a fuzzy bungalow came into view on one side and North Weir Point on the other. They were in the river.

Just after Dove Point the light finally went and from Chantry to the Quay they homed in on the street lamp. It was dark as they walked up Quay Street, the trees dropping moisture from the mist. John and Julia Waite had kindly, and with great prescience, left the remains of a roast lunch at 54 Church Street. That disappeared very quickly!

Few of us in those simpler years made much use of instruments beyond a compass. I don't remember a VHF radio on *Sea Swallow*. Charles was ahead of the game when he installed it on *Kehaar* in 1983 only to experience some embarrassment. Soon afterwards he was staying at Rosehill, where there had been some tension over phone bills. On a gentle sail downriver it seemed a good moment to try a link call to his mother in Fulham. This involved calling up North Foreland Radio, where the marine operator put you through, like an old-fashioned telephone exchange. His sister Mary, who was staying with her mother, picked up the phone.

Ann Iliff, assuming that this was a call from Charles at Rosehill, snatched the phone and gave colourful expression, influenced by her wartime service in the WRNS perhaps, to her views on the need to reduce telephone bills. She did not realise that she was being broadcast all over the southern North Sea. The radio operator formally cautioned her as to the language used. This too was broadcast across the air waves.

We were all 'learning from experience' and this was the title James Robinson gave to his description of a first venture in those distant days.

'After all it was the last century when very few boats had Decca navigation, there was no GPS, and there were no wind farms. On the plus side there were more buoys, and lightships you could talk to if you got nice and close.

In the early 1980s three young chaps from OSC set off in the good ship *Nerita*, a Snapdragon 21, with an outboard motor and some petrol for auxiliary power. We were going to Ostend with the Tweeds in *Wild Child*, their big Leisure 23.

The trip went well, all done by dead reckoning, and after some 18 hours Ostend was duly reached. Now the great thing was ship's stores were duty free and we liked beer, so several cases were ordered. As time came to leave the weather turned and the wind got up. Chris and Ruth Tweed decided to leave *Wild Child* and get the ferry back; we had a week to go, so we stayed but moved into the marina as the swell was untenable at the North Sea Yacht Club.

Every morning we trooped off to the main square for a coffee and a peek at the back page of the Telegraph to look at the weather charts; the internet was yet to arrive. The days rolled on. We did accomplish one good deed. A small youth had been sent aloft on the yacht in the next berth and the unlucky parents had managed to get the halyard tail over the mast winch; the youngster did not seem to be enjoying the parental debate as to how their offspring could return to deck level and started to make quite a noise about it. We assisted in getting him back down. Next morning there was a bottle of wine in the cockpit with a nice note.

At last the weather looked better, force 4 to 5 occasionally 6, SW to SSW – so, forward of the beam, but we could do that – oh, inexperience and youth!

Thus we departed Ostend well reefed; all went well and good progress was being made until the wind really started to build. We were crossing the shipping lanes, somehow we did it; in the troughs we were out of the wind, then bang! It hit us as we rode the top of the waves and all went mad. We had a knock-down. Peter and I found ourselves hanging in the guard rails, Paul was down below, as required by the system we were operating.

We had no wet weather gear, just some walking wet weather stuff; there was no spray hood; we did have safety harness and leads, but our life-jackets were so big you could not work the boat in them – they were for Abandon Ship. So every hour the Helm went below and the Crew slid along to helm and the one below deck came up to crew. Down below it took the best part of your hour to make a cup of soup, as the cooker, with two burners and a grill was not on gimbals. Paul had just got to the moment of success with his soup when the knock-down happened. No soup for him. His head appeared, and we were accused of spilling his soup. We noted his total lack of concern as to his two half-drowned shipmates.

Twenty Four hours went by and we were still not back, but after a few more hours the wind began to die down and the seas with it. Approaching the Shipwash a ferry from Denmark was heard on the radio to Thames Coast Guard asking why they had been broadcasting force 5 to 6 all night when it had been force 9, reaching 10 at times.

This was good news for us because we had been thinking. "Crikey! If this is a force 6 what on earth is a full gale like?" Now we had the answer. Back home on our mooring I went to phone HM Customs, as we used to do in those day to report arrival. For this I needed change for the call box – mobile phones were unheard of then. I went into the Old Warehouse Chandlery, as it then was, to get some coins. I got some funny looks. In the call box, fitted with a mirror – one must look one's best on the phone – I saw a white face, covered in salt with two very red eyes. Customs told us to wait for two hours and if no one came we could post the form to them. An officer did turn up and he did not believe we could have come across in such a small vessel in a Storm 10. He looked at the bedraggled crew. "Just make her secure. Go home, have a shower and go to sleep!" That was all he had to say.

What did we learn from this experience? First, the crew are the weak link. As long as the boat is watertight she will survive. Second, buy some proper wet weather gear; we were wet through. Third, make up a thermos or two before leaving. Fourth, be very careful with a rope to a wire halyard when winching small operatives aloft.'

Peter Norris, James Robinson and Paul Blaxhill were the team aboard *Nerita* on this tough crossing. James and Peter in this little ship, then in *Petronella*, their Victoria 26 and latterly in *Dura,* a Westerly Storm, have made many more since then. So too did Paul in his Contessa 26, *Rinjinn.* While Peter has serviced and installed our engines, James has passed on many of these lessons in his own way to more than one generation of would-be sailors over the years.

7. Four Ventures and a Rescue

Dr Henry Baker succeeded Commander Tony Pool as Commodore of OSC in 1978. At the AGM a year later the report by the Sailing Secretary, Dr Ray Glaister, hints at the recognition of 'cruising members', a category of which he would soon become a notable example, by expressing the hope that the arrangement of 'Sunday Cruises' would enable them to get to know 'racing members'. This suggests a kind of tension between the two groups, which did perhaps exist to some extent. Charles Iliff remembers a club newsletter item about that time suggesting that boats over a certain length should not participate in 'club events'. He raised this at the 1979 AGM, and Ray Glaister's Report on that year, given at the AGM in 1980, is minuted there, somewhat strangely: 'Mrs C. Iliffe (sic) raised the matter of yachts over 20ft joining handicap racing. The Commodore referred to the problem of handicapping and also of yachts with very different characteristics racing together; the matter would be discussed by the Sailing Committee.'

Although Charles does not recall Henry Baker mentioning these problems specifically, there was a positive outcome in the appointment of a Cruiser Class Captain, Charles Iliff himself, who served as such for the next five or six years, during which cruising events and general activity grew considerably.

In the Minutes of 1980 Dr Baker is also quoted as reporting that 'Christopher and Caroline Gill (his son-in-law and daughter) had made a notable cruise from Orford to Malta and back'. Here again the reference is to the previous season, 1979, and it is fair to say that, alongside the many voyages of Dr Craig, previously described, this was the most remarkable one from Orford so far recorded. Strangely, however, I myself was unaware of it at the time. Here is Chris Gill's own account of a voyage which clearly belongs in the 'notable' category, and was probably the longest up to then, taking them through the Straits of Gibraltar as far as Malta, Sicily, Sardinia and Corsica; then back through the Canal du Midi.

'In 1979 Caroline and I had the opportunity to take a few months off. We had married in 1977; we had as yet no children, and a career gap opened before returning to the family building business.

I had been on a cruise to Denmark with some university friends, had subsequently done the 1974 Round Britain Race, and a few North Sea yacht deliveries. So with this experience behind me I decided to plan to sail to the Med and to go to as many islands as we could working eastwards until it was time to turn round. It is strange that it all seemed so simple then – a paradox that the more help we get with GPS and electronics the more concerned and safety conscious we become. Perhaps it is just the adventuring of youth versus the caution and comfort of age.

Caroline had sailed in dinghies on the Ore and the Alde since childhood but her cruising experience was limited to one overnight delivery trip with me. She says she had complete faith in the skipper, and the prospect was very exciting.

I had formed a boat-building company with a designer partner some years before, building Samphire 26ft and 29ft traditionally shaped long keel cruisers. With 25% VAT and a strengthening pound affecting business we decided to call it a day (hence the career gap); but I kept a partially fitted out 26 footer and completed the internal fit-out myself. This was my first cruiser, and apart from sailing her to Orford, setting off to the Med was her maiden voyage. Her name was *Samara of Ore*.

She was an ideal shape for short-handed sailing and could be left to herself with the wind forward of the beam. We had a Mini Seacourse self steering hooked to the tiller which was very useful except downwind. The other electronics were a VHF Seafix for getting bearings on VHF stations and an echo sounder. Navigation was by dead reckoning and VHF fixes, when we could get them, and a Walker trailing impeller Log. (I still carry it as back up).

I don't remember much of the preparations. Charts were mostly second hand and pilot books were Admiralty publications. I took a plastic sextant and tables with Reeds Almanac to tell me how to calculate the position. I sewed a sea anchor in case of need and took spare warps. Food was mostly tins and dried fruit (who remembers those Vesta meals?) Our longest passages were five and seven days so fresh food was available most of the time.

We started out with our usual day trip to Ramsgate to get our sea-legs. Then it was overnight to Cherbourg for fresh food and finish sewing the sea anchor. Then our first long passage: six days to Corunna. We were lucky with the wind blowing north-easterly across the Bay of Biscay. In those days we only had 24 hour shipping forecasts and the station reports with which to draw our own pressure chart. It was warm, and at night we sailed by the stars. However, when we neared the coast the wind dropped and fog came down. I had taken a noon sight half way across the Bay and then I homed in on a radio signal from a mast behind the harbour. Suddenly we were confronted by cliffs. Which way to turn? I tried the west and in a few minutes spotted the breakwater.

From Corunna we hopped round the coast in day or overnight passages. The mornings were misty, clearing with some wind about 1100 each day. After a couple of stops we arrived at Cascais Marina where we took some time out and visited Lisbon. From here it was two nights to Gibraltar. I remember a long smooth swell, on the nose, off the coast of Portugal where a small boat like ours was blanketed from the wind in the troughs and only got a good drive on the top. In the Straits of Gibraltar it blew hard from behind for a while, when with only a small jib set, we were doing six knots and the waves were magnificent, long and smooth, and we could see through the tops as the white horses broke. And in the distance to the south were the tops of the North African mountains.

We spent some time in 'Gib' looking round, visiting the Rock and its monkeys and re-provisioning. Caroline went to the dentist and caught up with the washing. From there it was day sails and overnighters along the Spanish coast. Even then the development all along that coast was becoming evident. Altea was a milestone as we had friends there and spent nine days in their company. We helped them with the almond harvest and gave them a day trip to Calpe. We had picked up a rodent in Cartagena and we spent most of the last day moving everything in the boat to try and find it – not so arduous as it sounds in a 26ft boat, but to no avail, and it continued its munching under our bunk at night.

From there our destination was the Balearics. First stop was Elmeador, a low sandy island off Ibiza. We had been wearing very little in the Mediterranean sun and as we approached we thought we should don some clothes; but we needn't have worried; as we dropped anchor it appeared that it was a naturist area! We made for Ibiza harbour for the night. From there to Pollensa on Majorca, where I made another attempt to get rid of the noisy mouse, or was it a rat? I put rubbish in the cockpit and a stick under the washboard with a piece of string leading to me sitting up in my bunk. Patience was rewarded when the rodent – yes, a rat – appeared, and I pulled the string. Armed with a heavy winch handle I went out but it was nowhere to be seen. They can either walk down quite small warps or jump good distances. At least, and at last, it had gone.

From Cuededela and Mahon on Minorca it was on to Malta. This was a seven day passage starting with light winds and then two days beating followed by calm and some difficulty estimating where we were. I took a noon sight on the 6th of the month but by the 9th I wondered which headland it was 25 or 30 miles to the south. I plotted depths over 15 miles and made the correct guess, and the following night spotted the light on Gozo. Later that day we docked in Sliema, in Valetta harbour.

Malta was interesting with Moorish architecture but a British feel. Their religion was proclaimed by the shrines at the front of buses! However, Malta marked the point at which I thought we should turn back west, or in fact north to Sicily. We made a brief call in Syracuse taking in the famous ruins, then on to Reggio on the boot of Italy. Heading north through the Straits of Mycenae, avoiding Scylla and Charybdis, we sailed on to Stromboli. Unfortunately I lost my spare impeller on the Walker Log having forgotten to take it in as we manoeuvred alongside a ship occupying the jetty. It was rather exposed anyway so we carried on, minus a log. Sailing round the coast was not disappointing as the volcano spewed lumps of glowing lava into the air. We took our leave, heading for Sardinia and made Porto Rondo in a further two days. Space in Porto Cervo, the next day, was limited, but we squeezed in next to the Aga Khan's motor yacht! The following day the wind was force 6 so we stayed to do shopping and maintenance. That evening we enjoyed supper aboard a gin-palace, invited by the lonely delivery crew.

From Sardinia it was a fairly short sail to Bonofacio in Corsica and we anchored for lunch in a beautiful bay on the way. Bonofacio is like something from mediaeval history, situated at the end of a long deep cala and hanging on to cliffs between the sea and the port. We stayed for a day while a strong mistral blew outside. Then three day trips up the west coast were followed by an overnight passage to the Porquerolles Islands off the French coast. Our first sighting of life there was a naturist on a windsurfer! Apparently the islands are a well known naturist haunt but when we moved to another anchorage next day we were quite surprised to see a guy doing repairs up his mast 'sans culottes'!

From Cassis on the mainland a day later it was overnight across the Bay of Lions to Grau d'Agde to enter the Canal du Midi. This was the only passage when the navigation went wrong. Since Stromboli we had no log but I found that with two months' experience I could estimate the speed to a quarter of a knot, and I recorded it whenever I thought the boat speed had changed, giving, in theory, a five percent accuracy. Also our Mini Seacourse steering had been giving trouble and I had rigged up a self-steering system linking the tiller to the genoa sheets balanced by elastic on the lee side of the tiller, which seemed to work quite well. But when I thought we should be approaching the coast it didn't appear; not trusting my distance estimate I sailed on for some time until it did come up and we turned south for Cap d'Agde. In fact after a while it became clear that we were to the south of the cape and had to turn and beat back to the Grau d'Agde and the entrance to the Canal du Midi. My distance estimate had in fact been right but either due to the self-steering, bad helming or a south-westerly current we had gone 15 degrees off course.

In the morning we had the task of dropping the mast for the Canal. The mast was stepped in a tabernacle and I had rigged an 'A' frame using rope to the shrouds and the spinnaker pole. It was a bit wobbly but it came down all right. Getting it up again at the other end was slightly more difficult but we managed it.

The Canal du Midi was beautiful. It was autumn; so it was quiet and the trees had turned to autumn colours. We passed little gardens full of the late harvest of tomatoes and peppers and in the fields the vendange was in full swing. I remember a young man throwing Caroline a huge bunch of purple grapes. It was hard work opening the often ancient locks. The rush of water was quite strong so I stood by the helm with engine running and warps leading through blocks to me so that I could tighten or loosen them as needed. It was perhaps harder work for the crew who, in the absence of a lock-keeper, had to wind the sluice-gates up. The seven-staircase lock near Béziers and the ancient city of Carcassonne were memorable landmarks.

We joined the Canal Latéral which in turn opened into the Gironde estuary. We stopped briefly at Bordeaux but with a fast ebb tide running through the marina making the boat unsteady I thought it best to raise the mast elsewhere and we went on to Pauillac. With the mast up our next call was at Royan at the mouth of the estuary, and then La Rochelle. We set off from there for the Channel. We were held up at the Raz de Sein waiting for the southerly tide to ease in this tidal gate, but luckily there was no wind at the time and we carried the new tide through the Chenal du Four, arriving at L'Aberwrac'h 52 hours after departure.

We were now on the homeward leg and expected to run up the Channel with south-westerlies; but it wasn't to be so. The wind went easterly and gradually increased (with the forecast following behind) until it reached force 7 and by the following morning, after 24 hours beating to windward, I no longer had any faith in being able to estimate my position. The rock-strewn North Brittany shore in poor visibility is not a place to approach to try to find it. Devon has a much cleaner coast so I decided we should ease sheets a bit and make for Start Point which had a radio beacon to home in on. But there was still another test to come when I noticed us being swept down on a large buoy. The tide seemed very strong and there shouldn't be a buoy here anyway. Even when I turned away it was still getting closer. Then, looking back over my shoulder as it approached, I suddenly realised it was the conning-tower of a semi-submerged submarine. I doubt he saw us at all, obscured by the waves as we were half the time. Sailing on to Start Point we ran back to Plymouth for a well-earned rest and a day in port. There was a light and variable wind to sail up Channel and we made a stop in Lymington. Finally we arrived at Orford two days later having travelled in total a bit over 5000 miles in 15 weeks.'

By comparison with such a voyage the next entry in own my log book seems anti-climactic, but although I could not match the Gills' experience and expertise, and had lacked the opportunity to gain it at a comparable age, it was important to me for two reasons. I had a new boat, the one I have sailed ever since, and I was heading for France. The entry reads: '*Quantz* Poole to

Cherbourg Aug 2nd 1981'

In September 1980 we had moved to Surrey, at least in term-time, and the following spring I had succumbed to the temptation of an advertisement for a Wing 25 lying in a boatyard at Poole. I persuaded myself that she would have been well cared for by the yard owner, who had installed a 10hp Yanmar to replace the original air-cooled Lister diesel engine and various extra fittings, some of which I later removed. So I bought her without a survey, a decision I have never regretted, although she had been worked hard as a charter boat and still has some idiosyncrasies, including considerable weather helm, to which I have simply adjusted, but never cured.

Built at Robertsons in Woodbridge, the home of the class, in 1967, with sail number 17, she was one of the early versions. But I was already her third owner; the first was a Professor at the Royal Academy of Music, a flautist by training and admirer of Hans Joachim Quantz, court composer to Frederick the Great, who, apparently, also played the flute. This explains the Teutonic, masculine name, at odds with her nautical gender and personality. A year or two into my ownership, near Slaughden Quay, a passing yachtsman shouted "Do you play the flute?" It was, I thought, a very Aldeburgh question. Then in 2002, in a lock on the Gota Kanal somewhere in the middle of Sweden, a German skipper hailed me with another question. "Do you come from Potsdam?"

"Why do you ask?" I shouted back, gesturing towards my red ensign, often unrecognised in Baltic waters.

"Well, Quantz was born in Potsdam, where we come from, and there's a statue to him there."

On yet another occasion, alongside Orford Quay, a young woman called down to me. "Did that boat once belong to Sir John Francis?"

"Oh yes," I replied, "how did you know?"

"Because I was his pupil at the RACM, and he was forever talking about this boat he owned and kept at Ramsholt." Such claims to fame, I feel, have fully justified my loyalty to the name, and it is only right that *Quantz* returned to Suffolk.

Our first serious voyage, preceded during the Easter holidays by a brief return to the Solent and Isle of Wight, as earlier in *Sea Swallow*, was to be in August from Poole to Orford. But not directly: first across to Cherbourg, and then along the Normandy coast to Dieppe, Boulogne and Calais. Ralph and Don were again signed up as crew; by this time Jamie had left school and was not available. Wendy would cross by ferry to meet us in Cherbourg, taking her faithful moped 'Melody', on which to explore between our intended ports of call. This worked well with one fateful exception.

My log entries for that August morning do not reveal that we had intended to leave 24 hours earlier and had, indeed, left harbour – only to turn back after an hour, or less, at sea. Both wind and sea conditions had been distinctly unpleasant and we were back in time to warn Wendy of the delay. Despite the frustration I have never regretted this or similar choices, whereas more than once I have imposed on myself – and others too occasionally – the uncomfortable, even risky consequences of an impetuous or obstinate decision to press on regardless.

But on August 2nd the wind was helpful all day; a moderate north-easterly veering south-east and easing to force 3 later, the general situation encouragingly 'Fair' in the dawn forecast when we weighed anchor at 0530. It must have been a Sunday because an early note reads:

'0730 St Alban's Head bearing 290°, making five to six knots under all plain sail. Fine morning, all well. Divine Service held at 0715. (I hope this was not an irreverent comment, perhaps we were listening to a radio Service. Retribution may have come with rougher water.) 0930 Needles 20°. St Alban's Head just out of sight. Changed to small jib, wind SE freshening, sea choppier.'

By mid-afternoon we were clear of the shipping lanes in easier conditions and changing the jib to a large genoa with a hint of land looming ahead. Ferries passed us clearly heading into or out of Cherbourg. Was Wendy aboard one of them? This would be our first French landfall.

'1830 steering 180° closing Cherbourg slowly. 1945 Steering for Eastern Entrance. 2015 Passing Breakwater.'

I remember this first entry to a French harbour aboard my own vessel with great satisfaction. Wendy was there to meet us when we found a berth, and to occupy her bunk. August 3rd was apparently: 'a good day of recovery, meal out in the evening. Fog-bound next day. Visited exposition maritime and piscine'.

Then we went round to Barfleur, a short trip in light, hazy weather mostly under engine, with a moment of uncertainty in poor visibility when we went too far south of the entrance; but 'after enquiries from fishermen' – a crude but helpful check on navigation – by 1330 we were moored against the harbour wall – Barfleur is a drying harbour – 'comfortable but smelly'.

Most schoolmasters get married early in August and the 6th is our anniversary. My log tells me that flowers were delivered at 0930. At least I got that right. The rest of the day and following night were more problematic.

'Afloat 11.50. Left Barfleur for Ouistreham 1200. 125°, set main and spinnaker but wind too fickle, oily swell. Visibility 500 yards. Started engine and downed sails. 1400 sunshine calm, sail on port beam, under engine, sunbathing, visibility now 2 miles approx, helicopter overhead 1700 otherwise nothing in sight till 1830 then some yachts, fishing boats, Courcelles sighted 1900 approx. Some wind so sails set with engine. Then at 2000 with Les Essauts buoy in sight main fuel tank ran dry, topped up from reserve. But – AIR LOCK – no fuel, no engine, suddenly no wind either, so – drifted; finally, off Les Essauts about midnight, set course for Ouistreham entrance, wallowing and sails slatting, eventually picked up sight of entrance buoys but tide carried us south. Light breeze at last about 0300 enabled us to creep into harbour about 0430. Only 16 hours from Barfleur (32 miles) and eight hours for last eight miles! Moored on pontoons and went to bed at 0500.'

Ouistreham lies at the entrance to the Caen Canal. In 1944 it had been a strategic point on the left flank of the 'D Day' landings. Since the previous evening I had been all too mindful of Wendy on her moped, travelling the length of the Cherbourg Peninsula and then east along the coast to reach Ouistreham, expecting to find us there and her berth for the night in harbour. I could only hope she had found a bed ashore and was not too worried. It was not the anniversary I had planned

At about half past nine that morning we woke up to find that Wendy was standing on the quayside, apparently undisturbed by our non-arrival and having spent a comfortable night in a local 'pension'. My crew, understandably, were unwilling to sail on that day; rest, recuperation, laundry were decreed.

That afternoon I borrowed 'Melody' and rode off towards Arromanches to see something of the Invasion beaches and countryside. Not far from Ouistreham I came across a relatively small Commonwealth War Graves Cemetery, perhaps a hundred or so headstones. From the dates and inscriptions it seemed that there had been an engagement nearby a day or two after 'D Day', and that it involved, amongst other units, a battalion of the Gloucesters and another of the Suffolk Regiment. It was a strange and moving experience to read the names and ages, nearly all under 25, and to see so many surnames familiar to anyone with personal knowledge of both counties. None of the individuals was actually known to me, but they felt as if they were.

Our next two ports of call were Honfleur and Fécamp, reached without incident. The fact that in Honfleur we enjoyed an 'excellent fish dinner courtesy of W.E.R.' suggests that no grudges were held. In Fécamp we had time to visit the Benedictine Museum, before a noon departure which taught me another minor lesson.

'Weather fine but wind stronger than forecast off entrance with choppy sea. Should have set sails inside harbour but instead lost shackle, main halyard went loose, entangled with back stay. Object lesson in preparation before leaving harbour. Took nearly an hour to sort out and my cap went overboard in process not to mention my temper. Finally on course under reefed main and working jib at 1430 well offshore. We berthed in Dieppe at 2045 in time to enjoy 'dinner ashore – corbillard, steak etc, 24F menu, good value. Dieppe impressed as genuine and quiet.'

On August 11th we woke to a misty morning and waved sad farewell to Wendy and 'Melody' on the ferry, which left at 0800, *Quantz* having moved out of the inner basin to moor in the harbour. It was another long day from Dieppe to Boulogne in hazy conditions with a light northerly headwind, logging nine engine hours out of some 17 in total. We finally entered the yacht basin well after midnight, thankfully ate some stew and sought our bunks. I concluded that I should have headed further out into the Baie de la Seine to cope better with the tides.

A day's rest and tummy upsets, either from Boulogne's drinking water or the mackerel we had caught the day before and cooked in harbour, kept us there. The 20 miles on to Calais were again dogged by light winds and poor visibility, taking about five hours of which the engine ran for three despite a period in which it refused to start. Fortunately it did not give trouble on entry at 1415, but we had to moor to a buoy outside the yacht harbour gates, as the tide did not permit entrance until evening nor our planned early exit in the morning. This did not prevent us getting ashore in the dinghy for fuel, an evening meal and rides on the Calais 'dodgem cars'. As the log reminds me: 'a kind Belgian diagnosed poor battery connection and cleaned it up. Whisky appreciated in recompense. Good night's sleep despite wash and rolling from steamers. Calais, good show.'

The last leg of this, our first French cruise, was direct from Calais to Orford. We were clear of the harbour by 0845 with a moderate westerly and visibility for once at least five miles. But, by the time we reached my main area of anxiety, the Traffic Zones, fog banks were rolling in with visibility varying between 100 yards and half a mile, far from comfortable. Apparently we 'saw four or five ships but none too close'. My recollection is of listening fearfully for the beat of engines and hearing several more that were never seen. But with the afternoon, clear of shipping lanes, we were sailing in hazy sunshine. At 1520 the Drill Stone Buoy was in sight, showing that the tide had carried us helpfully north. The late afternoon and evening provided some good sailing with spinnaker or large genoa set. We were close to the South Shipwash buoy as darkness fell. It was just possible to identify Shingle Street but we decided it was too dark to attempt the entrance, so we anchored about a mile north, close inshore, just after midnight.

Although it was a calm night, the swell, I remember, caused us to roll continually, which did not deter the crew from sleeping, but did not help me to do so. We were up by 0615 in calm, clear conditions with a light northerly breeze.

'After boiled eggs etc, weighed anchor and proceeded to entrance by 0745; nice gentle sail up river, met Charles off quay and moored alongside him at 0915 approx. Wendy arrived on Quay five minutes later! A happy arrival and conclusion to a very successful trip. Only relative lack of wind and visibility reduced its enjoyment. Very nice to have *Quantz* at Orford.'

This is a fair summary, although I seem to have forgotten the problem off Ouistreham. Given that this was before the age of the mobile phone, Wendy's arrival to greet us was either due to her keen maternal instinct or, much less likely, complete confidence in my navigation and estimate of arrival.

In June that same year, unknown to me, Charles Iliff was exploring inland France, the waterways of Picardy and down the Somme, better described virtually in his own words.

'I have long been intrigued by the great inland waterways of Europe. For others it is *The Riddle of the Sands*'; for me Weston Martyr's *£200 Millionaire* and John Liley's *France the quiet way*. Some of my favourite cruises have involved mast-down elements.

In June 1981 Richard Waite and I sailed my Hunter Sonata *Kehaar* to Dunkirk. The harbourmaster locked us through, all alone, into the inner harbour and the canal system in a vast semi-derelict ship lock. It took 90 minutes for the level to adjust, time enough to take the mast down. Dunkirk is surrounded by a network of wide commercial canals and having seen them it is easier to understand the events of 1940 and 1944/5.

We took a detour via the tiny and very rural Canal de Bourbourg. Waiting for a lock we saw the keeper's children return from school for lunch; he put them to work for half an hour pulling a hand plough on the allotment. Then we were into the large Liaison Dunkerque-Escaut where Richard left, once he had seen me through the 45ft. rise of the lock at St Omer. After that I was solo on the broad waters of the Liaison, chugging along with my Tomos outboard. First World War battlefields lay on both sides, and often the battle had been about the line of the canal. I spent a night in a canal arm at Béthune. Along the southern side Hitler's blitzkrieg had thrust from the Ardennes to Calais in 1940.

Then we were into the hills of Picardy, just like the Downs, constantly climbing on the Canal du Nord. The summit section has a two and a half mile canal tunnel at Royaulcourt, single file with a long chamber in the middle where the convoys from each direction pass. I arrived just in time to catch a convoy that was preparing to go through, and was put at the rear behind six péniches. They lumbered into the tunnel and I followed.

Twenty yards into the tunnel the outboard stopped. It was too narrow to turn round. Frantically I restarted the engine and accelerated to catch up. A single white light ahead appeared to be looming towards me. I then realised that it was the stern light of the péniche in front; I was catching up and needed to slow down. Alone in the dark, and with a sense of being trapped in a tunnel, I have never been so frightened in a boat – and on a canal 500 feet above sea level.

Richard rejoined me in Péronne at the junction of the Canal du Nord and the Canal de la Somme. He failed to find me along another towpath. I wandered into town and just caught sight of a familiar and exhausted figure as he dived into a café. Howard Nash joined us at Cappy on the Somme. Truly it is an enchanted waterway, the northern branch of 'la France profonde' with its lagoons, lakes and lovely villages – and the wars again. There was a farmyard where every building, from the farmhouse to the dog kennel, had a prominent stone with date of reconstruction – 1921 or 1922.

We spent three days at Amiens. An English newspaper was full of riots in Brixton and Toxteth – and a couple had been turned down for fostering because their marriage was too happy, an inappropriate role model.

Finally to St Valery where the mast was quickly erected. A waitress refused to serve Richard coffee and chocolate ice-cream together – "mon Dieu ces Anglais!" Then we navigated down the tortuous channel of the estuary, and finally, with relief, past the deep water mark.'

1981 was also the year when Charles got involved with a project which became important to a significant body of Orford sailors – the 'Dalmatian Squadron' as I came to think of them. In July, just after his return from northern France, Charles joined the firm of Piper Smith and Basham, Solicitors, to do property work. The firm also specialised in tour operating, and a few weeks after he joined it, they received instructions to assist in setting up the first flotilla sailing operation in Tito's Yugoslavia. This meant negotiating a commercial framework with a nominally Marxist country and getting their law changed to enable British-flagged yachts to operate unsupervised in the Dalmatian islands. It would open up this beautiful cruising ground, and give access and economic benefits to the islands without the need for hotels and infrastructure.

The promoter needed additional funds and the senior partner introduced other clients who might be interested in investing, partly buying individual yachts and then leasing them for charter, a tax efficient arrangement, especially for higher rate taxpayers. Having introduced some non-sailing investors the senior partner called up Charles to say, unforgettably: "Charlie, you do something with boats don't you? You had better come in on this."

So Charles found himself in late 1981 negotiating the contract with Pelle Petterson of Sweden for the first batch of 24 Maxi 84s. Over the next decade many non-shareholders joined the scheme buying further batches of boats (well-equipped and at hugely discounted prices) and leasing them to the company, usually for five years. The boat could be used at nominal cost by the owner at the beginning and end of the chartering season, a system widely copied by other charter companies ever since.

Thus the Maxi 84s *Premuda, Ciovo, Susak, Hvar* and *Zut,* all named after Dalmatian islands, would find their way to Orford after their span of working in flotilla sailing. During these years many Orford people were involved in Seven Seas one way or another including Ralph Brinkley, John Oakes, various Waites, Iliffs, Tweeds, Pickthorns, Nashes, Foremans, Peter and Pippa Weir, Roger Oddie, Paul Blaxhill, Peter Norris, James Robinson, Jamie and Richard Roberts, etc. That included yacht delivery, maintenance, working in flotilla, sailing free or in flotilla, owner's use of and removal at end of charter. Many got used to a week's inexpensive cruising on this beautiful coast in and out of the islands at the beginning or end of the season. As a bonus Charles met Mo, his wife to be, organising a group to deliver a batch of new Maxis from Aprillia near Venice to Primosten near Split in March 1985.

In Chapter One I mentioned that Rosehill, once the home of Thomas Eve, and now of Charles Iliff and his family, might be regarded as the cradle of Orford cruising ventures. The Seven Seas ventures were not the only examples of this influence. In that same autumn of 1981 Charles and David Foreman stood together in shelter, watching a plucky Hunter Medina beat downriver in half a September gale. Both ex-dinghy-sailors, David had now acquired a J24, almost a racing dinghy with a cabin-top. Thinking aloud, although he blames David, Charles said:

"Wouldn't it be fun if…?" And David agreed. They were hatching the idea of something between a race across the North Sea and a sort of seaman-like fun-run, for everything from a J24 to an old gaffer. The idea took hold, and messages were slipped between wash-boards and cabin hatches up and down the moorings.

In February, Charles remembered a request for an Easter Saturday meeting at the 'Jolly Sailor'. This triggered another set of notes and draft Sailing Instructions. To be on the safe side: 'IT WILL BE THE SOLE AND CONTINUING RESPONSIBILITY OF EACH SKIPPER TO DECIDE WHETHER TO START AND WHETHER OR NOT TO CONTINUE.' Even that did not deter a number of potential starters or, at least, drinkers. In May a warm-up race in the river scraped a quorum but a proposed rally down the coast did not. Charles remembers the start well:

'Early August, the week before – a flaccid high, drifting easterlies, fog, and the prospect of a test for the outboard rather than the rigging. But on the day itself blessed with a light westerly and as the tide rises a motley fleet assembles, awaiting the ebb and the start: the J24, two Sonatas, a Trapper, two bilge-keeled cruisers, a Samphire, a Wing 25 and a Hunter Europa – Lymington and the Hamble might not be impressed but it is a high proportion of the cruisers then based here, and Flushing is 100 miles across a cold North Sea.

Flares were demonstrated and the forecast circulated – light westerlies and fog clearing. A bilge-keeler recruits a fourth crew member from the spectators. She reappears with moments to spare, clutching a bare minimum of kit and two tins of sausages but no passport. Meanwhile an old lady asks where the start is. She has driven miles to watch.

The 'slow' cruisers start and the Hunter Europa rockets off. But it is the two bilge-keelers that claim attention. On the wind-dodgers of one is a simple message: 'For Sale – Orford 262'. The other, helmed by a gentleman of the cloth, is towing a dinghy. Is the turnout nine or ten? It appears that the dinghy is propelled by sail, albeit slowly. Perhaps some devious handicap advantage is being sought. But it is the spirit which counts.

The 'fast' cruisers follow 50 minutes later, threading through the racing Wayfarers, Lasers and Squibs. The J24 and the Trapper soon cream past towards the river mouth. Then we are all out to sea, past a final group of well-wishers – and for Charles and David the reward for months of hand deliveries and gentle persuasion. This was our private Fastnet, with no press and no publicity. Weston Martyr and *Jolie Brise* would have approved.

With a light breeze astern and assorted spinnakers flying, evening falls, and the two groups draw together. The Trapper, the J24 and the Hunter Europa duel together, but then it is time for supper and the broadsides change to a salvo of beer cans. The J24 falls temporarily astern, seriously distracted. There is no corkscrew on board but a bottle of wine to open.

To the south the other Sonata heads off into the haze, and to the north the Wing 25. Shall we see them again, and from what direction? Masthead lights are twinkling and complete calm descends with darkness and a hint of fog. 'Yachts will be permitted to use engines for bona fide purposes' say the Sailing Instructions. By now the shipping lanes are near and good seamanship is surely a bona fide purpose. *Kehaar's* faithful Tomos breathes into life; soon distant lights and excellent night visibility return.

At the end of his watch off Charles wakes with the dawn, sleepily surprised to find himself on a boat. Is this the aggressive frenzy of offshore racing? The westerly breeze has returned and the little ship slips along. There is nothing in sight. This is the deserted area between the shipping lanes and the Scheldt known at Orford as the Empty Quarter. A fix with the RDF is distrusted, and twice repeated. Mistrust is rewarded and the Thornton Bank appears ahead.

As the wind increases with the low cliffs of Walcheren to port *Kehaar* streams into the Scheldt, hugging the twenty foot contour of the Plattebank and safe from the heavy traffic in comparison to which Harwich Harbour is a quiet backwater. There are many sails in sight but none familiar and they round Flushing pier head and enter the lock at 1324 on Sunday August 8th. Wendy, sketching on a grassy bank at the yacht harbour, has beaten them to it, courtesy of European Ferries and her Honda moped. The yacht harbourmaster assigns a deserted steel ketch we can raft up to and offers to lay on an evening meal for all. After some uncertainty as to arrivals the offer is gratefully accepted.

Other boats gradually arrive with a mixture of elation and fatigue. Navigational errors and surreptitious engine use are coyly admitted or justified. The Reverend Esmond Smith arrives at 1530, his dinghy still in tow, and protests are lodged against him for walking on the water ahead of his boat to pull her in the calm. Only the other Sonata, last seen heading south, is missing; but five minutes after we sit down to eat at 2000 she too arrives with a story about fishing boats.'

The *Quantz* version of this story is not wildly different. My log claims that we were second across the line in the 'slow' start. There was a short tacking duel with *Sea Swallow,* crewed by Jamie with Richard Waite as nominal skipper. She was still unsold, hence the message on her dodgers. Their choice of the Narrows rather than mine down the Gulls proved correct, so we followed them out of the river, closely pursued by the faster group. Then it was "up spinnaker" and past *Sea Swallow* though we were in company nearly as far as the Outer Gabbard. There it was calm again, with overfalls, and the use of the engine was irresistible. The Nord Hinder was sighted at 0400 with *Samara* in view and the wind returned. For several hours we had a good run with spinnaker set later and taking the northern channel past Westkapelle on a fast reach with a helpful tide we rounded Flushing pier at 1444 and reached the yacht basin by 1530 (BST). *Quantz* was the third boat to arrive but *Sea Swallow* was only 45 minutes behind.

As Charles noted: "no one asked who won; we were all winners." In the morning, minus two vessels, which left immediately for home, and a few crew members seeking Mediterranean sun or flying back to England, the main fleet went on to Middelburg, Veere, and Wohlfahrtsdijk in the Veerse Meer, where Wendy, dispatched on reconnaissance, had found a mechanic to fit a new impeller for *Quantz*. By Wednesday evening we were together in Goes having enjoyed the sail to Sandberg and the challenge of locking into the canal from the Oosterschelde. The canal voyage was notable for sun-bathing and swimming on the end of a tow-rope. It must have been somewhere during these two days that a puzzled Dutchman, reading the message painted on *Sea Swallow's* dodgers called out, with a continental accentuation of the final 'e'. "For Salé. That is a funny name!"

Kehaar, Mako, the J24, and *Wombat,* Howard Nash's little Hunter 19, left early the next morning bound for Orford. *Sea Swallow* and *Quantz* had less sense of urgency, and I was nervous about the immediate forecast. It was a breezy day with sunshine, once clear of the canal we had a fine sail to Willemstad reefed down and reduced for a time to the jib alone. The following day, Friday 13[th.] there was another fresh westerly force 5 or 6 at times. We sailed on to Stellendam, where the jib lost a clew, blown out. I kept wondering, bearing in mind the inauspicious date as well as the conditions – not without reason, as it turned out – how the other three, particularly *Wombat,* had enjoyed the sea crossing. Once again Wendy's moped was mobilised, this time to find a sail-maker in Hellevoetsluis to repair the jib. So we spent the night there and she left for her ferry early the next morning.

After a successful sail repair we sailed and motored back to Stellendam in pleasant, moderate conditions, and were soon through the lock. Beating down the Stikgat Channel we then set course due west on a close reach passing the Goeree Tower in early evening and the Euro Number One Buoy at 2000. *Sea Swallow* had remained in close company thus far but, as darkness fell, we agreed to continue independently. A good sailing breeze from the south came with sunset, so it was a fine night's sail with the wind abeam, only a moon or starlight, obscured by cloud, might have improved it. After negotiating the shipping lanes, by midnight we were alone, having lost sight of *Sea Swallow* some time before. With the dawn, however, the wind freshened and we soon reduced to jib alone, still making at least five knots. We sighted the Outer Gabbard about 0500 and passed the lightship at 0615. Here we set the main again but almost at once reefed, then double reefed, then lowered the main and finally the jib.

By 0700 force 7 gusts and rain squalls reduced visibility considerably.

Between squalls we caught sight of the Shipwash to the north-east. Under bare poles we motored towards Orford Haven, a wet and uncomfortable experience, but not impossibly so. Reaching the Haven Buoy at 1200 we lingered for half an hour; then entered against the ebb; 'considerable swell but no problems' – I suspect the entrance was deeper in those years as it seems to have been common practice not to wait for a flood tide, which I would not risk nowadays. I was anxious about *Sea Swallow*, given the discomfort of the last few hours, but as soon as we were in shelter we sighted her sails coming down the Hollesley Bay shore as pretty as you please. We waited for her at Dove Point so as to arrive at Orford Quay together. My log summary concludes:

'Received an enthusiastic welcome from other crews who had experienced a lively passage, with Aldeburgh lifeboat to the rescue of *Wombat*. Overall a successful trip, not least for *Sea Swallow,* whose captain and crew deserve high commendation as do crew and one-woman shore-party of *Quantz;* value of independent judgement on timing of return trip and weather shown by experience.'

Charles Iliff also had even more right to feel satisfaction.

'On the return, strong headwinds, and one yacht (*Mako*) gave continuous assistance to another (*Wombat*); courage and perseverance from both, and exhilaration too. The biggest of many lessons learned – the value of making passages in company. It has been a party, but undertaken with full seriousness. A group of small cruisers has done much in a few days' holiday. Of the nine skippers, three had never skippered on passage before, and of the 34 crew members 16 were new to passage making. Something like 7000 individual sea miles of experience were gained in the nine round trips. Orford feels that it knows a little more about the North Sea and southern Holland.'

The story of *Wombat* and *Mako* requires its own fuller narrative from the respective skippers and the perspective of the lifeboat crew. Howard Nash has written:

'What follows are intense but incomplete memories of a dramatic event when, as a relative newcomer to cruising and passage making, I sailed *Wombat*, my 19ft Hunter Europa, from Holland back to Orford in unexpectedly difficult conditions. Although tiny, the Europa 19 is very seaworthy – one came tenth in the 1972 Single-handed Transatlantic.

In August 1982 I took part in an informal rally for cruisers organised loosely under the aegis of Orford Sailing Club. A dozen or so skippers decided to sail their boats from Orford across to southern Holland. On the day of departure the weather was good, with every prospect of it remaining so.

It was my first passage in her across the southern North Sea. Navigation at that time was limited to dead reckoning and homing in on RDF. I was inexperienced in both, especially landfalls. Nevertheless we made it to Flushing and spent a pleasant week working our way through inland waters to Goes. My crew comprised my wife Monique and my son William, then just 16. It was quite a tight squeeze in the tiny cabin at bedtime.

We planned to make our return passage on Thursday August 12th. I checked the weather forecast the previous evening – the fine weather was about to break; a series of Atlantic lows were on their way. For the next 24 hours, gales and strong winds were predicted for many sea areas around the British Isles, although not in the southern North Sea. The longer term outlook was very unsettled. The 0600 forecast was much the same. This was a dilemma.

I didn't want to get stuck with my boat in Holland for an extended period. I talked to other skippers and, after some debate with my crew, I decided to join *Mako* and *Kehaar* and make a run for home.

We left Goes mid-morning, and once clear of the Roompotsluis and Customs we passed through the sea-lock into open waters in the early afternoon. From there we reckoned the crossing would take around 16 to 18 hours, so we should arrive at the Ore river mouth early the following morning.

The passage began with a fast sail to windward under reefed main and working jib. The wind was force 5 occasionally 6, from a south-west to west direction. My two crew and I were in the cockpit, taking turns on and off watch and at the helm, and drinking occasional cups of tea and hot soup. Although *Wombat* sails a little slower than *Mako* and *Kehaar*, she's a fast boat and we were able to keep the others in sight.

By early evening the wind had veered and strengthened significantly, and the sea state became more agitated. As night fell, we double-reefed the mainsail.

Our passage plan had been to take a direct course for the Sunk light vessel, passing south of the dangers of the Shipwash bank. The changing conditions headed us however and we could no longer lay a direct course for the Sunk. The only thing to do was to sail close-hauled and maintain boat speed, with a view to passing north of the Shipwash and seeking shelter in the lee of the coast as soon as possible. Despite the worsening conditions and her small size *Wombat* was still sailing amazingly well.

I took over the helm in the small hours of Friday 13th. Monique was on deck with me and William was below. As it turned out I was to stay there more or less continuously for the next 13 hours. William too. I shall never forget the dawn, when it finally came – an ominous red sky of wind-blown clouds mixed in with other strange sickly colours. They looked like streaky bacon gone off.

By then we were certainly through the shipping lanes, but I had only the vaguest idea of our position. The sea was now quite rough, with green water washing over the deck and into the cockpit. Although the wash-board was in place, water was finding its way down into the cabin via the loosely-fitting hatch. Everything below was soaked, including all our paper charts, not to mention poor William.

During the morning various things went wrong. First the inner fore-stay came away from its deck fitting – the plastic had snapped. Whilst dealing with this problem I dislodged the screw-down cap of the cabin ventilator, and it fell overboard, leaving a hole in the foredeck. I lashed a plastic bag over it, but this was only partially effective.

Sometime later we noticed that boat speed had dropped and that the mast was rocking back and forth as the boat pitched about. The fore-stay's bow fitting had sheared. The mast was now being held up by only the foresail halyard. I quickly took the spare halyard forward, attached it to an eye on the bow, and tensioned it as much as I could. Then I replaced the foresail with the storm-jib, partly because of the increased wind strength but also to take advantage of the strength of its wire luff. This improved boat speed but only to about three and a half knots, so progress was slow. I unsuccessfully attempted to start the Seagull outboard. It was always a temperamental old thing.

At some point a ferry bound for Harwich passed us, which was comforting. We must be approaching the coast, but whereabouts? When Sizewell Power Station appeared, I didn't immediately recognise it. We pressed on, accompanied by *Mako*, who knew we were in some difficulty and had no VHF. Their presence too was immensely comforting.

Closer to the coast we tacked for home. The huge waves had breaking crests and were now more or less head on to us. In the troughs, the wind completely disappeared. Somehow, instinctively, I discovered I could cope with the waves by luffing up so the bow would break through the crests, then quickly bearing away to gather enough momentum to carry us through the lull in the troughs and climb the next wall of water before breaking through its crest. Once mastered, it was an exhilarating dance, tinged with terror at the sight from each crest of a myriad more to come.

At some point in the afternoon, somewhere off Aldeburgh, I noticed an odd thing. The distance shown on my trip recorder was no longer increasing. The tide had turned – were we going backwards? Our prospects were diminishing.

Then Monique suddenly called "Look!" and pointed behind us. My first thought, when I saw the Aldeburgh lifeboat with ten burly chaps in bright orange weather gear lined up on the rail, was that I was hallucinating and seeing a Gilbert and Sullivan chorus about to burst into song. I had no idea they were coming but I am very glad they did. It turned out that *Mako* had been talking to them on VHF.

After coming alongside and taking my crew off they asked what I wanted to do. I asked them to tow me into the River. "We'll give it a go, but not with you on board, Sir." They replied. So I took down the sails and lashed the tiller whilst a lifeboat-man tied a long line round the base of the mast.

I watched from the lifeboat as *Wombat* slewed around a bit under tow, but she still kept going. An hour later they set me down on Orford Quay and I sailed *Wombat* back to her mooring. My crew and I owe a lot to David Foreman and John Oakes on *Mako* for their support throughout this adventure and to the men of Aldeburgh RNLI who came to our rescue. My deep and sincere thanks remain with all of them.'

The lifeboat *James Cable* had launched earlier in response to a call from a fishing boat in difficulty, which was towed into the river Ore and moored safely alongside another fishing vessel. At 1345, while heading back to Aldeburgh, they received a message from Thames Coastguard reporting *Wombat* 'in difficulties five miles south east of Sizewell.' The subsequent rescue was also reported in the East Anglian Daily Times with a further account in the Lifeboat Magazine later that year. A full 24 years further on the story appears again in a book about the history of the Lifeboat Service entitled *Never Turn Back*. The particular feature which attracted such attention was the role played by *Mako*, her skipper, David Foreman and crew, John Oakes. An extract from the chapter 'Why do they do it?' has the sub-heading 'Self Help' and speaks for itself:

'If there is any lingering doubt about the competence of some yachtsmen, and their ability to help themselves and others, an incident off Suffolk should dispel it. A 19ft yacht *Wombat*, on passage from Orford to Holland, got into difficulties in the night. Her rigging was damaged in rising winds which increased during the morning to gale force, so the crew made temporary repairs, but she was uncertain of her position. A companion yacht had to leave *Wombat* and go on ahead when her own navigation lights failed, to avoid collision. However, another yacht, *Mako*, kept company with *Wombat*, helping her with navigation. *Mako's* crew had an exhausting and difficult time, as they had to circle round *Wombat* to make enough speed to counter the very rough seas. Constant gybing and tacking took their toll on the crew and they worried they might damage their boat. Aldeburgh lifeboat was called, took the three crew off *Wombat* and towed her to Orford Quay, a relatively straightforward six hour rescue in a force 8 gale. For *Mako's* crew the relief was immense.'

David Foreman certainly endorses that sentiment, expressed in a letter of thanks to Billy Burrell after the event:

'When you and your crew of brave gentlemen arrived, the relief with which *Mako's* crew were able to shed the responsibility was enormous. Suddenly we could look to ourselves, put up the sail we needed to control the boat and start trying to avoid the breakers.'

As he has also told this author: 'the descriptions by the *James Cable* that the gale was force 8 and that the sea was "very rough" are measured scientific ones for their official logs. Their "force 8" is 39-46 mph, and sea state "very rough" is 4-6 metres, though I am not convinced we had 6 metres until later when we had to beat through the wind versus tide overfalls near the lighthouse after the rescue. Great big hills they were. I do recall that when we finally came up the river towards Orford I watched the seas visibly breaking on the seaward side of the Crouch, chucking spray way over towards the river, so it must have been pretty rough out there. It is most important to note that on this occasion I was not alone – John Oakes was with me, and he was a tower of strength and resilience.'

There must have been many moments during that night and morning when they wondered what the final outcome would be. At one point John Oakes nodded off and, waking all too soon, confided to David that he had just been dreaming of walking up Quay Street, back in Orford safe and sound, which, they convinced themselves, was a good omen.

Remembering my own blessed sense of relief at gaining the shelter of the river two days later in less strong winds, but after several uncomfortable hours– and with the image of the J24, to my eyes more like an overgrown racing dinghy with a bit of a roof than a cruising yacht– I am very glad I was not in their situation. Nevertheless they fully deserved the description in *Never Turn Back*: 'a well-found boat with a competent crew' – an accolade in itself. There is a photo taken over the bows of *Mako* with just the peak of *Wombat's* sail showing above the surging waves ahead (see page 128). That says even more.

8. Ditch-crawlers and other cruisers

After the excitement of those joint voyages to Holland and back, the next few years, at least for me and *Quantz*, were less adventurous. For various reasons I had less time for longer trips but there were still good moments. In 1983, during a solo visit to the Deben, engine failure forced me to practise the art of picking up moorings and anchoring under sail by myself. It also made me think more carefully about when and how to leave one river and re-enter the other without stranding on the shoals. This was a salutary reminder of the skills which earlier generations had taken for granted.

That summer we reluctantly said farewell to *Sea Swallow*, sold to Donald de Cogan from Nottingham University, who moved her to the Broads. To clinch the sale we sailed her round Havergate Island together in an ideal north-easterly breeze, which showed her off perfectly. Later, after Don had won the Aldeburgh Regatta Mirror trophy in *Pussyfoot*, he and Ralph, now an undergraduate student at Oxford Polytechnic, accompanied me on a quick voyage to the Colne and back. Tempted by fair weather, we left the river just as darkness fell and sailed south overnight. My log narrative describes this as 'a good sail' and continues:

'Slight swell to Cork and Roughs but then, with wind aft, rolled about rather in following breeze. But good progress to Knoll with half moon. Compass light malfunction, but able to follow a ship's stern light on same bearing 250° for a couple of hours and the lights of Clacton and buoys were usually helpful too. Poorer light and visibility and visibility pre-dawn gave us a little difficulty in finding the Colne entrance. Motored in as wind heading from North. Anchored in time for Rule Britannia. Bed.'

The reference to Rule Britannia is a nostalgic echo of many times at the end of a night at sea when our morale responded to the patriotic medley titled 'The UK Theme', which used to follow the early morning shipping forecast on Radio Four. Sadly it was replaced early this century by a depressing News Briefing.

At the end of that season I also had the bonus of two perfect late October days enhanced by the absence of the engine, which had been removed for overhaul. *Quantz* rode high and light in the water 'tacking like a dinghy'. This agility was useful going up Butley Creek above the Ferry in light winds one day and coming back over the river-mouth Bar after a short excursion into Hollesley Bay on the other occasion.

Meanwhile that same summer Charles Iliff in *Kehaar*, with Howard Nash aboard, undaunted by the *Wombat* experience, or seeking to exorcise it, had crossed to Ostend. They were in company with *Icterus*, sailed by Richard Waite, with his brother, Sam, and Peter Norris. Together they explored the canal system to Bruges and Gent. First, however, their masts had to be lowered in Ostend, which, according to Charles 'could be done quickly and by hand.' His account is entitled: 'The advantages of smaller cruisers.' It also reflects his taste for inland waterways.

'We then motored along the canal to Bruges and locked through the extraordinary ancient circular lock (with three exits, one to Zeebrugge) into the Bruges ring canal. We spent two or three days in an old canal arm in the historic centre. Then the 30 mile canal to Gent and on to Terneuzen in Holland. There the masts were erected and we sailed down the Scheldt to Flushing and Middelburg.

Yachts from Orford routinely sail to Ostend. But I am glad to have done the Bruges-Gent connection and I have not heard of anyone else doing it, whether or not from Orford. In a larger yacht than ours, 22 and 23 ft, involving a crane to remove the mast and then erect it again, it would not have happened.'

This mention of masts and cranes reminds me that in those years almost all the smaller yachts at Orford were lifted out for the winter by Ralph Brinkley. They were then parked in his yard behind the river wall or trundled behind his ancient tractor up Quay Street to some corner of a convenient garden. At the beginning of the next season the whole process was reversed. These rituals were not without a touch of hazard and uncertainty.

For many years Orford Quay was dominated by the gaunt triangle of a crane which loaded and unloaded heavy material for Orfordness. It was hand operated by a windlass. Ralph usually wound the handle and swung the crane himself so others were needed to fend off the suspended hulls from the edge of the quay, to handle ropes fore and aft, to unscrew rigging and to control the masts as they swung drunkenly ashore. Sometimes Chris Martin or A.N. Other was recruited but mainly it was down to owners and their friends. Exactly who might or might not be liable in the event of an accident and whether anybody's insurance would cover it was a matter of conjecture and faith. The other great uncertainty was the perennial difficulty of establishing a firm date and time when Ralph and the crane might be available. Wind and tide were other variables alongside the vagaries of Ralph's personal calendar. Getting all these factors lined up with the owners' working lives could be frustrating.

When the old crane was finally dismantled Ralph acquired a battered ex-military mobile crane, which did not inspire entire confidence despite his assurances that it passed annual inspections. To be fair, I am not aware of any serious accident or injury with either crane. Ralph did know what he was doing whether afloat or ashore, even if his business was conducted according to his own idiosyncratic methods and time-table – a characteristic Suffolk syndrome. Those who adjusted to it and remained loyal did not regret it; a few became exasperated and went elsewhere.

Later, of course, Larkmans at Melton became the preferred winter base for many Orford yachts, including my own for a quarter of a century. Chris Martin gave very good service to others; more recently, the watchful eye of Philip Atwood and the water-taxi service of *Chantry* have been invaluable to visiting yachts and Orford sailors alike.

Amongst arrivals in Orford during this decade were Clem and Judith Lister. They were soon established at Walnut Corner, off Ferry Road, and as pillars of the community. Following his Army career, stretching back to the siege of Malta and the liberation of Norway, Clem had enjoyed a second professional life with Marconi. When he finally retired they moved from Burnham-on-Crouch to the Ore with their Contest 33 *Hermione of Burnham* and a wealth of cruising experience.

The annual publication of the Royal Cruising Club *Roving Commissions*, for two successive years in the mid-1980s, contains contributions by Clem Lister. The first, from the 1984 edition, is titled 'To Paris and Back from the East Coast – Advice for Ditch-Crawlers' and contains much useful information, some of which I was glad to glean from him directly when I was planning the same voyage in 1986. Unlike *Quantz*, *Hermione* was equipped with a mast tabernacle, which with help 'from a few strong hands' enabled him to lower it independently in Rouen and raise it again on leaving the Somme. I have the impression that for Clem, an intensely practical man, skilled with his hands, as his wood-work and carving also proved, this technical achievement was almost as satisfying as the rest of the voyage. Tellingly his summary concludes:-

'We thoroughly enjoyed our trip. There was a great deal of variety in the country and types of canal. We visited many towns and met lots of interesting people, yachtsmen of course, but also bargees and other locals. As a change from sailing from one harbour to another, we can recommend it even if some of it can be called water-caravanning. It is slow and one must be prepared to be held up for the odd day. For those who have the time it is a new experience and for me it was the proof that my design of mast raising gear really did work, though in the event we could have managed without it.'

His second article: 'Hermione's Cruise 1985.' describes their voyage to Tréguier in North Brittany and back; this time, clearly, 'sailing from one harbour to another'. Two features stand out for me.

First, the frequent adverse weather, winds often force 6 or 7, secondly the Lister gift for making friends and enjoying the company of other yachts and crews. On arrival in Dieppe, for instance, they were 'promptly invited for a drink aboard the Dutch boat to which we were moored. This was our first meeting with Hans and Marion de Regt in their 36 foot ketch, *Spray*.' This couple and their boat are mentioned in several other ports, Fécamp, Ouistreham, Cherbourg and St Peter Port, on Guernsey. So too are their immediate neighbours in Orford, Dick and Libby Bizzey, sailing *Umtali*, whom they had met by arrangement. The Bizzeys, however, sailed under the flag of Aldeburgh Yacht Club, and did not moor at Orford. Later, both *Hermione* and *Umtali* returned to Fécamp and Dieppe before heading into St Valery, where even Clem had his moment of difficulty.

'We have been into the Somme several times but this time we ran aground due to a misplaced buoy off Le Crotoy. It took us twenty minutes to get off but it left poor Dick in a quandary since he draws more than we do. He had been warned by a German in Dieppe that one mark was out of place, but had not got his vital data. We got into St Valery tying up together in the marina at noon.'

One earlier reference bears witness to the length of Clem and Judith's cruising history as they approach Tréguier in better weather.

'We had a glorious trip with excellent visibility past Roches Douvres, which we had first seen 30 years before at 100 yards in thick fog...We had not been to Tréguier for 20 years and found the river very different, well dredged and buoyed.'

Finally, during the return passage, I detect further evidence of Clem's pleasure in making things work, whatever the weather.

'On Friday July 19th the wind was west 6 and we left Boulogne at 0930 putting in a reef in the outer harbour. We had to plug the tide initially to ensure we got to Calais in time to lock in. We had quite a beat up to Cap Gris Nez and put in a second reef, more to test my new reefing line than from necessity. It worked well. Soon we bore away and with the tide and a 6-7 behind us, we were doing over seven knots over the ground.'

Then, in a final sentence, he concludes: 'we did have some good weather and met lots of very interesting people.' They will have enjoyed meeting him too.

As will be apparent from Caroline Gill's summary of her parents' cruises, they also met the Listers while 'ditch-crawling' and probably on other voyages.

'Henry and Charmian Baker waited until they were retired before they started cruising. A windfall meant that Dad's dream nearly had an earlier realisation but the Fairey Marine Atlanta became a cottage in Snape and cruising turned into Wayfarer racing at Aldeburgh.

Their long-awaited first boat was an eight metre Catalac, *Cirrus*. Their plan was to cruise for at least six weeks every summer in comfort, i.e. without heeling. They enjoyed travelling down the Rance to Dinan and along the canal. George and Nancy McKnight joined them on at least one of these trips.

We all managed to meet up one summer, Chris and I and our two boys, aged five and three, in our 34ft Sparkman and Stevens, *Maratu,* managed to rendezvous in Dieppe, quite a feat in the days before mobile phones. I recall they had travelled slowly with a foul wind via Chichester and the Isle of Wight, while with small children tucked up in their bunks, we did the usual overnighter from Orford. We all sailed to Barfleur, where in those days you could dry out, tied to the wall of the harbour.

Cirrus travelled fast and was comfortable, but also a bit of a beast in a lock or mooring in a marina. That may be why you don't see so many now. After many successful holidays Henry fell overboard sailing north back to Orford. Charmian managed to get him back on board and made the requisite radio calls; but that was the end of catamaran sailing.

Their next boat was to be their favourite. *Withy* was a 26 foot Contessa, completely kitted out in a red colour scheme down below, as befits a Skipper and Mate celebrating their Ruby Wedding anniversary. After the catamaran, *Withy* sailed like a dream and in spite of her modest size took them to France and along the Seine to Paris, where they met up with Clem and Judith Lister. Henry found the lack of headroom difficult so, after much research, the Sabre 27 *Dolphin* was bought. Mostly they then sailed the East Coast rivers, which they loved. They made lifelong friends with a couple who kept their boat in the Woodbridge Tide Mill Harbour and spent many happy times with them. *Dolphin* is still on the river at Orford, owned by Ben Johnston and Geoffrey Smeed, and it is lovely to see her.'

Nick Oglethorpe, who lived in Quay House at this time, had graduated through smaller yachts to a Sovereign 35 ketch called *Sensibility*. David Foreman remembers a previous black Contessa 26 called *Sage*, sailed locally and traded in for a Contessa 32, his first *Sensibility*. David once sailed with him in lumpy conditions at sea; she was a wet boat but he thinks it was this one he navigated to Ostend for Nick, in murky visibility, to arrive dead on course, to his pleasant surprise. By 1979 or thereabouts Nick had acquired the larger, more comfortable Sovereign, his second *Sensibility*. In 1980 David sailed with him and John Oakes from Woodbridge to Holland early in the season. The crossing was cold and windy, sailing under genoa alone. David left them in Hoorn. Nick went on with a different crew to Sweden and it was there that John Oakes joined him again later in the summer. Nick had a friend with him from Ipswich, called Ted. They were not far from Stockholm and were guided into the main harbour by a very friendly former harbourmaster whom they met at the lock before entering. From their mooring they could see the building which housed *Vasa*, the Swedish *Mary Rose*, capsized in 1628 and now recovered. In 1980 she was still in the early stage of restoration, as they were able to see for themselves when they visited the imposing structure. In 2002 I had the same impressive experience, although by then the work was complete.

John has shared his memories of a series of interesting encounters and incidents. After mooring 'bows on' in the best Baltic manner at Vaxholm, just east of Stockholm, John went ashore for a walk. An attractive young woman waylaid him and invited herself back aboard. Hitching her skirt ever higher she suggested they might all go ashore. "I'll get my shoes," said Nick, and went below. The sight of Nick opening the oven door in the galley to retrieve his footwear apparently unnerved the girl because she suddenly rushed off the boat. As they watched her go, they saw several young toughs emerge from cover and disappear with their decoy. Nick's shoes had perhaps saved them from burglary, or worse. The explanation for their presence in the oven was that, earlier on, Nick had been on his way ashore with a bag of rubbish, which involved climbing over the pulpit, where he slipped, and was left suspended, half in and half out of the water. It was a little while before his shouts attracted Ted from the cabin to haul him back. His shoes and lower clothing needed to dry out.

On a more reassuring note, when they moved to an apparently private jetty, the owner not only made them welcome, but invited them to watch the Wimbledon Men's Singles Final, which proved to be the last triumph of the pride of Sweden, Bjorn Borg – incidentally confirming 1980 as the date of this cruise. After that they were not only treated to a barbecue supper but carried off to the nearest night-spot in town.

Another day, under No.1 jib alone, 'in a bit of a blow', they headed into a narrow fiord-like refuge, which only offered a pontoon alongside what appeared to be a yacht breaking yard. It was a relief to be waved in by an elderly lady to a secure berth. A beautiful, classic 12 Metre yacht was laid up on the opposite shore and they were invited aboard an equally splendid former Pilot cutter for supper with the skipper and his family.

The friendliness of Swedes, however, was sometimes tinged with amusement at the antics of *Sensibility* and her crew. Approaching one of the pretty island anchorages where a group of yachts was anchored by the bows to the shore with stern anchors also duly deployed, Nick steered in to the remaining space. With bow anchor safely ashore John was sent off in the rubber dinghy with another kedge on a line to drop astern. It was immediately apparent that the depth was much too great and a second warp, when attached, only produced the same embarrassing result. Nick managed to find a third line, which he hurriedly passed, yet again, to John – unfortunately forgetting that he needed to keep his end on board. "You had better hang on to your end, Nick"! shouted John, amid some hilarity from the spectators. This time the anchor held; John survived the cruise, and, so far as we know, so did *Sensibility*. (Baltic yachts, of course, carry drums of line on the stern pulpit all ready to reel out).

The summer of 1984 was saddened by the death of my Aunt Nan after two years of nursing home care. But in August my son Ralph, with a fellow student friend of his called Jim, accompanied me in *Quantz* to Ostend. It was a straightforward crossing from Levington in some 20 hours, which we all enjoyed. After a day's rest we made the short coastal trip to Zeebrugge. Instead of Charles Iliff's route to Bruges we went up the ship canal from Zeebrugge without lowering the mast. This prevented going further than the industrial outskirts of the city so we had to walk into the centre to see the sights and the evening 'illuminations'. When the bridges re-opened in the morning we retraced our course down the canal and sailed on up the coast to Breskens.

On our way into Flushing the next day we encountered the intrepid *Wombat* with Howard Nash and another Orford boat, Chris Tweed's *Wild Child,* a Leisure 23. We just had time in the next 24 hours to shop in Middelburg and moor for an idyllic overnight stay at one of the islands in the Veerse Meer, surrounded only by grazing sheep and roe deer. The return crossing was also quiet and calm, eerily so in the hours just before dawn when crossing the shipping lines in poor visibility under engine. Every five minutes we switched off to listen uneasily for the sound of other engines. Fortunately we neither saw nor heard anything before sunrise and better visibility returned with a useful breeze for the last leg. Jim had experienced an almost ideal introduction to North Sea sailing, although I am not aware he ever followed it up. He was, however, an amusing and cheerful companion on a voyage which was unusually easy for me with two young men as crew.

This would also be the situation in 1986 on a much longer four-week cruise up the Seine to Paris and back via the Seine-Oise Canal and down the Somme to St. Valery. This took place from May 23rd, following my early retirement from full-time work the previous autumn, which had released me from the bonds of the school term regime. It was a luxurious freedom which was shared by Don, our youngest, who was enjoying a gap year and had kept this time free to sail with me between working in the Alps and Camp America. His school friend William came with us.

As we headed down the Narrows towards Dove Point on the last of the ebb we gave William the helm so that he could get the hang of steering. He was doing well, so I said: "just keep her heading straight for that buoy at the end of the island" – and disappeared below with Don to sort out charts. William obeyed orders to the letter, but I should have remembered how shallow it is close to the Point at low water. *Quantz* came to an undignified halt somewhere short of the buoy and clearly was not going to move until the tide began to rise. Although it was late afternoon we were not in a hurry to leave the river until there was enough water on the bar so I was not unduly upset, except at my own carelessness. I was, however, both annoyed and embarrassed by the fact that the Glaisters were following us downriver and would witness our predicament. We decided to have an early supper down below and pretend to have 'parked' on purpose.

Finally clear of the river, passing the Glaisters with a cheerful wave, we had a fine overnight sail to North Foreland, then past Ramsgate about 0900. As we approached the French coast the tide was clearly adverse for Boulogne so we headed for Calais where we narrowly escaped a further embarrassment. My newly acquired Tillerpilot had performed well during the night but must have drained the battery. Approaching harbour, after a tedious beat eastward from Cap Gris Nez in choppy water, we were forced to enter under sail (clearly forbidden) closely followed by a large ferry and shouted at by harbour authorities. Once safely moored in the outer harbour the battery was re-charged with the help of a nearby catamaran. It was midnight by the time we passed into the inner harbour to find a proper bath and showers. No arrest, further rebuke or fines ensued. If William had started to wonder whether the skipper knew what he was about, he refrained from comment. Don and I put it all down to 'Archibald', a gremlin who lived somewhere below decks and was held responsible for all untoward events.

After a day's rest in Calais we departed at first light the next morning to reach Fécamp, always a favourite harbour, some 30 hours later at 0900. The same evening a short fast sail with favouring tide took us Le Havre for the night. Tidal assistance was also essential for the next stage from the mouth of the Seine to Rouen, where the mast would have to be lowered and *Quantz* would become a motor-cruiser, all the way to Paris and back to the sea. From a point opposite Honfleur at noon we averaged ten kilometres an hour, measured by each passing riverbank marker, with the wind astern and some engine use to maximise speed. Even so we were ten kilometres short of Rouen when the tide slackened and turned against us. We reached our goal, the Bassin St. Gervais, in fading light at 2115, exactly 12 hours from Le Havre. 'It might have been difficult to do in a day if there had been less tide or adverse wind', I noted in the log.

Friday May 30th, a week after our departure from Orford, started well enough. We located the hand-operated crane for lowering masts, manoeuvred underneath it, and carried out the operation successfully. The crutches, which I had prepared to stand on the stern locker, took the weight, and the mast projected only a foot or two over bow and stern respectively. Once all the rigging had been properly lashed and stowed we were ready to proceed. Then Archibald played his master stroke. As soon as we were ready to leave the jetty and move upstream the engine refused to start.

Assuming another battery problem I walked some distance to the yacht station at Villetard to borrow a spare and lug it back. But the engine did not respond. When I finally found a mechanic who was willing to have a look, the diagnosis was a defunct starter motor, with no possibility of spares, nor of a replacement until next week. It was inevitably a Friday, and *Quantz* was now a motor-cruiser without a motor. At this low point another British yacht, *Sabreur*, an East Anglian One-Design with a solo skipper called Stephen, arrived to use the crane. It was too late for him to start on his mast so he came aboard to commiserate over drinks with us until past midnight.

Sabreur was de-masted on Saturday as a combined effort, celebrated with wine and pâté, after which she towed us to a more attractive berth at the Ile Lacroix, which also offered 'douches' and was more central. Morale rose somewhat but it was not until the following Friday, that we finally left Rouen with a new starter motor delivered from Paris and fitted on the Thursday afternoon. Intervening days had been spent shopping, visiting the Cathedral and other sites of interest or finding cheap restaurants and bars, preferably those where the 1986 Football World Cup was being shown on television. These at least offered some evening entertainment to the crew.

Despite grey and chilly weather for early June it was a great relief to be under way that morning. Our first lock, at Amfreville, was negotiated at 1700 'with some drama but no scratches'. After that the Seine river-scape was increasingly attractive, not least the 'Bras Morts', backwaters or secondary channels. These were reminiscent of the Upper Thames or even Thorpeness, with smart riverside cottages, thatch-roofed and half-timbered, their lawns running down to private landing-stages or rougher fishing huts. It was easy to imagine a Simenon plot in some of these shuttered weekend retreats. In the background chalky downland hills rose on either side.

Late that first evening we moored at Les Andelys under the battlements of Château Gaillard, dating back to the reign of Richard Coeur de Lion. I climbed up to explore the castle early in the morning. A note in the log describes: 'a marvellous situation, dominating the river bend with wooded hills behind; had it entirely to myself apart from birdsong and the friendly ghosts of Norman knights.' Leaving at 1000 we kept going for a full day finding no real problems with various locks or passing péniches. Again the 'bras morts' were most attractive as was the reach past La Roche-Guyon. In sunshine with a following breeze we averaged 7.5 kilometres per hour or more. Finally we moored for the night at Meulan on the jetty of an empty house.

We were up early on Sunday June 8th to head for the capital. This would be Don's first arrival in Paris, probably William's too. To approach by river would, I thought, be a special experience. Drizzle at dawn gave way to long sunny periods and even sun-bathing on deck. We had two easy locks to ourselves until the last, alongside big barges, but with no undue difficulty. Conflans Ste Honorine, near the junction with the Oise, the capital of the barge world, where the bargees have their own church, was passed soon after midday and the river banks became more industrial and suburban. As evening came and the city itself hove into sight we started to look for a mooring. By 1900 we were abreast of the Eiffel Tower but the banks were full and the passing traffic of péniches was causing considerable swell, so we pressed on past the Ile de la Cité and Notre Dame to seek the lock entrance to Canal St Martin with its 'port de plaisance'. This we entered at 1950 with ten minutes spare before its Sunday closure. Arrival was celebrated in the nearest pizzeria, followed by the luxury of showers. Finally, after a session on the dodgem cars of a street fair in the Place de la Bastille, we retired to our bunks – 'tired but pleased'.

We allowed ourselves two full days of Parisian exploration visiting the main tourist attractions from the Eiffel Tower to Notre Dame, the Louvre and the Pompidou Centre, then relatively new. I dragged Don all the way to the great Cemetery of Père Lachaise, where we found the sadly dilapidated tomb of Sir Richard Wallace and his father Lord Hertford, once owners of the Sudbourne Estate and most of Orford. We also climbed the steps from Montmartre up to the Sacré Coeur one evening for my favourite view across the city as darkness fell and the lights shone out below. William sometimes preferred rest and contemplation to extra exertion. There was another bout of dodgem car rivalry on our last evening. Altogether the central location of the Canal St Martin close to the Place de la Bastille and its Métro station was a great advantage.

On our six day voyage back to the sea, we first retraced our route as far as the junction with the river Oise, which we followed upstream until we joined the less rural, more functional section of the Canal du Nord leading us into the upper reaches of the Somme. Before leaving the Seine we met *Sabreur* again, and for the last time, as Stephen made his more leisurely way towards Paris and onwards to the Med. Even Friday 13th did not tempt Archibald from his lair as we negotiated the narrow locks along these waterways. Some, on the Canal du Nord, are also deep and just long enough for two barges at a time. They tend, therefore, to operate in pairs, which may force a single yacht to wait for several openings before there is room to enter. We were lucky to find a single barge heading north and made haste to keep with it it as far as we could.

The gradual descent of the Somme valley over the next three days in warm, sunny weather remains, for me, the great memory of this cruise, alongside the early morning at Les Andelys and its castle. Together they almost erased the scars of the long delay in Rouen. The river was about three boat lengths wide, fringed with willow and rushes from which the rods and lines of anglers often protruded, especially at the weekend. To avoid their anger and the shallows on the bends it was important to steer down the centre of the stream. The locks were small, and almost always empty; we met very little other traffic. More than once we came across historic inscriptions carved into the masonry recording the names of the Royal Engineers who had repaired the locks damaged in the First World War. Passing through villages it was noticeable that the brickwork of most buildings, above foundation level, was almost always relatively new, in this case due to the Second War. More telling still, every few miles on some distant hillside, we could see the white lines of the headstones in war cemeteries, which seemed to march, like regiments, into the valley they had fought to defend or conquer.

Arrival at each lock aroused some nervous tension. They often had the rustic, abandoned air of a country station in the middle of England, like Adlestrop in the haunting poem by Edward Thomas. Here too: 'no one left and no one came.'

A blast on the foghorn is permitted, indeed advised, but the ensuing stillness often left us wondering if there was anyone to hear it. Eventually the lock-keeper, or his consort, would emerge, seeming surprised and even pleased to see some traffic. That pattern lasted until the Saturday evening; by then we were counting kilometres and calculating speed to reach the lock at Sailly-Laurette, due to close at 1900. If we arrived late we would miss the chance to cover another 15 kilometres before dark, putting us within a day's range of St Valery.

There is nothing at Sailly-Laurette except the lock, a bridge, a café-bar beside it, and a much smarter establishment on the other side, well beyond our means and style. We arrived with ten minutes to spare; but there was no sign of a lock-keeper. Enquiry was met with Gallic shrugs but no encouragement. It was unusual, it was indeed inexplicable, perhaps he would return within a few minutes; meanwhile, and in any case, it was not their business or concern. He did not come; at least not until past nine when it was growing dark. By then it was against all regulations to operate the lock gates: he was apologetic, but adamant. It seemed his little daughter was seriously ill in hospital and he had left early to take his wife to see the child, confident that no more boats could be expected. So there was nothing for it but to spend the night there and make the best of it.

Passing through Amiens for an overnight stop at Abbeville we reached the lock before St Valery on the Monday morning. We had checked on opening times in advance and knew we would have to wait till the afternoon to get through into the port itself. At low tide Don and I walked out about two miles following the edge of the channel, towards the dunes on the northern side of the estuary. The marker buoys lay marooned on their sides, like fish gasping for air. Between numbers 42 and 43 we waded in to swim 20 yards across and then sunbathe and build a castle on the further bank. The sea was far out beyond the horizon, lost in the haze. Flocks of sheep, hundreds of them, were grazing on that side, watched by a single shepherd. Half an hour later, having swum back across the channel, we were amazed to see the sheep and their guardian ahead of us, their trail in the wet sand marking the spot where they had crossed, like the flocks of Israel from Egypt into Sinai. Twenty Four hours later, or more, when we motored out against the flooding tide, past the same buoys swirling in the current, it was impossible to believe that any animals could have been there. We had enjoyed the hottest afternoon of the voyage but the expedition left us weary. After negotiating the final lock we were ready for a good meal in the Restaurant du Port.

It took us some time to find the necessary crane operative before the mast could be raised the next morning. Having stowed bulk stores from a huge supermarket some distance from the harbour we were 'advised' by the harbourmaster to move downstream to a berth where we were soon aground. We knew, however, that we needed to wait for the tide to rise in the long winding channel which leads out to sea. It was 1900 before we judged it possible to leave and even so we touched once in our tortuous progress between the endless series of channel markers. These did not always correspond to their charted positions; some were certainly missing. They were probably being repaired or re-painted like several others, which we had seen lined up ashore in the harbour. We were glad to follow a trawler for the last two miles of choppier, shallow water, until we were past the safe water mark.

In the last light of a fine evening we set course northwards offshore with a good breeze abeam which lasted till we were off Boulogne at first light. From this stage onwards, partly due to the adverse tide up to Gris Nez and to light variable winds, we motor-sailed for most of the homeward voyage. This lasted through the whole of Tuesday June 18th as we ploughed on in sunshine and good visibility which helped to identify our passage marks, the South Falls, Drill Stone and the Kentish Knock, until the familiar sightings of the Sunk Lightship and the Roughs Tower. At about this point in the early evening it was decided to head for Levington and the Suffolk Yacht Harbour where we berthed at 0015 on June19[th].

The choice of Levington was no doubt influenced by the fact that Jamie and his wife Frances, married the previous year, were then living in a cottage overlooking the Orwell just above the yacht harbour. Jamie had met Frances when working as a sailing instructor in the south of France and was now employed by Orwell Park School at Nacton. We were more than happy to enjoy breakfast with them that morning. At midday William and I set off for Orford while Don headed for an optician in Ipswich. Outside Harwich harbour we found a stiff north-easterly force 5 with an uncomfortable sea running over a slackening and soon hostile tide. I made one of my better decisions to return to harbour and thence by car to Orford, where we slept even more deeply. A brief note in my log book confirms that *Quantz* finally re-moored at home in lighter, easier weather, four days later.

We had been away for a full month, my longest continuous period of living aboard. I had also learned some lessons. I had not prepared the boat sufficiently, nor paid sufficient attention to engine servicing. Economy had proved costly: I should have replaced the battery at the start of the season, and, or, carried a spare. The experimental, wispy moustache I sported on return was not well received either. It came off before supper. But when it really mattered *Quantz*, and her crew, had done well; we had reached our goal, despite delays, and returned within the planned schedule. At least the study of tides and preliminary chart work had proved adequate, precautions it would have been fatal to neglect. Above all, I had the satisfaction of knowing I had accomplished at least one of my cruising ambitions, to see Paris from the water and the deck of my own ship. Another goal lay nearly two decades ahead, further north and east.

9. Maxis in the Med

The story which follows was published by *Yachting Monthly* in 1988 with the title: 'Just boring holes'. It is reproduced virtually as I then wrote it except for some concision and an addition to the account of our arrival in Bari from the skipper of *Premuda*.

'Premuda and Ciovo are the names of two islands off the Dalmatian Coast. Listeners to VHF Channel 72 in the Ionian Sea, on or about September 13th last year, might have been puzzled to hear a conversation between them.
"*Ciovo, Ciovo*, this is *Premuda*. Check course. Over"
"*Premuda*, this is *Ciovo*. Course 245. Out"

These were not, after all, the Wandering Islands of which Circe told Ulysses. *Premuda* and *Ciovo* are also the names of two Maxi 84s which happened to be at sea off the heel of Italy that morning. Their owners, Charles and Howard, had been grappling for at least a year with a problem which many yachtsmen would envy. Since 1982 the two boats had been leased to the Seven Seas Flotilla based at Primosten in Yugoslavia. The question had been how best to get them back, sooner or later, to Orford in Suffolk, their eventual intended home.

Charles and Howard knew Primosten and the Dalmatian coast well. Their arrangement with Seven Seas had included the use of the Maxis for at least one holiday in each season, and they had taken delivery of the yachts in Venice at the outset before sailing them down the Adriatic to Primosten, 30 kilometres or so north of Split. It is a cheap way of acquiring one's own boat and of fulfilling the dream of Mediterranean holidays afloat. But when the time comes to bring the boat back, it needs careful planning to decide the best route, the stages by which it is to be undertaken, and the crew to fit into these requirements.

"How would you like a trip from Primosten to Venice next September?"

This was the bait which Charles had dangled before me and others more than 12 months previously. I had never been to Venice, and the thought of seeing the city for the first time from the deck of a yacht was certainly tempting. From Venice, so the plan went, the boats would be taken overland to Holland to be sailed across the North Sea at the next opportunity. But by Christmas the plan had changed.

"We are thinking of going south round Italy and then leaving the boats in the South of France. Then the year after, or when ever it suits, we'll go on through the Canal du Midi, round Brittany and home that way."

"It's a bit further", I said, with truth. "Can you get that far in two weeks?"

"We would aim to get to France in 10 or 12 days. It's about 900 miles. After that it's a matter of coast-hopping along the Riviera to somewhere near Sète. We can manage the last part with fewer people if we have to."

A wave of nostalgia swept me back 40 years to a schoolboy exchange with a family in Nice and later undergraduate experiences. I had wandered enviously round the yacht harbours within reach, best of all my favourite, round the corner in Villefranche. One day, I had promised myself, I might even sail into one of these harbours in my own boat. This was the next best thing, a fair exchange for Venice.

As dawn broke on September 10th, 80 miles out from Primosten, I was less certain. The forecast on departure at 1300 the previous day had been for a moderate northerly; ideal if it had not blown up into a Bora. But here we were, plugging into a force 5 from just east of south. This was shovelling spray over the weather bow and causing me to regret I had not taken Stugeron much earlier. By midday the wind was even more awkward and any prospect of a dry, steady berth in harbour at Brindisi that night was long gone.

"*Ciovo, Ciovo.* This is *Premuda*. We propose change course for Bari, not Brindisi, repeat not Brindisi. Over." *Ciovo* agreed, and it was the right decision, bringing wind and sea rather more on the beam. Even so, the lighthouse at Bari was in sight for long hours before we passed the breakwater well after dark, and a bunk which lay still was very welcome.

Charles and Howard had been worrying about the Customs formalities for entry to our first Italian port involving the technical 'import' of two British yachts. Now to their relief, as with Yugoslav officials and tourist police in Primosten, the actual procedure went smoothly and without delay. Like those dire predictions in the Admiralty pilot books, the shoals of regulations were more fearsome in advance than in reality. Charles and Howard returned to announce that they were duly registered as *Commandantes* of their respective vessels. The rest of us, they emphasised, were listed as mere *marinaios*.

Nudity, however, takes no account of rank. Before this official designation Charles had gone in search of bread and milk. It turned out that we had moored in the Bari University compound. Kidnapping youngsters was a big problem at the time in Italy, security was intense, but he managed to get out to a grocer's close by. Perhaps he looked authentic. As he returned with the shopping a rowing coach told him that it was fine to have moored there, and invited us to make use of the shower block. Both crews were glad to take advantage of the kind offer and we prepared to ablute.

What we were not prepared for was sharing communal showers with a group of perfectly proportioned young Italian oarsmen. Orford's representatives did not come out of this well. Charles saw himself as a pasty-faced, desk-bound solicitor in his 30s, similarly John Pickthorn, a banker. According to Charles, I might, charitably, be described as a distinguished but retired headmaster.

Chris Tweed's figure was built for comfort; James Robinson depended on his crutches. Perhaps only Peter Norris and the Nashes gave us a little dignity.

The evening was fine and calm as we left Bari to reach Brindisi in the morning. Bari is the commercial harbour of a major provincial city; Brindisi has the maritime swagger of a naval base dating back to the Roman Empire. Frigates lay at their moorings and the crew of the jet-foil patrol boats entering harbour lined the deck to salute the Naval Memorial opposite the Roman column marking the end of the Appian Way. We would have liked to linger, but we were already behind schedule, with 800 miles or more still to go before our first French landfall. There was just time to lay in stores, sample *espressi,* and for Chris, wearing his towel like a toga, to emerge in imperial dignity from the showers on the quay. Then we headed south again.

More often than not throughout the voyage, the two Maxis were in visual range; only twice did we lose contact for more than a few hours. We gained support from sailing in company, easier in matched yachts. Being a crusty, conservative, anti-social kind of sailor, I have been inclined to disparage VHF. For a long time my boats were without it. But I had to acknowledge the value of discussing and agreeing joint decisions on changes of course or ports of call. On two occasions, James and Peter, our mechanical experts were summoned to repair minor engine faults on *Ciovo,* and once, when low on fuel, she received a transmission of *gasolio.*

Later, in the Ligurian Sea, radio contact with a larger vessel proved most helpful. In the background the disembodied shore stations provided a reassuring link with the mainland and became beacons of progress. The attractive, female, Slavonic cadences of "Split Radio, this is Split Radio" gave way to the shorter vowel sounds of Radio Bari, then Radio Crotone and Radio Messina. To prove that we had indeed passed into the Tyrrhenian Sea, we heard the operatic lilt of Radio Napoli , finally the sophisticated voice of Radio Monaco came on air to signal our approaching destination.

As we swung round the Italian peninsula the wind, at least until Elba was behind us, veered persistently with each new heading, to blow either from dead ahead or to offer only the closest of reaches in a light breeze. Usually it was so calm that this was just an apparent wind created by motor-sailing. In such weather, navigation was refreshingly simple, visibility never less than *discreta,* i.e. moderate. The main requirement of the helmsman was simply to stay awake, to watch the fuel gauge, to remain alert for other shipping and, above all, to hold a steady compass course. After Brindisi, and until we were north of Elba, even during my regular night watch from 0300 to 0500, one sweater sufficed; at midday, shade remained essential against sunburn even in September. To be alone in the cockpit in the hours leading up to a Mediterranean dawn exceeded all my fantasies. Apart from *Ciovo's* masthead light keeping us company, other vessels were rarely in sight.

As we left the Ionian Sea, Orion moved astern and swung onto the starboard quarter. Closing the land near Cape Spartivento the high mountain villages were like chaplets of fairy lights balanced improbably along the cliff-tops. Once I found myself enjoying the onset of dawn so much that I delayed waking my relief until the sun was well above the sea. Ironically, the calmest day of all was spent in the ominously named Gulf of Squillace or Bay of Squalls, notorious for sudden, dangerous gusts off the mountains. They left us severely alone.

The next morning I saw Etna for the second time in my life, first seen at the age of nearly seven from the deck of a British India ship, taking us home from East Africa. Now she unveiled her peak briefly and then withdrew into cloud as a sudden, brisk headwind whistled down the Straits to delay our arrival into Reggio by several hours. Large pizzas in the nearest restaurant and cool beers after a thirsty walk to reach it were our reward, and in the evening we dined on the terrace watching the sunset over Messina.

Navigation might be simple, but the skippers were still anxious about the direction to follow northward, complicated by calculations of fuel tank capacity and the willingness of the *marinaios* to stay with the voyage long enough to get them close to France before the claims of office, board meeting or family tore them away, like Scylla plucking the sailors of Ulysses out of his ship. Charles' original intention had been to follow the northern drift of current up to Ponza, then go westward between Sardinia and Corsica, and so up to a landfall on the southernmost part of the Côte d'Azur. This would take too long for some of us, so the best alternative was for Chris, James and Peter to disembark as far north in Italy as we could reach and to travel overland and pick up the car which they had left in northern Yugoslavia. John would catch his train from the same port of disembarkation to take him back for Monday morning in the City. I could stay with *Premuda* a little longer, as could William Howard's son, and his friend Roger, husky crewmen for *Ciovo*.

We steered well clear of Scylla, but even in flat calm the oily circles off Cape Peloro were a reminder that Charybdis was no mere poetic figment. At midnight we passed Stromboli. *Ciovo* got it right, choosing the western side with a view of the molten lava on the higher slopes; even from the east the dark cone shape which we saw from *Premuda* was still impressive. In the small hours of the next night the last of the moon silhouetted the outlying rocks of Ponza, and the heady scent of the scrub-land on these Tyrrhenian islands seemed to reach out to meet us at least as far as the lighthouse beams at the entrance. (More than 30 years on that memory remains precious).

More good pasta, wine, and a fine swim in a rocky cove made the 24-hour pause there a personal highlight. We left, as we had entered, in the early dawn, heading for Elba. The ferry from there to Livorno would take the departing crewmen to their trains. Provided the weather held, the remaining five could handle a 24-hour crossing to France.

On the strength of possessing an Italian phrase book and a taste for foreign broadcasts, I had been appointed meteorological officer, albeit with no promotion. But I failed to pick up the crucial forecast; the last I had deciphered spoke of more wind from a favourable quarter, the northeast. It did not sound like a gale and so, as soon as fuel was aboard and the galley restocked, foregoing the luxury of a night in harbour, *Premuda* and *Ciovo* were bound for Cap Corse – and on to Villefranche. This choice of port was a subtle ploy to keep me on board for this last stage, Charles having remembered a casual reference in conversation to my nostalgia for the place.

At about 0400, beyond the tip of Corsica the wind was gusting well above force 5 and both yachts had reefed down. At dawn *Ciovo* was in sight astern, just ahead of the grey shape of an American destroyer, keeping leisurely station on patrol or exercise. (There was a terrorist scare after bombs had exploded in Paris that week.) During the night Charles had seen a carrier of the Sixth Fleet and the voices of other units came up regularly on the air. We called *Ciovo* to discuss the weather: she might have a more recent forecast. The reply was not altogether reassuring.

"*Premuda*. This is *Ciovo*. Latest forecast radio Livorno last night. Northeast 5, increasing. Over."

"*Ciovo*. This is *Premuda*. Increasing indeed. Glad you have company astern. Over."

"*Premuda*. We've been dodging her for 30 minutes; clear now. Out."

A few seconds later, and before we could switch back to the listening Channel, an American voice came up on our frequency talking to a colleague. "There are two Limey yachts out here playing chicken with us." Howard, undeterred, interrupted.

"US Destroyer on my port quarter. This is yacht *Ciovo*. Request current weather prognosis. Over."

"*Ciovo*. This is *Donovan*. Sure thing. We heard your conversation and were trying to contact you. We have winds gusting 25 to 30 knots this morning, decreasing later 12 to 14 knots. Over"

"*Donovan*. This is *Ciovo*. Many thanks. Hope we are not a nuisance. Over"

"*Ciovo*. This is *Donovan*. No problem. We're just out here boring holes in the ocean and trying to keep out of other folks' way. Out."

"Boring holes in the ocean", an evocative phrase and, no doubt, from his steady platform in a snug radio cabin, it felt that way. Conversation with a small British yacht provided at least some break in the monotony. Bracing myself to stay on my feet in *Premuda's* swaying galley, the reassurance that this was not a rising gale was a comfort. I congratulated Howard on his initiative and privately admitted that VHF might have its uses. By noon *Donovan's* prognosis had been confirmed; the sea was calm and the sails limp, but with the diesels chugging away we were still boring our own holes across the ocean.

Towards evening Cape Ferrat duly came up over the starboard bow and Villefranche opened up ahead. For hours the image of a *bifteck et frites* had been tantalising me. In the restaurant overlooking the harbour the reality, in succession to *moules marinières*, and preceding that, a subtle sorbet was all, and more, that I had dreamed. Some time in the middle watch I woke and looked out through the fore-hatch. There had been many good moments since Primosten, but none better than taking in the silent harbour, sleeping in the shadow of the old fort facing the bay; one of those intense satisfactions which every yachtsman knows but no plan can guarantee; in its own way my own private Ithaca.

I left *Premuda* in St Tropez and she reached Marseillon two days later, there to await her skipper's pleasure the following spring. The Mediterranean, like Circe, knows how to delay seafarers, or to lure them back; I have accepted an invitation to join *Premuda* this year to explore Corsica and Sardinia. But I am not counting on those destinations. Like the voyages of Ulysses they should still depend partly on wind and weather.

Even that wily skipper had to depend on the whims of *marinaios*. Would the Odyssey ever have happened if the 'black ships' had been equipped with VHF? That would have been a loss, but I must allow that technology does have its merits. In an Ionian calm the throb of diesels leaves the men less exhausted than days at the oar-benches 'smiting the dark-grey seas' or, as USS *Donovan* had it, "boring holes in the ocean".'

That article did not appear in print until June 1988, when *Premuda* was already on her way to England via the Canal du Midi. There now follows Charles Iliff's account of her voyage from Menorca in 1987 and her return, a year later, through France, round Brittany and finally, as always planned, to Orford.

'Howard Nash and I had left *Ciovo* and *Premuda* in Marseillon (near Sète) for the winter after the voyage from Yugoslavia in 1986. They were in the kind care of Monsieur Pasquale near the Hôtel du Port, just a mile from Les Onglus, the entrance to the Canal du Midi.

We returned briefly at Easter 1987 for a fitting out session, and then in May with Monique and my sister Mary, to sail down the Spanish coast and across to the magnificent fiord of Fornells in Menorca. The boats were left tethered to stern anchors in Mahon harbour – everywhere Georgian villas that would not look out of place in Orford, and dating back to the 18th century when the harbour was a major British base. The ghosts of Nelson's and earlier fleets lingered; there are still gin distilleries there too, originally set up to meet naval demand.

Richard Roberts and John Pickthorn joined me to sail back to Marseillon. Howard was too busy and so *Premuda* left *Ciovo* behind in Mahon. Her stern line had been in the water only a few weeks, but it was encrusted with barnacles – painful to remove.

We had intended to sail to Sardinia, but the wind was adverse, so we headed towards Spain, stopping in Fornells for a bit of lotus-eating. Crossing over to Spain a 40 foot sperm whale surfaced just yards away, travelling away from us. It must have passed just under our keel. It was a very non-marine, Friesian cow-brown colour.

There was some coast-hopping as far as the French border. Richard insisted upon a nostalgic pause in Collioure, where he and Wendy had spent a happy week in 1964. We went on overnight past Sète to Aigues-Mortes in the western Camargue, finally back to Marseillon. Richard helped me prepare *Premuda* for another winter there – and had exactly the same menu as he had chosen the previous evening – "no point having anything else."

Richard retains no memory of those presumably tasty meals, unless they were the cause of the very uncomfortable night he spent in Arles (or was it Avignon?) where he broke his train journey north, but was in no state to eat at all. He does remember climbing up to see the view from the Sailors' Cemetery in Sète, famous for some magnificent lines by the poet Paul Valéry, and worth every step of the way uphill.

In April 1988 James Robinson was with me for the first leg of the voyage, Marseillon to Toulouse along the Canal du Midi. We bade farewell to Monsieur Pasquale, who had organised a mobile crane to lay the mast on the deck, and stocked up at the quayside winery. Then it was just across the Etang du Thau to the canal entrance.

The Canal du Midi, with the Canal de Garonne, extends about 300 miles from Bordeaux to the Mediterranean, with 152 locks. You allow 30 minutes per lock. We made steady progress through scenery which was initially Mediterranean, constantly climbing, thus entering locks with high walls dripping with water. James would put me ashore before each lock and manoeuvre *Premuda* in, taking care not to damage the mast, protruding beyond the bow and stern. He would then throw up the bow line, which I would put round a bollard, throwing the tail back, then the stern line. On the eastern section there were a lot of hire boats, and helpful lock-keepers. They were adamant as to draft: "cent cinquante passe":"cent soixante passe pas". *Premuda* required 1.5 metres precisely.

We alternated between groupings or staircases of locks (six at Béziers) and then long bounds between locks following the canal contour lines. The traffic diminished as we climbed past Carcassonne and Castelnaudary. We fed off fillet of horse and Dobbin went down a treat. Automated locks began to take over – a rod dangling over the canal two hundred yards before the lock, which you grab and twist. Generally, if the lock is vacant, the gates open as you approach. Then there is a knob to press once you are tied up. Finally we reached the summit section; James and I stopped for the night and to celebrate. The tiny harbour was part of a motorway service station. We discussed possible weather for the following day; it had been a bit mixed. We looked at the cabin barometer: 950mb! The sky did not suggest a mid-Atlantic depression. Then we realised – we were many hundred feet above sea level. The barometer had become an altimeter.

For the next 35 miles down to Toulouse locks were much easier; there was no need to throw ropes 20 feet into the air. This was still the eastern section of the canal, built between 1662 and 1681. In Toulouse we left *Premuda* for two months.

In July James and I returned, accompanied by Paul Blaxill, John Pickthorn – and Mo, who was cruising on *Premuda* for the first time. We made much faster progress on the more modern western section, the Canal de Garonne, built by Napoleon using Prussian prisoners of war. Most locks were automatic; we got through one in under five minutes. Paul sought to compete with the winding skills of a good-looking eclusière, but failed. He may still be exchanging billets doux with Écluse 19.

The canal joins the Garonne about 30 miles above Bordeaux. The speed of the river current varies hugely according to how much rain there has been, and the state of the tide below Bordeaux. Motoring at five knots we covered 12 miles in the first hour – life-jackets on – James called it white-water cruising. You have to line up for the correct bridge arch – always marked – no going back. And the names on each river bank read like an expensive wine list.

In 1988 Bordeaux seemed strangely derelict, at least along the river. The harbourmaster at the yacht club used a hand crane to help us erect the mast. There was no wine merchant nearby – again strange for the wine capital of the world – so I asked Madame behind the club bar whether I could buy a few bottles. She offered me the Ordinaire or the Spécial. And she produced modestly priced bottles without labels. We had them with supper in the cockpit; they were delicious, and ever since I have wondered – if the Ordinaire was that good, what was the Spécial like?

The next day we went down the huge estuary of the Gironde to Royan at the mouth. Going downstream you have to leave on the last of the flood, even so you arrive against the first of the new flood. Then we were into the Bay of Biscay. We left the estuary on the ebb – deep water, but even modest Atlantic rollers coming in combine with the ebb to make for a violent experience. The boat fell silent. I was standing on the stem picking out the lateral buoys. John did a brilliant job steering. Mo was co-ordinating between cockpit and cabin while James and Paul were keeping an eye on the engine and stopping things from being thrown across the cabin. A French pilot boat came over to check that we were OK – which we were. The last of the lateral buoys was passed; we turned north, and the violence stopped.

After the Garonne and the Gironde, La Rochelle and Les Sables d'Olonne were a bit tame. Then Belle-Isle, which, approaching from the south-east, meant motoring into a fresh wind. We all felt a bit seasick; once in Belle-Isle we found a simple quayside café. I ordered *steak tartare*, the sight of which left Paul queasier than he had felt at sea. John departed for Paris and Mo for a train and ferry to Jersey to see her parents. James, Paul and I began to contemplate a home run to Orford.

We made two swift passages round Britanny, the second along the north Breton coast to Guernsey, then from Guernsey to Newhaven, navigating the Alderney Race at night with running fixes every 20 minutes. I left *Premuda* in Newhaven for an engine overhaul, and to clear the paperwork and VAT on the import of a yacht that had been built in Sweden and then spent five years on commercial charter in communist Yugoslavia. In the end the bemused customs official gave me a form to fill in that was really for the personal importation of a car – it wanted to know which side the steering wheel was on – and agreed to levy VAT on the current valuation figure from a Newhaven firm of yachtbrokers.

Paul and John were with me for the final run to Orford; it ended with a flat calm and we arrived at Shingle Street bang on dead low water, ploughing our way through the deepest point. Richard Roberts and *Quantz* were there to greet us; he had been on board for at least 1600 miles of the odyssey. Oh! When I turned up at 71 Broad Street that evening, Mo mistook me for an intruder, and armed herself with a poker. I fell asleep in the bath and woke up with dead man's fingers.

Premuda was joined in due course by *Ciovo*, *Susak*, *Zut* and *Hvar* – all named after Dalmatian islands, each different but exquisite in their own way. *Premuda* made it all the way on her own bottom; I sold her when I bought *Katrina* in 2007, and in 2020 she is at Waldringfield, still with her 1981 engine, and much loved by the Stock family. *Ciovo* is owned by an Icelander in Reykjavik and has circumnavigated Iceland; *Susak* was last heard of in or near Hartlepool and *Hvar* has had a big upgrade but her current location is unknown.'

Charles Iliff's description of the voyage along the Canal du Midi resonates strongly with me and with Wendy, although we followed its course on our Brompton bicycles and never had to wind a lock. Our choice of route was partly influenced by the belief in a level towpath – not entirely justified – and by our son Jamie's affection for the region. In 1981 he worked as 'deckhand/steward' on the barge *Virginia Anne*, owned by the legendary Gerard Morgan-Grenville, usually skippered on his behalf for holiday cruises by John Turner, with whom Jamie remained in touch for years.

Morgan-Grenville himself skippered for one memorable week at the start of the season. The previous winter had been one of the coldest on record, with snow on the Canal. GM-G had failed to do his research on the height of Canal bridges so the wheelhouse did not fit underneath and had to be removed. As it was also supposed to provide the deckhand's berth this meant Jamie slept outside for the next nine months. GM-G's attempt to re-start the DAF engine when the starter motor failed involved putting a line round the engine block and pushing the barge out from the bank in a (futile) effort to turn the engine over. Later in life he became famous as an environmental pioneer, founding the Centre for Alternative Technology in North Wales.

That summer also provided other memorable moments in Jamie's experience. It gave him his first sight of the Tour de France as the race crossed the Languedoc with thousands of spectators on the hillsides and the newspapers dominated by the event. Jamie has followed the results ever since and, more recently, travelled to watch several stages. In 1981 the French Rugby Championship was won, yet again, by the ferocious Béziers team. Their stadium was next to the canal port, mobbed by spectators on match days. The team included the infamous forward Armand Vaquerin, who later killed himself during a game of Russian Roulette. Jamie was trying to keep in touch with the fortunes of Ipswich Town in the league Championship and European campaign via newspapers several days old in the pre-internet age. He watched the wedding of Prince Charles and Diana on French TV in a café in Capestang, and was surprised to learn that, according to French media, the British were anti-royal. On Bastille Day in Carcassonne, there was a magnificent firework display. Jamie claims this was also the first and last time in his life when he spent an evening drinking whisky. Picking up letters by Poste Restante was an important feature of his life. The constant winding of locks may have contributed to his breadth of shoulder and strength of biceps and other muscles by the time he got home. A year or two later, after a stint as a sailing instructor in the South of France, his mother failed to recognise the young man with a moustache standing at the door.

Those nine months on the Canal du Midi amounted, I suspect, to quite a rite of passage in the life of Jamie, which would lead indirectly to other important stages in his future, his marriage, his career, and leisure interests. But none of it might have happened without the background of messing about in boats on the Ore and even earlier in his childhood.

Jamie had a further experience, linked directly with Seven Seas and the Dalmatian Squadron, when Charles Iliff arranged a job for him doing end of season maintenance on the Maxis late in 1983. He was there for about six weeks during which beautiful windsurfing off the Dalmatian coast compensated somewhat for dismantling a fleet of marine toilets. The Communist flag still flew over the marina manager's office in that era.

Then all the sails and VHF radios had to be brought back to the UK in a Mercedes van with a hole in the floor next to the gear stick, so that the road underneath was visible. He was travelling with two other young men working for Seven Seas. They were faced with a long week of waiting in Sibenik while the local authorities decided if they were legal and could be permitted to take the equipment back. They were able to stay with a very hospitable Croatian family, who insisted on serving slivovitz for breakfast. Finally the paperwork was handed over, with the order to leave Yugoslavia within 24 hours. They drove up the amazing coast road as fast as they could to reach the East/West European border at night. There were searchlights, barbed wire and soldiers everywhere – lots of dodgy-looking truck drivers. Then they were ordered to leave Yugoslavia, at gun point, driving across several hundred yards of no man's land. Jamie felt he was part of a Cold War drama.

The reward was a wonderful *espresso* in Venice the next day before an equally impressive drive over the Dolomites. They stayed overnight in a farmhouse near Strasbourg where it was so cold there was a frozen rat next to the van in the morning. This was another stage in his course through the University of Life.

David Foreman's *Susak* stayed in Primosten until 1989 when her lease ended in September. David was busy at the time so Richard Waite, his wife Sue, Charles and Mo Iliff agreed to deliver *Susak* to Aprillia in the Venetian lagoons. Howard Nash and Simon, the owner of a Maxi 100, would do the same for his boat, which would be trucked to the Belgian coast sharing the same low loader with *Susak*. Charles recounts this voyage under the threat of a Balkan crisis.

'We all flew out in the first week of October; the Iron Curtain between Austria and Hungary had come down, the whole of Eastern Europe was in turmoil, and on October 9th Gorbachev visited East Berlin and made it plain that the Soviet Union would not intervene. Our delivery trip was going to be along a part of the fault line of the Cold War at the moment when that line was disintegrating.

At the harbour outside Primosten there were rumours of diesel shortages up the coast. We bought plenty and started refuelling. We began to think that the amount poured in was more than the capacity of the tank. A glance into the cabin showed fuel seeping in from the engine compartment. An inspection hatch on the tank had not been properly re-fixed.

There was poor visibility and mist on the first day, and that continued for the whole 220 miles, as we largely felt our way from island to island. This, and the great political events, made for an extraordinary atmosphere. There was undoubted apprehension on the part of Yugoslavs, and although the whole process in Eastern Europe was surprisingly peaceful, Yugoslavia subsequently suffered greatly.

We made our way first past Murter to Beograd in the Pasman Channel; there was *espresso* and cherry brandy for breakfast in a quayside bar; the mist was thickening and everyone was engrossed in the newspapers and the events unfolding. We crossed the Sound to the island of Pasman following the coastline in the fog; past Pasman and then Uglian, both inner Kornati islands. This was the sheltered route down the Adriatic, used by Venetian galleys to police their Empire.

The welcome heat from the engine filled the cabin and fended off the damp. We reached the island of Molat, where both boats moored by the tiny ferry berth. There was a time-warp village store, like Elliotts of Orford in the 1950s, but with few supplies. A fishing boat came in from which Howard bought four fish; but the process of killing and gutting upset Simon. Next day we crossed the Kvarner Gulf to the Istrian Peninsula, the last of the Kornati islands guiding us through the mist, which sadly prevented us from seeing the islands of Susak and Primosten. After three hours of staring into the damp gloom Cap Kamenjak suddenly came up ahead and we felt our way into Pula.

The following day we were coasting to Porec. From there it was ten miles across the Gulf of Trieste; visibility was now so bad that to increase the chance of finding the deep-water mark for the lagoon leading to Aprillia we motored side by side on the same heading and just in sight of each other. The buoy duly appeared. We entered the lagoon, an Italian Iken Water, surprisingly tidal. Then we were in the marina with a pizzeria and a huge wood-fired oven that chased out the all-enveloping damp. For David's *Susak*, as for Eastern Europe, this was not the beginning of the end, but the end of the beginning. As for her crew, the airline went bust as we waited at the airport. Freedom and the market economy have their disadvantages.'

'For Sale', *Sea Swallow* with *Quantz* and *Kehaar* (Wendy Roberts)

Tip of *Wombat's* sail seen from *Mako*, North Sea 1982 (David Foreman)

Quantz with mast down, Rouen (Richard Roberts)

Eiffel Tower ahead! (Richard Roberts)

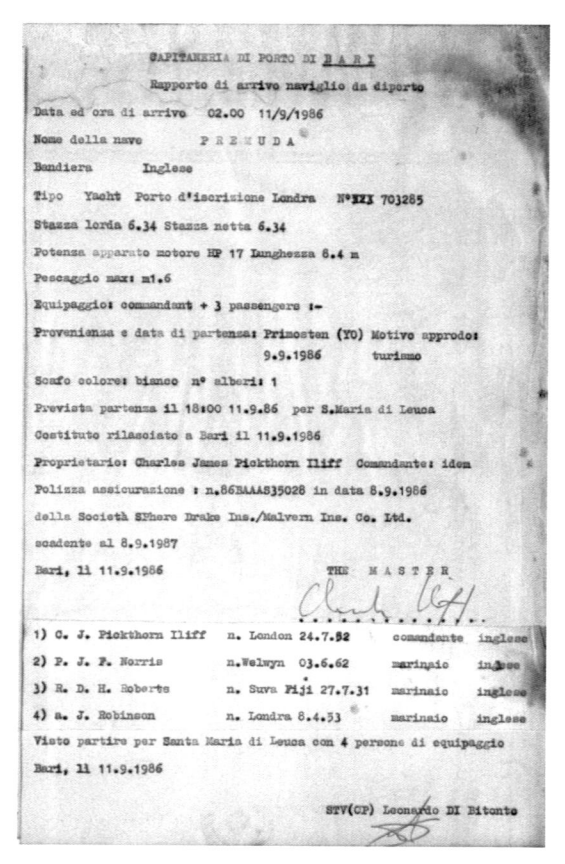

Italian crew list for *Premuda,* port of Bari, 1986 (Charles Iliff)

Mary responds vigorously to blue flag signal from Rhine Barge (Monica Iliff)

Automatic Lock on Moselle (Monica Iliff)

Cochem on Moselle (Monica Iliff)

Premuda at junction of Rhine and Moselle (Monica Iliff)

Simon Arnold in Friesland 1992 (Richard Roberts)

Traditional Dutch yacht rally Medemblik 1992 (Richard Roberts)

Low tide at Schiermonikoog AD2000 (Richard Roberts)

Babaji returns to Orford Quay (Glaister records)

Babaji in Sweden (Glaister records)

Babaji in Moscow, President Yeltsin's yacht in background (Glaister records)

Sail repairs by Dan, Denmark 2002

Quantz moored on Blue Coast in a typical 'naturhamn' 2002 (Richard Roberts)

Moored in the castle moat, Vadstena, Sweden (Richard Roberts)

Lacko Castle, Lake Vanern, Sweden (Richard Roberts)

Verdens Ende, Norway 2003 (Richard Roberts)

10. Round Brittany and Britain with *Babaji*

Towards the end of the 1970s Ray and Margo Glaister with their family had explored the Essex rivers, the Orwell and the Stour in their Wayfarer *Areopagitica*, notable not only for her name but for her striking yellow, almost orange hull. They slept aboard under a boom tent, sometimes with children somewhere aboard as well. In the summer of 1978, immediately after Alison's A Levels, she and her father sailed as far as they could to the top of all the local estuaries; the Ore and Alde, the Deben, the Orwell and the Stour. Alison particularly remembers getting over the side to push the Wayfarer off the mud just below the railway bridge above Mistley. Anchored off Pin Mill they went ashore for a meal at the Butt and Oyster. Wading back along hard to the rubber dinghy at high tide Alison fell off the edge, which was, as she put it "inconvenient"! Then they were invited aboard a yacht for a drink: "a real treat".

Alison suspects it was this experience which finally persuaded Ray to swap a centreboard for a proper keel and bunks to sit or sleep on. If so, it was a decision that inspired a truly remarkable cruising career over a quarter of a century. *Moette*, a Halcyon 23 provided more comfort than a dinghy and took them across to the Netherlands and France. She in turn was followed by *Iolanthe*, a Westerly Tiger and their cruising range gradually expanded. Finally they bought *Babaji*, a Colvic 'Sailer' Ketch, 31ft 6ins overall, built in 1980. Together, sometimes with friends or family, but often on their own, Ray and Margo covered many thousands of sea miles during the 1990s and first years of this century. I make no apology for describing early voyages in some detail as they were the foundation for much greater adventures in the future.

The first of *Babaji's* cruises for which I have Ray's Glaister's full log, took place in July and August 1990 from Falmouth to southern Brittany. After wintering ashore at Slaughden they had worked round the coast at weekends to a visitors' mooring at the Royal Cornwall Yacht Club. Judging from the introduction they had already made a trip to the Scillies in 1989 from the same base and repeated it in the spring of 1990 as a preliminary to the main voyage. There is also reference to having visited Ushant and the North Brittany coast in 1989 with their son Malcolm crewing. There is a general sense of familiarity and confidence among those rock-strewn waters reflecting these previous experiences.

In the light of Ray's professional expertise I was not surprised to read that *Babaji* was fully equipped with electronics: VHF, Autohelm, Vigil Radar, Navtstar and Decca, VDO fluxgate compass and wind instruments, Navico log, Navtex, RDF and domestic radio. This contrasts markedly with my own minimalist, perhaps foolhardy equipment of this nature; but I always sadly lacked the technical ability to operate and maintain more complex kit. Before setting off across the Channel with their first week's crew, two girls, possibly recruited from the Cruising Association, Ray was careful to make a short daylight passage to the Helford River. 'I have a fundamental rule', he wrote – 'learnt the hard way like most rules – not to do a night passage with an untried crew.'

The cruise proper thus left the Helford River early on July 22nd and reached Morgat in the Baie de Douarnenez on the following morning. It seems that Ray's passage plan worked perfectly as they were into the Chenal du Four, inside Ushant, at the intended time.

Ray and Margo took the first night watch. It was a busy one, as they sailed through the Walker Cup race (Brighton to Camaret) yachts; Ushant Radio was broadcasting warnings to shipping to keep a look-out together with polite requests for the entrants not to proceed the wrong way through the traffic separation zone.

From Ray's description Morgat now had a large marina, rather different from the sleepy place where Wendy and I had spent most of our honeymoon 30 years earlier. For nostalgic reasons we had re-visited it briefly with Don during the February half term of 1980, 20 years on, when it was still just a fishing harbour.

Babaji reached La Rochelle, the furthest point of the outward voyage, on July 29th. They had stopped each night at various attractive harbours and one anchorage. The two girls had disembarked the day before at Pornichet near the entrance to the Loire to get a train home. Ray and Margo appear to have enjoyed the freedom of the boat to themselves. The weather was fine and warm. There was time to swim, to unfold their bicycles and explore or shop, and for Margo to sketch and paint. The return voyage began two days later. On August 3rd their daughter Carol joined them for two more days until Vannes, where she left and their new crew, Graeme and Sarah Davies arrived, the former being an ex-Naval officer. This was a strong team for the next stage, which nevertheless began with an untoward event on the morning of the 6th.

'Up at 0600 BST to see Carol off to the station, then left at 0915. Bridge opens on demand and after passing through lock bridge opened for us as we approached. Sailed under genoa and rounded headland with genoa alone. Turned into wind under power while crew hoisted mainsail but this took so long and ended up by us being driven aground. Failed to get off under power or by rocking. A small fishing boat attempted to pull us off and Graeme went off in dinghy with line to masthead to heel us but with fast ebbing tide this was too late. A commercial barge saw our predicament and called for a line from our bows. Graeme gamely walked out with this. They successfully turned us through 90° and got us off leaving Graeme standing in the water; a passing inflatable gave him a lift to us!'

In Camaret, five days later, Ray and Margo celebrated their wedding anniversary with an 'excellent dinner, four courses for 86 francs', which sounds good value, although the cheapest Côte du Rhône wine added 52 francs. On Sunday August 12th they left at 0300 to ensure a fair tide through the Chenal du Four.

'Had fun identifying all the lights as we were swept through the Chenal on four knots of flood tide. Visibility dropped and we saw nothing more although we heard the Le Four fog siren in the distance. Navigated by Decca, keeping well clear of the rocky coast and decided to drift until the fog cleared off L'Aber Wrac'h. Had a short sleep then decided to locate the W. Cardinal off the entrance to L'Aber Wrac'h and simultaneously spotted a yacht emerging. Followed the reciprocal course of this and others emerging and sound found a well-buoyed channel. Could not reconcile buoyage with chart until I realised this was L'Aber Benoît not Wrac'h. Ironically I'd wanted to visit L'Aber Benoit but thought the entrance too tricky in poor visibility.'

The crew left that evening and Ray comments that they were now beginning 'a glorious week of freedom to do what we wished without pressure.' Like Ray, however much I have appreciated the vital assistance of a crew on longer passages, I have felt the same release from the responsibility of meeting other people's needs and schedules. In fact they needed less than a week to get back to Brighton on their own, first along the North Brittany coast with two overnight stops and another in St Peter Port, Guernsey. At that point they decided to make for Cherbourg to reduce the length of their final leg. This, however, brought them into the Alderney Race running under them at three and a half knots with some very rough patches.

After a night and a morning in Cherbourg for shopping and a minor sail repair, they were ready for departure at 1430 with a French forecast of north-west 4 – 5 becoming west 3 – 4; good visibility. As Ray's narrative shows, forecasts can be misleading.

'Left at 1430 with a south-west force 5 so cut engine in outer harbour and averaged six to seven knots for next eight hours during which our 030T course followed a yacht, first white against dark clouds, then a dark line before its white masthead light appeared. Margo prefers steering towards an object rather than to a bearing, so found this most helpful. Fortunately took in a double reef in main and furled genoa at watch change at 2215 as it was freshening, but it then continued up to force 8 which it held for five hours, the needle swinging up to 10 as the masthead rocked through the wind. The sea built up horrendously, the breaking waves being brilliantly illuminated with phosphorescence. This was all too much for Margo's wrist bands; she retired below. Ran engine to improve control as on a gybing course with frequent unavoidable and violent gybes as we were thrown off course. For a period forced to take a course 90° off correct. Decca was no help this night, having given a 3LOP alarm as early as 1630.

Very thankful to see the dawn and for the gale to moderate to a force 5 leaving confused seas. Decca was now totally useless and for a period the distance to our Brighton waypoint increased. It still showed 20 miles when at 0650 a chimney appeared through a gap in the mist. There is only one large chimney on the South Coast, being Shoreham Power Station's remaining one. Then another glimpse showed Beachy Head before it disappeared again. But the bearings had been taken and we were on the chart only a few miles off Brighton. Finally we arrived alongside the visitors' pontoon at Brighton at 1130 after 103 miles through the water. Never have I been so thankful to moor, and never was a hot shower so welcome.'

This narrative strikes me as a considerable tribute to Ray and Margo's competence and confidence, both in one another and in *Babaji*. Her sturdy build and the shelter of the wheelhouse made a bad night more tolerable. Reflecting on the experience he mentions that failure of his ordinary radio and RDF plus an earlier problem with Navtex had prevented them from getting up to date forecasts. If there had been a gale warning he would have sailed on the genoa and mizen alone, easily handled from the cockpit. While I admit to a wry smile at the fallibility of some electronics I also recognise his confidence about dealing with more severe conditions if necessary.

A week later *Babaji* left Brighton and returned to Orford with overnight stays in Dover and Harwich. It was the end of August and their last use of that home mooring had been, briefly, before Easter. It had clearly been a full summer's sailing. At the end of this log Ray appends a list of ports and anchorages with star ratings from three down to one and brief appraisals. For this cruise they total 27. Typical three stars include: Bénodet 'beautiful river'; Ile Hoedic, 'crowded but fun'; Ile Houatt 'Paradise'; Rochelle, 'lovely old town, superb marina'; and among the single stars: Audierne, 'plenty room, diesel in cans'; Cherbourg, 'real port, facilities excellent'; and Orford, 'home again, facilities – we manage!'

In the Introduction to his log of their 1992 cruise Ray Glaister mentions a voyage the previous year 'to Ireland'; unfortunately no details of this are available. No doubt it received the same thorough preparation and planning as their other cruises. They had then considered circumnavigating the UK in 1992; but with Alison's wedding scheduled for July 11th and the sad circumstance of his father's illness and death earlier in the year, 'a less ambitious' target was substituted. This was, in fact a voyage up the east coast to the Orkneys and back including passage through the Caledonian Canal and up to Stornaway and then to Stromness and Kirkwall on Orkney. Many of us, myself included, might still rate this as definitely 'ambitious.'

Alison has told me that she and her future husband and fellow doctor, David Ward, with friends, crewed for Ray on a quick trip across to France to buy the wine for the wedding. For once the Customs were on the Quay when they returned. The officers were offered a drink and, luckily, did not count the bottles. On another earlier cross-Channel foray she remembers being dropped off on Brighton beach to get back to work in Market Harborough. Having slept on a bench at Euston she caught the milk train and arrived, somewhat bleary-eyed, for morning surgery. I hope the authorities are not still looking for someone reported to have landed illegally on the south coast the day before.

Only five days after the wedding, but fully prepared as always, *Babaji* left Orford on July 16th.

This cruise lasted a full two months. James Logan, whose parents Tony and Bridget often crewed on other Orford boats, was with them for six days up to Dunbar; their daughter Carol joined them near Inverness for five days, mainly on the Caledonian Canal; otherwise Ray and Margo managed alone, apart from their dog Merry, whose daily walks were essential to the plan. Whatever happened they were determined to be within reach of Rosyth on August 26th to meet their son Malcolm, navigating officer on the minesweeper HMS *Dulverton*, due to hold an Open Day there on that date.

The overnight ports of call as far as Dunbar were: Lowestoft, Grimsby, Scarborough and Lindisfarne. The 119 mile leg from Lowestoft to the Humber included an overnight passage, as did the similar distance, later on, from Stornoway to Stromness, on Orkney, passing Cape Wrath. More often they were able to do relatively short day passages of between 30 and 60 miles or so. The weather that summer was far from ideal, often windy with a good deal of rain, and on the calmer days the wind was either light or contrary. Thus a typical day's run usually involved somewhat less under sail than power. (Ray noted the cost of diesel in Grimsby that July as 15p per litre!)

After dropping James in Dunbar they continued north and west calling at Montrose, Peterhead and Buckie before reaching Inverness on July 24th, only eight days after leaving Orford. It was just after leaving Buckie that they made a perhaps uncharacteristic snap decision to divert through the Caledonian Canal instead of meeting Carol at Lossiemouth and heading north towards Orkney. As Ray put it.

'It occurred to us that we could equally well go clockwise round Scotland starting with the Caledonian Canal, thereby giving Carol an easier return journey and spending the off-day in a more civilised place.'

Margo had been looking forward to a rest day but had to wait until they were about to enter the canal. The transit involved three days and the toll cost in 1992 was £89.50. Once clear of the last lock staircase at Banavie they had a fast passage to Oban under power, in a stiff headwind but with a strong ebb tide under them which, in the Corran Narrows, gave them a speed of nine knots over the land. Carol left them in Oban. They spent the next two days on passages to Mull and Coll but then returned to Oban for a repair to the mizen sail. Squally winds and rain prevailed for much of this period. After visits to South Uist and Harris they were in Stornoway on the afternoon of Monday August 10th.

After a brief exploration, including Lewis Castle, they listened to the evening forecast, confirmed by telephoning Marinecall for the five day outlook. This offered a short window of decent weather before possible gales; so they were under way again by 2000 heading for Stromness, on Orkney, some 120 miles to the north-east beyond the tip of the Scottish mainland at Cape Wrath. Once clear of the island Ray set the GPS on a way point one mile north-west of the Cape, 45 miles away on a course of 054T. They cut the engine and, in Ray's words, 'sailed into the night.' I know that feeling; besides, these were serious waters with the Atlantic on the port quarter and nothing between them and Iceland on the seaward side.

'Margo took over at midnight and handed back at 0320 with a distance of only 0.08 miles to the waypoint and the Cape Wrath light (Fl 3 30sec) spot on the nose! Speed had dropped to 3.3 knots so motor-sailed for the rest of the way. Saw two ships on same course. The first glimmer of dawn came at 0400 and the mountains became clear at 0430, some appearing snow-covered owing to a thin layer of cloud or mist. The Cape Wrath light was turned off at 0530 by which time its tower could be seen at about 15 miles. The sky became tinged with red at 0540 and the sun appeared but briefly above a band of low cloud. Rounded Cape Wrath at 0745 with a long Atlantic swell of about two metres and turned into an easterly headwind. Now changed to the Stromness way point 56 miles away. Margo now took over; got a reassuring Marinecall forecast at 0940 from Pentland Coastguard. Sun came out again at

1200 and shortly after saw the outline of the mountains on Hoy, with 32 miles to go. Picked up a mooring near the ferry terminal, so covered with marine life that it could not have been used for some time. Went ashore to have our wedding anniversary dinner of fresh salmon steaks at the Stromness Hotel. Night's run 119.6 miles in 21.6 hours of which 16 under power. Wind mostly east force 2-3. Barometer 997mb.'

They had certainly deserved their dinner so far to the north from their similar celebration in Brittany the year before. Judging by the barometer, they also made good use of a short weather window for a crucial stage of their cruise.

Undeterred by the possibility of stronger winds and reassured by a precise forecast from Orkney Radio, Ray was determined to press on the next day, August 12th, to Kirkwall. They successfully completed the 35 mile trip by sea and under power, making the best use of the tidal streams on the way despite a rough passage up the west coast and round Brough Head. Soon he felt they had no further navigation problems: 'as we sped into a new world, a vast smooth sea surrounded by lush green fields and with the shallow-domed Gairsay unmistakeable.' He made cups of soup and Margo served bacon sandwiches as they headed for Kirkwall, reporting arrival and being advised to enter the inner harbour with impending strong winds overnight. Once again Ray's judgement had paid a dividend with useful progress against the odds.

A gale warning kept them in Kirkwall for 24 hours but it was hardly a rest day. After they had visited the cathedral their bikes were unfolded and they rode off to visit the main archaeological sites on mainland Orkney, burial mounds, the Rings of Stones at Steness and Brodgar and, after a further seven miles of headwind, the remains of the prehistoric village at Skara Brae. Having ridden the wind-swept roads of Orkney myself, in the wake of Wendy, I am glad they had a tail wind on the return journey. On August 14th *Babaji* rounded the northern tip of Stronsay, the furthest point of their outward voyage, not quite the most northerly of the Orkney Islands. The echo sounder had an important role in the navigation of some shallow patches between skerries and reefs between the islets, with the compensation of numerous seals basking on the rocks. They moored on one end of the pier at Whitehall village, where they met an Orkney lady who sold wool. She was the daughter of a Norwegian who, at the age of 17, had escaped from Norway on a fishing boat and then served on the famous 'Shetland Bus' ferrying escapees and agents between Shetland and Norway during the winters of the war.

Soon they were heading south, stopping overnight in Deer Sound, just east of Kirkwall, then Wick and Helmsdale before crossing the Moray Firth to Findochty. The visit to Helmsdale was notable, not just for the beauty of the surrounding hills and river valley, but for the use of the showers in the

Helmsdale Hotel, their first such luxury for the whole of the past month. In Findochty Margo met her aunt Margaret, who, aged 72, managed the iron ladder down to the pontoon with aplomb, and whose local prestige seemed much enhanced by the arrival of *Babaji*.

The rendezvous with Malcolm in Rosyth was now an important factor, so they pressed on, calling at Fraserburgh, Peterhead and Stonehaven. Here they were held up by a deep depression and associated gale warnings. After two nights in shelter the next morning looked fine, so they set off for the River Tay, motoring into a stiff headwind with some heavier squalls. *Babaji's* wheelhouse offered vital protection on days like this. After nine hours and 41 miles of windward graft it was a relief to pick up a buoy off Tayport Harbour, open some tins for supper and retire. The delay in Stonehaven forced them to leave *Babaji* in Tayport Harbour for the next few days in order to reach Rosyth by road, collected by Malcolm early on August 25th to board HMS *Dulverton* before 1000.

They were on the bridge for a time while she manoeuvred in the Firth of Forth with a sister ship, intrigued to see how many men were needed to carry out the tasks which the two of them managed on *Babaji*. At anchor off Inchkieff Island they enjoyed a splendid lunch and had a full tour of the ship, after which she made a very cautious docking and Malcolm took them back to their own boat.

Following a further day for maintenance in Tayport they motor-sailed across the Forth to Fisherrow, on the edge of Leith Harbour, to allow themselves a three day break to visit Edinburgh and even to enjoy, or at least to attend, two Festival Fringe events, not wholly to their taste in some respects. This stay in harbour coincided with a report on the news of the second lowest barometer reading of the century.

On September 2nd *Babaji* and her doughty owners left Fisherrow for the final leg of the voyage lasting two weeks. The overnight ports of call were in turn: Eyemouth, Seahouses, Blyth – plus a day gale-bound there – Hartlepool, Whitby – a three night stay, Wells next the Sea, Yarmouth and Lowestoft. On September 16th at 1300 they went alongside Orford Quay to be greeted a little later by Alison and family. Ironically the weather that morning was the hottest of the whole cruise with the only north-westerly breeze they had experienced on the southward voyage, lasting as far as Thorpeness to give them a fine four hours of sailing.

During those two months the total distance covered was 1720 miles, with 46 days of sailing (or motor-sailing) and 18 spent in harbour. Ray's log was entered for the Cruising Association's Hanson Cup. I know that he was a frequent winner of their trophies and may well have done so, this time, although we have no actual record to prove the fact.

A year later Ray Glaister was preparing his first full circumnavigation of England, Wales and Scotland. 'In 1992', he wrote in the note on pre-planning, which prefaces his very full log,'we had explored the Hebrides and Orkney and fallen in love with the latter. Time and weather had stopped us reaching the Shetlands, and this was a major target for 1993.' Should it be clockwise, with a westward passage along the south coast, when easterly winds early in the year might help, followed by south-westerlies later in the season, or the reverse, because 'the tidal gate in the Pentland Firth favours an eastern crossing?' The complication of crewing arrangements and dates were another consideration: 'experience had shown us the pressure such deadlines place on cruising schedules. We decided to use no crew this year, although family were invited to join us at our convenience.' 'Wise man', I thought to myself, reading that.

In fact Ray chose to go 'east about' taking some 100 charts. Many were never used but gave him freedom to make choices dependent on weather and timing. Because they wanted to explore the Orkneys thoroughly and the Shetland Islands, for which their experience the year before suggested that the better weather occurred early in the summer, they would leave as soon as possible. Ray was undertaking a good deal of consultancy work, which reduced somewhat during the summer. By taking a PC, printer and cellular phone he could 'not only round off some work under way and tackle some new work; the availability of fax machines around the coast made this possible, although I had hoped to couple the PC to cell-phone.' These comments illustrate the level of commitment Ray brought to both his professional life and cruising ambitions, allied to his technological expertise.

His very detailed log, prepared for the Cruising Association, bears the title:

Babaji Rounds Britain including Orkneys and Shetlands 1993

It is divided into six parts of which the first, London to Berwick, covers nine days and 358 nautical miles, from May 26th to June 7th. After a night in the Walton Backwaters they were held up in Orford for three days by bad weather, so the northward voyage was completed as swiftly as they could, following a very similar route and ports of call to the 1992 trip. Ironically their trickiest moment in this first stage may have been the entry to the Ore which was timed for half flood. It fell calm as they passed the Deben.

'Cursed myself for failing to get the 1993 chartlet showing the entrance, which changes every year, sometimes quite dramatically, but fortunately a yacht was coming out, so assuming it knew what it was doing took the reciprocal course. All went well until the engine stopped dead at a depth of only 2.2 meters, the shallowest point over the bar. Fortunately God was with us and provided enough wind to sail into the river.'

In fact, once clear of Orford, they only needed five days to reach Berwick and were able to allow themselves a full 'rest day' in Whitby, 'as attractive as on our first visit'. In Ray's case the concept of rest was relative since, besides their visit to the Captain Cook Museum and climbing the countless steps to the Abbey, he had himself hauled to the masthead by a helpful garage attendant delivering fuel. This enabled him to fix the Vodafone aerial permanently on the mizen mast to assist communication for his consultancy.

Part Two of the log covered 11 days and 305 nautical miles from Berwick to Orkney between June 7th and 18th. Their intermediate ports of call were largely familiar from the previous year. They stayed two nights in Montrose, after aborting their first departure into a strong north-east headwind, a decision approved by the Coastguard as 'wise'. Between Stonehaven and Fraserburgh they saw the wreck of the vessel *Sea Reefer* stranded on the rocks in 1992, while they had sheltered in port listening to the Mayday and the crew's rescue by helicopter. In Findochty they had another meeting with Margo's Aunt Margaret and then timed their arrival in Helmsdale to ensure access to the showers 'the first since Amble.' Their Orkney landfall, from Wick, was just inside Scapa Flow anchoring off Burray, just inside the Churchill Barrier or causeway built by Italian prisoners of war to protect Scapa Flow from U-boats and, ironically, only completed just after the end of the war.

Part Three is entitled 'Orkneys, Fair Isle and Shetland.' It lasts 29 days from June 18th to July 17th, covering 474 nautical miles and takes them round the northernmost point of Great Britain and back to mainland Scotland at Scrabster, across the Pentland Firth, thus achieving the main aim of the cruise. In Kirkwall they had two days in port, on the Sunday they attended morning service in the Cathedral and an evening concert of 16th century music. The Monday was described as a 'rest day' but involved a cycle ride back over the Mainland hills and across the first Churchill Barrier to Lamb Holm overlooking Scapa Flow. Here they visited the beautifully decorated Italian Chapel built by the Italian POWs from a converted Nissen Hut. I have done the same ride and it is not restful, although the chapel was certainly worth the effort. After Kirkwall they called at four of the other Orkney islands in the space of a week; Rousay and Eday, where they anchored in the Bay of Carrick; Sanday and Westray. The passage through tidal currents between Rousay and Bay of Carrick sounds far from pleasant.

'Set off at 1630 having made superficial check on the tides... and made good progress under sail as far as Little Green Holm. Shortly after we struck terrific eddies which made steering very difficult. Despite adding engine power to sail, and touching an indicated 10 knots at times, our speed over the ground was only about 0.9 knots; then checked direction and found this was 0.9 knots almost backwards... After wasting thirty minutes and much diesel, and having made an alternative passage plan on the hoof, turned round and sped out of the race and due north towards Fers Ness, the entrance to the Sound of Foray.'

Eventually, after some rough going with wind against tide and passing through another moderate race they anchored in Carrick Bay with the GPS on anchor watch. Ray had a meal. Margo was 'emotionally exhausted' and had no appetite. The day's run was noted as '24 miles to make good 14(!) in four hours of which three were power-assisted'.

The compensation was an enjoyable day at anchor while they explored the island of Eday, saw more burial chambers, enjoyed glorious views from Red Head and admired the splendid Carrick House, where the notorious pirate John Gow was imprisoned in 1725 after his ship ran aground in the Calf of Eday. Perhaps he had trouble with tidal currents too. He was conveyed to Greenwich and hung in chains. Their weather was now good but cold with a north wind. (Temperatures in the Northern Isles for much of their voyage were rarely much above 10C and photographs of Margo at the helm show her well-wrapped in wind-proof gear). Nevertheless Ray rated this: 'a very good day, capped appropriately with a CD of the Pirates of Penzance. The sun set dramatically in the dip between Vicquoy Hill and Noup Hill. The wind dropped to six knots giving only slight ripples. The only sounds were from birds'. Times like these are indeed the real rewards for voyaging.

It was a short run from Eday to Sanday, where a gale warning detained them for another 'easy day'. The wind did reach force 7 and having discovered that 'gales have an equally adverse effect on cycling' they were happy to walk to see a ruined church, the remains of a Viking settlement and photograph seals and their pups on the shore. An 18-mile run in the evening of their second day at Sanday took them to Westray. The timing was dictated by the tide but the wind was against it giving them some uncomfortable short seas for a period. This was their last Orkney island heading north, the jumping off point for the sea crossing to Shetland, with Fair Isle on the way. They spent a further whole day on Westray, with another ruined church and a roofless castle to be explored. An elderly islander told them he had been to London, once in his life, but not impressed: "it was a bit of a mess with those flying bombs". He may have seen the capital in less than ideal circumstances.

The voyage to Fair Isle was a day's run, 53 miles to make good 45 in 12 hours, four under power. There was a southerly wind between force 3 and

5 assisting, but some confused seas that made them glad of the shelter once they had rounded the headland into the North Harbour. They found ample room to moor ahead of the *Good Shepherd*, the island ferry converted from a fishing vessel but still easy to recognize as such. Ray and Margo had set sail at 0455 that morning after rising at 0400 to give Merry, the dog, a walk first. I am amazed that they still had the energy to walk the full length of Fair Isle to the South Light House, to shop from the back door of the shop, officially closed by that time of the day, to meet several of the local population (then 80, less than 60 now) and admire the multiple roles like meteorologist and airport fireman, or builder and ferry skipper, which are common there. One highlight of the day was the phone call they had received at sea from Malcolm who had just arrived at St Peter Port, Jersey, on the maiden voyage of his newly purchased J24. He had experienced thick fog and a seven hour calm with engine failure tied up to a navigation buoy (with approval of the Coastguard sought on VHF). The two Glaister vessels could scarcely have been further apart in UK territorial waters.

Babaji's crossing to Grutness Voe, on the southern tip of Shetland was unusually smooth for that stretch of water. When I had a similar experience years later aboard the *Good Shepherd*, after my second visit to Fair Isle, I asked the helmsman how rare this might be. After a moment's thought, he said he had been doing the trip for 20 years, whenever the weather would permit, but he could only remember one comparable day. Passengers are welcome in the wheelhouse if it is not over-crowded; on a windy day it is preferable to the open deck or a stuffy saloon, converted from a hold in the bowels of the ship. On my first outward trip I had felt distinctly queasy. The skipper became aware of my discomfort. From earlier conversation he knew I had some acquaintance with the sea. Disconnecting the auto-helm he gave me the wheel and the compass course for Fair Isle. "That will take your mind off it", he said. Indeed, with wind and sea on the port bow, it did the trick. This probably would not happen on Townsend Thoresen.

On Day 40 of their voyage, with 61 still to go, *Babaji* was about to round the northernmost point of the British Isles. They had allowed themselves three nights and two full days in Lerwick, which Ray described as: 'a truly international harbour; we were the only English yacht. There were two Norwegians, one German and one American motor-cruiser (brought over as deck cargo). Another American yacht came in during the night, having crossed in 17 and a half days, en route to Oslo. Margo's first priority was to buy quantities of real Shetland wool.'

Now it was Thursday July 8th, two days north of Lerwick, and they were leaving Baltasound with the advice of the harbourmaster and his reassurance about the North Channel which "should only be used with local knowledge."

'We left at 1230 after most welcome showers, and were careful to advise the Coast Guard that we were rounding Muckle Flugga, not the best place to get into trouble in fog, the visibility being about one mile and cloud base only 50 metres. I had set a waypoint two miles off the Skaw to avoid the notorious Skaw Roost, but the wind was a light south easterly and like the Sumburgh Roost it failed to materialize and we kept quite close in. Rounding the Skaw we were off Britain's most northerly coast, comprising high and jagged rock cliffs, an awesome and lonely experience. To the east lay Norway, to the north, Iceland, and to the west, Canada. As we approached the Noup, a promontory east of Burra Firth, Muckle Flugga with its fine lighthouse, and Out Stack, the most northerly island, came into view. I had planned to sail between Muckle Flugga and Hermaness, but then thought it would be more interesting to go between Muckle Flugga and Out Stack. Muckle Flugga is the most northerly of four huge sawtooth rocks some 66 metres high. The ledges on the third were crowded with bright white gannets in contrast to the black rock.'

Four days later they were in Scalloway where they spent two nights. Ray needed to complete some consultancy work and send the results by fax.

'At 1900 the fish man arrived on our pontoon and offered to open up his office to send my fax, driving me there! He would not accept a penny for faxing and would only take £2 for the smoked mackerel and kippers Margo bought. Such is the hospitality of Shetlanders.'

It is 85 miles from Scalloway going south to Papa Westray, in the Orkney group. Ray chose to do this in a single 14-hour voyage, by-passing Fair Isle, although, with good visibility, both Fair Isle and the distant island of Foula to the west were in sight for most of the passage. Calm conditions required the use of the engine much of the time. A further 43 miles the next day took them back to Stromness where they celebrated Ray's birthday in style ashore in the Hamnavoe, a highly-rated restaurant.

From Stromness a short three-hour afternoon trip took them to South Walls inside the island of Hoy and across to the southern side of Scapa Flow. Now they were poised for the challenge of the Pentland Firth. The Pilot advised that this should not be attempted with wind against tide, winds above force 4, nor during spring tides, nor with poor visibility or a swell running. On Saturday July 17th all these conditions were in place – except one: visibility was down to about a quarter of a mile. Ray decided to talk to the Coast Guard. They forecast that the fog would clear in the afternoon and that, with the wind over the tide, the dangerous overfalls on the west-going ebb, known as the Merry

Men of Mey, should not be a problem. Although the fog was slower to clear than expected, the Coast Guard then checked with Orkney Harbour Radio to confirm there was no shipping present. With this reassurance they were under way with all possible speed to reach Scrabster harbour, 20 miles away on the mainland, in a three and half hour passage.

An hour out they got a clear radar target but then heard Orkney Harbour Radio call it with their position. A German vessel confirmed that it had them on radar and passed at a distance of half a mile, although without either visual sight or sound. At the charted position of the Merry Men the sea remained smooth. Crossing Thurso Bay they saw the harbour at Scrabster at a distance of one mile and knew the Merry Men had been thwarted.

Part Four of the circumnavigation ran from Scrabster to Arran, 403 miles and 20 days – July 17th to August 6th. Once past Cape Wrath, on the second day, they were often in waters or harbours which they knew from their voyage the year before. Finding safe moorings or anchorages was sometimes a problem as when a furious expatriate Englishman complained that they had anchored on top of his scallop beds in Lake Eriboll. A night at anchor in a 'secret bay' on the tiny islet of Poll Domhain made up for this as did their visit to Iona. But on July 29th, as they made the rock-strewn approach to a new marina at Craobh Haven (pronounced 'croove'), *Babaji* came to a sudden halt with a crunch and a lurch to starboard. They had hit a reef – and the tide was falling.

The marina work boat and another yacht were soon on the scene and they were pulled off, not without some unpleasant noises. It was five days before they could leave again, during which, after some delay, they were hauled out on the slip, an 18 inch gash in the keel was repaired and they took the opportunity to anti-foul, which they had been hoping to do, whenever convenient, since leaving St Katharine's in May. They then made their way through the Crinan Canal taking the inside route to Arran where they spent two nights. Ray re-lived a boyhood visit to the island in 1946 when he had made daily observations of wave height, wind force and direction, which he then submitted to the junior section of the Sir Napier Shaw competition for meteorology to win first prize! No wonder he still showed some confidence in his reading of the weather.

Part Five of this epic took them 19 days and 533 nautical miles from Arran to Padstow, where they arrived on August 28th. On the way they spent two nights in Peel in the Isle of Man, including their wedding anniversary dinner, followed by a risky three-mile cliff-top walk in the dark returning to the boat. This was followed by a breezy run to Holyhead, one of their best sailing days, and a further two nights in harbour there, while Ray worked for a good 12 hours of the intervening day on discs of consultancy work, lying in wait at the Post Office. Rounding the Lleyn Peninsula from an idyllic island anchorage at Pilot Cove they enjoyed another two night stay in a luxurious new marina at Pwllehi and carried out maintenance before crossing to Barmouth, where they had a rendezvous with Ray's brother, David, and his wife.

By comparison with earlier legs there were more days in harbour than before, although time was never wasted. From Barmouth to Fishguard and then on to Milford Haven there was good progress, though less under sail than engine. They were now bound for Bristol, where Ray expected more mail, calling at Swansea and Penarth en route, locking into harbour for both nights.

Having navigated the entrance to Avonmouth and moored on the waterside by the Arnolfini Centre, Ray needed to do another day's work in Bristol. It was also the city where he and Margo had first met; so they visited the digs where she had once lodged and went to the Old Vic Theatre to sit in the 'gods' for £2. The seats were just as hard as when they had cost 2/6d in the 1950s but they enjoyed the evening. From Avonmouth they returned to Penarth for a very short night, locking out at 0200 in order to cross to Lundy Island.

This was a 12 hour passage in two-hour watches, half under sail, to cover 57 miles. They anchored off the island and were determined to go ashore, not least to buy and send post cards. It was one of the sunniest days of a poor summer and they enjoyed exploring the island. But launching the dinghy from the beach with an onshore wind, to return to *Babaji,* and the row out, proved extremely challenging. It was also an anxious night at anchor with some violent motion and noise from the chain. They were probably glad of the calm conditions and light winds of the following day which took them to Padstow, even if they had to motor more than sail.

Now they were in waters even more familiar from previous cruises with only the final stage to come: round Land's End, along the south coast and into London; 10 days from August 28th to September 7th, 480 NM. They left Padstow at 0600, cautiously, because of thick mist giving way to a red sunrise. This was the first time Ray did not advise the Coast Guard of destination and ETA, since both were still undecided.

'Closed in on the Cornish coast to get a good view of the old tin mines, and rounded the Longships Light in the only rough water of the passage. With plenty of time in hand and with a favourable wind and tide for the Lizard we decided to continue and crossing Mounts Bay rounded the Lizard at 1800. Picked up a mooring in Gillian Harbour, a bay on the south side of the Helford estuary.'

That day's run was logged as 98 miles in 14.4 hours but only 0.8 under sail, whereas from Helford to Plymouth they had a following wind and could sail for six hours out of nine with a jib pole and preventer rigged. The remaining ports of call were Dartmouth, Swanage, Newhaven, Dover and Queenborough. Ray's last log entry is surprisingly non-triumphant, with an undertone of quiet pride, well justified.

'**Day 101 Tuesday 7th September.**
Queenborough to London (South Dock).
After a short shopping expedition left mooring at 1000 crossing the meridian at 1550 (a nice Ray touch) and locked into South Dock and "home" at 1600.'

Part Seven of this impressive 75-page document contains three full pages of day by day analysis in tabular form, with mileages both daily and cumulative, wind speeds, barometer readings, nature of harbours, moorings etc, with a note of charges where applicable, and a quality rating. Lerwick, Scalloway Papa Westray; Pilot's Cove Pwllheli, and Bristol were among those which rated 10; poor old Swanage only 3 (although they liked the town) and Orford (this time) 6.

There is also a table of statistics including harbours visited, 82 in total, of which only 25 were for the first time; total days 107; sailing days 79; hours under sail 181; under power 373. Average day's log distance 34.7 on sailing days. A note also compares these totals with LP (Libby Purves). I assume this refers to her 1988 circumnavigation of mainland Britain, with her husband Paul Heiney and their two children, narrated in her book *One Summer's Grace;* LP is credited with 57 harbours, fewer anchorages, 54 sailing days, average log distance 17 (understandable with small children); hours under sail 210, under power 180. It would appear that this was a shorter, less extensive voyage than *Babaji's,* but with less use of the engine. Their boat, *Grace O'Malley* was a gaff-rigged cutter, a larger version of the Cornish Crabber range.

Before the end of the millennium, as we shall learn, the Glaisters would carry out another complete circumnavigation of the British Isles, including the west coast of Ireland, and several Baltic voyages, including at least two into the heart of Russia and one back round the North Cape.

11. Water music and war

From the late 1980s into the next decade, the Orford cruising fleet grew significantly in numbers and experience. Boats tended to get somewhat larger as the relative cost of GRP building and maintenance fell in relation to disposable incomes. Some of us were reaching retirement age and were less constrained by other responsibilities such as flag office, as was the case with the Bakers and Glaisters, and now.

At the end of the 1987 season *Quantz* was re-wired at Frank Knights Yard in Woodbridge. In 1988 Simon Arnold, who became such a congenial and valued companion and crew for many future voyages, joined me and Don, two years into his university course, in a short round trip to the Belgian coast, Ostend, and Nieuwpoort, then to Dunkirk and Ramsgate. Then in 1989 Simon and I explored the Ijsselmeer harbours, including a first visit to Friesland, which was to be another favourite destination. Neither of our crossings was straightforward, a problem with the mainsail track in rising wind forced us to run for Scheveningen, which we entered under foresail, with a following sea and a prayer. After enjoyable visits to Amsterdam, Hoorn, Medemblik and across to Hinterloopen, we experienced awkward contrary winds and a short-lived engine problem on the return from Ijmuiden, which shepherded us further north into Lowestoft as first port of call before I brought *Quantz* back to Orford a day later, Simon having had to answer the call to work.

At the end of that season a survey indicated patches of osmosis requiring some treatment or at least a prolonged period of drying out. The responsibilities of being Commodore, which I had taken on in 1989, were reducing the time available for longer cruises as did the chairmanship of a Sea Defence Action Group pressing for government finance to reduce the risk of a breach at Slaughden.

Quantz was therefore laid up at Larkmans in Melton and left to dry out fully for the whole of 1990 and not re-launched until the end of August 1991.

In the summer of 1990, Charles Iliff, with his love of rivers and canals, once across the sea, made another cruise further east into the heart of Europe. This account is his own abridged version from the Royal Cruising Club's 'Roving Commissions'.

'We reached our first lock in descent, 95 locks and nine days from Antwerp through Belgium and the north of France. The gentle winding Meuse had given us a helping hand upwards through the gorges of the Ardennes and the upland meadows of Sedan and Verdun. Without it the Rhine and the Moselle would have been unattainable to *Premuda*, the 28ft Maxi 84. For this part of the voyage the mast was laid on the pulpit forward, a pile of tyres amidships, and wooden crutches at the pushpit. Of overriding importance was her engine – the Rhine below Koblenz can flow at five knots and *Premuda* just about squeezed six knots at full throttle.

But something was different about this lock. It was musical. Not water music, but no less classical, the first stanza of the duet from the Merry Widow. Not from myself, my wife Monica, her godson Douglas, or his mother Jo. That left only the elderly lock-keeper. He manned the first five of the flight of 15 locks down to Toul and the French Moselle, only a few hundred yards separating each. He let us through, the music stopped, a moped whizzed along the towpath, and he was waiting at the second lock – with the second stanza. By the third lock I had summoned up the courage to ask what the name of the music was, by way of learning the French title of the opera. He did not know: "c'est une vieille chanson, monsieur". But we still got the fifth stanza at the fifth lock.

The canal from the summit connects with the Moselle at Toul. We were now in Alsace-Lorraine which has an uncomfortable history. Airey Neave's *They have their exits* describes interviewing a Waffen SS officer from Alsace in 1945. He was told: "my great-grandfather fought for the French in 1870, my grandfather for the Germans in 1918 and my father for the French in 1940."

Coming out of the first of the two locks through to the Moselle there was a sudden grinding noise. I slipped the engine into neutral and it ran smoothly, suggesting a propeller problem. Goggles on and clothes off – the water was warm and slightly opaque from the chalky uplands of the summit section, but clear and otherwise clean. I surfaced with a sheet of plastic and some relief.

The French Moselle, sometimes canal, sometimes river, and wider above the weirs, with the channels marked by buoys, flows through wooded country like a large scale Upper Thames. The locks all the way down to the junction with the Rhine at Koblenz are large, 172 by 12 metres, with drops of 6 to 9 metres. The banks are usually granite rocks, unsuitable for mooring given the barge wash, and often the only places to moor are close to the locks themselves. But there are some pontoons where yachts can moor overnight.

Metz, the capital of Lorraine, is a magnificent city, situated by virtue of numerous river arms, canals and lakes on a series of islands. The Port de Plaisance was in the centre. Like an old-fashioned Oxford and Cambridge rowing club with a building to match in the centre and some pontoons for visiting yachts, it was surrounded by green gardens, handsome buildings, old bridges and cathedral spires; it was as if we were mooring on the lake at St. James' Park in Westminster. The following morning we moved *Premuda* to a deeper pontoon in case the level of the water dropped. It is never easy leaving a boat but she was to be well looked after for a few weeks.

Monica and I returned to Metz on August 18th, this time with my sister

Mary and two friends from Cambridge, Michael and Gill. Monica, Mary and I had a fortnight off, which we thought would give enough time to descend the Moselle and the Rhine, get the mast up, and cross the North Sea to Orford.

Next day we motored out of the Port (whose level had indeed dropped) to the first lock and waited with the engine idling. The lock opened, I pushed the throttle forward to enter – and nothing happened. The engine merely continued to idle – in forward gear. *Premuda* edged forward into the lock. A frantic removal of engine panels suggested that the throttle cable had parted, but I could not see where. The engine would only idle, in forward, neutral, or reverse, probably enough for lock work. To open the throttle I made an arrangement of string leading out of the cockpit with the engine cover off. Nothing is more permanent than a temporary arrangement that works, and it was still in place at the end of the season.

That evening we reached Sierck, only about a mile from the border, and already there were the beginnings of a considerable change to come – the first of the deep, sinuously curving valleys beneath the slate hills, covered with vines, that border the river for the rest of its length. Apache Lock is the border point, itself in France, the weir and vineyards beyond in Luxembourg and the bridge connecting the two banks in Germany. The French Customs office was closed and the German officer only wanted to chat. Of Luxembourg Customs there was no sign.

I had counted on using the automatic mini-locks or 'bootschleuse', particularly further down the Moselle, to avoid sharing large locks with 2000 tonne pusher trains. At the second of the two Luxembourg locks, Gravenmacher, I asked whether the bootschleuse would be available. Yes, but we should enter "doucement".

Premuda squeezed herself into this tiny lock, not much wider or longer than herself. She did not ground as she entered. There were detailed instructions and a notice disclaiming all responsibility. You turned a lever either to 'bergfahrt' – towards the mountains – or 'talfahrt 'towards the valley.' 'Talfahrt' it was. Then press 'go', with an emergency button just in case. Hydraulic sounds started to grind from the machinery and the open upstream gate closed very, very slowly. When this had been completed a small hydraulic arm pulled open the sluice on the downstream gate and we began to descend, ever so slowly, down a narrow, tight, wet slot. Thirty feet is not a small drop but when the lock is only 12 feet wide, just a foot wider than the boat, and you have committed yourself to the safe working of the automatic machinery, it seems enormous. Eventually the slow descent ended and the high and narrow lock gate ahead of us edged open.

Now with only three on board, we stopped that night at a pontoon at Wasserbillig, the last town in Luxembourg. The slopes of the high hills along the Moselle are covered almost everywhere with vineyards. The vineyard slopes themselves are a slatey black whose own darkness holds the sun's rays and boosts the temperatures for grape growing. These slopes are often very steep, with elaborate arrangements of terracing, access ladders and pulley cableways. Interspersed along the slopes, and particularly on the river's edge, are the characteristic whitewashed and half-timbered small towns and villages with their Romanesque churches.

The barge traffic, up to 2000 tonnes, increased gradually as we approached the junction with the Rhine. Although it was late August there were few yachts. On the Moselle as on the Rhine there are few bridges and local communication between opposite banks is often served by tiny car ferries.

I wanted to buy some Moselle wine. Bernkastel seemed the right place and I explored before breakfast to find a suitable wine merchant and to buy bread. The baker's shop was in a street of half-timbered houses. I paid for my loaf of landbrot and asked where I might find a wine merchant. The baker took me outside. "You see my shop?" "Yes". "You see that house over there – No 11?" "Those are the only houses in the street that are not wine merchants."

We loaded with Auslese and Spätlese and left for Cochem and its fairytale castle. The following day took us down the rest of the Moselle to Koblenz, relishing this great river, current still hardly noticeable, but not relaxing as much as we had – the Rhine was tomorrow, and that would certainly be different.

From Koblenz down the Rhine to Cologne is about 100 kilometres. *Premuda* did this in six hours, which meant an average speed over the ground of 16kmph. However, there are sections where the river is squeezing through the shoulder of a valley with the rate of drop increasing, and where we went faster. It was a lot less than the current through the gorges above Koblenz, but it was quite enough for *Premuda*.

The lower level of the river this August did mean that the current was a little slacker than at other times, but on the other hand the water was less deep, bringing the risk of striking the bottom. The narrower river also meant that traffic had less room to manoeuvre. This is a beautiful river, but also a very busy one. Barges stream in both directions, perhaps one every two or three hundred yards. This means wash; so the mast and rigging must be securely lashed down. It also means keeping constantly alert and observing the rule of the road as amended by the system of blue flagging.

Because the current is strong and the river takes large sweeping bends, an up-going barge may benefit by proceeding on the inside of a bend. It has the option of taking oncoming barges on the 'wrong' side, in which case it hoists a blue flag or slatted blue board. The down-coming barge acknowledges in like fashion. I had read advice to keep to the side of the main channel, but in many places it was not possible to do so. A two foot square blue flag was lashed to the mop handle and flashed up and down as required

We began to feel that we were masters of the Rhine! But hubris deserves retribution. We set off from Cologne early the following morning and raced out of the Rheinauhafen, throttle wide open; then there was a faint smell of burning – and the engine stopped. We drifted under the main road bridge at Cologne. There was very little barge traffic but, with the mast stowed on deck, we were helpless; the Rhine swept us on our way.

A quick check revealed no obvious problem. The string throttle was adjusted to minimum. I turned the ignition key, and the engine fired. We set off again at a moderate throttle level.

Below Cologne, past Düsseldorf and the Ruhr basin, the Rhine imperceptibly widened, although the strength of the current was little changed. Gradually the granite stones of the banks gave way to shingle and then to sand, with prolific bird life on the shores; water fowl, and above all herons, standing in groups every few hundred yards, holding committee meetings and apparently tamer than their French cousins on the Meuse – perhaps they are not shot in Germany. The Rhine appeared to be a very clean river, with little or no debris floating in it. The birds (and herons can only mean fish) suggest that it is relatively pollution free.

The next day we would be exchanging the Dutch for the German courtesy flag. I got out John Liley's *Barge Country*, to reintroduce myself to the waterways of the Dutch Rhine delta. The book fell open – 'Fog' was the heading, with vivid descriptions in the text. But in this heatwave it scarcely seemed relevant.

The next morning though we were enveloped by – fog. We decided to set off, if only for the Customs Post a few kilometres away. We hugged the bank and checked the 10th of a kilometre and kilometre marks on the Rhine atlas against those appearing out of the fog on the bank. Very occasionally the shapes of barges edged past, proceeding slowly and with radar antennae swivelling. They had abandoned blue flags.

We moored in the little Dutch Customs harbour at Lobith and sought out the joint Customs building to obtain our German 'Quittung'. Meanwhile the fog had been lifting, windmills and steep gables came into view (on this border the cultural change is abrupt) and barges poured out into the river from side canals and harbours.

We arrived late that afternoon at Goringchem, just before the Rhine divides, the narrower section turning off south towards the Hollandsche Diep, Zeeland and the Oosterschelde. Here, below the last bridge we needed to find a crane to erect our mast. Magnificent weather and magnificent scenery, with the inland 'secret water' of the Biesbosch on our left. Although I know

Zeeland itself well, I had not been to this part of southern Holland before, and resolved to return. At Strijensas, just below the last bridge, not only did they have a crane, but we were invited to help ourselves, and at no charge. With the help of a kind Dutchman the mast was quickly erected and I had a sailing boat again.

We sat that evening over supper, overlooking the yacht harbour and out across the Hollandsche Diep to Willemstad under a wide sky towards low horizons. The scene had little in common with the muscular current of the Rhine and the deep valleys of the Moselle, and even less with the little lock above Toul. Yet some small proportion of the waters here at the mouth of the Rhine had been sent on their way by our elderly French lock keeper. The Merry Widow was still audible, however faintly.'

Once the main events of the 1991 OSC sailing season were over I was very happy to see *Quantz* re-launched at Larkmans on August 29th, free of osmosis, as far as we could tell, and with a new, lighter weight mast. Michael Collins was with me to sail her round to Orford and my log-book also mentions the valuable help I received from James Robinson, Peter Norris and David Foreman trying out sails and testing the engine. Simon Arnold joined me early in September for a celebratory 12-day cruise to Holland, during which I introduced him to the inland scenery of the Veerse Meer, the canal up to Goes and some exploration further inland for nights in Wemeldinge and Kortegene before returning to Middelburg and Flushing.

We emerged from harbour into the Scheldt with the idea of heading for Blankenberge but a fresh headwind and rough water re-directed to Breskens for the afternoon and evening. After an agreeable supper ashore the wind seemed to have moderated and conditions seemed good enough to set out on the return crossing. This was not my best decision. We were off Westkapelle by 1100 with two reefs down. It was distinctly choppy and later rough, gusting up to force 6. One wave broke into the cockpit, unusual for *Quantz*, both of us suffered some nausea, or worse, during the night hours. Heading somewhat further north to avoid the Gabbard and Shipwash we finally sighted Sizewell and made for Southwold, entering in time for a drink in the clubhouse, a meal aboard, and welcome sleep. The reward for an uncomfortable 24 hours was a lovely early morning, motor-sailing under full canvas with a favouring tide, at least to Orfordness, and only the early ebb to contend with upriver. Of course if we had waited overnight in Breskens, we might have enjoyed those conditions all the way home.

Not many of us have chosen to sail through a war zone, but early in 1992 two Orford sailors did just that. Their story appeared in the December issue of *Practical Boat Owner* under the title 'Collection in Croatia'. 'AJ Robinson agrees to attempt a dangerous delivery trip'. With James' permission and very slight abridgement, the story of how the last of the Seven Seas Maxis was rescued from the Balkan War is now re-told.

'When Chris, the owner of *Silba* invited me to join him in a spot of early sailing in March 1992 I thought: what a charming fellow to offer me the chance! News of the civil war was thin on the ground at home. It might be now or never to go and see if *Silba* was still in one piece and with luck move her to safe waters. So armed with a plentiful supply of nine millimetre hardwood plugs it was 'Holiday Time'.

We caught the midday ferry to Calais on March 8th and were in Rijeka the following night. The guard on the Croatian frontier was surprised to see us, but, after all, we told ourselves it was early in the season.

In the morning the skipper was up early, while I was still dreaming of sand-bags and sticky-taped windows. He returned with good news – there was either a jet-boat or the ferry running, but if we caught that night's ferry we would gain at least half a day – and anyway he had bought the tickets. We spent the day in the car looking for a berth but all the northern Adriatic was full of boats brought up last summer. After a drive to Pula, with only one stop by the Police/Militia, we struck lucky: the AYC Marina had room. There was a destination for *Silba*.

The ferry leaves Rijeka at 1800 and the trip to Split takes about 12 hours. It was packed with people and belongings – all the cabins and reclining seats had been booked for weeks. We found somewhere to stow luggage and retired to the bar for a much needed beer. The restaurant was operating; we had a good meal and the staff seemed genuinely pleased to see some Brits again.

Chris had tuned his amazing Sony to the World Service for news of the Budget. This attracted the attention of a Croatian, who spoke some English, a merchant seaman it transpired, who was returning home after a year away, knowing only that his village, outside Dubrovnik, was reduced to rubble: he gave us his view of the Serb Chetniks. It was not such a good idea to listen to the 2300 Radio Croatia English broadcast. Zada, Sibenik and Split were mentioned, Split having undergone its first air raid for weeks, plus rockets. Incendiary bombs had been dropped and the population was being kept indoors. What on earth were we doing here? We talked the situation through. Short of swimming for it (swiftly discarded) we were bound for Split regardless. It was time to find some deck space and, if possible, some sleep.

As we disembarked early on Wednesday morning the strain and tension on the faces of the people waiting to meet relatives and friends was quite apparent. Not a taxi in sight until Providence, in the shape of an elderly gentleman driving an ancient vehicle, halted at our feet. A young lady got out to catch the ferry on to Dubrovnik, and we persuaded him to take us on to Primosten.

It was a taxi ride with a difference: as soon as we neared the outskirts of town speed limits were totally ignored – overtaking on blind corners – no problem –squealing tyres the norm. Admittedly there was very little traffic, and for very good reason – snipers – who seem to like the coast road. A tip to remember on the M25: "Sorry, Officer, but speed does reduce the target."

Suddenly there we were, standing beside the boat on Primosten quayside, no need of the hardwood plugs – not a mark on her. After all the months of worry and not knowing, here she was. In Dubrovnik 85% per cent of all boats had been sunk by gunfire. Chris paid the driver with a fistful of Deutschmarks, it made his day. (No Euros then). Now it was off to settle the bill for *Silba,* find some fuel and obtain the navigation certificate and we would be on our merry way. Wrong! No problem with the bill, nor the fuel; not even the Duty free, although the staff were not expecting Englishmen and we bought the one and only case of beer in sight. And, oh yes! – the biggest Croatian courtesy flag available, nearly as big as the yacht's ensign. Even the harbourmaster sought us out and did the paper work. A great chap, who looked after us well and notified the gunboats up the coast of our intended passage just inside the Kornati islands, travelling by daylight, definitely.

No, it was the exhaust manifold, which had a big split in it. In the end only a temporary setback, the marina staff got hold of an engineer who spoke no English but removed the manifold and took it off to Sibenik for welding, only to come back without it. The power station had been bombed, and they were trying to restore power. To pass the time we looked round the marina for old cans, tubing, or any object which might enable some sort of repair. Alongside one of the quay walls a boat was being converted into a gunboat with much coming and going of militia. We kept a low profile. During the afternoon there was a burst of gunfire in the hills. At about 1800 the man from Sibenik turned up again with one repaired manifold. Were we pleased to see him! He seemed to think it should last to Pula.

We cast off and gently motored round to Primosten town for fresh food to supplement our stores. We had a drink in the bar beside the small harbour, the girl serving us told us of her English studies and how all the schools had been shut for months. These people just wanted a normal life, they suffered, but still smiled and were just as hospitable as they were when I was last here, a few years ago.

First thing in the morning and *Silba* was on her way north, steering 280° magnetic from Primosten to start with, until we could leave Zirje to starboard, putting us outside the first islands and well off shore from Sibenik. The plan was to get as far north as possible and hope to make it beyond Zadar, after which the fighting seemed to have quietened down.

Having set the sails in a light north-west wind and sunshine – things were looking up – we motor-sailed for speed. Chris made a link call to his wife Ruth, and I called Charles, the owner of *Premuda*, acting as UK agent for the trip; both calls made through Split Radio. The sun shone, the wind built up and we were soon in the channel between the islands of Zut and Kornat. From here there would be islands between us and the mainland. The harbourmaster at Primosten had shown some concern that if sighted visually or on radar we might make a target. I hoped he was being over-protective, but it was reassuring to be among the islands. The wind was cold but the sun had some warmth in it and progress was good. During the afternoon we saw one gunboat which ran parallel with us for a time but always a mile distant. Our friend's call from Primosten seemed to have done the trick. That night we lay in Bosava on the northern end of Dugi Otok.

We were woken in the morning by the swell coming in from the south, the only unprotected quarter in the harbour. We left quickly; whereas the night had been flat calm this wind turned out to be the Sirocco, giving the swell from a breeze blowing the entire length of the Adriatic with an average force of 4-5. It can last for nine days and bring a rough sea, but the waves are long and regular, and it proved most helpful to us.

Friday was much greyer but the south wind was warm. We left Zwerinac to starboard and cut through the channel that runs between Tun and Molat, staying close to Molat we skirted the small island of Tovarnjak. The islands are greener here and we passed over rocks and sand more than 330ft below but crystal-clear; it is a superb cruising ground. (Better still in peace time?).

Closing the island of Silba itself Chris tried once more to get a radio station, but could not raise anyone. Perhaps we were in a blind spot. Then Rijeka Radio answered...

"Rijeka Radio, this is *Silba*. One link call, please."
"Silba, this is Rijeka Radio. What is your position?" "Five miles south of Silba."
"Yes, your boat is called *Silba*, but where are you?" "I am five miles south of Silba."

So it went on with Chris spelling out the fact that *Silba* was south of Silba. It was no good, we could almost feel the operator shrug his shoulders and say: "OK what number do you want?" After the call to Ruth, the operator came back to tell Chris how long it had been and, to general amusement, told us he had worked it out – the boat was named after the island!

We had passed Ciovo in the taxi from Split and now we could see Premuda and Silba. Later on we would pass close to Susak. There was something emotional about seeing all the islands after which the Orford Maxis were named. We spent an hour and a half on Silba, just time for some supplies and a beer, the first visitors for some time. As we rounded the top of the island and headed for Ilovik, water appeared in the bilges: the manifold was leaking again. The engine was turned off to save it for later and in case the split opened right up. Our speed dropped and Chris got busy with bucket and mop. By now we were clearing the island and with the full benefit of the Sirocco, soon picking up speed over the longer, larger waves. 'George' could not cope with the surfing.

For the last 55 miles or so it would have to be 'hands on wood'. And a cracking sail it was – soon past Susak. At dusk we closed the headland at the tip of the Istrian Peninsula. The Satnav had not given us a fix all day, and now we could have used one. There are two lights and with our angle of approach the more distant one appeared to be the closer. Get it wrong and you are on the rocks. Once this was sorted out it should have been easy to find Pula.

We got there in the end. The old rule – 'if in doubt, stand off in safe water' – was put to good use twice. Matters were complicated by lights not working and some appearing that were not on the chart. As we motored up the channel all the wind was lost but we kept the mainsail up so if we were spotted, it would be clear we were a yacht. Nobody hailed us, and we tied up at 2230. A couple from Slovenia took our lines. They were a bit surprised by our port of origin and took us aboard for meat, cheese and wine. It was well into the small hours before we turned in.

On Saturday Chris took the bus to Rijeka, returning late in the afternoon with the car. I spent the day cleaning the boat which we moved to an inside berth with a good view of the Roman Amphitheatre. On Sunday morning, after making a job list, we set off home. Our work was done.

The last time I was out here helping to move a boat the crew were 'paid' one dinar a day (see Chapter Nine 'Maxis in the Med'). This time I was treated to a day in Venice and a drive through Czechoslovakia, a country I had always wanted to see. Looking back, the time of greatest risk must have been on the German Autobahn but it is always unknown dangers that bother us most. I remain very grateful to Chris for the chance to do the trip – a unique experience for me, one I shall never forget.'

There is a sad sequel to this story. *Silba* never did return to the UK. Some time later, after this article was published, a severe storm dashed her against the quayside where she still lay, and she was damaged beyond repair. Chris Tweed became the owner of *Zut,* another of the Dalmatian sister ships, which had reached the UK safely a year or two earlier.

James has made an earlier appearance as one of the *marinaios* aboard

Premuda and *Ciovo* on the voyage round the foot of Italy. But his role in helping others to make the most of their cruising by developing their confidence and competence goes far beyond being a crew member. Ever since 1982 he and Peter Norris have been part owners of a series of boats, first *Nerita*, a Snapdragon 21, then *Petronella* their Francis 26 and now *Dura*, a Westerly Storm. James and Peter, together with Paul Blaxill had grown up in Knebworth but James' first experience of sailing went back to his school days at Framlingham College, where boys sailed dinghies at Orford under the tutelage of Philip de Whalley, a member of staff, and also of OSC.

The effects of a serious accident resulted in James' move to live permanently in Orford. Despite the pain and some disability, which has been his lot ever since, he has never allowed these disadvantages to prevent his sailing nor the encouragement of others, above all younger sailors. Two generations will bear witness to this. He obtained his Yachtmaster certificate and by 1989 he had qualified as an Instructor. He worked alongside Philippe Taylor and, subsequently, Graham Bush helping many Orford sailors to obtain offshore qualifications as skippers or competent crew. Often the presence of James aboard our boats with a helping hand or a word of tactful advice, only given when requested, perhaps alongside the club pontoon or in the clubhouse, has been invaluable.

By comparison with *Susak's* adventures and the ambitious Glaister voyage of 1992 my own effort that summer seems small beer, although it had its moments. With Simon Arnold as crew I took *Quantz* back to Fécamp, stopping overnight twice in Ramsgate and Boulogne with an enjoyable night passage past Dieppe. We then returned to Dieppe, a fine spinnaker run for much of the day, as we were due to meet Wendy there from the Newhaven ferry. Simon left on the midnight ferry after dinner ashore that evening. The whole purpose of Wendy's trip was to visit Monet's famous garden at Varengeville, which was not far by bus. Her enjoyment was, however, much reduced by suffering increasingly from acute pain in her neck, which may have been brought on by sleeping aboard, and got worse still during the second night. She plainly could not travel back by ferry and then drive the car, on her own, all the way from Newhaven back to Orford. I hurriedly arranged to leave *Quantz* in Dieppe and we took the very early morning ferry back together. I then drove direct to Ipswich Hospital, where she was diagnosed as having a 'wry neck'. I took her back to Orford and she went straight to bed.

To this day I remain guilty about my decision to head back to Dieppe only 24 hours later, leaving Wendy still in bed, although somewhat more comfortable. It was influenced by anxiety about having left *Quantz* so abruptly in a large foreign harbour where I had no personal contacts. Also I had crew lined up to join me, our son Don and James Logan, only just back from his assignment with the Glaisters. Both were scheduled to join me there on July 26th. I travelled on the overnight ferry from Newhaven and they arrived the next evening. Meanwhile I had re-stocked *Quantz,* reassured myself that she had come to no harm and moved to the outer harbour ready for an early departure.

My log admits that in my haste to leave, and get back to Orford, I had made 'the classic mistake of under-estimating the weather' so that two hours from Dieppe at 0800 we needed to change to a smaller jib. Leaving Don asleep below, my second mistake, I went forward to change head-sails and allowed the smaller working jib, which I was about to set, to slip overboard. James, on the helm, had to put up with my anger at myself. The sail disappeared before we could pick it up. Having reefed the main, we motor-sailed on, consequently making rapid progress. By 1600 we were off Boulogne breakwater where the sea was 'nasty' and the dinghy, under tow, capsized and broke adrift: unlike the sail, earlier, we managed to recover it with no harm done.

A quarter of an hour later we were happily motoring up the harbour when we were accosted by a boat-load of fierce-looking customs officers. They escorted *Quantz* to a pontoon berth, where we were boarded and searched. No contraband was found and the officials became increasingly friendly. They had problems, they said, with yachts bringing in drugs, although more often under Dutch than other flags. I put our 'arrest' down to the dark glasses Don was wearing at the helm, and his sun-bleached hair. He might easily have been a dodgy young Dutchman.

After a night's rest we pressed on, under power alone till Gris Nez and then motor-sailing to enter Ramsgate by mid-afternoon. We left again at 2215 that evening after a short rest some quick shopping, showers, and fish and chips. The log records 'a great sail overnight' with a force 3-4 easterly. Near the Kentish Knock, about 0200, there was 'a moment of concern' when we heard the sound of breaking waves, but veered off and sailed safely on. Having made the most of favourable tides all the way we were approaching Orford Haven Buoy at 0745, nine and a half hours out of Ramsgate.

Just inside the entrance we allowed ourselves the respite of anchoring for breakfast in a shingle lagoon before North Weir Point. The final sail upriver was thoroughly enjoyable, feeling sleepy but satisfied. Best of all, waiting on the Quay was Jamie, who had interrupted his holiday to come and look after his mother, and was able to report that she was much better. Without my strong, young crew I could not have got back so quickly, and James Logan was kind, or polite enough, to say how much he had enjoyed the *Quantz* experience.

It was now Tuesday July 30th and I had returned with just two days to spare before an OSC Sail Past as part of the Riverside Fun Day, a major village event that year. The following week would also be the last training course to be run by Ray Maunder, in which I was contracted to participate, with our Mirror, as one of the mostly unqualified and somewhat elderly instructors on whom we then, to a great extent, relied. We were looking for a successor to Ray, who had done so much to train a whole generation of young Orford sailors. Roddy Webb had given us the name of a certain Liz Feibusch, who, with her husband Johnny, had a caravan base at Waldringfield. She had taught Roddy's children with great success on sailing courses in the south of England.

My 1992 diary tells me that I met Liz, for the first time on the Sunday afternoon, August 2nd. Tania Bielecki, as a committee member with children of Mirror sailing age, joined me for the 'interview'. It was immediately obvious that we did not need to look any further, but we were committed to seeing another possible candidate a day or so later. With heart in mouth I had to tell Liz that we would be in touch as soon as possible. I hope she has forgiven me, but at least she did agree to take it on – and the rest has been a great step forward in the Club's history.

12. Orford to the Indies, and less far

The 1994 *OSC Year Book*, compared with its smarter and much more detailed 21st century equivalent, only contains a very basic list of members, their addresses, names of boats and classes or types to which they belong. Wayfarers and Mirror dinghies are most numerous and a few Lasers and Toppers are mentioned. There are also about 25 boats 24 feet or more in length, which might be classified as cruising yachts. Most are under 30 feet, including the Maxis, with half a dozen larger boats, among them the Glaisters' Colvic (misspelt) *Babayi; Hermione of Burnham*, a Contest 33 and the Gills' *Maratu* of similar size. Some have moorings elsewhere rather than in Orford. Other smaller keel boats are listed but used mainly as day boats or for local cruising to nearby estuaries.

The list also contains several significant arrivals, two of whom were also members of the Royal Cruising Club, Colin Barry and 'Clem' Lister. I find a mention in my log of giving some help to the Listers on the Quay at the start of that season, then, more typically, of receiving their hospitality aboard *Hermione* in Butley Creek. Frequently I was on the receiving end of Clem's offers of help or some piece of equipment which he insisted on giving me. I have been unable to build a full picture of the Listers' cruising range in earlier years but at this period they were content with coastal passages and occasional visits to the Netherlands or France. His accounts of 1984 and 1985 cruises have already appeared in Chapter Eight.

Colin Barry started sailing at the age of seven in a Lymington Scow. Since these early beginnings he bought his first 24 foot cruiser in 1975 and has clocked up some 70000 nautical miles, 15000 of which have been ocean sailing. He is proud that his first crossing of the Orford Bar was from seaward in his 24 footer coming round from Lymington over four weekends. His boats progressed in size to a 28ft Trapper, 32 and 34ft Sadlers followed by his current 38ft Beneteau.

Cruises took place every year. For a time Colin had a mooring in the Solent but tended to winter on the East Coast. Summer voyages included the Channel Islands, Cornwall, North and South Brittany, Holland and Germany, the Hebrides and the Scillies. It is the Sadler *32 Bosham Dreamer* which appears in the 1994 Year Book. She is also noted as having won the Ore Challenge Cup, one of three 'Cruiser trophies' awarded in 1993. Paul Blaxhill's *Rinjinn* a Contessa 26 was the winner of the North Sea Trophy usually awarded for a praiseworthy crossing, the third trophy being the Barry Cup for a race at sea, won by Barry Hitchcock in the Seal *Flapper*.

These 'races' were run in a very informal way, with trophies awarded somewhat arbitrarily on the subjective judgement of the Cruising Co-

Ordinator, James Robinson, in a spirit characteristic of OSC, resembling the annual award of the Snape Cup or Monnington Mug, often given for a novice effort and for an event which rarely gets to Snape. Nobody would dream of challenging the result.

In 1995, anticipating retirement, Colin bought *Te'Aroa* a Sadler 34 in Plymouth and sailed her back to Orford. This was the vessel for his first Transatlantic Circuit and the subject of his account in the 1998 edition of *Roving Commissions*. This is reproduced now, with his permission and that of RCC, with some abridgement, which I hope will be forgiven.

'Having the Time of One's Life

As one approaches 60, the evening of life appears to draw in. You realise that you have achieved some things but failed to achieve others. One also considers goals that are still outstanding.

Born to a naval family, with two Flag Officers in the last two generations, I have thought about the sea since a very early age, falling in and out of boats since the age of seven. A short period in the Navy taught me the basics of old-fashioned seamanship and rudiments of Coastal Navigation. I really became interested in cruising when I was about 40 and spent the next 20 years planning and executing a series of summer holiday cruises which put us as far afield as Copenhagen, the Outer Hebrides, the Isles of Scilly and halfway round the Bay of Biscay. In 1990 the RCC were kind enough to re-instate me as a member. I suppose I was a bit like a lapsed Catholic, having been a cadet member!

At the age of 60 I decided that I wanted to achieve at least an Atlantic circuit and possibly more. With this in mind I exchanged my yacht for what I perceived as the minimum size for such a voyage, settling on a Sadler 34. I put my affairs in order and, early in November 1996, I was poised for action with the boat in Lagos, on the Algarve. We flew down to the Algarve on a Monday morning – the contrast was amazing. At Gatwick it was raining so heavily we could hardly see the plane, while the Algarve was enjoying an Indian summer.

Next morning saw us alongside the scrubbing wharf and the following few days were spent getting the ship ready for sea so we could leave on the Friday morning. Waiting for the final provisions to arrive, I went up the mast for a final check, to be told from the deck that my boss was on the mobile. Perhaps I should have taken the call aloft, but I rang back half an hour later.

The 400 miles to Madeira were achieved in two and a half days, a cracking sail giving us our first experience of running with two jibs. We stopped a couple of nights in Santos, which I highly recommend, and two more in Madeira, which suffered then from a small marina with little room for visiting yachts.

Anchoring in 35 feet of water with a strong wind and ground swell proved quite a task for my East Coast crew. Communication between the two ends of the boat improved with time. We obtained permission to visit the Selvagen Islands and had also planned to go to Lanzarote. However, with the angle and strength of the wind (force 6-7 ENE) we could only manage a close reach to Gran Canaria and were unable to anchor at the islands as the sea was too rough.

The first day of a 48-hour passage saw our highest daily run of 161 miles. We went to take part in the ARC and, although there were two weeks to go before the start, we effectively got stuck in Gran Canaria, largely because yachts were piling in, and if we had left we would have lost our marina position.

Jimmy Cornell's ARC is a remarkable event in many ways, with a good deal of build-up before the start. This happens about November 20th each year, with the object of getting between 150 and 200 boats to St Lucia in time for Christmas. The average time taken is about three weeks and for most of the voyage there should be a useful amount of trade wind. In truth the Rally is a little earlier than it perhaps should be as the north-east trades usually don't develop until early December.

Yet in 1996 we picked up a north-easterly breeze on the second morning and, steering down the rhumb line, kept wind with us to within 150 miles of St Lucia. I had three crew members: Andrew Curtis – the boy (aged 55), Philippe Taylor (59) and myself at 60. For most of the voyage we used twin jibs, on occasions we had the cruising chute up, and sometimes just the smaller jib. Most of the time we had between 12 and 25 knots of wind and someone claims to have seen 35 knots over the deck one night! But largely it was a fast, uneventful passage and we arrived in just under 20 days, a day shorter than *Slip Anchor*, another Sadler 34, which won the ARC in 1997.

St Lucia in December is a lovely place to be and wives began to join us. Philippe moved off the boat with his wife to a very comfortable hotel and Caroline joined us. Before Andrew went home for Christmas we staged a short cruise to the south part of St Lucia showing him the Pitons and Marigot Bays.

The six weeks after Christmas were taken up with entertaining three sets of guests, travelling as far south as Petit St. Vincent, the ultimate millionaires' paradise, and as far north as the tip of Guadeloupe, spending a windy night in Deshaies. In Bequia, one of the most attractive places in the West Indies we met several RCC boats. With more wind than normal we were involved in some spirited anchor-dragging in Bequia and turbulent sailing, rarely with less than two reefs in the mainsail.

The lowlight of the trip came in Wallilabou from one pushy local individual in particular – often hassled, bumped by boats without fenders, surf boards and so on. On a subsequent visit there was a demand for 'insurance money' or "he would bump the boat", at which stage we left to anchor in the delightful if rather spooky Cumberland Bay. By contrast the 'Saints' small island was charming with a population largely of French descent and very civilised. Martinique was way ahead of other islands, with Dominica probably the most fascinating, having as much as 300 inches of rain in the interior, which we visited.

Having returned to the UK in February 1997, my wife and I, with Katrina Milnes Gaskill came out for a break in May. We sailed down to Bequia again; then called it a day for that year, laying up at Rodney Bay in St. Lucia. Later in the year Trevor Wilkinson was kind enough to invite me to help him sail *Wombat*, his 52 foot ketch, from Gran Canaria to St Lucia, a relaxed, largely uneventful passage.

Having returned to UK for Christmas I was back in St Lucia early in 1998 for a series of trips with different parties coming and going: with the Logans south to Grenada, dropping them off in Bequia, picking up the Johnstons back in St. Lucia and leaving them in Antigua, and so on. During this four month period we called at virtually every island in the so-called Lesser Antilles, apart from some of the smaller French ones, getting all the way up to the British Virgin Islands in time for Race Week in Antigua.

The weather seemed different this year with reasonable winds. We sailed through the Salee River in Guadeloupe, a fascinating experience, starting at five in the morning when the bridge opens. The mosquitoes were large – we were trying to eat our breakfast: so were they! A rollicking sail to Antigua was our reward. After due exploration, we moved on to Barbuda, and via Nevis, St Kitts, St Eustatius and St Barts to St Martin, where a medical problem for one of us required a 10 day stay. After popping into Anguilla we reached the British Virgin Islands, where two younger crew – Ben Beddard and 'Shakes' Shackleton – joined us to sail back to Antigua.

The Annegada Passage is a horrible piece of sea. It had taken 11 hours to cross it from east to west, but the return took 31 against a one knot current and a force 6 to 7 wind. We proved to ourselves that sailing against the Trades is not a good idea!

Engine trouble and a crack in the boom had to be fixed but cost us three days' racing during Antigua Race week – disappointing for the young crew headed by my son and his three friends who joined us. One unforgettable experience there was a helicopter trip round Montserrat, eerie and sinister, albeit very sad.

In early May I headed north with three crew towards Bermuda. We had expected Trade Winds for the first four days, making a fast passage, then light winds, probably south-westerly, or none. In fact the wind expired after one day, we had calms for three days then strong north-westerlies for four, against all predictions! After a nasty electrical storm we entered St George's Harbour, older and wiser, eight days and some 950 miles after starting.

After a few days we joined the ARC fleet to the Azores. Most of the suggestions in the pilot books for June are to head north, edging up to 40 degrees north to keep reasonable winds. In fact, there were useful winds down on the Rhumb line, roughly 33 to 38 degrees north, but 40 knots or more along the 40th Parallel. We set a middle course and experienced many calms and three hours of a force 9 gale. At one point we found that the shroud fastenings had worked loose on the deck and we were in imminent danger of losing the mast, which we quickly put right. Sixteen days out we arrived in Horta, having sailed close alongside a 70ft sperm whale the previous afternoon. Heavy rain cleared the next day to reveal the magnificent sight of Mount Pico, the tallest in Portugal at 7500ft.

Our return passage to England after the memorable Azores Meet was remarkable in that we had myself, the Langdons and their two young sons 13 and 9 aboard. Despite predictions by several old and bold RCC members, it went very well, possibly because the weather was kind.

After a few days in Falmouth, the Logans rejoined to see me back to Orford. We had a delightful passage along the South Coast, enjoying a thoroughly relaxed style of sailing. Cally, my wife, joined us in Eastbourne and on Tuesday August 11th we entered Orford Haven. Ten boats were there to greet us, including Clem Lister. We provided some amusement by attempting the entrance too early and spending an hour and a quarter on the bar.

We were then piped home in traditional style, thus ending a memorable cruise which involved some 12000 miles' sailing, 36 different islands, 14 nation states and 26 crew members in addition to Cally and myself. Fifteen members of OSC participated; Andrew Curtis and Philippe Taylor sailed from Gran Canaria to St Lucia and Geoffrey Smeed from Antigua to Bermuda.

(Note. *Te'Aroa* is a Sadler 34, launched in 1986, having been the Boat Show model that January, a GRP sloop with a 20hp Bukh engine. Modifications for the trip included a deeper and heavier keel, hydrovane self-steering, SSB radio, a towed generator; inner fore-stay and running back-stays.)'

John Fulford's cruising history is an example of what might be termed as the Orford Sailing Diaspora, members of OSC whose boats have often been based abroad for considerable periods – Colin Barry's *Bosham Dreamer* prominent among them. It also exemplifies the gradual increase in size of boats during many sailing careers.

John's first cruising yacht was *Mary Alice*, acquired when he was living and working in India. She was a 28ft sloop, a sister ship to Robin Knox Johnston's *Suhaili*, built in the same Bombay yard in 1963 of solid teak. They cruised off the beaches and creeks of Western India, flying a defaced blue ensign with the Union flag in the corner (only recently replaced by the Indian flag). Life was good in the lingering shadow of the British Raj.

Back in the UK he had a 22ft Pandora, kept on a mooring at Ramsholt. When he moved to Belgium he bought a Westerly Centaur, moored at Kortgene in the Veerse Meer, 'that inland sea full of delightful islands and mosquitos' as he describes it. His next boat was a 32ft Jeanneau Attalia *(Semiramis1)*, moored first at Ramsholt, then for a while in London Docklands, now Canary Wharf. There followed a 36ft Jeanneau Voyage *(Semiramis 2)*, kept in Carentan, Normandy and cruised widely in France and Holland. Carentan proved to be an ideal location, despite a somewhat challenging entrance, especially in bad visibility, which was frequent. Virtually every port between Flushing in Holland and Pornic in Brittany was visited at some stage. These cruises included frequent visits to Orford with a mooring at Ramsholt.

From Carentan John's base moved to Roche Bernard and the story is best continued in his own words:

'This delightful town up the river Vilaine was well-placed for cruising in Brittany, especially places like the fascinating Morbihan and the numerous islands off that coast. In the year 2000 came *Semiramis 3*, a 40ft Beneteau, Centre Cockpit, with a vast aft cabin, a very comfortable and competent vessel. She was kept for a while at St Peter Port in Guernsey, a congenial location with wonderful cruising potential. Hankering after warmer climes, we set off from Vannes in Morbihan for the Mediterranean. After an uneventful Biscay crossing we reached Gijon in northern Spain and carried on round the dreaded Cape Finisterre. Popping in and out of the 'Rias' along the coast we were foolishly towing the inflatable and misread a forecast. We duly hit a force 7 and lost the dinghy! We had an exhilarating run down the Portuguese coast with a following wind and a small jib before running into dense fog – a common future. We helped to guide a small British yacht with no radar for a whole day. Arriving at Lagos in the Algarve we liked it so much we stayed and did not proceed into the Med.

The southern coast of Portugal and Spain provides an interesting cruising area from Cape St Vincent to Gibraltar. Unlike the Med it has an Atlantic climate, more predictable weather if on occasion more ferocious. There are numerous interesting ports and anchorages. Two of our favourite trips were up the River Guadiana from Vila Real to Alcoutin, or from Sanluca de Barrammeda to Seville. About 20 members of OSC shared these enjoyable trips, whilst the boat was berthed in Lagos, where she was eventually sold and is still berthed.

I briefly shared a Westerly Centaur again at Orford with Michael Flint until anno domini prevailed. Despite plenty of mileage in my cruising experience we had no real catastrophes – just happy memories of excellent boats in very pleasant parts of the world.'

During these middle and later years of the 1990s many of the OSC cruising fraternity, some mentioned above, often took part in small group rallies across the North Sea, to Ostend or Flushing in particular. For some it might be their first such venture. My own activities in *Quantz* extended, whenever possible, to the French coast as far as Le Havre and Honfleur. My companion, most summers, was Simon Arnold. He was not only a willing and uncomplaining crewman but blessed with an unfailing ability to find the restaurant with the best menu, franc for franc or guilder in every port.

Sometimes I went alone, as in 1993 to spend some time in the Walton Backwaters exploring the headwaters at Landermere and in Kirby Creek, where I woke up at anchor and was surprised to see a seal basking, not on the muddy bank, but on the middle thwart of a rowing dinghy moored nearby.

Our cruise to Zeeland in August 1994 was special because my son Don was now engaged to Veronica. He crewed me to Flushing, where Wendy and Veronica joined us from the ferry. For the next six days, the last week of July, the four of us, living in close quarters, visited or re-visited those favourite places from Middelburg and Veere to Zierikzee and Goes. It was unusually fine and warm, too hot in one lock, where a Dutch yacht with a cabin thermometer claimed to register 100ºF. Don and Veronica spent a day on their own visiting art galleries in Amsterdam, otherwise we had every opportunity to get to know and approve one another. It seemed to work. In Breskens, after a thunderstorm which broke the spell, Wendy and Veronica left to catch a ferry. Don and I waited till that evening before setting sail in fresh, choppy conditions with lighter winds later. By this time I had graduated to the use of a very simple 'Dinghy Decca' as an advanced navigational aid. It was used mainly to confirm our position against dead reckoning or observation, but it might be seen as progress.

Towards the end of the 1995 season *Quantz* and I went through a strange crisis, which might have resulted in the end of offshore sailing for me. It followed a successful solo trip to the Blackwater and the Crouch, my first visit to Burnham. But, near Stone Point at the entrance to the Walton Backwaters, where I had anchored for a swim on the way back, I pulled a muscle in my back when scrubbing the deck. It was a struggle to get back to Orford on my own, and the condition came and went with varying severity over several months. I began to think I would have to settle for a smaller, lighter boat. *Quantz* spent the winter at Levington, placed in the hands of brokers and advertised for sale. Very fortunately, only two potential buyers even came to look, and no offers were received. My back recovered and I remember, early in 1996, being firmly advised by James Robinson and Peter Norris that I would be stupid to get rid of a boat that suited me well and which I could manage on my own if necessary. They were entirely right, as another 25 years have proved, including the cruises which have given me most satisfaction.

My confidence was further restored sailing in company with *Petronella*, *Susak*, *Rinjinn* and *Zut* to the Walton Backwaters; then, mainly alone, to the Blackwater and back. Early in July I covered much of the same ground with a first visit to Heybridge Basin and a return to Brightlingsea thrown in. Then from Brightlingsea I crossed the Thames Estuary to North Kent and Ramsgate. The use of the Tillerpilot and some motoring reduced the strain of a long day. My log also contains several entries of positions noted as co-ordinates – evidence that I was making more use of GPS. I needed and enjoyed a day off in Ramsgate. Then I saw a notice on the pontoon asking whether anyone would like a crew across the Channel and directing enquiries to a Dutch yacht nearby. Alef Burghouts and his father had arrived from Holland in their boat, and his mother would be joining her husband to cruise further along the South Coast, but Alef needed to get back to Holland as cheaply as possible. He was hoping for a lift to Calais and to hitch-hike home from there. Father and son joined me for a drink on *Quantz* and mutual inspection. I knew at once that I had struck lucky.

The early morning forecast was more encouraging, but it would have been too breezy for me alone when we left harbour at 0615. Alef proved to be excellent company and an equally proficient helmsman and crew. We both enjoyed the trip apart from some queasy moments on my part approaching Calais, when his presence was all the more helpful. Once we had locked through to the inner harbour and tidied up Alef departed in search of a lift. A bond had formed, however, which brought the Burghouts twice to Orford in their new, larger boat *Tilman,* named after the intrepid solo sailor. We remained in touch for many years until they gave up longer voyages. This was one of those extra rewards that cruises unexpectedly provide.

Before returning to Orford I sailed happily round Gris Nez to Boulogne, spent two nights there and most of another in Ramsgate. The last day began at first light and gave me a very enjoyable 10-hour passage to Orford Haven. Log entries show that I was making proper use of GPS and waypoints to skirt the outer banks of the Thames Estuary. The weather was set 'Fair' with a friendly south-east breeze; 'George', the Tillerpilot, gave me the chance to relax from time to time. 'This has been a great voyage', I wrote in my notes.

'*Quantz* must stay.'

With this confidence re-building season behind me, 1997 had much to offer. The Burghouts and *Tilman* paid their first visit to Orford in May. It was good to see them again, to pilot them upriver, offer some hospitality ashore and accompany them down to Orford Haven for departure. Between sessions of A Level marking and Parish Council meetings, which were a constraint for much of this decade, I managed a solo trip to the Stour and Orwell early on; then a cruise south to Maldon and eastwards across to Sheppey and the Swale with Ben Johnston, who demonstrated how I should really be trying to use GPS. We experienced a breezy run back from Queensborough with two reefs down, when his presence was doubly valuable. In late July I headed north to Lowestoft and up the Waveney to Beccles and then back to St Olave's as far as the bridge, so that I could claim to have sailed on the Broads.

In September there was still time for Simon Arnold to join me for a fortnight's cruise south to France, during which we visited both St Valery sur Somme and St Valery en Caux. I was keen to experience the entrance to the Somme again from seaward, a challenge, which did not disappoint, and also to see at first hand the war memorials of St Valery en Caux where the 51st Highland Division had made its last desperate stand in June 1940. It was there too that Commander John Pryor, as we now knew him, but then a young sub-lieutenant, had been captured when trying to evacuate troops at low tide. Perhaps this steered him towards his later expertise as a naval hydrographer, regularly charting the entrance to the Ore for the benefit of OSC and AYC yachtsmen until Trinity House eventually surveyed and buoyed it.

Quantz remained afloat well into November that year. My last sail of the season was unforgettable. Despite the shortness of daylight hours I found time to glide gently northwards in Hollesey Bay that magical afternoon. As we approached the Haven buoy on the way back, the sun was setting over Shingle Street and, at the same time, an almost full moon rose slowly over the sea astern. 'He who has once been happy', wrote Emerson, poet and philosopher, 'is forever out of destruction's reach.'

During that winter I ordered a new genoa and furling gear and *Quantz* was treated to a new coat of paint on the topsides. These improvements led to a later launching date than usual with valuable assistance from James Robinson, once more, in setting up the new foresail rig. Short early trips either within the river, or into the Deben and the Orwell, gave me increasing confidence in handling the furling gear from the cockpit, a great help for single-handed sailing. In July I set off again for Ramsgate, Calais and Boulogne, managing successfully on my own.

As once before, I found myself in France during the Football World Cup, with the added interest that this was now the host country: the tournament had reached the semi-final stage; the French team was still very much involved, England was not, so I was free to enjoy a neutral status. The bars and restaurants of Boulogne were busy that week with supporters crowded round screens. The first evening after arrival I found myself commiserating with devastated Dutchmen as they lost to Brazil. Twenty four hours later I squeezed into the only empty chair at the Bar César, which throbbed with anticipation as France faced Croatia. The evening exploded into euphoria as the home team reached the Final, scoring two goals to one. Convoys of hooting cars kept the town awake well past midnight.

In the face of a poor forecast for several days to come I decided to leave *Quantz* in the marina and take the Seacat across to Folkestone in order to pay a visit to my sister in the Isle of Wight. I had toyed with the idea of doing this under sail, but discretion wisely prevailed over foolishness. Two days later I returned, delighted to find that the seat I had reserved in the Bar César for the night of the World Cup Final had indeed been kept for this strange, solitary Englishman. Admittedly it was next to the toilets in a very crowded corner, but some of the screen was still visible. Anyway the progress of the match was easy to follow from the faces of the crowd and the noise in the room. This rose in a crescendo: France 3 – Brésil 0: Gallic joy abounded – into the small hours.

I remained in harbour for three more days, taking care to ensure that *Quantz* was dressed overall early on the first morning, which was appreciated. Since the day following would be July 14th I decided to catch the first train of the day to Paris and to witness the Parade on the Champs Elysées, as close to the Arc de Triomphe as I could manage on this doubly triumphal national occasion. That was memorable too, and would have been even more enjoyable if I had not been suffering the first symptoms of a violent, viral cold. With a force 5 – 6 westerly blowing across the harbour in the morning I was not sorry to have the excuse to stay there.

I did manage to reach Ramsgate the following evening, but felt increasingly unwell and in need of rest and comfort. In the end it was nearly a week, following convalescence with friends in Kent and back in Orford, before I re-joined my ship with John Wadge as crew. John had started his career as an apprentice at Camper and Nicholson, the famous yacht builders, and knew his way around a boat. Examples of his carpentry skill adorn our home to this day. He was also a tolerant, helpful extra pair of hands. This time we took the Edinburgh Channel into the Black Deep before heading for the Sunk. Light, variable winds, but mainly from the south east or east, were a help not a hindrance, but it was a slower passage than usual. The sun was going down and the tide looked dangerously low as we sneaked over the bar against the last of the ebb, unlike the yacht behind us, which grounded. Darkness had fallen by the time that Wendy and Ann Wadge met us on the Quay. But such arrivals have special quality.

13. Routes into Russia

Compared with my forays to the French ports or across the Thames Estuary, whether solo or accompanied, the voyages of Ray and Margo Glaister between 1994 and the Millennium were on a very different scale of ambition and extent. His account of their 1995 Baltic venture reveals that this was already their second cruise to Scandinavia.

'Last year we rounded the North Sea and fell in love with Scandinavia, especially the Norwegian fiords and the west coast of Sweden. But we realized that there was another world just round the corner in the Baltic.

The 1994 crossing from Bergen had been smooth but we were lucky, and the passages up the east coast had taken a month. My wife and I are finding long crossings tiring (both were now 64), whilst additional crew impose enormous constraints on freedom and time schedules. This year we would take additional crew for the initial leg to Gothenburg, enabling us to get 550 miles behind us within one week of leaving Lowestoft, where Dick Blamey and Roger Winn would join us. Then we could enjoy our own pace across Sweden and make detailed plans as we went on.'

Other than this reference to the crossing from Shetland to Norway and a few clues in his later narrative, we have no detailed picture of this 1994 voyage. But the evidence suggests that from Bergen they followed the Norwegian coast south and east until they crossed to Sweden, then down the Swedish west coast and through the Danish islands south-west to Kiel. Having entered the Kiel Canal they took the route of the Eider River to the North Sea, and thence, probably, calling at one of the Friesian Islands and Ijmuiden, or possibly taking the inland route further south before the final return crossing. Most of these waters would become familiar to me seven or eight years later.

Returning to Ray's summary of the 1995 cruise this began on June 1st and lasted until September 2nd, 102 days, covering 3042 nautical miles. Its furthest point was Helsinki. The outward route crossed from Lowestoft to the Limfiord in eastern Jutland, traversed by the fiord, which becomes a virtual canal to the Kattegat; onward to Gothenburg, where their crew departed. At a gentler pace they proceeded north and east right across Sweden by way of the Trollhattan Canal, Lake Vanern and the Gota Canal. Ray describes this stage as follows:

'We took 14 days to do 230 miles and traverse the six Trollhattan locks and 58 Gota locks, reaching 92 metres above sea level. A highlight was mooring in the moat of Vadstena Castle. We entered the Baltic at Söderköping and took the back-door entrance to Stockholm via the short Sodertalje Canal. Highlight of Stockholm was the new *Vasa* museum.'

So much of this reads nostalgically for me since I did the same inland voyage in 2002 but from east to west and, as it turned out, on my own. The Glaisters, however, now went further north and east to reach Helsinki, first following the islands, where they would have liked to dally, after one night moored to a rock. A short 40NM sea crossing took them to the Aland archipelago, stretching to Helsinki and beyond. In Helsinki they enjoyed the bicycle tracks round the city, the Sibelius memorial and the Church in the Rock. They arrived there on July 20th, leaving two days later.

It seems they were tempted to press on to St. Petersburg but 'even paying the exorbitant express fee for a visa' meant a week's delay plus mooring charges, so they went south for a 'fascinating and most enjoyable visit to six ports in Estonia and four in Latvia, amongst the most friendly people', before heading westward to Farosund in Gotland Then came a night passage to Kalmar and two very enjoyable days in Karlskrona with Swedish friends, met earlier on the Gota Canal. Now on the homeward stretch, they rounded the south of Sweden, crossed the Oresund to Rodvig in Denmark before returning to the North Sea via the Kiel Canal. They were in Cuxhaven on August 21st, Langeoog the next night and Ijmuiden two days later. Here, as in 1994, the weather turned against them so they took the inland route to Flushing, finally crossing from Ostend to Ramsgate and so to Limehouse. Happily, for the greater part of the Scandinavian stages and in the Baltic States, they had enjoyed fine, warm weather, swimming and sun-bathing whenever they could, especially in Sweden.

It is the very extent of voyages like this, which together really deserve their own volume, which forces me to summarise them at this stage in Ray and Margo's remarkable story. The next is still more ambitious, clearly building on this foundation. Ray gives his 1996 Log a fuller title than usual:

To Russia with Apprehension
From Russia with Love

Babaji visits Pertrozavodsk, 330 miles inland from St. Petersburg, exploring East Germany, Poland and the Baltic States en route.

Beneath this he adds a Russian Proverb.
'Love is so strong a feeling that one can fall in love with a goat.'

In his Introduction Ray explains that the inspiration came partly from the account by Wallace Clark of a voyage in *Wild Goose* through Russia 'from the White to the Black Sea.' This had appeared in the National Geographic in 1994 whetting their appetite to go beyond Helsinki, where visa problems had frustrated them in 1995. In 1996, he made sure that visas were obtained well ahead. His further research in the Library of the Cruising Association revealed information from Alan Logan on a Rally, Blue Onega '96, inviting Western yachts to visit Petrozavodsk on Lake Onega. Ray then contacted Alan Logan and, with greater difficulty, the Rally organisers. Eventually they learned that their application had been received and, from a Russian yachtswoman in Bristol, that the total cost should be about 250 dollars.

It appeared that Alan, a Russian speaker and former Consul-general in Moscow, was keen to find a place on a yacht joining the event, which Ray was pleased to offer. Rather to his surprise the offer was swiftly accepted, although it then transpired that *Babaji* was, in fact, the only foreign yacht signed up! It was also agreed that they would meet initially in Calais and that Alan would join them in Helsinki for the crucial stage including the Rally itself. With these arrangements in place, having loved Latvia and Estonia during their cruise the year before, Ray and Margo planned to set off early enough to visit East Germany, Poland, Lithuania and the islands off Estonia, before arriving in Helsinki on June 26th. It should be said that the Reunification of Germany in 1990 was still recent history and this was the Russia of President Yeltsin, only four years after the collapse of the Soviet Union. The hesitation of other Western yachts to venture that far, so soon, is understandable.

Babaji left Limehouse on April 26th to reach Calais via Ramsgate two days later. They planned to remain there till May 10th, partly so that Margo could visit their daughter Hilary, who lived in France, after the recent birth of a baby, but also because Alan Logan was flying from the USA to France where he would have his exploratory meeting with Ray in Calais. Meanwhile *Babaji* would be careened and anti-fouled. Ray and Margo set off on May 11th passing the familiar Belgian ports to call in Flushing, Scheveningen, Ijmuiden and Den Helder. They then took the inland route, later well-known to me, via Harlingen, Leeuwarden and across the Lauwersmeer to regain the open sea and sail to Borkum. This was all very much the territory of Erskine Childers and *The Riddle of the Sands*, especially when they passed south of Borkum then out to sea again past Memmert.

By this time the passage from Langeoog to Cuxhaven and onward through the Kiel Canal would have been routine for Ray and Margo. The next stage, however, along the German coast, calling at the ancient Hanseatic ports like Lübeck and Rostock, was new territory and, as they had hoped, an enjoyable experience. By June 2nd they were in Gdansk and soon re-visiting some of the harbours along the coasts of Latvia and Estonia which had given them so much pleasure in 1995. The various frontiers to be traversed did cause some bureaucratic problems, but they had learned how to be patient in dealing with these, and officials were not hostile. Some windy days delayed them but they were also pleased to see something of the Estonian islands. After a couple of days in Tallinn they made the 45-mile crossing to Helsinki on June 18th to meet Alan Logan that evening as arranged.

Four days later *Babaji,* now with a crew of three, arrived in her first Russian port, Kronstadt. A team of four customs and immigration officials arrived, eventually, by launch. The formalities were not rapid, but friendly. They were surprised to find no yachts, let alone foreign ones, assembled for the Blue Onega Rally. Two years before it had attracted three foreign yachts, in 1995, none. Now there was one! This was, however, a good base from which to spend two days exploring St. Petersburg, travelling by an elderly bus to the Metro station and a fast, clean train to Nevsky Prospect.

At 0215 on June 26th, with two pilots aboard, one being an English speaker, they were waiting to proceed through the succession of St. Petersburg bridges, after which they were due to be towed, owing to the fast flowing currents on the Neva, for the early stages of the onward river voyage to Lake Onega. There were further delays before the *Yunga Severa*, a youth training vessel could take them in tow. The experience was not altogether smooth, at times distinctly unpleasant; 'the wind 15 knots on the nose, *Babaji* pitching violently and unnaturally, with the tow-line in danger of jumping out of the bow roller.' Conditions then improved and they were sometimes able to motor or sail independently in Lake Ladoga and on the River Svir to reach their target destination Petrozavodsk, on the shore of Lake Onega on Friday June 28th, with the Festival starting the next day.

This city is the capital of Karelia, situated at the north-western corner of the lake, about half way in waterway distance between St. Petersburg and the White Sea. Blue Onega was taking place during the main annual holiday when the lake attracted many visitors. Peter the Great had encouraged sailing and built 141 yachts in 1741; unfortunately, they were told, Yeltsin preferred tennis. A replica of one such vessel, named *Peter the Great*, was launched on the Saturday. They would also celebrate 300 years of the Russian Fleet. The ceremonies included reference to the freedom of the Karelian Republic. This may well have been a propaganda exercise as the status of Karelia has historically been a matter of dispute, and even war with Finland. As recently as 1939-40, there was 'the Winter War'; then in 1941-44, the 'Continuation War', as it is known in Finland. In both struggles the Finns, led by Marshal Mannerheim, fought with great tenacity against the overwhelming force of the Soviet Army. *Babaji* as the only foreign arrival, was given a great reception and a good number of Russian yachts were present. Cannons were fired, fireworks set off, speeches made, burgees exchanged, loud music played, food and drink consumed amid general enthusiasm. Ray, Margo and Alan were made thoroughly welcome.

During the following three days they explored the city, took a hydrofoil to the island of Kizhi, famous for its wooden nine-domed church, and were filmed aboard *Babaji*. The main focus of the cameramen seemed to be a demonstration of the folding, unfolding and mounting of their bicycles. More speeches and presentation watches were given in exchange for tins of English Teas and Tower of London Tea Towels. On Wednesday July 3rd it was time to make sad farewells as they started to retrace their route, downriver this time, following the Svir out of Lake Onega, across the bottom of Lake Ladoga (the largest inland lake in Europe, Onega being the second) and down the Neva. Towage was not required in this direction but in one lock the propeller wash from a ship ahead tore the centre cleat, to which their warp was attached, from the deck. They reached St. Petersburg four days later, needing a further night for the piloted descent through its eight bridges. The word 'night' is used deliberately for a northern 'white night' passage starting at 0205 and ending just over three hours later when they berthed and went to sleep.

'Compared with the ascent, engine flat out and only one waiting period the descent was a doddle, mostly slow speed or waiting, although the ten knots over the ground through the bridges did seem very fast.'

It was now Monday July 8th. I am astonished that, after such a short, busy night, Ray and Margo had the energy to get up in time to move on to their berth at the Baltic Shipping Club, tidy the boat and catch the Metro into the city for more sight-seeing at the Peterhof. On return that evening they invited a Russian, whom they found talking to Alan Logan, to join them for barbecued sausages at a table overlooking the marina, where they opened a bottle of Mouton Cadet they had been given before whole voyage started. In Ray's words: 'a great ending to a fantastic day.' Alan left them that evening to catch the night sleeper to Moscow.

There was another day of sight-seeing before they left for Kronstadt, their last Russian harbour, where, in a slight, final contretemps with Customs, their passports were held overnight but returned, as promised, by a smart young guard at 0500, in time for their planned departure five minutes later. (I hope they slept better than I would have done in that situation.) On the way towards the buoy marking the border with Finland they spotted a red ensign on an approaching yacht. This they identified as *Athene,* owned by a fellow Cruising Association member, Robin Guilleret, and called her on VHF. Ray does not mention, and perhaps may not have known, that Robin was also a member of OSC and her home port was Orford. So, after all, more than one Orford boat was in Russian waters that year. (Robin Guilleret remained a member of OSC for at least another ten years and cruised extensively in the Baltic and up and down the Norwegian coast. *Athene*, his Victoria 30 is listed in both 1994 and 2000 OSC year books).

The homeward voyage from Helsinki began on July 16th. The Glaisters were now experts on the route to Gotland, Kalmar, Karlskrona and Kiel, re-visiting many places known to them from the previous year. *Babaji* was left in Copenhagen for just over two weeks in early August while they flew home for their son Malcolm's wedding. The voyage recommenced on July 14th and they sailed into Orford on the 20th having left Den Helder at 0635 the previous morning with a very hot, calm day to come, reaching 30°C by the afternoon. Weather in Russia and in the Baltic had also been very warm, often allowing them to enjoy their swimming, as both did.

The final grey dawn was different, very English weather. They entered the Ore three hours after LW and to quote Ray's last entry in this log: 'roared up to Orford, arriving at the Quay just after Alison and her family. So ended our exciting 3700 NM cruise!'

In 1997 this experience propelled them back to Russia and further still inland, all the way to Moscow. During the previous winter they had received details of Blue Onega 97 and 'a typically over-ambitious rally via Moscow to the Black Sea'. Ray had also prepared an Information Pack for the CA on Russia and established a website on Cruising to and in Russia. The idea of visiting Moscow via the rivers and canals used by the very popular cruise ships was now irresistible.

They had a contact in Moscow, Professor Leonid Lesnevsky, the owner of *Spray,* encountered in St. Petersburg in 1996. They therefore asked him to suggest a Russian who might join them for the trip to Moscow. His daughter liked the idea but then pulled out when she decided to get married instead! However, she persuaded her father to join them himself. Ray appealed on his web site for other yachts to join them but only one other CA boat signed up and, in the event, travelled independently. The Association had been asked by the Royal Ocean Racing Club to organize a cruise in tandem with their planned Millennium Race to St Petersburg, so a secondary aim would be to establish suitable stopping places for this cruise in 2000.

As in 1995, Ray thought it prudent to have additional crew for the outward North Sea crossing. This time they left Lowestoft for Helgoland at 1900 on May 17th 1997, with 'two excellent crew, Geoff Doggett and his friend Colin.' They arrived in Heligoland 48 hours and 240NM later. As Ray wryly comments. 'We must sell our services to the Met Office or get sponsorship from an oil company: wherever *Babaji* goes we get a headwind.' They had motor-sailed almost the whole way passing close to oil rigs but not seeing them in fog. Geoff and Colin left them in Cuxhaven. Ray and Margo pressed on through the Kiel Canal and up across to Bornholm, Kalmar, Gotland, then inside the Estonian islands off the Gulf of Riga.

June 9th found them in Tallinn, where they greatly enjoyed a two night stay. Summer had come, but also calm weather. 'If the Millennium race has weather like this the cruising boats will be waiting for the racers,' wrote Ray. His log this time takes the form of a series of letters written from key ports, summarising progress and experiences on the way. The sixth of these begins in the Gulf of Finland as they approach St Petersburg from Estonia, missing out Helsinki on the outward voyage but not on the return. They cleared customs unusually quickly in Kronstadt, thanks to 'an intelligent girl'; and the CA's honorary representative in St. Petersburg, Vladimir Ivankiv, warned of their approach, met them at the central Yacht Club, 16 NM further into Russia on Friday evening June 13th.

Although some of the dates in these 'letters' appear confusing, it seems that they spent nearly two weeks in St. Petersburg, with much to enjoy and further decisions to be made. Their arrival was, however, saddened by news of the death of Alan Logan, their crew on the crucial stages of the 1996 Blue Onega rally. Professor Leonid Lesnevsky (Leo to them) arrived on the Sunday morning. That evening they went to the opera at the Marinsky Theatre. Excellent dress circle seats cost the equivalent of £4.30.

On Monday morning crucial decisions were taken. A ban on foreign-flagged yachts using Russian waterways unless for specific events like the Blue Onega had not been rescinded, as previously expected. Three bold changes of plan were now agreed; they would go to Moscow under the Russian flag with Leo in nominal charge; they would lower the masts for the passage through the St Petersburg bridges and thus avoid the need for a pilot; *Babaji* would be renamed *Babai* after the fairy-tale Russian witch who pursues naughty children! Ray went to work cutting out letters from self-adhesive sailcloth numbers. Later they were invited aboard *Peter Duck*, once owned by Arthur Ransome, but at that time by Greg Palmer, a lecturer in English and History at the University.

During the following week, insurance and other administrative issues were gradually overcome as were arrangements for lowering the masts. One evening Margo provided dinner aboard *Babaji* for five Russians. Leo returned from a visit to Moscow in pursuit of further documentation. Finally, equipped with a large Russian flag made from spinnaker cloth provided by a nearby sail loft, they left the Yacht Club basin at 0545 on the morning of Tuesday June 24th. There were no undue problems under the bridges or on the way to Petrokrepost on Lake Ladoga, where the masts were re-erected at minimal cost. Two Spice Girls posters presented to the operators were a great success. They had now covered 331 kilometres from St. Petersburg and 250km non-stop in 36 hours. There were still more than 1000 kilometres between this point and Moscow.

The route they followed is a succession of rivers, lakes, and canalised waterways including the upper Volga. At times these are very wide and they made several night passages. As Ray says: 'Stalin provided a magnificent waterway connecting St. Petersburg to Moscow and the Black Sea'. The human cost was huge; 700 villages were flooded in the process, labour provided by political dissidents from the gulags with an average of 100 deaths per day during the many years of construction. One incident during this voyage caused serious anxiety and is best described by Ray himself.

'At a bend in the river by Kalazin Church we slowed down to take photographs. Suddenly we were approached by a fast aluminium runabout with five or six young men. They banged into us and held on while one tried to board. Hurriedly, Margo put cameras and other valuables out of sight while I went full ahead weaving to try to stop boarding and Leo negotiated with them. They would have been happy with a bottle of vodka, I suspect, but Leo eventually managed to reason with them and they left leaving us all badly shaken. Leo had done a magnificent job.'

Nine days after their departure from St. Petersburg, at 1800 hours on July 4th, *Babaji* arrived in Moscow, mooring at No1 Navy Yacht Club within sight of President Yeltsin's huge motor yacht. Ray later describes this voyage as 'exhausting, almost non-stop except huge delays at locks': but also as rewarding... 'and at least we know what we face on return'.

Those rewards would be an increasingly hospitable reception during their six-day stay. They dined at the home of the President of the All Russia Yacht Federation, were taken to see all the major sights, met and were entertained by several friends, students and family connections of Leo. He was unable to accompany them on the return journey but there was much concern that no more unpleasant incidents should occur and that 'full protection for the honour of Russia' should be provided. It was agreed that Vladimir, a young neurosurgeon, who knew the Moscow Canal well, would accompany them at least as far as Lake Onega, and a mechanic, Vadim (but with no English) might be able to go all the way to St. Petersburg.

The return voyage began early on July 9th with the arrival of Vladimir and Vadim at 0615, accompanied by Vladimir's mother, aunt, and champagne to see them off. The temperature that scorching day was 35°C at six in the evening. Apart from delays at locks, interspersed with fast runs to keep up with lock companions, the whole passage back went without mishaps or attempted piracy. One lock-keeper, learning that it was Margo's birthday, presented her with flowers. Six days out they were moored on Kizhi Island in the centre of Lake Onega and were welcomed back the next day in Petrozavodsk, the scene of the festival in 1996. There they learned that the ban on foreign yachts navigation had been lifted, enabling *Babaji* to resume her true name and nationality.

From there back to St. Petersburg, and indeed all the way to Orford, Ray and Margo went on alone. Vadim's friend, due to replace Vladimir as interpreter, had turned out to have little English and they felt they could manage. With the confidence of previous experience they were able to take the last Russian stage at an easier pace. On arrival in St Petersburg the fact that they had left as a Russian registered vessel and returned under the red ensign caused problems for the officials, which Ray felt relaxed enough to enjoy. Four days later they were under way again to Kronstadt; they faced a fresh headwind and unpleasant high-running waves as they approached Finland. In Helsinki they had arranged to meet Finnish friends who insisted on putting them up for two nights in a luxury hotel managed by their daughter. It was a strange feeling to stay in a huge bedroom after a small ship's berth, watch the CNN news and tuck into a buffet breakfast.

On Sunday August 3rd 'much refreshed and cleaner' they left Helsinki. The route home was very similar to that of the year before, except that from Brunsbüttel, at the western end of the Kiel Canal, they decided to head straight for Heligoland and then endured a horrid wet passage out of the 'cruel Elbe'. There was a nasty short sea despite neap tides and only a force 3 headwind. Ray promised Margo it would get better but it did not. Unsurprisingly almost all the yachts leaving at the same time opted for Cuxhaven. But, as others like me have found, the Elbe can stay cruel for days on end with wind over tide blowing remorselessly from the north-west.

Undeterred, after a rest in harbour, showers and the delivery of diesel and 'duty free' they were under way for Orford at 1105 on August 15th. Next morning they were off the Dutch Friesian islands, passing Ameland, Terschelling and Vlieland, one by one, until they cleared Texel in the late afternoon. The second night of the passage was lit by a bright moon as they motored with a light easterly. The Suffolk coast, however, was veiled in mist as they approached in the morning until, suddenly, Orfordness Lighthouse appeared at one NM distant. At 1300 on August 17th *Babaji* passed the Orford Haven Buoy to enter on the flood and moor at 1430. Unfortunately the appendix containing daily log distances is missing from this file, so it remains uncertain how much longer this challenging cruise had been than its predecessor, surely not less than 4000 nautical miles, 92 days from Lowestoft to Moscow and back to Orford, including the non-sailing days.

As the return voyage suggests, undertaken on their own, Ray must have been increasingly confident in himself, his ship and her mate. He was by now, it seems to me, one of the few experts on cruising to Russia at this point in the post-Soviet era and clearly a leading figure in the Cruising Association. There is clear evidence, in the shape of a certificate from Blue Onega 2000, that *Babaji* returned there for the Millennium Rally, but no detailed log has, so far, come to light. Ray and Margo's daughter Alison has, however, confirmed David Foreman's belief that the return voyage was via the canal to Murmansk and round the North Cape and Norwegian coast. Thus they followed the route of the notorious wartime Arctic convoys as far as the Lofoten Islands, where *Babaji* was left for the winter. This must surely have been a rare British sailing venture.

As if these exploits were not enough, Ray and Margo's 1998 cruising record involved another UK circumnavigation, which might almost be defined as a clockwise tour of the main British Shipping Forecast areas Thames – Dover – Plymouth – Fastnet – Malin – Hebrides – Fair Isle and so on. Ray does not provide his usual Introduction for this log but it is prefaced by ten 'Rules for Crew on *Babaji*' (appendix) and a full page list of Safety Equipment with particular points to be understood. From the narrative it appears that they had crew aboard at least as far as Cork. Thereafter I assume they continued alone round the Atlantic coast of Ireland in a series of shorter daily passages until they were on the way to Scotland, in waters which they already knew.

Their starting point this time was Woodbridge, where they were joined by Ian, recommended by Geoff Doggett, who had been with them as far as Cuxhaven in 1997, and Mike Perkins of Woodbridge Cruising Club, recently returned from the Channel Islands in his own boat. They left the Deben on Saturday May 23rd on a 24-hour passage to Brighton. By Sunday 31st they were at their favourite anchorage in the Helford River before sailing to St Mary's in the Scillies. This would be their jumping off point for the crossing to Crosshaven (Cork) arriving on June 4th. Mike left them to fly home, replaced by Dick Blamey, who had been with them on a previous voyage.

Despite the attractions of their day's rest in St Mary's, the Atlantic swell made their mooring very uncomfortable at night, and they were probably glad to get away. The potential challenge of the passage across to Southern Ireland proved relatively calm; leaving at 1815 in good visibility they were able to dispense with the engine the next morning with a fair wind and the jib pole rigged.

After a day's rest and a short passage to Kinsale, bad forecasts delayed them until June 11th. No mentions of crew are made from Cork onwards.

Sailing towards the Fastnet Rock with double-reefed main and five rolls in the genoa the sea became rough 'as the fetch for the north wind increased and combined with the Atlantic swell we had all day. Fastnet Rock appeared looking like an approaching frigate until becoming unmistakably Fastnet. Two yachts that had passed us earlier had rounded the Rock and were on their way home. Fortunately we had rounded Fastnet in 1991 so didn't feel the urge to do this again.'

During the next week the weather improved somewhat with a helpful wind as they rounded Mizen Head, called at some attractive harbours, such as Dingle Bay, and were sometimes escorted by dolphins. At least a dozen saw them off from Fenit and even more welcomed them into the Shannon. The Shannon got very rough with wind against tide as it narrowed so they anchored round the corner out of the tide with good holding for a quiet night. It was now June 18th; the day's run of 25NM in five and a half hours being fairly typical of others.

The weather, however, was not set 'Fair'. Four days later they were in Cashla Bay, west of Galway. They had been stuck in harbour for a couple of nights and had already made one abortive attempt to leave. Ray was asking himself questions as he wrote his log that evening after more frustration.

'Delayed by fuelling and left at 1115. After battling two hours into headwind and rough seas I asked myself: why do we cruise? To enjoy ever-changing scenery? Fog! Sailing? Making 3 knots motor-sailing into rough sea! Outdoor living? Heavy rain! U-turned and sailed back at 7 knots feeling somewhat sheepish as our French neighbours took our warps again.'

Two more days passed before they got away, while the French yacht still waited for a north wind. Ray was relieved to pass Slyne Head 'another major headland hurdle' with a fresh force 5 on the beam. Two miles offshore 'it wasn't too bad, long Atlantic rollers of about 3M and not too rough.' This was not always the case as his account of June 28th suggests.

'A day of rest started just before 0520. West wind steadily rose and we had a real roller-coaster, the sea building to 4/5 metres. Much over genuine six knots speed. Ended up with single reefed main with preventer and 17 rolls in the genoa. In attempting a second reef we inadvertently gybed, the preventer breaking off the rivet through the swivel on the main sheet block. Fortunately we only had 10NM to do before turning into the shelter of Killibegs, a magnificent harbour, when all was quiet again.'

These daily entries leave the impression of a wild, lonely, often spectacular coastline, but also of good shelter and friendly people. 'Saw only one fishing boat all day....Each meeting of a yacht qualifies for a log entry.' They reached Portrush, their last Irish harbour, on July7th, remarking on the difference from those further south. 'Northern Ireland contrasted strongly with Ireland, looking very English and reminiscent of Paignton.' They allowed themselves a day to visit the Giants' Causeway and Londonderry before the ten-hour crossing by day to Craighouse in the Sound of Jura.

On Sunday July 12th they had reached Tobermory on Mull. I was intrigued to learn that they too were ashore watching the Football World Cup Final in a crowded pub just as I was watching it the same evening in Boulogne. I dare say the reaction to the goals and the final whistle was more neutral, less euphoric than in France. The weatherman, Michael Fish, provided a window of opportunity for the passage from Kinlochbervie to Stromness, requiring only under 14 hours of daylight motoring in a slowly increasing headwind. July 20th qualified as a rest day and they did not move on to Westray, another favourite place, for three days. Twenty Four hours later they were moored, for the third time, in the North Harbour on Fair Isle, where they spent two nights, saw some old friends, showered in the Bird Observatory hostel, and counted innumerable puffins. Then they headed back to Kirkwall, leaving Shetland out after two previous visits.

For these seasoned sailors the voyage south, now traversing more shipping forecast areas – Cromarty – Forth – Tyne – Humber and back to Thames, was a well-trodden path. Whitehills, in the Moray Firth, where they called for a few hours only, seems to have been the only port they had not used on one of their previous cruises. Several days were blessed with unusually good weather and one or two even with ideal north-westerly winds.

For three days they enjoyed 'a real holiday' in Berwick-on-Tweed, impressed by the ancient town walls and the third largest colony of swans in the UK. There was, however, one bad moment. On the second day Ray hauled the bikes out on to the quayside and left them erected against a bollard while he went back on board to tidy up. Margo was first to climb the ladder.

"Where are the bikes?" she said. Gone! After being used all over Europe, including Russia, they were stolen in England! Ray rushed to a newsagent to get the police station number and reported the loss. On return he met a fisherman who had offered them some crabs earlier.

"Would you like some crabs?" he asked. "Blow the crabs, someone has stolen our bikes!" Without a word the man went off in his car, returning shortly with two bikes in the open boot. The police car then arrived and Ray pointed out their hero. "That man" said the officer, "I won't get much out of him, he's always in trouble with us over his fishing." Nor did he obtain any information: but they had their bikes back, as well as the crabs, and were duly grateful.

Spurn Head was the scene of a difficulty which Ray felt he should describe as a 'useful confessional'. It had been rough off Flamborough Head and very rough off Spurn Head with little shelter in the anchorage inside. Eventually he anchored 'with some difficulty' in the dark with three knots of tide or more running. He was careful to avoid two moorings, one occupied by the reserve lifeboat. When he called to Margo to let go, the anchor jammed in the hawse pipe and he dived below to free it.

'Before it could hold I found we were almost on the vacant mooring buoy. But fast. It had clearly dragged and caught the ground tackle of the mooring. I called the Coast Guard to advise of our predicament; they called the lifeboat that had just refuelled at its jetty to our east and it came out to see us. Their (correct) prognostication was that we should have to abandon the anchor, but Humber VTS called us and suggested we tried to get free at low water slack. At 0130 the stream stopped and although the chain was slack my attempts failed. After an exhausting hour by which time the flood had started I admitted defeat and retired to continue the night's rest.

They did manage to leave in the morning, minus the anchor and ten metres of chain which had to be sawn through. Perhaps it was a good thing to have a boring day of motor-sailing across the Wash in poor visibility before they reached Wells-next-the-Sea ten hours later. On Wednesday August 12th they sailed from Yarmouth to Woodbridge arriving at the Tide Mill at high water on the hottest day of their cruise, 26°C. Ray's log concludes with a modest summary:

'So ends our second (and last!) circumnavigation of the UK, with the addition of Ireland this time. In 81 days away we had 22 non-sailing days, mostly through bad weather in Ireland, and stopped at 63 ports or anchorages. Total charted distance was 2449 NM in 467 hours' sailing time of which 337 were motor-sailing or motoring. It was very good to be home again, despite the amount of gardening to be done, mail to handle, the CA web site to work on and – ghastly thought, tax return to complete!'

If Ray's inclusion of the word 'last' suggests finality, this was far from the end of their cruising life. There was the major Millennium Cruise, with its Arctic prolongation, still to come. *Babaji* and *Quantz* were also destined to meet in 2004, entirely by chance, in the Friesian Islands; and I came across mentions of her presence in the Baltic several times during my own voyages.

14. Crossing Thresholds

When *Quantz* took to the water again at the end of April 1999, with a new engine installed by Peter Norris, I was looking forward to the season with keener anticipation. It was not only the quieter, lighter Nanni diesel chugging away with less vibration than the older, clumsier Yanmar. I knew that in a month's time I would be free of commitments to regular meetings and committees of the Parish Council and Orford Town Trust or any other similar body. Neither would I have to find time for marking A level or GCE examination papers during the summer. I was now officially too old for this academic work or for supply teaching which had sometimes kept me ashore. But in my own eyes, at least, I was not too old to go on sailing and make the most of this welcome freedom.

I was also expecting the arrival of the Burghouts, whose son Alef had crewed me expertly from Ramsgate to Calais the year before. I had persuaded them that Orford would be an ideal destination for their spring voyage in their new, larger boat, *Tilman*. The Dutch often seem able to take holidays in May and profit from the likelihood of more easterlies to help them across. There was no sign of them when I went in and out of the river entrance for reconnaissance; they were delayed in Rotterdam, but two days later, on a fine morning, I called them up on VHF as they approached Shingle Street. By the time I reached the Orford Haven buoy they were anchored waiting for me to pilot them in, which I was glad to do, especially when I was invited to lunch aboard as soon as they had moored not far from the Quay.

We were able to return this hospitality a day later, but their appreciation may have been reduced by the loan of my dinghy which Peter and Alef managed to capsize on the way back to the mooring, being unused to rowing an unstable boat across tidal water through choppy waves. Leida Burghouts and I witnessed the event with some anxiety as we stood on the Quay, but they were soon rescued by Chris Martin in his motor boat. I think they used their inflatable dinghy and outboard thereafter; luckily they had another full day to recover and spend more time with us before departure.

Another Dutch connection influenced my plans for the summer, as OSC had been invited to send some yachts to join others from the Deben taking part in a Rally at Rhoon, near Rotterdam, which was celebrating an anniversary of some kind. This would take place early in July. I signed up for this and also to take the examination for the Certificate of Navigation on European inland waters or CEVNI. This now seemed to be necessary, although if it had been required previously I had not been aware of it nor asked to produce it. The test was taken at the Sailing Club in June, under the benevolent eye of James Robinson as Instructor, without whose discreet intervention I would not have scraped through with a minimum pass mark.

In mid-May another little group of yachts had set off for Lowestoft together, Michael Pearce and Suki in *Naivasha*, their Halberg Rassey, Philippe Taylor in *Crossjack VI*, a Freedom 33, with his son Charlie, *Hvar*, one of the Maxis, part-owned by Ben Johnston who had an ex RAF friend with him that day, and myself in *Quantz*. Conditions were benign, with a light southerly, only slightly tiresome when dead astern after Orfordness. *Quantz* behaves better with the wind either on one quarter or the other. But even in ideal weather things can go wrong. Just past Benacre Ness, north of Southwold, I realised that something must be amiss with *Crossjack*. On *Hvar* Ben had heard a radio call from Philippe about a medical emergency. He speeded up and went alongside to find Philippe nursing his son in the cockpit. In fact Charlie Taylor had received a nasty blow to the head from a swinging boom while Philippe had been on the foredeck. Ben acted as contact with the emergency services while his friend went aboard to assist on *Crossjack*. An RNLI rib soon arrived as well as a rescue helicopter to winch the young man aboard and take him to hospital. *Hvar* and *Crossjack* headed back to Orford while I went on to Lowestoft to moor alongside *Naivasha* near the RNSYC. We dined there in company with a Dutch yacht rally group. It was a relief to have reassuring news of the casualty. I made my way back to Orford on my own two days later in equally gentle weather.

I was due to join others in Holland for the second weekend in July but had decided to do the crossing independently since Jamie had offered to crew for me a week earlier than that. His presence proved to be essential on a lively passage. We left the river early on a Saturday morning with one reef down when two would have been wiser. The second had to be put in off Shingle Street, harder work than in calm water. With a fresh breeze on the starboard quarter and a following sea we made good speed but my stomach was not reacting well. Fortunately Jamie seemed unaffected and took the major share of helming. After dark the wind eased, the waves reduced and the moon shone; everything became easier. We were in Flushing by 0600 on Sunday and Middelburg in time for lunch. Jamie had to catch a train from Goes back to the ferry on Monday, so we motored into the Veerse Meer as far as Wohlfahrtsdyk which was in taxi range. I saw him off from Goes station and returned to *Quantz* on my Brompton bicycle, now an invaluable cruising adjunct.

Two days later I met *Crossjack* and *Hvar* again in Willemstad, where I was invited to dine, rather too well, with the Taylors and James Robinson. It was a fine evening and I caused some surprise by taking a shower in the cockpit of *Quantz* from a bag rigged up on the boom. Ben Johnston was in charge of *Hvar* with Neville Spinney and Keble Paterson as crew. In Hellevoetsluis the next day we found Tony Carr's *Lady Dane*. Together with *Quantz* these four boats formed the OSC representation at the Rhoon event, for which we arrived on the Friday afternoon. The reception committee cast Ben Johnston as the official representative of Orford and he duly received a presentation on our behalf and was treated as a VIP throughout. I made sure that *Quantz* was 'dressed overall' and we all attended a Mayoral Reception before the Orford contingent defected to a local pub for a good meal. On the Saturday we were taken on a conducted walk through attractive osier beds, took a ferry to visit a local fair and swimming pool and were entertained to a barbecue at Portugaal WSV the host Sailing Club. I spent the Sunday morning on a quick visit to central Rotterdam by bike and Metro and the afternoon sailing or motoring as far as Bruinisse on the way towards Willemstad.

My plan for the next ten days or so was to explore that part of Holland, particularly another large expanse of inland water, the Grevelingenmeer, an artificial lake resembling the Veerse Meer further south, formed by a high dam at the seaward end of a former estuary. But this is much bigger, nearly 20 kilometres long and five wide at one point with many islands and little harbours. The weather was warm enough for me to enjoy swimming most days although there were some squally showers. It was a relaxed sailing holiday and a rehearsal for living aboard by myself for an extended period, as I hoped to do frequently over the coming years. I do not remember ever being bored. There were always jobs to do on the boat, short voyages to make and plenty of activity to watch, since it was an ideal place for family holidays afloat or youth groups.

Occasional shopping trips ashore, encounters with other yachts in harbour or going through the lock at Bruinisse on entry or exit, provided sufficient human contact, apart from the radio and a couple of telephone calls to home. I needed to confirm arrangements with Ralph, who was coming all the way from Scotland to join me at Hellevoetsluis for the return crossing. Much depended therefore on the weather outlook for the crucial weekend, which luckily sounded promising several days ahead. I made my way slowly back in that direction and berthed there with some hours to spare before his arrival from Hook of Holland ferry at midnight on July 21st. This was a Wednesday and we needed to be back in Orford on the Sunday. The immediate forecast was not good but set to improve, so we sailed back as far as Willemstad for one night and then returned to Collingsplaat, near the Rompootsluis, on the Friday evening, ready for an early departure.

The crossing that followed was one of the easiest and most relaxed in my experience. We had to motor in calm conditions to start with, then motor-sail until we were clear of the shipping lanes by early evening. There was even time to sit and read when off watch. Then we were able to sail on properly into the night, with the moon rising and, for a time, with the helm lashed, *Quantz* sailing herself on course. The visibility remained good and we made our landfall, at first light, south of Aldeburgh. With the wind now northwesterly we could sail gently round Orfordness and down Hollesley Bay to reach Orford Quay at 0800 on the Sunday morning. For once everything conspired to provide enjoyment rather than challenge. Ralph's journey from Scotland to Holland and back had been worthwhile for both of us. I was also grateful to Jamie for his vital help on the outward voyage. Other short trips in August, and September took me back to the Deben, the Orwell and Walton Backwaters as well as up and down the river. *Quantz* stayed afloat until early November and I felt even more hopeful about future plans.

Quantz was launched into the new Millennium early in May, equipped with a spray hood, which soon proved its worth as Don and I approached the Dutch coast about three weeks later bound for Ijmuiden. We had left the river with one reef down in a moderate north-westerly, but put in a second one north of Orfordness as the wind freshened. During the day the wind backed round and decreased, which persuaded me to shake out the second reef. We were still surging along, making between five and six knots with a following sea, even surfing the waves from time to time. This was fun for an hour or so in the afternoon but, as evening came, the sky clouded over and the wind grew stronger again. Now we needed that second reef, but it was not an easy operation with a plunging deck and a flapping sail. Worse still, a tear along a seam in the mainsail had suddenly appeared. We had just got things under control when there was a violent thundery squall which threatened to lay us on our beam ends. I was below at the time and shouted to Don to let the sheets go. Unfortunately he followed orders, so that, by the time I emerged from the cabin, the furling jib had wrapped itself round and round the forestay in a complete tangle.

A long struggle followed while we lowered and stowed the mainsail and I sorted out the situation on the foredeck, head to wind under engine, with a very unsteady platform to work upon. "One hand for yourself and one for the ship" is all very well, but sometimes you need both hands, and, although I was glad of my safety harness, that was also a hindrance. Finally we got ourselves back on course sailing under the jib and later using the engine as well. One way and another it seemed a long night. Don took longer spells at the helm while I recovered from my battle with the jib sheets. We were very glad to find a berth in Ijmuiden harbour at 0930, especially as the wind was now forecast to back right round to the east and reach force 7.

In fact a full gale blew up and we did not move for two days. My plan for the summer ahead was to explore Friesland and visit as many of the Friesian islands as possible before laying up for the winter somewhere in the north of Holland as a jumping-off point for the Baltic in 2001. Simon Arnold and Ben Johnston had agreed to join me for separate spells in July and early September. I was not in a hurry, but a celebration of our 40th wedding anniversary in August was also an important factor. Meanwhile I needed to find a sail-maker to repair the mainsail tear and the local advice was to try Volendam not far beyond Amsterdam.

Don was able to stay with me for three more days, during which his company was as good as his efforts on the crossing had been vital. We negotiated the Ship Canal to Amsterdam, spent a night in the Sixhaven and another in Volendam, where the sail was repaired at minimal cost. When John Seymour arrived in Volendam with *Willynilly* he was full of enthusiasm for the attractions of Dutch national costume and the girls who wore it. Don and I agreed that the girls were still good-looking but felt that the costumes were now worn almost entirely for tourist effect. Also we were in haste to catch a bus back to Amsterdam because we had identified a bar advertising that the TV that evening would show the English Football Championship Play Off Final at Wembley, in which Ipswich Town might gain promotion to the Premier League. We were there in time to join a lively crowd of Dutch Ipswich fans. The connection between Dutch football and Ipswich has often been strong, dating back to the great days of the 1980s and the skills of Arnold Muhren and Frank Thyssen. It was a great night for the fans, for us, and for Ipswich, who won by four goals to two against Barnsley. I did not know then, as I have since discovered, that Muhren was born and grew up in Volendam, where he once played for the local team, otherwise I would have made the most of it in harbour there.

The repaired sail was ready for us in the morning so that we could enjoy a broad reach taking us to Enkhuizen, where Don had to leave me, catching a train to Schipol and a flight to Edinburgh. As with Jamie, the year before, I felt lonely that afternoon, despite having so much enjoyment still to come.

This began with a still, almost windless, warm day for my crossing of the Ijsselmeer to Stavoren, in Friesland. I sailed gently for two hours before starting the engine as I tried to outpace a cloud of may-flies. Stavoren offered the slight challenge of a lock to negotiate on my own but without harm. Mooring was cheap and I logged the pretty waterside village as one possibility for a later base where *Quantz* might be left when I returned home. Apart from the very real pleasures of navigating the canals and lakes stretching continuously northwards into the heart of Friesland, this was something I needed to arrange during the next week. The landscape reminded me of the Norfolk Broads but the waterways were less crowded. There were islands where I sometimes anchored overnight, large stretches of open reed-fringed water like the Sneekermeer, where I could carry full sail, using the genoa alone on the canals for greater control, assisted by the engine if necessary. Each day was different and none caused stress. I could chose between a mooring in a small town like Grouw or somewhere more isolated, riding my bike to the shop for stores.

Finally, after six days I found myself in a village called Earnewald, where the nearby Westdijk Jachthaven offered surprisingly cheap prices for good facilities, including winter storage if required. This, I decided, was the place I had been looking for. It was now early June and I needed to head home. I left *Quantz* in good hands, hoping she would not be lonely, and was away for some four weeks.

I was back aboard at the beginning of July with a few days to potter round the nearby lakes, islands and canals before Simon Arnold met me, as arranged, in Grouw. I really enjoyed this watery land and felt at home among the Friesians, whose distant forebears may well have colonised East Suffolk. Almost every house has the Friesian flag flying. I decided that *Quantz* should also have one at the yardarm as well as the Dutch courtesy flag. The weather for several days after Simon arrived was changeable and we did not hurry back to more open water. Other British yachts were rarely to be seen in these parts, so it was a strange coincidence, when we moored in Sloten, Friesland's smallest city, to bump into someone I knew. It was nearly half a century since he and I had been in the same batch of National Servicemen marching off the Passing Out Parade at Mons Officer Cadet School in Aldershot. We had met just once since then, in Orford, when he was visiting his friends the Waites, our close neighbours. Now he and his wife were in the process of collecting a Halberg Rassey 29, which they had bought from a local boatyard.

My ambition was still to explore as many of the Dutch Friesian islands as possible during Simon's holiday, but we wanted more settled weather. So we spent another five days on shorter trips back and forth round the shores of the Ijsselmeer in and out of places like Lemmer, Hindeloopen, Medemblik and Makkum, all of which have their special charms and culinary opportunities. Then we could wait no longer to make our way through the lock which opens into the very tidal, Waddenzee, stretching west to den Helder and north-east between the string of islands and the Friesian mainland. We spent one night in harbour at Harlingen working out the ideal tidal timings for the day ahead. Our target was to reach the harbour on the island Ameland having crossed the tidal watershed as near high water as possible. Otherwise we would be stranded for twelve hours surrounded by sandbanks. High water was 1044 BST, and we reached the crucial point half an hour early, touching the bottom briefly and gently on the way. Then we took a detour towards a deeper channel to reach Nes, on Ameland, at 1330, just as the tide withdrew and miles of sand dried out behind us. This was the Walton Backwaters on a vast scale.

A northerly wind, gusting to force 7 detained us for another day. With a hired bicycle for Simon, and my Brompton, we rode into the wind to see as much of the island as we could. A detour to a beach on the seaward side, where the waves came crashing ashore, confirmed the unforgiving nature of that coast. We also received more local advice on "wantijs", the various watersheds or thresholds between each pair of islands.

With a less hostile north-westerly we set off in the morning with HW 1230 BST on the intervening 'wantij' before we headed either for the sluis into Lauwersoog on the mainland shore or, if we got there in time, for the channel to Schiermonikoog. Our timing must have been right because we never had less than three feet under the keel, according to the echo sounder, which was now the most important gadget on the boat. So we turned to port following a winding trail of withies which reminded us of the approach to Iken multiplied and complicated several times over. Proceeding with great caution but never touching sand, we found our way into the tiny harbour on Schiermonikoog in time for a late lunch. The sun came out; we explored the one small village and enjoyed an evening meal ashore at the end of a day which had given us exactly the experience we hoped for.

Simon was running out of time but we had to wait for the next morning tide to fill the channel. We launched the dinghy and rowed to the harbour entrance only to confirm that there was no water there. So I went for a bike ride further into the island, a pleasing mixture of dunes, copses and water-meadows. When the tide rose sufficiently we had a fair wind down the channel and across to Lauwersoog, where a lock gives entry to the a wide expanse of the non-tidal Lauwersmeer. Once inside we moored in the nearby Jachthaven to seek information on bus connections to Groningen so that Simon could start his homeward journey the next day. After his departure I sailed quietly across the Lauwersmeer to another small yacht harbour, from which I cycled in search of shops and a bank.

Over the next five days I followed the canal route south again through a succession of small places with opening bridges, where I sometimes had to wait, and the occasional lock. It was a route I would follow at least three times in the future and always enjoyed. Ironically the weather had become warm and sunny with light winds. Overnight stops included Dokkum, a very agreeable small town, and Leeuwarden, where it was possible to moor in the central park-like gardens within easy reach of the main square, shops, banks, cafes and the railway station. On the morning of July 27th *Quantz* was moored once more at the yacht harbour near Ernewald, which was now her Friesian home. I had a date in Orford for our Anniversary Party early in August. Phase Two of our Friesian ventures had been dogged by periods of rain and strong north-westerlies but, as I wrote in my log: 'we had at least achieved two Friesian islands and learned a great deal.'

Phase Three was still to come, and I returned at the end of August with almost four weeks at my disposal. Ben Johnston was due to join me in Leeuwarden two days later. The journeys out and back were part of the fun. I have always loved ferry crossings, short or long. They probably remind me of the much longer ocean voyages on cargo-liners in my early childhood, watching the crew cast off the mooring lines, the swirl of water between the ship's side and the dock as she edged away, standing on the after deck with the wake foaming astern or near the bridge to catch a glimpse of the officer on watch, then peer over the rail to see the waves breaking away from the ship's side. Even waiting for the gangway to be brought aboard for the small crowd of foot-passengers; this was all exciting for me. Then I would be sitting in a Dutch train while a different landscape sped past the windows.

On this occasion I reached Leeuwarden in the early evening with my Brompton, and biked the seven or eight kilometres to Ernewald and *Quantz* in time for supper aboard and bed. There is a complex of canal junctions and bridges on the south side of Leeuwarden, which requires some patience, particularly at rush hour periods when the road and rail traffic understandably take precedence. It took me six hours to negotiate these obstacles at about one knot per hour including waiting time. But I had a full day in Leeuwarden to prepare for the next stage and for Ben to arrive, as he did by train that evening, September 1st. Our target was to reach at least some of the German Friesian islands, the stage on which *The Riddle of the Sands* had reached its climax.

To get there we retraced the same canal route to the Lauwersmeer which I had used in July, with two overnight stops, the second being in the centre of Groningen, where there is also a series of bridges opening in sequence at particular times, which impose inevitable delays and trials of patience. Beyond Groningen there is a much wider, straight ship canal with bridges that open automatically by remote control as traffic approaches. So it was desirable to follow in the wake of a barge or coasting steamer as we did successfully in the morning, as far as Delfzijl, where the canal joins the Ems estuary, with Germany on the farther shore. After a three-hour pause in the yacht harbour to shop, check the weather and get some advice on the tidal streams in the direction of Borkum, our first objective, we left the shelter of a long breakwater and headed into the estuary.

As expected, the tide was against us for the first two hours; so was a light north-westerly wind. But, as the tide eased and turned, we made faster progress under engine and then, for the last stretch up the channel into the harbour on Borkum with help from the genoa, mooring in time for a celebratory drink ashore, which turned into supper.

For the next five days, until we returned to Delfzijl, our daily progress was entirely regulated by the tide, as we crossed and re-crossed the thresholds of the German Waddenzee, even more extensive and tortuous than its Dutch counterpart. Sailing the Suffolk estuaries is a helpful background but the Thames Estuary, writ large, is more comparable, although this is a much lonelier, empty water-land, when the water is there. Every six hours it becomes emptier still, with hard, unforgiving sand rather than mud on either side of the narrow runnels, which become navigable only with the new flooding stream. Writing of the shoal spaces between the islands Erskine Childer's fictional narrator, Carruthers, remarks: 'two-thirds dry at low water and the remaining third becomes a system of lagoons whose distribution is controlled by the North Sea as it forces its way through the intervals between the islands. Each of these intervals resembles the bar of a river, and is obstructed by dangerous banks over which the sea pours at every tide scooping out a deep pool.' John Seymour had come this way too in *Willynilly*, equally fascinated and baffled sometimes. 'To navigate these waters you need a computer in your head. There are a hundred variable factors, and they change from hour to hour – even from minute to minute. A map made of the sands is invalid in half an hour's time. Creeks that were plainly visible when your map was made are now merged in an endless flood.'

It was this Riddle of the Tides that had to be solved every day to get anywhere. There was no point in leaving Borkum for Norderney before mid-morning. Then we made fast progress, seven knots over the land with the early flood, to cross the first of two water-sheds, after which we stemmed an adverse current with the help of the engine, until the buoy which marked the Memmert channel. For another ten miles or so we enjoyed perfect sailing parallel to the coast of Juist, the second in the island chain, and over another water-shed into the Busetief, one of Carruthers' lagoons, close to high water, with never less than six feet under the keel. We berthed at Norderney at 1830 that evening in time for a drink ashore and supper back on board. It had been, I noted: 'the best day so far on the whole trip.' It was also the fulfilment of a dream, inspired by the gift of Childers' seminal book, and nursed ever since the age of 13.

The wind blew up with intermittent showers to force a not unwelcome rest day before we continued towards Baltrum. As we were enjoying another good sail that afternoon we decided to follow the channel between Norderney and Baltrum out to sea and return at the far end of that island in the gap before Langeoog. There were big waves surging into that gap as we sped back in. As we made our way westward to the harbour on Baltrum, along the narrow twisting channel we had a seal-watching steamer behind us and were suddenly confronted by a mussel-fishing boat at the narrowest, most shallow point on the chart. Her stern wash pushed us sideways into a withy and the tiller broke! Fortunately Ben mastered the art of steering with the remaining bracket until we were safely in harbour. Next morning, while we waited for the tide, the tiller was repaired. I have carried a spare ever since.

We paid the penalty of impatience, leaving Baltrum for Norderney earlier in the afternoon than we should have done; we went the wrong side of a buoy separating two channels and were aground for 20 minutes or more, without any damage other than annoyance. Acting on the advice of the harbourmaster in Nordeney we made an early start for Delfzijl at 0550 in the morning, three hours before High Water. With the confidence of previous experience navigation presented few problems although light, variable and mostly contrary winds meant that we motored or motor-sailed for the whole trip. I felt a tinge of guilt at my willingness to use this artificial aid, which the fictional Davies and Carruthers in *Dulcibella,* like the real John Seymour and Mogador the Oar Breaker in *Willynilly,* never could. We thought about continuing up the estuary to Emden but were happy to moor in Delfzijl by the time we reached the harbour entrance. I rated this: 'a good day, despite tiresome wind direction, the only southerly so far – on the one day when a north-westerly would have been ideal.'

On September 10th it was time to head for Groningen after an easy morning run, minimal delays at the one lock and various bridges on the ship canal. We had time in hand to see more of the city and reconnoitre the station from which Ben was due to depart the next day. I still had the luxury of more than two weeks available for further ventures on my own, with the remaining Dutch Friesian islands in my sights. Perhaps because I knew what to expect, the bridge system out of Groningen seemed easier and faster that afternoon. Over the next two days I made unhurried progress along the canal route and across the Lauwersmeer to Oostmahorn, the small yacht harbour where I had spent a night in July.

Provided I was not delayed by the sea-lock out of the Lauwersmeer and got the tidal timing right it should not be a difficult business to reach Schiermonnikoog, for the second time, the next morning. It was only a half hour trip to the lock, where I slipped in conveniently behind a barge. There was sufficient water outside to head directly across, with the help of a gentle breeze, to the withies leading up the winding channel to the island harbour. Even that tortuous passage was easier this time. Now it was mid-September the place was almost deserted, but another British yacht, *Dutch Link,* arrived soon after me. We were moored before noon and the tide was already dropping outside the harbour sill. So I had every excuse to enjoy the rest of the day, including a ride to Nordstrand on the seaward side and along the hard sand surface of the beach. This island had already laid some spell on me and every hour needed to be stored in my memory.

Over the next few days I made my way westward, crossing the inter-island thresholds when the tide served, first to Nes on Ameland, which Simon and I had visited earlier, then Terschelling and, lastly, Vlieland. High tides were in the middle of the day, so there were no early starts or late arrivals. Light winds made boat handling straightforward although visibility was sometimes moderate. This caused me some problems in identifying navigational marks but was preferable to rushing along under straining sail with no time to correct an error before it was too late. Motor-sailing with the genoa was the prudent option for controlled progress. In Nes, Mike and Janette from *Dutch Link* joined me for drinks and then invited me to supper with them, which was a happy evening. We were all surprised to be visited by Immigration for a passport check the next morning. I cannot recall any other such check in Holland.

I gave myself a day's rest on Ameland before continuing to Terschelling. Again there was an end of season atmosphere in the harbour but the town felt older and somehow more grounded in history than Nes. The harbourmaster assured me that conditions the next morning were suitable for the short crossing to Vlieland, despite a fresh wind just south of west. I made it, but did not enjoy the process, which involved following the harbour channel out against the wind and across the 'seegat', the open gap through which the sea swept in, kicking up the waves. You might imagine a much wider version of the Orford Haven Bar, taking two hours to negotiate in a stiff breeze. On the way out *Dutch Link* passed me, well-reefed-down and going like a train, bound for Den Oever.

As it turned out I spent longer on Vlieland than any Friesian island, and did not regret it. The forecast for the day after my arrival was windy so I had a good excuse to stay, although the sun shone. I cycled into the main village, where the museum and the lighthouse were open to visitors, and to the western end of the island, returning after lunch through woods and dunes along the sea coast. Overnight an easterly gale arrived followed by rain in the morning. Later that day I found the Education Centre in the village and an interesting, sometimes daunting exhibition on sea-defences, beach-combing and wrecks.

On the third morning the forecast was better but I had to wait for the tide until noon, which was probably too soon anyway. My intention had been to reach Harlingen on the mainland but in mid-afternoon I decided to turn south towards the lock at Kornerzand which would take me back into the

Ijsselmeer. The bridge and lock-gates opened conveniently on approach, as if to approve this decision, and I moored in Makkum an hour later. No harbourmaster ever appeared so I also had the berth for free.

Although visibility the next morning was poor there was a useful south-easterly breeze. With some waypoints entered in case of need, I ventured out of harbour and enjoyed one of the better sailing days of the season as visibility improved and I tacked steadily south towards Stavoren. By 1600 I had made my way through the lock into the canal where I re-fuelled and pressed on with the genoa pulling me along. Finally I moored just ahead of a small traditional Dutch yacht. The young skipper and his girl friend immediately invited me aboard for supper, which was a delightful end to a special day.

Perhaps that was too good to last. The next day was a Saturday, September 23rd. The nearby village of Heegh was attractive and provided a telephone box from which to book my return ferry and a night's lodging in Earnewald before my final departure. I was not feeling energetic and it was well past lunch-time before I moved on in fair weather but with an unfavourable wind. The canal was very busy with week-end traffic so it was not a relaxing afternoon. The last bridge before Grouw is a railway bridge and I waited there, with others, for over an hour, only to learn that it was closed for repairs until October 2nd. The only option, to avoid retracing the whole of the last three days progress all the way back to Harlingen, was to make a detour inland through Akkrum, hoping that the bridges that way would open. I turned round and headed in that direction to moor in Akkrum at 1930.

More patience was required on the Sunday. I started in good time and the first bridge let me and several others through. Next came a railway bridge, which showed no signs of opening. Eventually it did – six hours later, by which time a large fleet had gathered. At least their presence was some encouragement. I took the opportunity to clean stanchions, remove or dismantle some things that were no longer needed, and clean more of the ship. Finally in mid-afternoon the bridge-keepers relented, and an hour later I moored in Grouw, not far beyond the previous day's obstacle.

With hindsight I might have realised that by late September those responsible for bridge maintenance felt justified in giving it priority over non-commercial canal traffic. But there were no more bridges between Grouw and Earnewald, where I was due to leave *Quantz* for the winter three days later. This was just time enough for various arrangements – repair of an awning, maintenance of the genoa, general washing down and clearing up. The last short morning's voyage to the Yacht Harbour was blessed with sunshine and a perfect sailing breeze. I knew I was leaving her in good hands, at a ridiculously low price for winter storage. "If you were Dutch it would be twice as much, for Germans, three times, but you are British!" (I wonder if this would still apply?)

I had arranged bed and breakfast ashore with a local family for the last night before departure, but could not resist a farewell visit to berth number 88 before I set off for Leeuwarden and the train south, with as much luggage as I could manage on a Brompton and on my back. I was grateful to *Quantz* and my crew companions for – as I wrote in my log – 'carrying me safely through a long season, achieving all our goals, despite often discouraging weather, leaving her in a good jumping-off situation for 2001 – a Baltic odyssey?'

15. Into the Baltic

Ever since my second year as an undergraduate it had been my ambition to sail my own boat one day into the Baltic Sea. This was partly fired by the early chapters of *The Riddle of the Sands* but then reinforced by a week in Denmark with my college rowing crew which was competing in two regattas at the beginning of the summer vacation. The first took place on a lake near Arhus in Jutland, the second on the outskirts of Copenhagen. Although the crew, with which I travelled as one of two 'spare men', had just become Head of the River at Cambridge, they were twice soundly defeated by the strongest Danish Club, Kvick, which lived up to its name. The distinction between a college and the University as a whole was lost on the Danes, and we were received everywhere as 'Cambridge University.' The entertainment, often too generous for our fitness to race, culminated in a great party on the harbour shore somewhere near the Little Maiden statue, lasting until dawn. Towards sunrise most of us plunged into the water for a swim, only to discover that harbour water is often impregnated with a film of fuel oil. I was determined, however, that I would return, and that it would be at the helm of a yacht. It just took the best part of 50 years to do so.

Having explored both Dutch and German Friesian Islands in the summer of 2000 it was now time to press on from the winter berth where I had left *Quantz* at the end of September. I rejoined her there in the middle of May 2001 and after four days' work, including varnish and anti-fouling, moved to Leeuwarden, where my crew and companion for the next important stage would arrive.

Paul Shipman had been installing a new heating system for us and, in the course of casual conversation about my plans, I mentioned that I was still short of a crew. "I think I'd quite enjoy doing that," he said. Although Paul had no sailing experience, he was clearly competent, resourceful and used to discomfort when travelling abroad. We seemed to get along well together and I was confident that he would pick up the essentials quickly. That proved to be entirely the case.

We followed the now familiar canal route to Groningen and Delfzijl. Paul had mastered the art of steering on the canals before we crossed the more open water of the Lauwersmeer, where we practised sail-handling on various headings; he was soon proficient with ordinary conditions. We left Delfzijl early on Ascension Day, a holiday in those parts, so there were plenty of other boats accompanying us down the Ems and across the watersheds south of Juist and Memmert, where Ben Johnston and I had found our way the year before. The harbour in Norderney was very full, but the harbourmaster, whose memory was impressive, recognised *Quantz* and waved us into almost the only vacant berth.

Preliminary study of charts, pilot books and discussions with Dutch and other yachtsmen had persuaded me to avoid the passage into the Elbe in favour of Heligoland and the Eider River, which leads into the Kiel Canal beyond the half way mark. We spent another good day sailing south of Baltrum to Langeoog, which would be our point of departure. It was again advantageous to have followed the same route with Ben previously. Only one moment of anxiety came when it was necessary to squeeze past a cruise boat in a narrow, shallow section of the inter-island channel. The harbour on Langeoog struck me as pleasantly quieter than Norderney though still busy. When a group of German yachts arrived together the peace was less evident. We needed an early night and did not appreciate Auld Lang Syne sung at midnight by drunken Teutonic voices, when we had to be up at first light.

Other boats were also on the move that Saturday morning and it was easy to follow them out to sea. Despite the almost calm conditions and a good eight feet under the keel it was choppy over the bar, or perhaps it was a long period spent in sheltered water that gave me that impression. We were clear of the entrance by 0630 on a heading of 50°, with plenty of navigational marks to check our progress and use as waypoints. Lack of wind forced us to motor with the main up as a steadying sail and a slight rolling swell. By 1030 Heligoland was visible, 20 miles away; we berthed four hours later after a very easy passage. Owing to the holiday weekend we had to raft up with at least six yachts inside us. Heligoland was flattened by wartime bombing, so the town lacks character, but there is still a sense of history and isolation; the cliff top views were worth seeing and a visit to the Duty Free store essential before heading towards Denmark. That night there was no singing to prevent our sleep despite our near neighbours.

Without GPS I would have hesitated to aim for the Eider River entrance in the moderate to poor visibility of the following day. We left harbour at 0900 in cloudy, calm weather with a forecast of a light westerly breeze, which never materialised, although there were signs of something from the south-east gradually filling the sails. The Schleswig Holstein coast is very low-lying even by comparison with East Anglia, and it is also shallow a long way offshore. The Eider offing buoy was an essential waypoint some 20 miles distant on a bearing of 78° but still far from land.

With a favourable tide under us and some help from the wind we made decent speed, but it was reassuring to be overtaken by a motor cruiser on the same heading, the only vessel we had seen for several hours. Paul was enjoying his spells on the helm more and more. Eventually, in the early afternoon, the Eider buoy came into view on the port bow. From this point a series of some 20 channel buoys duly appeared in turn. The approach was reminiscent of St

Valery in the Baie de la Somme, though more straightforward, with reliable buoyage and less tidal stream. Nevertheless two full hours elapsed before we sighted the land itself as we steered between buoys numbered 21 and 22. An hour later, as we approached the lock-entrance to the river itself, the gates swung open – just for us! This was a moment of considerable satisfaction but we still had several miles to go to find a berth in Tönning, the first place upriver, where we moored that evening.

Next day we were content with a two-hour morning trip through two opening bridges, which responded helpfully to signal blasts on the foghorn, as advised, and an equally obliging lock into Friedrichstadt. Once berthed there we declared a rest day. It was a pleasant town to visit, the architecture and lay-out almost Dutch, with a complex of little canals; there were laundry facilities, shops, and we found a restaurant for supper, an unusual event, since Paul's talents included the ability to produce a good meal from a basic galley. That night I managed to ring Wendy at a bed and breakfast in the Hebrides, where she was touring Scotland on her Brompton, as was now her habit during these summers when I was away. I am inclined to think she was the more adventurous.

On leaving the lock channel soon after departure I cut the corner unwisely and ran aground. By dint of raising the mainsail and unfurling the jib to heel the boat in a gusty breeze we came off, but it had been a disconcerting moment since there was no prospect of a rising tide. Later that day a chatty lock keeper told us the last British yacht he had seen passing through had been three years previously. It would not surprise me if his memory was one year adrift; if so it could well have been the Glaisters in *Babaji*. Larger, deeper draft yachts would avoid the Eider. There were pleasant, winding tree-lined reaches along the river, not unlike the Kentish Stour, and more open reaches where the rising wind gave us about six knots sailing with the jib alone. Paul greatly enjoyed this and during the last four hours of that trip we scarcely needed the engine.

By midday on May 30th we were in Rendsburg, having joined the main Kiel Canal soon after breakfast. We found it surprisingly peaceful, with wooded banks and more yachts than commercial traffic. The town was worth an afternoon and overnight stop. Another four hour run the next morning took us to the final locks at Holtenau, passing on the way a naval patrol boat which duly acknowledged our dipping ensign. By 1215 we had entered the lock and at 1240, as I wrote in my log we were: 'through, into the Baltic!'

Thousands of British yachts must have passed that way since men like Erskine Childers and EF Knight a hundred years or more earlier. But it was still a big moment for me. After an excursion ashore, to buy charts and withdraw money we pressed on down the Kieler Fiord in search of a berth at the British Kiel Yacht Club where we moored expertly, stern to pontoon, to the satisfaction of the military berthing master. The facilities were impressive, although no food was available that evening and the charge of 24 deutschmarks was higher than usual. It was also the only harbour anywhere from Holland to Denmark, Sweden, Norway and back again over the next three years, where I was ever required to produce my passport and prove my nationality.

Amongst the yachts berthed there were two of the beautiful classic boats built for Hermann Goering in the 1930s. 'Liberated' by the British in 1945, they had been handed back to the West German government some years later but then leased to the British Forces for adventure training. The soldier skipper of one of them, *Flamingo*, was generous with advice on Danish waters before we left, just before noon. It was a brisk, breezy sail down the fiord and then a fast broad reach as far as the entrance to the Schlei Fiord, where we moored at Maasholm a mile or so inside. In Chapter Six of the *Riddle of the Sands* Carruthers describes beating into the Schlei in the *Dulcibella*:

'I could see no sign of the entrance he had spoken of, and no wonder, for it is only 80 yards wide, though it leads to a fiord 30 miles long. At once we were jolting in a tumble of sea, and the channel disclosed itself, stealing between marshes and meadows and then broadening to a mere.'

So now I could really feel I was sailing in the wake of Davies and Carruthers, those joint, very different heroes of the novel. Perhaps it should be said that 'fiord' in most of the Baltic countries has nothing to do with the same word as used in Norway, with mountains on either side. These are much more like tide-less versions of the Suffolk rivers. In fact I am willing to claim that Orford, or Oreford, which is plainly not a ford, was originally the Orefiord to its Viking invaders.

Willynilly had also moored in Maasholm, which I described in my log as pretty and picturesque, almost 'twee'. John Seymour seems to have felt something similar:

'Maasholm is almost too beautiful. You wonder why it is not flooded with lady water-colourists. It would be in England. It has little streets of tiny houses, some thatched the rest tiled, and the walls are all painted with different vivid colours...They are miniature houses – dolls' houses.'

He also mentions that EF Knight, author of *Falcon on the Baltic*, had been to Maasholm in the 1880s, where he found that the islanders would not intermarry with the inhabitants of the mainland and were all related to each other, with only four or five surnames among them. I suspect this is a common feature of coastal places, not unknown close to home.

From the Schlei we sailed on another fast sailing day to our first Danish harbour, Sonderburg, on the northern shore of Flensburg Fiord, raising our courtesy flag in sight of Denmark at 1418, another landmark for me. Sonderburg was too good to leave in a hurry, and we were happy to spend a further, windier day in harbour, where Paul did more laundry, we explored the town and, like Carruthers in Chapter Five of the *Riddle*, I climbed to the higher ground behind the town, where the monument stands to the Dybbol Bank and Mill – 'the Dybbol of bloody memory; scene of the last desperate stand of the Danes in '64 'ere the Prussians wrested the two fair provinces from them.'

Here Carruthers is referring to the loss of Schleswig and Holstein to Prussia at the end of that war. Like him, and presumably Childers himself, I enjoyed the view of the whole bight in the fiord below, where his fictional character – 'could see the wee form and gossamer rigging of the *Dulcibella* on the silver ribbon of the Sound.'

Paul and I now had another week before we needed to leave *Quantz* and head home. We spent it sailing west, crossing the Kleine Belt towards Fyn or Funen. Unknown to us we were following the same track as *Willynilly*. And the area we were exploring is well described by John Seymour:

'Between the island of Aero and the 'mainland' of Fyn, (not a mainland at all of course but a big island), there is a piece of shallow sea that is almost enclosed by islands. The sea thus enclosed is like a great lagoon, and is itself filled with islands. Islands from tiny uninhabited strips like the one to which we were sailing, to small countries with towns and villages and great beech woods, like Taasinghe and Thuro. This big lagoon, or little sea, is quite a world apart: cut off from the rest of the Baltic, although open to it at many points.'

This was now our perfect cruising ground for seven days, often breezy, sailing well-reefed or under jib alone. On successive nights we moored, or sometimes anchored offshore, visiting Skoby on the tip of Aero; Faaborg, lying across the strait, on Fyn, is a Hans Andersen sort of place, but that is hardly surprising since Odense, his birthplace is the major town on Fyn, some 20 miles north; we went on to Svendborg, Dyreborg, and back to Faaborg. After various enquiries I had decided that this would make the best base for *Quantz* until I returned in July, possibly even for the winter, unless I found better. Like the Seymours we had enjoyed the clarity of the water, so that the bed of the inland sea was often visible, and learned once, the hard way, that it was sometimes shallow. This was not a soft landing. My last log entry I before we left *Quantz* in the hands of the harbourmaster made the point. 'It is clear that depth sounding and attention to buoyage are essential in this area and probably through much of the Baltic. It remains wonderful cruising with lovely places to visit and moor.'

I rejoined *Quantz* on August 3rd and spent the next week making my way gently north towards Arhus where I had a rendezvous with Simon Arnold. The weather was very warm and I was often able to drop anchor and enjoy a swim. The winds were also helpful for easy single-handed sailing. In different harbours, like Fredericia, I made enquiries about possible winter storage, which remained a preoccupation. The last morning, as I approached Arhus, was typical of this trip, providing – 'very pleasant reaching conditions with no strain but good speed all the way. Into Marselisborg Jachthafen past the Royal Slot (a villa rather than a palace, which is the royal summer residence) for late lunch and a snooze.'

It was a casual, impulsive decision to head into this large new yacht harbour, on the southern side of the city, instead of the central, more commercial harbour, also used by some yachts. I was not to know how fortunate this choice would prove to be. It was then, and still remains, the smartest, most luxurious facility I have ever experienced, with a big chandlery, a choice of restaurants, and a first-class shower and toilet block. It was also very moderately priced, although this may have been a special arrangement due to the harbourmaster at the time, Christian Vinberg, who apparently made up his mind that this elderly Englishman, sailing on his own in a small boat, needed to be taken care of. For *Quantz*, and for me, this would become a winter base and a summer home for three years.

I had four days to spare before Simon arrived, which allowed me to reacquaint myself properly with Denmark's second city, the largest also in Jutland, which I had visited briefly in 1954 as a student oarsman. It is not a large place but has a great deal to offer, attractive shopping streets, a fine cathedral square, cafes and restaurants overlooking water, a major commercial and ferry port, interesting older houses and several museums including the eerie Museum of Occupation, situated in the wartime Gestapo headquarters. I spent an hour or so there by myself and felt relieved to emerge into sunlight. There were always jobs to do on the boat including electrical repairs with help from a kind and resourceful Canadian skipper with a Danish wife, charts to be bought for onward use and other useful tasks. One evening Christian Vinberg entrusted me with lowering the Danish flag, from the flagstaff at Marselisborg. Then I felt I was really at home. The sacred red and white 'Dannebrog' is flown outside nearly all official buildings and many private houses. It must be lowered and folded carefully, and never touch the ground.

Simon and I had nearly two weeks together for a very relaxed cruise northward, usually sailing for about four or five hours each day in good weather. Our twin main objectives were the exploration of the Mariager Fiord half way up the east coast of Jutland from Arhus and the island of Laeso well out in the Kattegat towards Sweden. Between Ebeltoft and Grenaa, our first two intermediate ports, we sailed along a coastline of low hills and sandy cliffs. The Mariager Fiord runs for a good 20 miles inland, about as wide as the Orwell or the Stour with a well-marked, winding channel, but no mud-flats. Its pastoral fields and woodlands stretch down to the shore with occasional farmhouses or larger country houses standing in spacious grounds. We spent one night at Hadsund, half way along, where there is an opening bridge, another at Hobro, the top of the fiord, the third at Mariager itself, between Hobro and Hadsund, the most picturesque of the three.

Two days later we sailed across to Laeso from Hals at the mouth of the Limfiord, with a fair wind and the rare experience of a good spinnaker run. The island is diamond shaped, about ten miles long and five wide at one point, and deservedly popular with visiting yachts and other holiday makers. There is only one road, connecting the western harbour, where we lay, to its eastern counterpart. We allowed ourselves a full extra day and hired another bike so that we could both ride to the small central village of Byrum, where there is an exhibition centre showing the process of salt-making for which Laeso was famous. Later we found our way back along woodland tracks and swam in the clearest of water beyond the harbour wall. The day was crowned by filled sole in the harbour's fish restaurant accompanied by Chablis, followed by sharing our whisky and some cheerful conversation with the crew of the nearest yacht.

It was a pity to leave Laeso on a fine, still morning but we headed out, steering due west and then south of west, to make harbour on the mainland at Hou, just north of the Limfiord. The sea remained flat and calm all the way and the one event was the sighting of a dark grey shape, a submarine, nationality unknown, about a mile to starboard, going north. Hou is a small harbour which has only two metres of depth, so the yachts tended to be smaller, more like *Quantz*, but at this time it was still busy, with family crews on holiday.

Bonnerup, our next port of call, faces due north on the projecting coast of Djurland, and Grenaa, where we spent another night, is at the western end of the same promontory, a ferry port to Sweden. From there we sailed due south to reach the large island of Samso, which lies about 15 miles south-south-west of Arhus and forms the southern screen of the wide Arhus Bight. The weather was set fair but the wind shifted south, and, as so often in the Baltic, produced an adverse current. I had also begun to realise that, although there is no tide, changes in wind direction, or some more mysterious force, can bring changes of water level of at least half a metre.

The coastline of Samso is lovely, with rolling uplands, cliffs and chines, resembling a mini Dorset. We rounded the headland into the harbour cove of Marup Vig, which was packed full of yachts. Nevertheless we were waved enthusiastically in, to squeeze between others. It seemed easier to eat aboard, with a bottle of red wine, since it was, after all, my 70th birthday. From Samso we headed back to Arhus because Simon's holiday was running out. Happily it was a fine reaching sail with a south-westerly 3 to 4. Less happily, although we did not know it then, he was already experiencing some early symptoms of the illness which would eventually prove fatal, and this was the last occasion when we sailed together.

Three days remained before I was due to follow him back to England. These I spent, with great enjoyment, just to the north and east of Arhus, where the Mols promontory juts out, like the fat central prong of a fork, enclosing two bays or inlets, Knebel Vig and Kalo Vig. Both offer very sheltered, quiet anchorage, although not perfect holding, as I discovered on the second day, in Knebel Vig, where I dragged twice. I swam, explored beaches, woods and farmland, and made friends with a couple aboard *Megan Louise*, from Fambridge, moored not far away, which, I noted, was only the third British yacht I had seen in Denmark so far. In Kalo Vig I lay at anchor surrounded by woods and cliffs and overlooked by the ruined castle of Kalo Slot, which I landed to explore. This was almost as good as being in the shelter of the Crusader Castle at Les Andelys on the Seine, 17 years before. Days like these were, in their way, just as fulfilling as the completion of a longer voyage or series of passages to a chosen objective.

I needed to be in Orford for the first three weeks of August, crossing, as now became habitual, from Esbjerg to Harwich. The departure from Esbjerg, that time, was notable for the presence in harbour of some of the Tall Ships Race fleet including a magnificent Mexican three-master, and, as the ferry headed out of the long seaward channel, we passed others coming in. On these passages over the coming years, I always made a point of finding a place on the starboard side just after breakfast to watch Orfordness Lighthouse, the Castle and Church come into view.

The return trip to Denmark, however, was different. I was very keen to show Wendy some of the places I had just discovered. The plan was that we would both take our Bromptons, use *Quantz* as a floating base, and visit one or two nearby islands like Samso, if necessary by ferry, to avoid much sailing. For some reason which I have now forgotten, we were booked on the overnight ferry to Hamburg, and would take the train north to Arhus. Perhaps I wanted to show her something of the territory I had just covered.

Wendy was not keen on a stuffy cabin down below, so we slept, or tried to sleep, in very cramped, alleged 'reclining chairs', which did not justify the description. By the time we reached Marselisborg her sensitive back was showing signs of protest and one night on a bunk aboard *Quantz* left her in nearly as bad a state as in Dieppe once before. Enquiries showed that the few equivalents to B&B on Samso were fully booked, owing to some Congress, and anyway she was too uncomfortable to go far. Instead I booked her into the Marselisborg Hotel for at least 24 hours of proper comfort.

The compromise solution, suggested by Christian Vinberg, who was becoming a mentor and friend as much as a harbourmaster, was that we should take a train to the Silkeborg Lake District and spend a few days there, using our bikes if we felt like it. This worked out happily. There are several attractive lakes in that area, some 30 miles inland, with low hills, woods and farmland on either side. The longest, perhaps ten miles long and up to a mile wide, takes its name from the town of Silkeborg, which lies at its head. This is the Ambleside of Denmark's Windermere, minus mountains and fells. We found a good self-catering B&B where we stayed for two nights.

Wendy felt better, and we cycled the length of the lake to Ry at the further end. On the way we reached the summit of Denmark's highest hill, the Himmelburget, perhaps a few hundred metres up, without having to dismount. Having lunched we took a boat trip back up the lake. On our third day we made another short train journey to Sonderborg, half way back to the coast having booked another B&B at Hov, the little port which I had used on the way to Arhus. For some miles we rode through undulating pastures. Then Wendy sustained a puncture. Brompton tyres are high pressure, difficult to change and almost impossible to repair. We were on a very secondary, empty road miles from anywhere. But we folded the bikes and waited in hope.

Perhaps five or ten minutes later a van, pulling a trailer, stopped beside us. The driver insisted that he would take us into Odder, where there was a bicycle shop, which, he was confident, would solve the problem. First he needed to pick up his grandson from school. He himself was a retired head teacher, and he was determined also to show us his home, and give us a tour of the district on the way. This was all delightful, as was Pieter Nielsen, his house, and the refreshment and information he pressed upon us, although I was anxious that the shop would shut before we ever got there. We had a few minutes to spare when he dropped us, full of thanks, in Odder, where a new tube was soon fitted. This episode was characteristic of so much help given to me in Denmark with no expectation of recompense. Our hosts in Hov were equally friendly; in the morning we cycled back to Odder and took the train to Arhus with enough time left in the day for me to show Wendy 'Den Gamle By', a re-constructed museum village of historic houses, one of the city's main attractions.

After one more night in another friendly B&B, Wendy left by train to Hamburg and her return ferry early on the next day. It was a relief to hear that the she had not suffered the same discomfort on that journey. Just under three weeks of my sailing season remained and Ben Johnston was due to join me on September 3rd, five days on, for one more cruise from Arhus to Roskilde and back. Roskilde Fiord runs south for 20 miles from the north coast of Sjaelland, very close to Copenhagen. Apart from the fact that it was a convenient distance eastward from Arhus, the harbour is famous for its Longship Museum, where replicas are also still built by traditional methods.

While I awaited Ben's arrival there was time for another visit to Samso and also for a night on Tuno, the tiny island just to the west of Marup Vig, my last port of call with Simon in July. Both were well worth seeing and Samso was much quieter than a month before with only six yachts in the harbour at Marup Vig. I managed bicycle explorations the short length of Tuno and for several miles north on Samso and across to Langor on its eastern coast, all useful future reconnaissance.

I had a spare Sunday in Marselisborg before Ben arrived, when I tried to catch up with Queen Margarethe of Denmark who was attending a service in the cathedral. She must have been sitting in the balcony, because she was not to be seen in the nave, and at the end of the long, formal Lutheran service, I just got a glimpse of her departing Rolls Royce. In the main harbour I found the splendid Royal Yacht *Dannebrog* lying at the quayside with smart, white-uniformed sailors, shouldering cutlasses, on guard at the gangplank, but still no sign of 'Daisy' as she was affectionately known.

Ben and I set off for Roskilde early in the afternoon of September 3rd; a good beam wind took us round the northern tip of Samso and close-hauled down to Langor on its eastern shore, navigating a channel through rocky shoals under engine for a time. We were not in a hurry to leave before midday, as our next harbour on the little island of Sejero was only 17 miles to the east on a sunny calm afternoon with no option but to use the engine. From this quiet little haven we needed to round the northern headland before crossing the 21 mile stretch to Odden, the ferry port between Sjaelland and Arhus, which lies near the end of a long finger-like promontory. It was necessary at one point to find a gap through the rocky Griben reef and we were suddenly disturbed, soon after, by a series of explosions and the realisation that we were sailing into a naval firing range, where a target-towing tug signalled us to head south into safety and towards our destination – a less dramatic encounter than *Sea Swallow's* approach to Lulworth Cove all those years before.

Fredriksvaerk, just inside the entrance to the Isselfiord, was our third port of call, and this in turn leads into the narrower Roskilde Fiord, running south to the town itself, 20 miles inland, which we reached by early afternoon on September 7th. This was good timing, since we had several hours available for a worthwhile visit to the Viking Museum, where we could watch the actual building process of longships still being carried out, much larger equivalents of John Seymour's little coble or the Shetland yoals, which are their descendants in line and shape. The town was also vibrant with a 'festival of music and culture' so that, unusually, we were not in our bunks before midnight, when the sounds of music were ceasing.

A steadily freshening north-westerly greeted us in the morning, but we did progress back north beyond the large opening bridge at Frederikssund in time for its noon opening. Under threat of heavy showers and still more wind I opted for shelter in the port of Lynaes two hours further on, which proved a wise decision. There were good facilities and a restaurant, compensations for the delay of another full day waiting for a force 7 north-easterly to decrease. We were also invited for a drink aboard a beautifully equipped 26 foot Swedish yacht *Luffe*, which arrived to find us occupying her berth, but their crew insisted we should remain – yet another instance of Scandinavian kindness.

At last the wind seemed less aggressive and had shifted further east and we found our way back to Odden, *Quantz* handling the swell left over from the last few days with confidence. It was windy again that night but the harbourmaster was optimistic so we headed out, bound for Langor, once more, on Samso. There was a big sea running that morning, but this, and the wind, eased once we were through the Griben reef gap, and we avoided any trespass into the firing range. One way and another September 11th, 2001, was, according to my log: 'much more satisfactory than seemed possible to start with. Langor seemed very peaceful.'

But this was before we knew what had happened in New York and it was, of course, one of those days when everyone remembers where they were. Ben had gone off for a ride on the Brompton while I prepared supper and, casually, turned on the radio to listen to the news. It was probably a worse shock for Ben, as a former airline pilot, to hear about the attack on the Twin Towers of the World Trade Centre – all this happening while we were sailing happily towards this quiet, isolated, empty little harbour. Later that evening we lay on the pontoon and looked up into a cloudless sky, dense with bright stars in the absence of the slightest sign of light pollution. It was hard to believe that the world could contain two such different skies. Meanwhile in Scotland, that same indelible day, our granddaughter, Rose, was being born.

Ben was on his way home two days later from Arhus, while I had another three days to make arrangements with Christian for the storage of *Quantz* that winter, rinse and bag sails, pack up instruments and other items I could not carry, but did not wish to leave aboard, which he also collected for safe keeping. I had still seen no television footage of the Twin Towers, but read accounts in German newspapers, more accessible to me than Danish ones. I also attended a Three Minutes' Silence among a large crowd on the Cathedral Square. Finally, confident that my ship was in safe hands, I left for Esbjerg once more on September 17th.

As things turned out there was to be one more trip to Arhus that year, one more sight of *Quantz*, and another example of extraordinary Danish hospitality to come. Ipswich Town FC qualified for European competition and were drawn against Helsingborg in Sweden, the away match scheduled for November 1st. My sons, Jamie and Don wanted to be there, as did a friend of Jamie's. Their research indicated that the cheapest, quickest route would be a flight from Stansted to Arhus with onward train and ferry journeys. Would I like to come? I agreed, and rang Christian Vinberg, asking him to put me in contact with a B&B for four of us, in Arhus, before the return flight. He refused to cooperate, unless we would agree to stay with him. In the end I accepted gratefully. All went according to plan. On the ferry trip across to Sweden it was not a great surprise to meet Jamie Beddard, amongst the most faithful of Ipswich fans, also on his way to Helsingborg, and we were all rewarded by an eventual victory after a frustrating first half.

Back in Arhus by the next evening, we paid a quick visit to *Quantz* in Marselisborg. She was in good order, but Jamie's friend, Patrick, fell through a gap in the pontoon, gashing his leg in the process. The Vinbergs patched him up, entertained and lodged us in style and comfort, vacating their own bedrooms to sleep downstairs, and leaving us embarrassingly grateful as we flew home.

For 2002 I had set my sights on Sweden. I returned to Arhus in May and spent the first week of my stay as the guest of Christian and Ulla Vinberg working on *Quantz* before she was re-launched. Not only did this allow me to carry out anti-fouling and other jobs with a comfortable bed to sleep in, but it was a very enjoyable introduction to life in a Danish family home with two delightful children, Freja, probably aged 13 that year, and Aske, about eight or nine. They watched my taste for marmalade and other strange breakfast habits with amused fascination. I was taken to an evening show of drama and dance at Freja's school, and we all went to the circus together on another night. I discovered that, at least for the female members of the household, the broadcast of the Eurovision Song Contest was an unmissable event.

During the second week I slept aboard, but continued fitting out jobs. As I was experiencing some pain and discomfort from a swollen knee Christian eventually took me off to the A and E ward at Arhus Hospital one evening. I had to take my turn owing to a problem with casualties from local gang quarrels, then received helpful diagnosis and treatment for a strained ligament and signs of arthritis. In so many ways I was made to feel at home. But there was only time for one short sailing excursion in the bay before I had to return to the UK for a couple of weeks in order to attend a family wedding in Scotland. Nevertheless I was poised for the next stage of my Baltic exploration, in its way the most challenging so far.

Verdens Ende from above

Lock gates on Telemark Canal, Norway 2003 (Richard Roberts)

Quantz near Dove Point after return from Baltic

'One reef down' *Quantz* in Medusa Channel off Walton (David Foreman)

Tuesday moored near Svartisen Glacier, Norway. (David Foreman)

'Shake Down' for *Tuesday*, force 7 off Denmark (David Foreman)

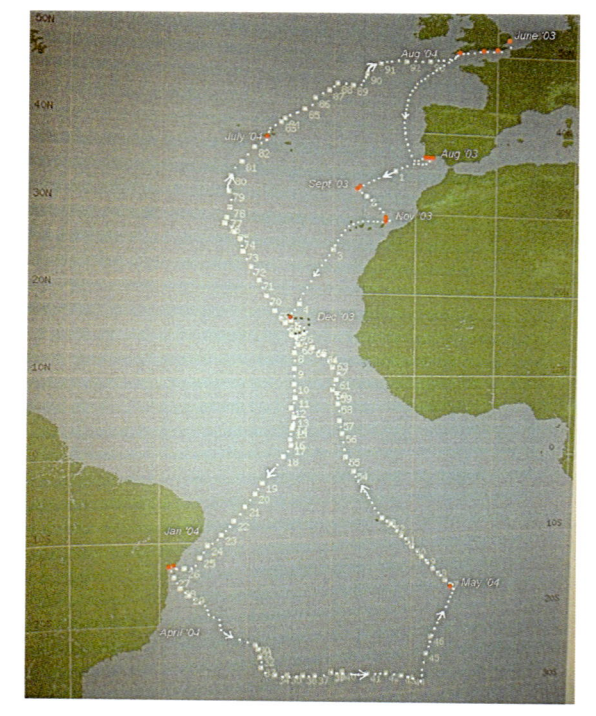

Atlantic Figure of Eight (David Foreman)

Father Christmas on the Equator (David Foreman)

Whizzbang! Lighting damage to electronics (David Foreman)

Welcome back *Tuesday!* Orford, August 2004.

Tuesday moored at Orford (David Foreman)

Lasers at sea (Sheena Barrow)

White Water off the White Cliffs (Sheena Barrow)

Katrina in Helsinki (Love Hansell)

Katrina on the Blue Coast (Richard Waite)

Katrina on the Blue Coast (Joel Chadwick)

Katrina on passage Gotland to Estonia (Tina Exley)

Who's Who? Young Instructors with Liz Feibusch

Sailing Course and Instructors

16. Canals and Castles

When I returned to Arhus in June 2002 it was for a prolonged cruise which would last until late July and take me round the south of Sweden and back through the Gota Canal, across the whole country. Much of this was to be accomplished on my own, partly because other people were not available, and because I was happy for it to be so.

I spent one night at the Vinberg home before settling in to my berth on *Quantz* and a further full day of preparations for departure. On the afternoon June 12th I left harbour in calm conditions motor-sailing for some five hours before picking up a buoy in a sheltered bay on the eastern side of Samso a short distance from the harbour at Langor. I berthed in harbour there the next morning, staying long enough for some shopping and an encounter with a journalist who seemed keen to interview me until he discovered that I had not, after all, sailed alone from the Caribbean through hurricanes and other potential disasters. My passage plan was essentially to follow the same route eastward as Ben and I had taken the previous September. This would lead me to the north coast of Sjaelland from which I could easily reach Helsingborg, in Sweden, where I was due to meet Dan Spinney ten days later. I had time in hand for relatively short passages and to pause in harbour in case of bad weather or simply to rest and explore.

The conditions on the second day should perhaps have detained me. The wind was blowing towards Sejero, my next destination, but the squalls were nearer force 6 than 5, accompanied by showers. Accordingly I returned to my overnight mooring and waited until the wind appeared to moderate somewhat after lunch. Even so, the following seas, as I sailed on under the genoa alone with the wind dead aft, made steering hard work and I was glad to reach harbour by 1730 that afternoon. During the night the wind strengthened again and it seemed wise not to move on too soon. In the morning two friendly skippers of neighbouring yachts, a Dutchman and a Dane, offered coffee laced with whisky, and helpful advice, including the exact coordinates of the gap in the Griben reef which I would need to find on my way. Later I enjoyed a bike ride to the south of the island past wheat fields dotted with scarlet poppies with a sun-flecked sea always in sight. As there were also plenty of white horses riding the waves I did not regret being ashore. That evening I returned hospitality aboard my own ship only to be invited later for Irish coffee on another. A printed list of useful Danish waypoints was also pressed upon me. Altogether I had every reason to be glad of the decision to stay in Sejero that day even if a surfeit of coffee led to a wakeful night.

Short of sleep or not, I was under way by 0600 for the short trip to Sjaellands Odde and moored there by 1030. This passage planning probably had something to do with yet another World Cup football match, four years after my sessions in Boulogne. This time Denmark were drawn against England in a match scheduled for broadcast that afternoon. I remember standing, as inconspicuously as I could, at the back of a crowded Bar Bodega with a television screen, trying to look neutral, while England scored three goals to none against. In truth it was not a good game, apart from the result, and those nearest to me in the room were extraordinarily tolerant as my real affiliation gradually became obvious.

Over the three days that followed I progressed in relatively short stages of some four hours each at sea, stopping overnight at Hundstedt, in the entrance to Roskilde Fiord, and Gilleje on the north coast before mooring in Helsingor under the walls of Kronborg, Hamlet's castle. It was now the evening of June 18th; I still had several days to spare before meeting Dan in Helsingborg just a few miles across the Oresund which separates Denmark and Sweden at that narrow point. If the worst came to the worst the ferry we had used the previous November would take me there in 20 minutes. I had already been excited the previous afternoon by a glimpse of Sweden on the horizon. Now I could enjoy the experience of sitting in the cockpit in the shadow of the battlements on which the ghost appears in *Hamlet, Act One, Scene One*. "In the same figure, like the king that's dead." As if on cue, as I prepared for bed, the sky darkened and a dramatic storm of thunder and lightning broke over the castle.

I gave myself a full day's holiday, partly to provision and tidy the boat in preparation for the arrival of a new crew member and because I wanted to visit the Kronborg properly. The royal apartments were impressive and there was an interesting collection of ship models in the maritime museum but, rather to my surprise, no mention of Nelson or the Battle of Copenhagen, when he allegedly put his telescope to his blind eye. It must surely have been fought within sight of these walls or not long after his fleet had passed below. The empty case-mates were suitably dark and spooky as I wandered round them on my own.

Later on June 20th, a Thursday, I motored gently across to Helsingborg in a flat calm with the added pleasure of raising the Swedish courtesy flag for the first time, half way over. As recommended by one of the skippers I had met earlier, I found a convenient berth at the Sailing Club pontoons marked 'fri til som' (free till Sunday). With another day to spare I gave myself the luxury of breakfast ashore the next morning in the nearby Hotel Karnen, where I could also watch England versus Brazil in their next match. Predictably, this time, England lost. Removal of an errant sock causing a blockage in the bilge pump was a compensating satisfaction, reinforced by the refusal of the harbourmaster to accept any mooring fee – plainly not a Swede, he spoke with a strong Geordie accent.

Dan arrived exactly as planned in time for lunch on June 22nd after which we set off, crossing to the Danish coast south of Helsingor, thence rather slowly in light fluky winds onward to Vedbaek for our overnight mooring, perhaps ten miles north of Copenhagen. I was much reassured by the presence of a strong, young crewman with transatlantic experience for the next stage, through the busy Oresund past the Danish capital and then round the southern tip of Sweden. He had just six days free, but if he could get me as far as Karlskrona I would be well-placed to go on at my own pace up the east coast to the Gota Canal entrance south of Stockholm. Within 24 hours I was doubly grateful.

After several days of light winds we woke to a fresh south-westerly gusting between 5 and 6. With a double reef and in the lee of the coast we were happy enough to press on past Copenhagen itself and enjoyed a fine reaching sail for two or three hours. Then the gusts seemed stronger still and I decided to head into the harbour of Dragor just to the south of the city. As we were in the process of lowering the mainsail the goose-neck fitting came adrift and the sail flogged badly and split, yet again, as off Ijmuiden two years before, along the top batten seam. The spray-hood also got detached in the struggle for control.

We found a berth in Dragor, coincidentally the place where *Willynilly's* Baltic venture had concluded. There was a chandlery, run by an Englishman, with an uncanny resemblance to Commander Pool, former Commodore of OSC, who thought he might get hold of a sail repairer in Kastrup, but not that day. It did not take us long to re-fix the spray-hood and the goose-neck. We allowed ourselves some rest, then caught a bus and a train into the city centre. There we walked to the main harbour and back, in tourist mode, before a visit to Tivoli, where we enjoyed the ambiance and a steak each. Back aboard we slept well.

In the morning the chandler advised us to tackle the sail repair ourselves to avoid further delay, for which purpose he provided a sail-maker's needle, strong thread and tape. Armed with these and some friendly advice from an American lady tourist observer, Dan set to at 1100 with great efficiency and persistence, apart from a short lunch break, until 1605 when the sewing was done and the tape was setting. Lacking a thimble he improvised with a bottle-top. At 1845 we left Dragor, heading south-east across to Holviken on the Swedish side, where a short canal saves the detour round the awkward hook-like promontory of Falsterbo. We sailed with the foresail alone and a fresh westerly cross-wind causing some swell and consequent difficulty with steering, until we used the engine for easier control. After some hesitation in identifying the channel into harbour we were able to follow a coast guard vessel shepherding a motor-cruiser, which had called for help. So we docked near the canal entrance at 2100, had supper and took to our bunks. Dan fully deserved both food and rest.

Broken cloud and a fresh breeze greeted us on waking. With four other boats we waited for a bridge over the canal to let us through at mid-morning, and by noon we were sailing on a beam reach with two reefs down initially, later reduced to one. Our goal that day was the ferry-port of Ystad, 30 miles away. We made good speed until the later afternoon when some auxiliary power was added to sustain progress. Berthed by 1915 that evening, we had time to enjoy good showers and dinner in a proper restaurant, the 'Old Brevey', as due reward for Dan's sail repairs. Ystad is a ferry port, such as I always rather enjoy, mainly from Germany and Poland, but also to and from the island of Bornholm to the south. Some years later, watching TV, I realised it was also the setting for the Swedish police drama series *Wallander* which became a nostalgic reminder for me of this cruise.

Another good day's sailing took us a similar distance to Simrishamn and then, on Thursday June 27th, Dan's last full day, the last 55 mile stage into Karlskrona. Dan was able to set the spinnaker for a while, but found that sailing goose-winged with the genoa boomed out was just as effective. As the wind freshened so the swell increased and our heading turned further north; we lowered the mainsail and ran on fast enough with the foresail alone. Finally we were following the channel across the wide bay between islands which leads into the central harbour.

Dan left *Quantz* to catch his train soon after breakfast. As my log states his contribution over that last 151 miles had been vital, setting me up crucially for the rest of this long mid-summer cruise round and through the heart of Sweden. It took me nearly two weeks of relatively short stages to make my northwards to the entrance of the Gota Canal.

Two days further on, in the Sailing Club at Bergkrava, I watched Brazil defeat Germany in the final of the World Cup. This coast is a favourite German cruising ground so it was not a happy outcome for some of that audience. A helpful Swede gave me excellent advice on the location of the many 'natural harbours', islets offering 'steep to' mooring and shelter all the way up that beautiful 'Blue Coast' which, although strewn with rocks and little wooded islands, has a well-marked channel winding between them.

The next morning, July 1st, I was under way early and moored in Kalmar by midday. My log records exchanging enthusiastic waves as I was passed by a Russian yacht, from St Petersburg, as I later learned. They were, like many, somewhat surprised to see a British yacht at all, but at least they recognised the ensign, which was not always the case. "Where do you come from?" being a not unusual question. Feeling tired that day I did not move on for a further 24 hours. There were also interesting things to see. Kalmar has a fine castle, an impressive cathedral and I was interested by a visit to a World War Two Soviet submarine, which strayed into neutral Swedish waters and is now a floating museum artefact. Their cramped, spartan crew quarters made *Quantz* seem luxurious, to say nothing of what they would feel like when submerged. That evening I was given drinks aboard a Hallberg Rassey by Fred and Laura, a friendly Dutch couple, but it was pleasant physical weariness rather than alcohol which caused me to keep knocking things over, so I was glad of a full night's sleep. Borgholm, only 16 miles further north on the island of Oland was my next harbour, where another Dutch yacht, from Stavoren in Friesland, took my mooring lines ashore for me. The town has its own imposing ruined castle; I also visited the grounds and garden of the Swedish royal family's summer residence at Solliden, wishing that Wendy could have seen it too.

From Borgholm I needed to cross back to the mainland shore, a passage which turned out to be one of the more testing stages of the trip so far. To begin with progress was fine in calm weather. Then came rain and poor visibility, which I had not detected in any forecast. *Quantz* was steering herself well under engine so I decided to press on aiming for Oscarshamn 27 miles away and further north. Before long we were enveloped by fog and the worst visibility I could remember. GPS was a godsend, particularly as I needed to find the channel into Oskarshamn and stick to it. I was also rightly nervous of shipping; one vessel went past on the port side, merely detectable as a vague shape without lights. On the final approach the outline of what I assumed to be a harbour wall turned into a container ship moving slowly out. I nosed in prudently to moor safely, with relief and satisfaction. The lifeboat was just bringing some other people in. Big ferries, I learned, use the port regularly and one had been due 15 minutes before my arrival. Perhaps I had just been lucky.

From Oskarshamn to Figeholm was only a 10 mile afternoon's sail under blue skies with force 4-5 offshore wind so I was content to set the genoa and leave *Quantz* to do the rest, apart from navigating carefully along the coastal channel between myriad rocky islands. That morning I had met a rather distressed Dutch couple who had hit a rock the day before and done significant damage to their boat. Figeholm proved to be a long, land-locked inlet, with a friendly atmosphere. In return for the use of his mobile phone I shared some of my whisky with a Danish skipper, Jens Andersen from Holbaek, near Roskilde. He had won a silver medal in the Sydney para-Olympic regatta, and had hopes for Athens in 2004 in addition to having won a transatlantic event. It was difficult to detect any sign of disability, certainly not when he sailed past me the following day. The harbour mistress told me that an Ipswich yacht had been there the day before. The whole place reminded me of Thorpeness if one could imagine the Mere dotted with rocks and deeper between its islands. Altogether I was pleased to be there.

The day after that I could say the same in Handelop, 27 miles north. True, the engine had been required a good deal in fair, calm weather. I had almost expected Red Indians in war canoes to emerge from the wooded coves and islands on the way. I stopped for lunch, mooring bows on to a tree with the kedge dropped astern in Baltic style, although I must admit to two attempts and accepting help at the last minute from a kind lady on a Swedish yacht, already moored up. I allowed myself a siesta before sailing on.

That afternoon the crew of a German yacht, *Crystal*, which I had moored alongside on two occasions elsewhere, passed me coming south, waving wildly. It was nice to feel recognised. Soon afterwards Jens Andersen in *Sara Sofie* overtook me with his spinnaker drawing powerfully. We exchanged greetings on VHF but he soon disappeared ahead.

The little fishing harbour of Handelop was another special place to moor, completely sheltered, not unlike Iken Cliff or the 'Rocks' above Ramsholt, with the significant difference that I could step straight off the bows onto the shore. There was only one other (Danish) yacht and the evening mosquitoes to share the peace and quiet. I had been warned about insects. Most regular Baltic cruising boats had mesh or netting contraptions over the hatchways. I relied either on burning anti-mosquito candles like joss-sticks, which worked up to a point, or shutting myself in and hunting down the one beast which had inevitably got into the cabin first.

A short early morning trip took me to Vastervik in search of supplies, but it was a delightful couple of hours in sunshine, and a special moment when passing through the Sparosund, a narrow cleft between shoulders of rock. I shopped and lunched ashore during a short spell of rain, then sailed on with thundery clouds in the offing until I could anchor, more expertly this time, in the 'naturhamn' on the little island of Kalmalso. There were four other yachts there but it did not feel at all crowded, more like some cove in British Columbia in my imagination. At this stage the entries in my log narrative seem increasingly lyrical. I even started to parody Wordsworth on Westminster Bridge at one point.

'This place is like an inland lake, lovely this morning. Just now (0945) I have it to myself. Three Germans and a nice Swedish family have left. I am reluctant to go – Shangri-La – but must set off soon. "Bliss was it on this day to sail and be alive".

After navigating an inner channel short cut, I motored with little wind until St Grindo, a most pretty little bay with red ochre timbered houses selling smoked salmon etc. Could not resist popping in. Big yacht flying red ensign waved vigorously. Very beautiful stretch followed: stopped engine and set pole, speed and wind increasing. Did not stop for lunch as conditions so good. Headed in to St Alo with Swedish yacht and moored to buoy in natural harbour, but more developed and patronised with buoys and pontoons available. Lennart Kindlund from the Swedish boat rowed over and invited me for dinner – pickled herring, chicken and potatoes etc – so salmon still untouched – charming couple, built boat themselves, beautifully done.'

Kindness and invitations like this are one of the unexpected advantages or compensations of solo sailing. If there had been two people aboard *Quantz* we would have been left to our own devices.
'Better and better' I wrote the next evening.

'If yesterday scored 9/10 this had to be higher; only the unnecessary reef, though wise (the wind did get up as forecast late pm) and consequent slow if tranquil progress to start with, denies the Full Monty. Scenery more grand early on, then some wider, major lake-like stretches followed by a straight run, almost like a canal, through pretty islets, one, strangely, with cows basking on rocks. Only pain is big motor-boats and their wash. The Dutch, as ever, then the Germans, react enthusiastically at sighting the 'red duster'; the Swedes reach for binoculars.'

Ormoarna, where I moored that afternoon was a wild little archipelago. I had a version of Ransome's Wild Cat Island to myself; cleaned the topsides from my little plastic dinghy, went for a row, read a book, snoozed and prepared yesterday's salmon for supper. Then, on July 10th, under a cloudless sky, I headed for the entrance to the Gota Canal. It was faster, down-wind sailing with a freshening easterly breeze, close to force 5 by mid-afternoon when I moored at Mems outside the first set of lock-gates. Here I paid my Canal dues for the whole transit (2400 kroner or £185) and sorted out my ropes for lock use.

The *Baltic Pilot* and other literature suggest that it is unusual and unwise to attempt the procession of locks between one side of Sweden and the other single-handed because the lock-basins are crowded in season, and the swift ingress of water can cause loss of control for the unwary. I had worked out a system, with a pulley on the bows, which would, theoretically, allow me to hitch the bow rope over a bollard and lead it back to the cockpit where I could control it and the stern warp together. But going east to west I would be ascending in every lock for about five days until we reached the highest point. This meant entering each lock when it was empty, with a high wall on either side, and a long, optimistic, upward throw required for each warp.

The Danish skipper of *Cream Lady* observed my preparation and, typically, suggested that they could give me a hand in the lock, which made the whole manoeuvre easy. Similarly in the second lock that evening, Gustav, the 'lockvart', was on hand to take my warps from me, and at the third a group of watching tourists were keen to do so. There was a swinging bridge before my intended berth near Söderköping, which opened every half hour. A motor-cruiser radioed ahead on my behalf to warn them I was coming. I could hardly have expected more assistance and it was all spontaneous. I found a quiet berth beyond the crowded yacht harbour; ahead of me along the bank was a yacht with 'Lerwick' on the stern, but no ensign or sign of life. A Swedish girl skipper from another boat astern told me her father was on a solo round the world voyage, he had been away for nine years, so far, and was now in Tahiti. Like the crew of Captain Cook's *Endeavour* perhaps he was reluctant to leave.

The pace at which I was progressing, between 20 and 30 miles a day was about right for my physical resources, but I always knew it would not allow sufficient time in my overall schedule to sail further up the coast to Stockholm and back. On the other hand I was now within two hours' reach of the capital by bus and train, so a day-trip to the city was the best alternative. A comfortable seat on the Copenhagen – Stockholm express, at a discounted rate, was worth waiting for and I thoroughly enjoyed my tourist experience, lunch in the Old Town, a walk past the royal palace to the ferry, which took me to see the *Vasa* Museum across the harbour. The great ship was now very impressively preserved and displayed. This is a city dominated by water, a mixture of Venice, Paris and Amsterdam; I was glad to have seen it, however briefly.

Most of the following morning was required for a staircase of eight locks on a perfect summer day. Two more in the afternoon added to my confidence and technique, although assistance from *Seeschwalbe – Sea Swallow*, no less – was not refused. This was also the day when a yachtsman from Potsdam wanted to know if that was my home port since Hans Joachim Quantz was its favourite son. The enquirer himself played the French Horn and his son was a professional bassoonist in the Cologne Philarmonic. Actual distance covered was only 12 miles but the sense of achievement was not diminished and we were now 33 metres above sea level. It was good weather for swimming even if the water was cool on entry. My new friends aboard *Cream Lady* moored alongside.

Each day provided variety because the Gota Canal connects a series of lakes, which occasionally, like Lake Roxen, the day after, allowed me to sail properly for a while through pastoral scenery, past high wooded bluffs and a ruined castle or two. I stopped for lunch and a swim before tackling another eight lock staircase in the afternoon. Growing confidence allowed me to take the leading position in the first basin, but I was happy to drop back after the third and accept some help from a Dutch family. *Cream Lady* was in the group of yachts behind so, as soon as I was through, I was able to take her lines in return for earlier assistance. At some stage in our canal progress the delightful Aviaja Norskov Nielsen, aged 11, daughter of the skipper of this boat, had decided I was her responsibility when we were in locks together, climbing ashore to take my lines from me at the crucial moments. Sadly they were having engine trouble and tending to arrive later. I kept in touch with this family for a year or two at Christmas but lost contact later. I sometimes wonder what life has had in store for Aviaja over the last 17 years and hope it has been good.

Progress improved slightly day by day. I learned the trick of jockeying for position before the first lock or bridge, the latter often opening automatically one after the other if a larger vessel was at the head of a group. If Aviaja was not available to give assistance the lock attendants often did without being asked. Most of them were students doing this as a seasonal vacation job. The girls wore blue shorts and yellow shirts, the national colours, and being blonde, tanned and long-legged, this was both a distraction and a compensation for occasional delays. The further we went the more I was able to enjoy the landscape of canal and lakes. Sometimes I might have been on the Upper Thames above Henley. School holidays were in full swing with groups of children jumping into the water with admirable disregard for health and safety and making the same noises as they all do from Iken to Zanzibar. The weather seemed to be set fair and sometimes I also stopped to swim. Once, drifting across a lake in flat calm, I did not bother to anchor, and had to swim faster to catch up when a little puff nearly blew *Quantz* and my lifeline, the towed dinghy, out of reach.

One night, in Vadstena, on the shore of Lake Vattern, my mooring, alongside others, was in the castle moat, one of the attractions of a town which was clearly a magnet for tourists. Lake Vattern is the second largest on this route but only some four or five miles wide at the crossing point. Military firing ranges lie on either side but the artillery, like the children, seemed to be on holiday.

On July 17th, the day after this lake crossing, I reached the canal summit 33 metres above sea level. Even this slight elevation had removed the mosquito problem for several days past. From this point the locks were full on entry, making life much easier, provided one's ropes were free to cast off after the descent. The slussvakt (there seemed to be a change of title here from the earlier lockvart) told me she thought about half a dozen British yachts had gone through that year so far. *Babaji*, of course, had been that way seven years before, but in the opposite direction. On this day I even clocked up 24 miles, with only two locks and three bridges to negotiate, passing through wilder, less populated country with a North American feel to it. Then on the 18th there were three locks and four bridges, but I still managed 21 miles, of which just one was covered under sail. When the wind did freshen a day or two later, in the open waters of Lake Vanern, it blew from straight ahead and I had neither time nor energy to beat to windward the 40 mile length of that inland sea. That was perhaps the only disappointment of the whole summer.

In fact I experienced a moment of slight regret on leaving the last lock before the lake and the end of the Gota Canal proper but the first of two days on the lake offered a major compensation. The harbour at Lacko sits at the tip of a peninsula jutting into the lake 18 miles west of Mariestad, where I had left the canal. The yacht basin lies in the shadow of a fairy-tale castle and I had fortunately arrived by mid-afternoon just in time to discover that Danish National Opera Touring Company were going to stage a performance of Donizetti's *Don Pasquale* in the castle courtyard that same evening. I am no expert on opera, but this is not a demanding work, and there was an enchanting Norina in the cast. I was lucky to get a ticket and sitting in those surroundings on a summer evening listening to that music was an intense, joyous experience.

From Lacko to Vanesborg at the southern end of the lake is a 38-mile passage so I was under way by 0730 despite a late night. Just over an hour later, some of it actually sailing, I anchored for a second breakfast and put in a precautionary reef before clearing the last of the little islands near Lacko. Lake Vanern seemed vast by comparison with the enclosed waters I had been used to for a fortnight and now the wind backed unhelpfully, or, I suspect, was tunnelled up the lake against me. I resorted to motoring with a steadying sail, forcing myself to stay awake, keep an eye on the compass and make minor adjustments to the steering. The Tillerpilot would have been helpful but 'George' had gone on strike somewhere on the east coast. As if to tease me, an ideal westerly breeze filled in just as we reached the narrow channel leading into Vanersborg, where it was not safe to sail. That night, my log tells me, I slept for nine hours undisturbed.

Much refreshed and re-fuelled, I headed for the first of two bridges and the entrance to the Trollhatten Canal – with some trepidation. This is a serious commercial waterway, designed for real ships, at least small cargo-carrying vessels, not the leisure craft or little tourist steamers, which use the Gota Canal. These locks are much deeper, wider and longer. Fortunately the bridges opened on cue and the skipper of a Swedish motor-cruiser took one look at *Quantz* and waved me alongside. So we descended together to the depths of the first basin, while his crew did all the rope handling fore and aft, climbing up and down vertical ladders if necessary. I did not hesitate to ask for similar help later. Those on *Jocarna of Kastrup*, Danes again, looked after me for the last four locks of the second series. It would have been a tricky operation for me single-handed, although I admired one expert who confidently operated a single midships loop and moved it down by stages without apparent difficulty.

This operation began about 1130 and took four hours. After that I pressed on downriver through pastoral reaches where the current ran strongly and we moved at about five and a half knots over the ground. This took us to Little Edet just before the one remaining lock between here and Gothenburg. It was now July 23rd and I was booked to fly from there, as I thought, four days later. Meanwhile, somewhere in between, I needed to find the right berth for *Quantz* until September, and, as if home now beckoned, my little radio suddenly picked up the BBC World Service and even Radio Four, which had been out of range for at least a month.

One lock remained to be negotiated in the morning – thanks to the crew of *Anaconda*, from Ebeltoft, north of Arhus, and we were soon speeding on with the strong down the craggy river valley which gradually flattened as the cliffs retreated and began to resemble a version of the Thames again. Twenty miles on, at lunch-time, I turned into a quiet backwater at Kungalv, dominated by the mediaeval fortress castle of Bohus. I had spotted the masts of a dozen or so yachts on pontoons with a few free. In the afternoon I clinched a very reasonable deal with the attendant, who also looked after a camp-site, to leave *Quantz* in his charge for a 30 day period, exactly what I needed. In the next berth I found two German lads in a little Silhouette, who I had met twice before. Further reconnaissance revealed that Kungalv itself was a very pleasant village with shops and cafes, a tourist office, which gave me useful information on buses to Gothenburg and the airport (some of which turned out to be erroneous) and a fine baroque church. The view from the ramparts of Bohus was also worth the climb.

I now had a spare day. I moved *Quantz* to a better berth, facing into the prevailing wind and where the stream ran less strongly, and tidied up generally. For once there was rain about and I headed into Gothenburg by bus for a further reconnaissance there. At the dockside I spotted one big British yacht *Firecracker*, with 'Dover' and 'R.O.R.C'. written on the stern. I did not invite myself aboard – they looked too smart for me – but I bet myself they were not going through the canal. In the maritime museum area there was another submarine, Swedish this time, and marginally less cramped and uncomfortable than the Soviet one I had boarded in Kalmar, as well as a 1950s era destroyer, also worth the visit.

On my return to Kungalv there was a pony-tailed German sailor called Martin in a little red yacht, whom I had met in Kalmar. He and his crew invited me for supper, but I had food to finish up, so I declined as tactfully as I could. Having eaten, and not wishing to appear anti-social, I went over with some wine, which needed emptying and some whisky, which did not. They had other friends aboard and we had a cheerful evening, good exercise for my German, during which the wine and the whisky vanished, supplemented by Martin's bottle of Irish.

Just 24 hours later Wendy was meeting me at Stansted. I had spent a morning preparing departure before catching an afternoon bus into the city and the Flybus out to the airport. Only after a leisurely supper in the terminal, but no sign of any Ryanair information, did I discover that my flight was meant to be from a quite different, ex-military air field, miles away, not far from Kungalv. I dashed for a taxi, costing almost the same as the flight. I arrived just in time, only to find the flight delayed anyway, but came close to arrest before boarding, when the scanner detected my Leatherman tool, lurking in my hand-luggage.

After four weeks in Orford I flew back to Sweden and found *Quantz* safe and sound in an almost empty yacht basin. Ben Johnston was coming to join me in Gothenburg for the voyage south to Arhus but I had several days to spare during which I sailed down to Gothenburg and then up the coast to Marstrand a wonderful enclosed island harbour which might be termed the Cowes of the Swedish West. This is a perfect sailing ground with a screen of small islands offshore; the coast runs north-north-east so that the prevailing winds most often provide a good reach. The Baltic season was virtually over, nowhere was crowded, but the weather still warm enough to swim.

I was back in Gothenburg to meet Ben as arranged on August 26th. Unfortunately I had received bad news of a serious accident and injury to my niece, Jane, and was anxious to get back to see my sister Ann, her mother, as soon as possible. With Ben's help we were able to undertake longer daylight passages, with three nights in port, one on the island of Anholt, well south of Laeso. I left Ben and *Quantz* in Ebeltoft and flew home from Arhus. There are not many people to whom I would I would entrust my ship but he not only saw her safely back to Marselisborg, but, from the evidence of his entries in the log book, clearly enjoyed his own cruise in charge, visiting Tuno and Samso on the way. Into the bargain he found the source of a recent persistent leak, a worn engine water hose, and cured it.

After a week in the Isle of Wight with my sister and her family I was able to return to Arhus in September. Primarily I needed to make arrangements for *Quantz* during the winter, but I allowed myself three days for a short final cruise at the end of a great season, one night in Begtrup Vig, across the bay from Arhus and two on Tuno. 992 miles, that summer's total, may not sound a great number when I had spent so many days aboard, but the quality of most of that voyage had been, and remains, among the best of my life.

17. To the World's End and Back

If it had not been for a remark by Anders Frostrup I would never have sailed into Verdens Ende and I would have missed one of the best experiences in my sailing life.

I returned to Arhus in the middle of May 2003 with southern Norway in my sights. But it was two weeks before I set off northward to meet Ben Johnston in Aalborg on the Limfiord. During this time several modifications were carried out aboard *Quantz*, mainly by the expert hands of Christian Vinberg. He had parted company with the yacht harbour and resumed self-employment as a general builder and carpenter. For at least a week of this time I lodged with him and the family. When I finally set sail I had the assistance of 'George II', the re-wired Tillerpilot, who was functioning better again. During the winter the sails had been overhauled and some repairs done. Christian had fitted new wooden strips on the cockpit seats and made new floorboards.

I enjoyed familiar overnight stays in Ebeltoft, Grenaa and Hals, also spending one night at anchor just inside the entrance to the Mariager Fiord. Aalborg, sounding almost like Aldeburgh if pronounced in broad Suffolk tones with a silent 'g', lies nearly 20 miles inland from Hals, but it is an easy channel to follow. I was able to sail most of it with a favouring wind. It must be the major town in North Jutland, almost as large as Arhus. I had a day or more to spare before Ben arrived on June 3rd, valuable for some rest, re-provisioning and sight-seeing. It remains a regret that I never found time, or opportunity, to follow the Limfiord right through to the North Sea.

Once Ben had embarked, we returned to Hals that evening as a launch-pad. On Laeso, where we spent the following night, Ben hauled me to the mast-head, not as an act of discipline, like hapless midshipmen banished there in Nelson's navy, but to sort out a fouled halyard. He let me down again. From Laeso we had a fine brisk sail to Skagen at the northern tip of Jutland, arriving in a flurry with a jammed jib sheet which I finally sorted with a stroke of the sheath knife I always kept handy. It was also 'Constitution Day', the start of a holiday weekend. The harbour was busy with Norwegians who had sailed over to collect beer and spirits owing to the high tax paid on alcohol compared with Denmark. It was delivered to the quayside in vans; pallet loads were swung aboard the larger yachts. Their crews did not wait to reach Norway before starting on the cargo. We slept surprisingly well considering the sounds of merriment and attempts at song which surrounded us.

With one reef in the main, when two would have been better, we left Skagen at 1800 on Friday June 6th. The forecast was SW 4 – 5, but in reality we had a westerly most of the way across the Skaggerak, a solid force 5 with stronger gusts. Only the first hour was deceptively lighter. By 2100 the waves were distinctly higher, two metres according to my log. 'The motion was not comfy but *Quantz* coping as wind freshened', I noted. The boat was managing better than the skipper, who felt queasy and was having problems with motions of another kind. I was grateful for a calmer period after midnight, although the wind freshened again at dawn; we also made use of George and were both able sleep a little between watches. At 0700 the first peaks of Norway were a welcome sight and our decision to head into Lyngor, a little further east than I had planned, was fully justified. By 1000 we were moored near a sail loft and I was heading fast for the toilets. After a late breakfast we caught up on sleep and then moved a short distance to an idyllic island where we could moor alongside smooth rocks forming a natural quay. We had it entirely to ourselves, a little wilderness of varied trees, wild flowers and birdsong, well worth a night's discomfort on the open sea. After drinks and supper we were asleep early and slept long.

Five days later in Larvik, some 70 miles further east, Ben left for home, but his handiness, company and experience had been essential to this crucial stage of the voyage. I now had almost four weeks before Don, our youngest son, was expecting to join me somewhere near Oslo. Originally Simon Arnold had hoped to spend some of this time with me but, sadly, his health was now worse and he was going into hospital.

For a few days I explored the attractive Viksfiorden before heading back westward and then inland to find the entrance to the Telemark Kanalen. This system of lakes, rivers and canals leads right into the heart of southern Norway and the mountainous region famous for the exploits of the wartime Resistance, dramatised in the film *Heroes of Telemark.* A series of 18 locks, several rocky straits and three big lakes, with depths of 200 metres and mountainous shores up to 700 metres above water level, led me to Dalen, 60 miles inland. The whole voyage there and back required at least ten days, as it involved waiting for locks and bridges to open. There were also several fixed bridges which, fortunately, provided just sufficient clearance for *Quantz* but not for larger yachts with higher masts. Their only option was to lower and de-rig the mast, and I saw none who had bothered to do this. Perhaps for this reason a British yacht was a surprise to the lock-keepers, although one had come that way a few years previously.

"What was the name?" I asked the harbourmaster at Ulefoss. "A funny name", he said, 'it began with B". "Could it have been *Babaji*?" "Yes, that's right, it was *Babaji*." I might have known; this was just the sort of route the Glaisters would have been unable to resist. It amused me to think that OSC might have a monopoly of recent British visitors to this waterway.

Although the main lakes were deep, the approaches to locks, and their exit channels, were narrow, with shallow places on either side. I ran aground twice, once on the outward trip when a passing speedboat towed me off, and again, on the return journey, when I was hurrying to get into a lock before its evening closure. This time I strayed into a backwater and hastily swung round to escape; but it was too late – and this was more serious. No one else was likely to come that way; no tide would lift me off. With the help of the dinghy I tried kedging off, without success. The main anchor fouled and was difficult to recover. Eventually I took a warp across in the dinghy to a solid tree trunk on the opposite bank, heeled the boat by every means I could think of and wound in on a cockpit winch with as much strength as I had left. This swung her slightly but not enough. In the end, once the anchor was aboard, with the engine 'Full Astern', we edged slowly into deeper water and escaped. I had to settle for a night above the lock, but at least I could progress in the morning.

Otherwise the lake passages offered some splendid sailing, sometimes enlivened by gusty down-drafts from the hills. I reached Dalen at the head of Lake Banak on the eve of the longest day. To my delight there was still snow lying on the summit of the mountain above the little town. It was the first and last time I have seen snow from the deck of *Quantz*. I celebrated this landmark with a beer in the stunning Dalen Hotel, a period piece from the 1890s, but beyond my means, I guessed, for dinner. Later the tourist steamer *Henrik Ibsen* disembarked just ten passengers. She and her twin *Victoria* plied the canal and the lakes regularly. Though picturesque they filled each lock on their own so I preferred to meet them in more open water.

I had been looking forward to St Hans Day on June 23rd, when the Norwegians celebrate Midsummer with parties round bonfires in every town and village. I had noticed preparations wherever I had been over the last two weeks. The evening before that date I moored in Brevik, near the entrance to the fiord. In the morning there were heavy showers; then persistent rain set in for the rest of the day and well into the evening. Fortunately I had good books aboard, sufficient supplies and the awning rigged over the cockpit. It was at least a week before I did in fact attend a bonfire party somewhere else.

I was now heading for Tonsberg about three days further east at my gentle pace. I had been given a contact there, Anders and Randi Frostrup, a Norwegian and Danish couple. Anders was a yachtsman and Randi's cousin was married to a friend of ours. I rang them to see if they would be at home and to invite myself to visit. They were predictably welcoming, and Anders made a suggestion. "Make sure you call in at Verdens Ende," he said. "It's on your way – the World's End – not to be missed." I found it on the chart, in small writing, at the end of a rocky promontory, a little horseshoe basin or gap between the rocks.

So I found my way gingerly round the southern tip of Tjorne with rocks on either side and headed, even more cautiously, towards a narrow gap, beyond which I could see two or three boats anchored or moored. Last minute, agitated signals from an angler saved me from grounding and suddenly I found myself in a land-locked, craggy little natural harbour. There was a stone quay and a wooden pontoon, where I moored, one yacht and a couple of motor-cruisers at the quay. Otherwise I had the World's End to myself on a warm summer afternoon and evening.

I swam, re-visited the entrance in my dinghy, and realised exactly why the fisherman had been waving at me as I approached. A friendly family on a Bavaria 33 offered me their vacant private berth at Naersnes near Oslo and other local advice. When I had finished supper I went off to the basic shower and toilet block above the quay. This took me past a group people from the other boats sitting on crates, consuming the contents and singing folk songs. I recognised the accordion player as the angler who had piloted me into harbour from his rocky perch. On my way back they insisted that I joined the party. After some time, and having contributed some of my whisky, I felt compelled to offer an English song. I still cringe at the memory of my embarrassing attempt at the words, let alone the tune, of the *Foggy Foggy Dew*. Somewhere towards the end of the first verse I gave up, to the relief of all concerned.

It was well past midnight, but still not really dark, when I decided I must be the first to leave the party. As I drifted off to sleep in my bunk I could still hear tuneful singing in the distance. If I had never experienced anything else in Norway, except that place and that evening, it would have been well worth the voyage on its own.

On arrival in Tonsberg I rang Anders Frostrup, who collected me from the harbour and took me to the family home on the edge of the town for supper. When I mentioned a persistent leak from the propeller shaft on *Quantz* he contacted the boatyard he normally used, on the island of Notteroy, 20 miles further up the coast, and arranged that they would attend to it. Randi, who is a nurse, took one look at my swollen wrist, which had reacted to an insect bite and insisted I called in at a pharmacy in the morning. Thanks to her and the pharmacist it gradually improved. On the way back, Anders showed me his own boat, a very smart Contest 33. He also recommended some anchorages for me to visit in the next few days. Altogether, quite apart from a very tasty meal, they could not have done more for an unknown visitor.

Nearly two weeks still remained before Don could join me. From the earliest planning stage for this cruise I had made a firm decision that I would not attempt to reach the west coast of Norway, but I did want to see Oslo. If *Quantz* was going to be laid up in a boatyard for a time, I decided that it would be sensible to visit Oslo by train, and while I was about it, go on by rail to Bergen and back. This has been described as one of the great scenic journeys of the world and I might be able to see a little of the western fiords after all.

Anders' recommendations for two intervening places to anchor or moor both worked well. At Sandosund, on the second evening, a Saturday, I was able to attend a postponed midsummer bonfire party on the shore nearby, but carefully avoided any involvement in the singing. At the boat yard on Notteroy *Quantz* was lifted out, and it was agreed that the shaft would be re-packed and an electric automatic bilge-pump fitted, setting my mind at ease during periods when she was left afloat unattended.

By late afternoon I was in Oslo booking my train journey and finding overnight accommodation in a tower-block, where I not only slept in comfort for two nights but wallowed in the bathroom. During that 36 hour stay I managed to see some of the city landmarks, the Parliament buildings, Royal Palace and the Cathedral. Using buses, a ferry boat and my invaluable Brompton, I also visited the Maritime Museum, the excellent Viking Museum and the 'Fram' Museum of Polar exploration. I was equally impressed by the displays in the small 'Home Front' Museum situated in the imposing Akerhus Fortress, much moved by the inscription in English over the doorway on leaving the exhibition, which read, to the best of my recollection.

> 'In the skies over Britain
> In the deserts of North Africa
> On the beaches of Normandy
> You gave us back our Country.'

The very strong bond formed between Norway and Britain during the Second World War is equally evident on Shetland, where, coincidentally, Wendy was, at about the same time, discovering the full story of the 'Shetland Bus', the converted fishing vessels that ran between western Norway and the Shetland Isles on long winter nights, conveying Resistance fighters or escapees across the North Sea. As the Glaisters had also found, many of the Norwegian sailors who manned those little ships married Shetland women and have proud descendants there.

On the outward journey to Bergen, leaving towards midday, I had chosen to sit and not to sleep, so that I could make the most of the scenery, which my diary described as 'increasingly impressive and from about 2pm overwhelming – glaciers, patches of snow, foaming waterfalls, rapids – at one point a tunnel through over-arching ice and snow – and finally the long descent beside the fiord.'

Bergen is notorious for the few number of days without rain each year. I arrived in a heat-wave and it never rained. The Tourist Office consigned me to a Youth Hostel which was some distance uphill on my Brompton, although the return descent made up for that. I slept reasonably well after the journey in a 'mixed' dormitory, where I must have been by far the most senior occupant. In fact there was only one woman, and she had a husband to protect her. There was also a communal open-air jacuzzi, which was fun.

I needed to make the most of the next day before catching the overnight train back to Oslo. I took the Funicular to the highest available viewpoint and then found a bus running along the fiord to catch a small ferry over to the island of Lysoen, once the summer retreat of a virtuoso violinist, Ole Bull, who built a wonderfully exotic villa there in 1873. The house and its memorabilia were fascinating, but the secluded island paths through woodland and views of the fiord were even better.

My train left at 2258. This time I had booked a couchette, shared with some chaps with whom I could find no common language for communication. It was a very warm night and I stripped to my under pants. Well after midnight – because it was certainly dark – I felt the need to visit the WC, and left the compartment as quietly as I could. On my return I realised, with some dismay, that the only means of reopening the door was by using the card which had been issued to me with my ticket. This was still in my trouser pocket, hanging by my bunk. I tried to get some response by knocking on the door but my companions were not to be disturbed. So there I was – in the middle of Norway – in the middle of the night – in my pants – standing in the corridor.

In the vain hope that a train attendant might come along I waited a while. Then there was nothing for it but to see if one existed. It was a long train and he, or she, might be at either end. After traversing nearly every carriage I stumbled into the buffet car, where three or four train employees were playing cards. They seemed neither impressed, nor amused by my dilemma. But one of them, in a bored tone, said he would come along in a while and let me in. Which, eventually, he did. My fellow sleepers never stirred.

Apart from this mishap everything about this overland trip, Oslo and Bergen and the scenery between, was a great experience. *Quantz* was re-launched that afternoon and I found another island anchorage in a perfect setting as evening came. My log says I slept well and there was no sign of any leak in the morning. Before my rendezvous with Don I made several short voyages to islands and inlets within easy reach of Tonsberg. One was the harbour of Hanko, the headquarters of the KNS, Norwegian equivalent of the Royal Yacht Squadron where the Royal Yacht was moored. Perhaps predictably I spotted two British ensigns there – less predictably – red not blue; one was a snooty power boat, the other a classic yacht.

Don arrived early on the afternoon of July 9th, courtesy of Ryanair and a short bus journey. As he would only spend one night in a Norwegian harbour I was determined that it must be at Verdens Ende, where we moored in time for supper. Our 28 mile crossing to Stromstad, on the Swedish coast, was trouble free, with several hours of good sailing until the wind shifted and fell away. The next five days, as we progressed south-west to Marstrand, rank among the very best sailing I have known. We enjoyed beam or following winds, just one day's rain with a solid force 5 or 6, otherwise warm sunshine, sheltered waters inside the island chain, and a succession of ideal moorings or anchorages. We took a short cut through the Sote Canal, which cuts off a headland north of Grundsund. It was on our approach to the canal that a larger yacht behind us hit a rock, which we must either have passed over or narrowly missed, both of us failing to respect starboard channel markers in company with others ahead. It was disconcerting to see her bows rear up and come to a complete stop; an object lesson in not following the herd instead of the chart.

This idyllic voyage finished in fine style, with a long spinnaker run into the Marstrand approaches, then a final relaxed day of sailing round Marstrand before Don had to return to Scotland. I well remember the feeling, almost of bereavement, when I saw him off at the ferry to the mainland. I recovered soon enough, however, to enjoy three more days taking *Quantz* through Gothenburg and on upriver to Kungalv where I left her, as in 2002, for my August 'holiday at home'.

A month later Christian Vinberg came over by ferry to meet me in Gothenburg after I had flown back to collect *Quantz* a few days earlier. This gave me time to make preparations for the voyage back to Arhus and to see more of the city, which improved on better acquaintance. Before departure I paid a courtesy call on *Tryad*, flying the RCC burgee, home port Argyll, and owned by a barrister whose name I failed to note, but who received me kindly. (He was, I have since learned, a Scottish High Court judge, the Hon. Lord Weir, and still owns this classic yacht).

About an hour after leaving harbour I learned exactly what it feels like to hit a Swedish rock. I had gone below to sort charts and blithely informed Christian there was nothing in the way; he could hold the course set. In fact we had gone the wrong side of a buoy and were about to hit the only obstacle for miles on either side. There was a loud bang, a nasty jolt, and we slid off immediately. Anxious inspection did not reveal any signs of a leak or serious damage. When *Quantz* was lifted out for the winter there was a scratch on the forefoot of the keel but nothing more. It must have been a nice round, smooth boulder.

We spent that night in Tangen, an island harbour before crossing to Laeso. One of Christian's many skills was his ability to cook. Either that evening or earlier I learned more about his experiences refitting a barge in Holland and taking her up the Rhine and down the Danube to the Black Sea with a Danish television crew making a documentary. We left Swedish waters in variable weather, crossing to the eastern end of Laeso. Here Christian introduced me to the delights of *Skipperslabskov*, a very strong, thick, Danish fish and potato dish, the ideal lining to a sailor's stomach. Another 50 miles or so further south, the island of Anholt was our next harbour, from which we crossed to Grenaa on Jutland. That evening Christian took me to supper at his mother's home, not far away. It was a delightful old house in a very rural setting and she was a most interesting lady. Then he headed home, my third invaluable and equally tolerant cruising companion of the season, while I went on south round Samso and back to Arhus to lay up for my last winter there.

There was much more in the Baltic I would have loved to see but I had decided it was time to bring *Quantz* back to Suffolk and this was my plan for 2004. I expected to leave Arhus, very reluctantly, in May, sailing south to the Kiel Canal but exploring several places in southern Denmark and northern Germany on the way. I still needed to cover some of *Dulcibella's* route in *The Riddle of the Sands*, which I had missed in 2000 and 2001. James Robinson was going to meet me in Schleswig early in June and I hoped we might get through the Kiel Canal and reach one of the Friesian islands before he had to leave. Later, my grandson Joe hoped to join me, after his exams were over, somewhere in Holland. The timing and point of departure for the final North Sea crossing would depend on progress.

When I arrived in Arhus on May 8th 2004 *Quantz* was parked in the Vinbergs' front garden as there were more improvements Christian had offered to make, probably as the result of spending several days aboard the previous September. His lorry-owning friend Lars had delivered her there from the yacht harbour. What Ulla thought about having a boat outside her front door I do not know. Freja and Aske were not displeased, since few, if any, of their classmates could match this, especially not one from England. But Christian also had other work commitments, so it was nearly two weeks before she could be re-launched, again with help from Lars. Christian had re-built and re-fitted the battery box, replaced all the sea-cocks, and a pair of stays to the cross-trees. I had replaced the gas cooker with a spirit stove, for which Christian had fitted a stainless steel surround. He had also re-built the cabin table, installed and wired new a new electrical switch-panel and fuses, a new stern light and fitted a new exhaust outlet. Although I covered the cost of all materials, he stubbornly refused to make any charge for labour. For all this time until she was afloat again I was lodging with them. For the use of his lorry and crane Lars suggested that a crate of beer would be more than sufficient.

Quantz was re-launched on May 21st but I was not ready to leave for five days; then with sadness, after all the kindness and friendship I had received in Arhus over the last three years. I promised to return a year later for the occasion of Freja's Confirmation Party, a major rite of passage for teenagers in Denmark, whether or not they have any church affiliation. As I eventually discovered, it resembled an 18th or 21st birthday party with elements of a wedding reception or major anniversary in England.

There was no pressure to hurry at this stage. James Robinson would meet me in Schleswig on June 10th. So I made my way gently south to Sonderborg on the northern shore of Flensburg fiord, where Christian joined me for a few days. This was very much the territory described by Erskine Childers in the early chapters of *The Riddle of the Sands*, when the unsuspecting Carruthers is lured into joining Davies on the *Dulcibella* in Flensburg with promises of autumn duck-shooting. As I headed into Sonderburg I was on the reverse track of their first two days together. Soon, after Christian and I had been up to Flensburg, we would be following the *Dulcibella's* route south into Schlei Fiord, spending one night at Kappeln, near the entrance. I needed to reach Schleswig at the top of the fiord, where Christian would catch his train home and James Robinson would arrive. Davies, in the novel, dislikes towns, preferring isolated anchorages. It is at one of these in the Schlei Fiord that he gradually reveals the story of his earlier meetings with 'Herr Dollmann' and his suspicions regarding this man's activities in the Friesian Islands, including the attempt to wreck and murder Davies himself.

As things turned out for me and *Quantz*, just ten days later we would be running into serious danger after rounding the Scharhorn Reef at the mouth of the Elbe, just a few miles from the place where the *Dulcibella* so nearly came to grief in Childers' story. Meanwhile I spent two restful days in Schleswig harbour, doing some of the odd jobs that a boat always requires, and even attending a concert for organ and choir in the Cathedral.

With James' reassuring presence aboard we headed back down the fiord on and stopped overnight in Maasholm, as Paul Shipman and I had done three years before. By early afternoon on 12th we had negotiated the lock at Holtenau into the Kiel Canal. Both days had given us good passages with a brisk south-westerly wind either astern or on a reach. We berthed in Rendsburg that evening and were under way before breakfast on the next day. Early in the afternoon we emerged from the lock at Brunsbüttel into the Elbe. The three-hour trip to Cuxhaven on the fast-running ebb with a fresh cross head-wind was not all comfortable – a reminder of the effects of wind against tide which I had almost forgotten in the Baltic; but we travelled at seven knots or more over the ground.

So far this important stage of the voyage home had gone very much to plan and within schedule. I was very keen to have James with me for at least one more passage out of the Elbe, round the projecting sandbanks of the Scharhorn, where the *Dulcibella* so nearly foundered, and back into shelter inside the screen of the Friesian islands. From there, if necessary, I was confident that I could reach Delfzijl and Groningen in Holland. The harbourmaster in Cuxhaven was very friendly, but pessimistic about the weather pattern for the days ahead.

The mouth of the Elbe is a bad place to be with north-westerly winds blowing against the ebb tide, which you need to use – and for four days running, and much of the fifth, they blew from that quarter, never less than force 4 to 5, and up to 9 one afternoon. James did invaluable work locating a leak at the base of the remote greaser to the stern gland, then finding someone to make up the fitting, which he replaced. After three days, however, he had no option but to meet his own schedule and start his journey home. Later that evening I received a message from him about the sea-state observed from the deck of his ferry, which at least convinced me I was better off in harbour.

On the morning of the fifth day I took a ferry trip to the island of Neuwark which lies about eight miles down the estuary, leaving at 1000 and returning six hours later. It was an enjoyable trip in better weather, which I was treating as reconnaissance. This seduced me into a dangerous, nearly fatal decision. As I wrote in my log: 'a classic case of impatience and optimism/over-confidence.'

The combination of calmer conditions during that afternoon plus an apparent weather window at least until midnight persuaded me to set off immediately with the ebb 'towards Wangeroog' (with a 'worst-case' refuge in mind up the Jade at Hooksiel, half-way to Wilhelmshaven). The wind was still WNW but only force 3-4 as I left, well reefed down, in case. Certainly *Quantz* made good speed in relatively calm water with the tide under her. We were doing seven to eight knots at times and averaging six plus. Thus by 2015 I had sighted the Elbe No1 Buoy and at 2100, clear of the Scharhorn, was able to head on a bearing of 211° for the gap between Wangeroog and Spiekeroog. This was still over-optimistic; it would have been wiser to head further south for the eastern end of Wangeroog.

As the last of the light faded the situation began to get tricky. The wind was veering north and then north-east, strengthening as it did so. This meant that I would be heading for a lee-shore and trying to find a channel which was completely unfamiliar to me, in the dark. Several squally rain showers seriously reduced the visibility and the chance of identifying navigational marks. Fortunately I had the sense to realise that I would have to give up the idea of reaching harbour on Wangeroog and head up the Jade estuary instead. One major risk remained. This was a highway for shipping and, although I had the right chart, I had not worked out the necessary waypoints in advance or entered them in my hand-held GPS. To do this I would have to go below, where I could use the chart and the instruments properly. There was nothing for it but to heave to, have a good look round to see if any ships' lights were visible, dive into the cabin and get on with the job. Every few minutes I put my head out and looked round again.

Quantz was cooperative and lay quite comfortably hove to, although the motion down below was not so steady. It probably took me 15 minutes to finish my calculations, interrupted by nervous checks on the very limited horizon outside. As I finally emerged into the cockpit I suddenly saw the lights and shape of a vessel coming up fast on the port quarter. I just had time to bear away to starboard and watch a small coaster surge past less than 100 yards away. I doubt if her helmsman had any idea that I was there at all. At the time I just felt relief: but, ever since, I have re-lived that moment often and it has brought on the real shivers of fear that I should have felt at the time.

By 0100 I was heading safely south-east up the Jade, keeping out of the main channel but progressing slowly against the tide, our speed had dropped to less than three knots. The main problem now was simply the need to stay awake and keep warm – it was cold, wet and dark. I took the sails down and proceeded under engine to ease the strain of steering.

At last the signs of dawn appeared; I could steer more confidently from one channel marker to the next and by 0600 I was approaching the little harbour of Hooksiel. This was made easier by the sight of several yachts coming out. By 0700 I was safely moored in the outer basin and content to wait for the lock to open. Later that morning I went through the lock and up to the actual village a couple of miles inland. In retrospect I knew I had been lucky. The margins had been small; *Quantz*, the GPS, and some sensible later decisions had made up for rash earlier ones. But as I wrote in the log book, later that day. '14 hours on the helm are not recommended for gents of 72 nearing 73.'

Hooksiel was a pleasant village with all the basic facilities I needed for at least 24 hours' rest. The names of almost all these coastal places in German Friesland end in 'siel', meaning 'sluice'. Chapter 26 of *The Riddle of the Sands* is headed 'The Seven Siels' and it is in one of them that Carruthers hides on board a tug and finally discovers the proof of Dollmann's guilt and the motive behind his mysterious behaviour, the answer to the riddle. It was my vague intention, if time allowed, to visit at least one of these villages on the mainland opposite Norderney. This was the nearest I would ever get.

By 0830 the following day I had left the outer harbour and was retracing my route back down the Jade with a strong ebb tide to speed me on and a light south-westerly on the beam. Even the sky was clear and bright during the morning. It was, I wrote: 'a satisfactory day of competence and almost all correct decisions.' Spiekeroog, where I moored six hours later, was far enough, although I could have reached Wangeroog using the inside channel if I had pressed on. I realised when I passed the buoy off the Wangeroog entrance, that I had entered its co-ordinates as a waypoint incorrectly on my previous approach. Besides, these small red buoys were not that easy to see even in daylight and there was some swell on the bar even in these benign conditions. One way and another it was just as well I had turned away before.

The next morning was more satisfactory still. Benefiting from useful previous experience when Ben Johnston was with me in 2000 I took the route out to sea between Spiekeroog and Langeroog, the Baltumer Balje, and motor-sailed in light airs the length of Langeoog, Baltrum and Norderney, before rounding the western end of the last and into harbour through the Dove Tief. Both this channel and the Baltumer Balje had a serious swell running despite the calm weather and I was glad not to be attempting them when it was rough.

Norderney harbour was pleasantly calm, and warm. I had been up since dawn and it was still not midday, but I had a sense of achievement in reaching this important staging point. Later I went into town and, on my return, saw that a yacht with a British ensign had occupied the berth opposite my bows. There was something about her shape that looked familiar. Then I saw the name. It was *Babaji*! Ray and Margo were probably just as surprised as I was to find that the only other British vessel in sight belonged to a neighbour who lived within a hundred yards of their Orford home.

Strong wind warnings, well-justified, kept us all in Norderney for two more days. The three of us had several sessions of coffee or drinks aboard our respective boats and had a meal together in the harbour restaurant. They must have told me where they had been cruising that year but I failed to note it down.

I would have preferred to avoid the delay in Norderney, but there were compensations. These would be my last few days in Childers territory. Like Carruthers I drew money from the Post Office and visited the Vier Jahreszeiten Hotel, although I found it in the town centre, whereas the novelist places it overlooking the sea. Nevertheless, I decided, it did retain some of the early Edwardian atmosphere I was hoping for. On the other hand the more modern Mariehofe Cafe did face the beach, where I had a fine view of seething waves breaking on the sand, and was pleased to be on land. With hindsight I regret not taking the ferry to the mainland on one of these days and exploring at least one of Childers' 'Seven Siels'.

On the afternoon of the third day wind and tide gave us the opportunity to leave. *Babaji* came too, but stuck to their planned destination of Borkum, while I headed south to Delfzijl, making harbour in time for a late supper. On the following morning I negotiated the lock into the canal, which opened just for me, with the series of bridges on the way to Groningen also swinging or lifting, one after the other in sequence, as if to my command. Joe was due to leave Harwich on the ferry to the Hook the next day, where I went to meet him. This was his first trip abroad alone and the train journey to Groningen was not straightforward, although familiar to me. All went well and we were back in Groningen in time for an evening meal.

The trip through the complex of bridges in Groningen and along the canal was a useful introduction to inland cruising for Joe, along a route which I remembered well. I was in touch with Ben Johnston by phone and we met him and his wife Sue in their Westerly Storm *Shelanda* in Zoutkampf, 18 miles west of Groningen. A meal in an Indo-Chinese restaurant in the village and card games aboard *Shelanda* went down well with my new crew. The evening after that we moored in Leeuwarden, where we were able to find a cafe with a television showing a European Cup football match in which Portugal defeated the Netherlands by two goals to one, not a happy outcome for the fans around us.

It was important that Joe should have more to enjoy than the relative monotony of canal passages. Before we left Leeuwarden for my former winter base in Earnewald, we saw more of the town and went swimming in the big municipal indoor pool with its flume and jacuzzis. In Earnewald, which I was keen to revisit for old time's sake, an exciting match between Greece and the Czech Republic provided the evening's entertainment. Then in Sneek, the next night, we moored next to the Glaisters in *Babaji*, who were following the same route. Joe enjoyed meeting other people and we played cards together. Our last night in Friesland was spent in Stavoren after a windy day. I was glad to be in shelter but Joe had relished the waves and spray crossing the Heegemeer and other lakes on the way.

The passage from Stavoren to Enkhuizen across the Ijsselmeer was also fairly rough with a fresh breeze, which gave us some fast sailing but was a test for Joe's sea legs. He was probably glad to reach harbour that day, but we were in time to explore the attractions of Enkhuizen, to enjoy a solid meal ashore and watch the European Cup Final, in which Greece triumphed over Portugal by a single goal. Enkhuizen also provided another good swimming pool before our departure in the morning.

At some stage, probably well before this, I must have rejected the possibility of a direct North Sea crossing from Holland either with Joe or on my own. It would not have been sensible to give him the responsibility of watch-keeping while I rested, or coping with an emergency if I was somehow incapacitated. Nor did I think I could manage 24 hours single-handed even in the most favourable conditions. I did not wish to repeat anything like the experience of my night between Cuxhaven and Hooksiel. On the other hand I was pretty confident that I could cope with relatively short daytime passages down the coast to Dunkerque or Calais, across to Ramsgate and home to Orford. In any case the delays in Cuxhaven and Norderney already meant that Joe would have to return to England before we reached a suitable port of departure. From Enkhuizen we had an enjoyable reaching sail to Volendam during which Joe helmed very competently and was promoted to Able Seaman. We went on in calm, warm weather to the Sixhaven in Amsterdam.

In preference to a coastal passage from Ijmuiden I was keen to join the mast-up convoy that leaves Amsterdam after midnight to follow the inland canal route through opening bridges into the southern waterways of Holland. Accordingly, on the advice of the Sixhaven harbourmaster, we moved to the Westerkanal and waited for the arrival of the north-going procession about midnight. Finally at 0205 our own convoy set off. Progress was slow at first, because the whole group had to be marshalled in each basin while the bridge behind was closed and the next one ahead then opened. I was glad of calm conditions as I imagined that windy weather might easily cause collisions. I found it difficult to keep awake and alert, but coffee and biscuits helped. After Schipol and its complex of bridges, progress was faster and by this time it was daylight.

At 0800, however, as we approached the bridge at Woubrigge we were informed that the next one, at Alphen, was going to remain closed for three days. Joe was due to catch a ferry from the Hook the following day. Accordingly we moored at Woubrugge and sought information on train connections from Alphen. A fortunate encounter with a friendly German Air Controller who kept his boat in Woubrugge was most helpful. Klaus insisted on driving us to and from Alphen station on both days.

By this time I had become relatively philosophical about the tendency of Dutch bridges to remain closed for extended periods without much warning. Like the onset of bad weather it was a phenomenon which simply had to be accepted. Thanks to Klaus, Joe and I made a satisfactory train journey to the Hook of Holland and he boarded his ferry in mid-afternoon. I was sad to see him disappear up the gangway before my return journey to *Quantz*. I met Klaus that evening for a drink, which cheered me up.

In the morning there were signs that the offending bridge might open earlier than expected, as indeed it did. So I reached Gouda that evening. As if to compensate for recent frustrations Saturday July 10th proved to be one of the better days of this voyage. The weather was better than forecast. There were stretches when I could motor-sail with the foresail at over six knots. There was one lock and several bridges including a major one in Dordrecht to pass through, but all went well despite some interesting manoeuvres with a large container ship, which was positioning herself for the same bridge at the same time. That evening I moored, as often before, in Willemstad, happy to be there, with 32 miles covered during the day.

A similar distance plus three locks, as opposed to bridges, took me into the Veerse Meer. I was looking for a quiet island mooring when I was hailed by a British yacht already moored at Spieringplaat. *Quantz* had been recognised by Graham Bush in *Curlew V*; Graham was the owner and chief instructor of Seatrain Sailing, which he had taken over some years before from Philippe Taylor. Between them, and with the assistance of James Robinson and David Foreman, Seatrain had steered many Orford sailors through the various grades from Competent Crew to Yachtmaster. Perhaps I should no longer have felt surprised by meeting an Orford boat on my travels but it was an agreeable encounter and reassuring to learn that they were planning a similar route via Dunkerque.

I was content with a short trip to Middelburg, leaving time for rest and re-stocking supplies before I went on down the coast during the following days to Ostend, Nieuwpoort and then Dunkerque. This time it was not a surprise to find *Curlew V* in the yacht harbour, and I was given the adjoining berth. Graham and his wife joined me on *Quantz* for a drink and we went to the nearest Brasserie for *entrecôte et frites*, followed by a nightcap aboard *Curlew V*. I stayed up later than was wise working out waypoints and worrying about the forecast, which included fog patches.

Tidal timing dictated an early start, forcing me from my bunk at 0415. Two hours later I was leaving harbour. For rather less than an hour we punched our way through choppy water in moderate to poor visibility. When the weather report from Sandettie mentioned force 6 and fog patches I decided to turn back, and was safely berthed by 0745 for a second breakfast. *Curlew V* went on undeterred.

Saturday July 17th is described in my log as a day of 'great contrasts, but eventual satisfaction.' Calm weather had replaced the strong winds of the previous morning and the tide bore me swiftly towards Calais. Heading across the Straits, visibility was a slight but not a serious problem. I kept to the north of, and parallel with the ferry track, before rounding the South Goodwin at 1245, six and a half hours from Dunkerque. I made good progress past Deal, but heavy clouds were gathering over Kent, with flickers of lightning and rolls of thunder getting closer. Near the East Brake mark the wind became variable and gusty followed by half an hour of very heavy rain, hail, thunder, and lightning which seemed uncomfortably close: in the squalls there was almost no visibility. For a while I could do nothing except heave to and hope for the best. Finally the rain eased and the hail stopped. I was extremely glad, and somewhat relieved, to enter Ramsgate harbour and moor safely at 1530, after a nine-hour crossing. I was wet through but soon dried out; a couple of hours rest, a visit to the showers, a meal ashore and a telephone call to home fully restored morale. *Quantz* had returned to a British port in good order after five years away.

Partly influenced by the forecast of afternoon rain, which I thought would make for a depressing trip across the Thames Estuary, I was happy to observe Sunday as a day of rest. It seemed equally appropriate to attend a service in the Sailors' Church and to visit the Royal Temple Yacht Club for a drink and enter *Quantz* in the Visitors' Book. *Curlew V* set sail regardless of mere rain, but they had avoided Saturday's thunderstorm.

On balance mine was a good decision. On Monday I left Ramsgate at 1020. This was to be, although I did not know it, my last crossing of the Estuary. More often I had gone by way of the South Edinburgh Channel; this time I made for Foulger's Gat. This was before wind turbines proliferated. By 1450 I was sailing happily down the Black Deep with a light ESE wind just ahead of the beam. At one stage I hove to for a five-minute snooze and some refreshment, allowing the tide to carry me rather further north-east than I had intended, so that I had to push against it for a while. At 2000 I hove to again off Orford Haven and waited for the tide to flood over the bar. I also rang Wendy to tell her not to expect me before the morning. An hour later, with just sufficient light to identify the buoys, I slipped into the river. Graham Bush had given me a copy of the entrance chartlet, for which I was grateful, since the shingle banks had changed and the buoys themselves were a new feature since my last departure.

I remember a lovely quiet run under the jib towards Havergate as the light faded. There were too many masts in Abraham's Bosom and Butley Creek, so I anchored below Dove Point for supper and went to bed. Perhaps because this is not the best place to lie at anchor, or because I was both tired and excited, this was not a very restful night. In the morning it took me some time to do the necessary packing up and to raise the numerous courtesy flags of the different countries I had visited over the last five years. Unaccountably, the most important one, Denmark, had gone missing.

At 1025 I hauled up the anchor for the last time on this voyage and headed into the Gulls behind Havergate Island under sail and engine. This was a deliberate choice since I prefer that approach to Orford with the changing angles between the Castle and the Church Tower. I made a point of switching off the engine at Chantry and sailing the last leg to the Quay properly. On the river wall a flag-waving shore-party, headed by Wendy, was there to greet us.

I recorded a final distance of 881 miles since leaving Arhus on this voyage. The equivalent distances in my log book for 2002 and 2003 were 992 and 959 miles. I did not record the mileage for 2000 and 2001 in the same detail but it would be safe to say that the combined mileage over five seasons was close to 4500. I have never had the ambition, or the nerve, to sail across the Atlantic, and on this basis it would have taken me years to do so. But at least I had put some distance under the keel and achieved my own private goal. Best of all I had sailed into lovely places; I had gone to the World's End; I had met scores of friendly and interesting people of different ages and nationalities. *Quantz* had brought me home.

18. Brazil and Back

While I was indulging myself with my personal little odyssey of a few thousand miles in mainly coastal, sheltered Baltic waters, David Foreman had embarked on a single-handed transoceanic voyage lasting 14 months and 15000 miles. David has published his own vivid account of this epic accomplishment and the lightning strike off the coast of Brazil, which would have forced most sailors to abandon the project there and then. His book *Tuesday 'n' Me* was published by Bosun Publications in 2006 and is available also from Amazon. The accompanying DVD enables the reader to share a direct visual experience. But for the purpose of this book David has very kindly given me permission to reproduce extracts from *Tuesday 'n' Me* so that it may take its place as the longest, most adventurous, continuous voyage in the history of Orford cruises – at least to date.

I have taken cautious liberties with minor alterations to conform to the style or pattern of other stories told so far; otherwise the words are those of David himself. Here and there you might even catch the voice of *Tuesday*.

'Why?
Ever since I was a schoolboy I have always wanted to see, hear, (perhaps even to smell) the different weather systems and ocean wildlife in the various climate belts of this planet. Reading books about the old sailing ships' explorations kept reinforcing this wish. I wanted to experience it myself. I longed to LIVE in the open ocean for a while, to feel what it was like to become a tiny part of that world and to see some of the wonders as sailors of 500 years ago saw them. It would be nice to visit all sorts of islands and foreign places, but for me this would be a bonus, not the main reason for my travels.

The Route
Because of the circulation of the winds and currents (clockwise in the north Atlantic, anti-clockwise in the south), and in order to cut across the weather systems, a giant figure-of-eight route seemed best. Starting in the UK this meant sailing south to the Algarve, then out to the islands of the Madeira archipelago. Thence to the Canaries and on southwards to the Cap Verde Islands, before crossing through the Doldrums, staying well east and upwind for the south-east trades to Salvador in Brazil. From there I originally planned to go southwards down to Argentina, before turning east towards the Falklands and Tristan da Cunha. This would be the approximate half way point.

The return trip would involve turning north to St Helena, past Ascension Island, over the Equator once more, before slicing across and upwind against the north-east Trades and eventually into the calm of the Horse Latitudes. Then I should be able to work the ship slowly through the calms northward to the Azores and thus homewards to the UK.

Unfortunately both the ship and myself were severely damaged by a direct hit by lightning in Brazil, causing four separate fires on board. So, after three months' hard work achieving only basic repairs, the journey continued south-eastwards towards Tristan da Cunha. However, the early winter weather down there turned particularly aggressive, so to protect the damaged ship, the course was changed direct to St Helena as soon as I could pick up some easterly winds off the African coast.

When?
The intention was to have a northern hemisphere summer, then a southern summer below the Equator, followed by summer again in the north. The plan was to avoid bad weather if at all possible, leaving England in June/July to avoid gales in Biscay, but delaying the crossing to Brazil until November/December to avoid the hurricane season. The last bit of the return voyage would require leaving the Azores for the UK by August 1st the following year.

Overall Policy.
I consider ocean sailing to be like tiptoeing past a vast dragon in its cave. Try to choose a time when it is asleep, be prepared to run back when it stirs, but make sure both you and the ship are strong enough to survive if by chance it rolls over on top of you. There is nothing personal in its behaviour, it's so big it doesn't even know you're there, but it's lethal if you get it wrong. The ship and the crew become a single entity, each unable to survive without the other: just as the ship is there to protect me, it is up to me to look after her carefully.

Why alone?
Most certainly I was not out to prove anything, nor was I running away from anything. On ocean voyages it is often simpler to sail alone, so long as the ship is suitably arranged for one person (which will require considerable forethought). The single-hander is able to alter the voyage plan if necessary and to adapt to circumstances if he does not have other people to consider. The responsibilities are less, and so far as emotions are concerned the Lows may be deeper but the Highs are much greater. Many natural events witnessed will be a source of absolute wonder and delight. I longed to be able to share these emotions but the presence of someone nearby would have diluted them perhaps.

The downside is that the single-hander must be prepared for the total absence of reassurance and advice when things go wrong; at times he will have to remain a detached 'observer' of this little human, who may then be considered as merely part of the boat's equipment – and a very fragile one. This ability to detach yourself from the drama of the event will enable you to prevent 'panic' by reducing it to 'fear', then to 'worry' and finally to 'concern'. Personally I get frightened very easily, and seasick easily too, but a balanced outlook carried me through, so that I could continue to think ahead and work out what to do.

The Ship.

I found *Tuesday* in Majorca in 1997 after a long search. She is named after a derelict Thames barge whose bones are still visible just above the Orfordness landing-stages opposite Orford Quay. Built in 1975, she is a centre-cockpit Rival 41, modified by a small but massive bowsprit bringing her to 43ft overall. When fully loaded with stores etc. she displaces fourteen tons and draws 2.1 metres. I knew she had severe osmosis, which meant the removal of quite a thickness of glass before we reached something we could work with, but the outer three layers are now glass reinforced-epoxy, much stronger than the original. It was a 15 months job, but it gave me time and opportunity to make many other improvements.

I had very clear ideas of what I needed from her sail power. So, with a new mast and rig to my specifications, she now has a taller, boomed stay-sail cutter rig giving her 38 per cent more sail than the standard plan, which has transformed her power and performance, while remaining within the capabilities of one person. This cutter rig has proved to be an excellent choice for me. The most comfortable rig for downwind sailing was not twin genoas, but a single-reefed main with firm preventers, and a poled-out genoa, with the stay-sail pinned in flat fore and aft to kill any vortices from the other two sails. This dramatically damped down the rolling. A longer than usual genny pole means that the sail can be carried well onto a beam reach, maintaining full power with a lighter helm. As the wind rises sail area is reduced progressively until we end up running under a pinned-in stay-sail only (slab-reefed on its own boom if necessary). The storm sails were always ready to hoist, but never actually needed on this trip.

A replacement five-cylinder Nanni engine has proved to be nearly twice as powerful as the original Perkins 4.108, with greater fuel efficiency. In fact I hardly used the engine at all, and certainly not for simply charging the batteries, as there are solar cells, a towed generator and a wind-generator for the electricity supply, with full spares for each. The simplest, cheapest radar I could find was very reliable and ran virtually continuously until the lightning Whizzbang.

The general rule I followed was to keep everything as simple and repairable as possible, without needing specialist tools. I had to be able to do all the maintenance and repairs at sea myself. This policy paid off very well indeed when the electrics were destroyed in Brazil, as the repairs had to be done using the ship's stores only. Almost none of the replacement parts sent out from England reached me, which caused much anguish, and was still a matter of legal discussion a year later. Unfortunately most of the spare electronics on board had been ruined as well, but lateral thinking found temporary and primitive solutions, sufficient to enable me to sail for home

After the primary refit, the whole ship was first tested in 2001 by a horribly rough North Sea crossing from Harwich to Ijmuiden and back, undertaken with my two older children. This included a 25-hour beat to windward in a full-blooded force 7 to 8 westerly. Then in 2002, she was even more thoroughly challenged during a ten-week cruise up the western coast of Norway. On the outward voyage my oldest son was with me on the crossing from Peterhead together with Chris Tweed, as was James Robinson for some stages. On departure from Scotland we sailed through some vicious seas in order to catch the midnight sun north of the Arctic Circle, just short of Lofoten. Parked under a glacier at midnight, we scraped off samples of overhanging ice with a screwdriver to take home to friends. I had expected to be the only yacht in these waters, so I was slightly disappointed to find two at anchor nearby, one German and one Dutch. Other encounters, as with Tom Cunliffe, veteran ocean sailor, were most rewarding and encouraging.

The final test, for me, was the stormy single-handed voyage from Norway to Orford, particularly the conditions off Denmark early on. I sailed upriver on a Sunday evening, approaching the Quay to the strains of the hymn 'For Those in Peril on the Sea' sung by the congregation of the annual Seafarers' Service, held early in August. "How long did it take you?", somebody shouted. "Three and a half days," I replied. The questioner may well have been Robin Guilleret, who was then a member of OSC, and was later to serve as President of the Cruising Association – no stranger to Norwegian waters himself. The fish and chips brought to me for supper were especially welcome.

Throughout her travels, whether during this shakedown cruise north of the Arctic Circle or south of Capricorn in 2004, the ship did her job admirably; time and time again I was thankful for the genius of designer Peter Brett. To watch the sea-kindly way she dealt with awkward conditions, sitting in the water comfortably with a soft motion, making it all look easy, was a joy. Her passage times were always respectable, although I admit her windward-pointing ability in light winds is nothing special. However, as soon as it gets rough she quickly shows why she is the shape she is. Truly she is a very civilised and safe means of transport – and in my opinion, elegant and graceful too. In combination with her Aries self-steering gear, combined with some modifications made by me, she looked after me very well.

Navigation.
  I enjoy the ability to navigate by traditional methods (such as daylight Venus transits etc.), and this was a great help during the return journey when the damaged electronic gear was unreliable. It was very reassuring to be able to check one method with the other. Observing the night sky I was surprised to discover a comet all of our own, which I called the 'Tuesday Comet' partly because I confirmed its direction and rate of travel in the early hours of a Tuesday. (I know now that it had been discovered some months before and given the name 'Comet C/2001 Q4 NEAT', but nevertheless I was able to experience a glimmer of the pride those ancient sailors must have felt when they named a new phenomenon.)
  As a general rule I aimed to make landfalls at sunset, heave to 30 to 40 miles off, and then make harbour late the following morning. I consider most night arrivals require more than one pair of eyes to be safe.

Health.
  Illness or injury would incapacitate a single-handed vessel. I spent time and effort before each leg of the voyage trying to get very physically fit. Early on in the journey I would be covered with bruises by the time I sighted land again, but I learnt rapidly and one or two simple modifications round the cabin helped enormously. However, a damaged elbow caused several weeks of trouble; I had to find a way round the difficulties it caused.
  I had spent a long time getting dental treatment before the trip; even so I unluckily cracked an upper tooth just as I was leaving Brazil. So I super-glued the carefully cleaned remains together, kneeling, forehead on the floor, balancing a mirror and torch against the motion, while dripping glue into place. It held together, with some repairs, until I was home, when it sadly became apparent that the tooth did not survive the event.

Sleep.
  The biggest problem was making sure I could get enough and yet maintain a good weather eye. I found it best to try to sleep for 15 minutes of every hour, day and night regardless, as I did in 2002 coming back from Norway. When shipping was about, rest periods would be shorter and more frequent, often in the cockpit. I was frequently convinced I hadn't slept, but stopped worrying about it once I realised I had been dreaming. Kitchen-timers, a minimum of two at a time, under the pillow, were used to ensure regular waking. Later in the open ocean I was happy to extend sleeping times to 30 minutes, depending on conditions. It required great discipline to keep to this regime when I didn't want to miss anything on deck, but tiredness causes mistakes, injuries, and (as is well recorded and I know from personal experience) eventually delusions. Storing sleep is like re-charging a battery – easy to manage if you keep topping it up – but there is no point in over-charging. The most tiring

bits of the whole voyage were the 36-hour passages in the English Channel, amongst all the other ships and radar-invisible yachts, when I wasn't able to rest at all. The price I paid for all this was that it took more than four weeks before I could sleep normally again on my return home.

Clothing.

With so many times when I was taking off and replacing my waterproofs and life-harness, I found it useful to wear thin nylon overalls, so that outer clothing slipped over them easily. Near the equator clothes were unnecessary – for a single-hander – but protection was still needed from the sun when it was overhead and the sea when rough. A life-jacket was no use to me in the open ocean but a comfortable harness definitely was.

Provisions.

I found this particularly difficult to sort out before setting off owing to the absence of refrigeration, particularly as I am the world's worst cook. So I devised a simple system of three categories: fresh stuff for the first seven to ten days: the third and last category was about six weeks of emergency rations (tins of high protein meat etc.) in case I was dis-masted and stuck out in the middle. For the rest there was three months supply of tinned meats, soups, beans, vegetables and pastas. I preserved six dozen eggs before each of the longest legs by flash-boiling them in very weak vinegar for ten seconds on a rotation system in a large saucepan, which was most successful. I learned to make bread but had to be careful with adequate vitamins if at sea for more than six weeks at a time.

The diet was supplemented by fresh fish, mainly Flying Fish and Dorado. I was careful not to eat anything I wasn't sure of. In fact I ate everything I caught except two poisonous Puffer Fish, hooked by accident. I used a weak line to avoid catching anything too big to deal with.

I collected rainwater if it was easy, which came in handy when the main water supply went bad in mid-ocean. I had also evolved a simple way of making up an emergency supply by filling empty fizzy drink bottles, leaving them in the sun for a week and, if there was nothing growing in them by then, stowing them in the bilge. In the end this was unnecessary as I made a filtering/precipitating system for the bad water and lived on that for eight weeks.

Islands.

I landed on ten separate islands, six still actively volcanic, and was fascinated by the variations of landscape, geology, animals and plants. The island people had an almost universal 'island mentality', slower, peaceful, tolerant and friendly, yet each island was completely different. There were fascinating contrasts: on the Azores some rock samples actually FLOATED in water but wood samples from Itaparica in Brazil would actually SINK.

Wildlife.

I found the ocean teemed with life in some places and seemed deserted in others. To mention a few: in the Azores mullet will clean the weed off your boat without scrubbing. Dolphins of many types were curious about the boat and were a never-ending delight to watch. Whales, mainly Sperm Whales, often passed close by, ignoring the ship altogether, but when 'breeching', leaping clear after a long dive, I was very aware this was their territory not mine. There were vast Fin Whales in Biscay, virtually twice the length of *Tuesday*, which was a bit daunting; then one night in the South Atlantic a Humpback Whale became amorous towards the ship's bottom. I didn't know whether to sit down, stand up, or jump overboard.

Albatrosses, the large southern variety are very large creatures, their body-size comparable to a swan, but with twice the wing span. Their gliding, soaring flight is beautiful to watch; I understand the awe that sailors of old felt for them. For three days millions Portuguese-Men-of-War covered the sea continuously. You would certainly die from their stings if you fell overboard there. I saw a group of Gannets fishing happily 234 miles from the nearest land or rock. This worried me since I believed they went only 70 miles offshore. Was my navigation wrong? A hasty sextant check confirmed my position, and I have since found they have been seen up to 200 miles off land.

In Brazil there is a yellow-crested bird with a characteristic cry of "Fifty Quid! Fifty Quid!" – at least that's how we interpreted it. The Brazilians call it "Bem-ti-vi" ("I saw you") and the French name is "Kiscadee" (Qu'est-ce qu'il dit?) suggesting that the bird is deaf. Personally I think "Fifty Quid" is best. Also in Brazil, when scuba diving, I came across the very ugly Walking Batfish. It cannot even swim! If you pick it up, it flails about and sinks rapidly to the bottom. But there it will set off walking, hopping and jumping on its pelvic fins, just like a rabbit – weird but wonderful!

People.

I was privileged to meet some truly remarkable sailing people, whom I would never have got to know if I hadn't been sailing single-handed. It is impossible to mention them all but they are among the most resourceful, adaptable and resilient human beings I have come across. I am still in contact – and they made me proud to be human, when there is much in the media to cause doubt. They are modest, unsung heroes and heroines, and they will remain deep, sincere friends for the rest of my life.

Island officials were almost always helpful, although one in the Azores was an outright liar and two separate officials in Brazil verged on the certifiably insane. Nearly everyone else was courteous, helpful and friendly, more so than I suspect the British would be in similar circumstances.

Emotions.

I was surprised how emotional a Suffolk Anglo-Saxon could be in the circumstances in which I was living. There were episodes of tears of elation, or, rarely, of despair, and others of simple happiness while listening to gentle music reminding me of friends and home – very un-British! Bad temper was easily recognised as a sign that I was not coping well with a situation; it needed to be controlled, then calm returned. Recognising early signs of 'Mr Cock-up Day', saved me no end of problems, breaking a chain of events which might have led to injury or damage.

Even though I have been sailing all my life, I had to learn to live with my own fears and lack of confidence, but both feelings may actually help survival. I had not anticipated the mountain of support and encouragement from my family and those few true friends I consider as family. I was surprised to find that emails enabled them to do the journey with me in spirit, and it was an absolute joy to meet up with those who came to join me briefly on some of the islands. The downside was the empty coldness of the ship for a day or two when they left.

I was surprised at my reaction when a Brazilian in a motorboat rammed poor old *Tuesday* while she was moored in a marina and then blamed me for being in his way. I frog-marched him to the authorities; not my scene at all normally, but I felt exceptionally protective towards the ship which had become my home for over a year.

At sea I tried to save 20 minutes most evenings for a concert, either on cassette or learning to play the chromatic harmonica, as a way of having some precious time off. Other joys were making pairs of earrings out of Mid-South-Atlantic barnacles for my daughters (very rare jewellery indeed) and artistic pictures from flying fishes' wings. Ham Radio allowed me to speak to my brother in Yorkshire and to chat virtually every day to special members of the Maritime Mobile Networks in a variety of countries. I felt, very rarely, truly alone, as when leaving Plymouth, and Portugal for Madeira, when I promptly ran into unforecast 45 knot winds. Another time was in Brazil when the lightning strike suddenly left both myself and the ship physically disabled, 6000 miles from home – then again with a rudder problem casting doubt on the ship's ability to stay afloat: I was wrong, and worrying unnecessarily, but did not know it at the time. A further episode occurred 1600 miles from the nearest mainland when I discovered the freshwater supply was going bad, and another when the replacement ham radio blew a transistor near St Helena.

I tried to record as much of the voyage in the ship's diary, on stills camera and on video. I took comfort from talking to the camera I think.'

The full narrative of this exceptional voyage is, of course, best followed in the pages of David's own book and the accompanying DVD. For the purpose of this shorter record I have selected extracts from some of the emails from which he constructed his own unique account. For me they are vivid illustrations of the moments and emotions described above. I have tried to reproduce the form and style he uses, which does not always conform to those I have attempted to standardise elsewhere. David's emails are often punctuated by… which adds to their immediacy. In my version this is limited to indicating that some intervening words, sentences or paragraphs have been left out: instead I have used more commas or semi-colons. David begins each message with the greeting **Dear Everybodies** and more often than not signs off **With love from Tuesday 'n' me** (hence the title of his book). I have compromised by limiting this to an early example and his last email in the series. I would have loved to include more of this material, but space and time have prevented this. I have, however, deliberately chosen just one reply email, sent by David's mother, in response to news of his arrival in Brazil.

It also seems appropriate to preface these emails with the lines which appear on page seven of his book before his story begins and are reproduced in the same form.

RISKS
The greatest hazard in life is to risk nothing…
To laugh is to risk appearing a fool…
To weep is to risk appearing sentimental..
To reach out for another is to risk involvement.
To expose feelings is to risk exposing your true self.
To place your ideas, your dreams, before a crowd is to risk their loss…
To live is to risk dying…
To hope is to risk disappointment..
To try is to risk failure…
But risks must be taken,
because the greatest risk is to risk nothing.
The person who risks nothing has nothing, knows nothing,
and IS nothing.
They may avoid suffering and sorrow,
but they cannot learn, feel, change, grow, nor love nor live.
Chained by their certitudes they are slaves;
they have forfeited their freedom.

Only a person who risks is FREE.

Sat 19/07/2003 01:10

Arrived in Vilamoura, Portugal, 16/7/03 after an 11+ ½ day, solo, non-stop 1340 mile, slow passage outside Biscay, keeping about 150-200 miles off the headlands, just for practice! And the things you see! When was the last time you saw a 35' ketch being towed at 14+ knots behind a large ship? You should see its wash! (Got it on film).

Absolutely fascinating the Highs (and Lows) of life.

For example, a Low was during the days before setting off on this trip, going through the "horrors" when I wasn't sure I would be able to manage. Another was when it was too rough to be able to rest and cook, being thrown around a lot, as well as feeling cold and a bit "tom and dick"...

A High was when completely becalmed by night, the ship was surrounded by scores of Dolphins (5-8 feet long), feeding in formation on sprats shoaling under the ship, for over one and a half hours, all within touching distance... but the cream of this High was two days later when three pods of Fin Whales came up doing about 6-7 knots 400 yards away, heading west. The first lot were four in number, the second lot maybe six (one of the last had a smaller bushier spout than the others, perhaps a calf). But boy are they BIG (and I mean SERIOUSLY). The book says 50-70 feet, but all I can tell you is that they are a LOT bigger than *Tuesday* and me and I'm not at all keen on getting any closer to them. And the spout seems so remarkably high too. I thought it was distant smoke at first, got it all on film. These animals are so very noisy when they breathe, when it's calm you can hear them from a long way off; small dolphins go "fpa!", Minke go "ff-ah!", but Fins go "FFFFFfffff!". I can really shout "THAR SHE BLOWS CAP'N!" now, certainly didn't hope to see these things so early in the voyage.

But the whole point of this saga is that if the sea had been lumpy, or if we had been doing the conventional thing and motoring through the calm, I would have missed it all! I wanted to feel a little of what the ancient sailors felt centuries ago, and they clearly HEARD a lot more than we do today, and they had a lot more TIME too...

...Spending 3-4 weeks on the Algarve coast, planning to move every few days... after that, hopefully, further progress south and west.

There's so much more, literally could write a book, but you've suffered enough, so Stay Well, and once again, thanks for all your support, each and every one of you.

"TUESDAY"

Thu 21/08/2003 2318
More Highs and Lows.

The Forest fires in Portugal were really quite worrying, and the cinders could easily damage sail-covers etc. (they still reek of woodsmoke), but no harm done, spent hours washing the decks.

I needn't have bothered. Left Alvor on 14.8.03, but everything went wrong from the start (just as though the ship didn't want to play that day). The final blow was charging headlong into 35-40 knot winds (certainly NOT forecast) in the 'acceleration zone' off Cape St Vincent; gave myself one hour to see if I would stick it, but gave up after another five minutes and turned back; found a small bay tucked under the Cape itself, and, feeling rather 'hammered', tentatively clawed the way in against the wind, first time I've used ALL the reefs in anger, to anchor in about 20 feet on good sand, still heavy gusts to 45 knots, so a wretched night at anchor-watch with ruined confidence and little sleep. I thought I was stuck there forever, but noted it calmed down a bit at dawn so after 36 hours, took a big breath and had another go on 16.8.03...

...But on the second day out, still literally battered and bruised, got miserable again (usual on the second day I think?); couldn't tell the difference between Fear and Hunger and Seasickness (same symptoms), and I certainly didn't feel inclined to cook, although the sailing was excellent in 25+ knots of wind, I was tired and fed up with the motion in a decidedly awkward sea...gave myself a blunt talk, had a cup of tea and felt a bit better...

...Settling down nicely into life, when suddenly all change again at sunset on 19.8.03. LAND HO!   At 40 miles, approx 450 miles in three and a half days. To avoid entering the place at night...hove to at 30 miles out, at 0.5 knots for 12 hours; overslept, twice, getting a grand total of four hours in all that night knowing I was heading AWAY from land, in a more comfortable motion.

Got her going again at 0500 (the sun here is an hour behind yours), and fetched up in this enchanting spot in the large sheltered bay that is PORTO SANTO Island, Madeira; clear pale blue water, clean sand, palm trees, volcanic ash hills, hot sun, temperature breeze,(strong at times), and the occasional brief and warm rain-shower, and CHARMING people. Harbourmaster came haring out to see me in his little speedboat, and said in English, with a big smile, no need for formalities today, have some sleep and food, and come and see Immigration, Customs, Police, and himself tomorrow... Lovely welcome!...

...Blimey, this was a long waffle, sorry about that, take good care of yourselves, more soon.
        Love
        Tuesday

Mon 15/12/2003 11:53
Dear Everybodies

   Now running down towards the Equator, 530 miles ahead (still can't grasp that it's all real!). December but cabin temp is 29-30ºC, wind force 3 – 4, broad reach with boomed out genoa staysail and main, flying fish, bright and new (to me!) stars at night, etc. MAGIC!...

Had a wild and fast beam close reach south-EASTwards from Mindelo, max speed, and taking quite a lot of water on deck, noted a beautifully clear example of wind and wave patterns 20 miles to leeward of one island; waves look chaotic, until you study them carefully, and NOW I understand one of the Polynesians' methods of navigation as described by David Lewis!

Had intended to explore Praia harbour on Santaiago Isle, but lighter winds meant it was VERY dark before I got there... so sailed straight by it, feeling a bit guilty (I'd already suggested to Jack in Pennsylvania that I would look for one particular boat for him there).

   Very solid wind shadow effects that night, nasty, steep, confused and broken seas and light airs, the heavy boom trying to smash everything in sight as I prepared to gybe the ship, in spite of preventers etc. Surprised and cross in the morning to note a complete mainsheet winch missing, bolts sheered cleanly... anyway it's not a problem, and it was a tired old winch anyway...

...Then westwards for 70 miles to confirm the other islands are really there; it means I have actually seen ALL the Canary Islands and eight of the ten Cap Verdes; most impressive of them is FOGO Island, a single massive volcano straight out of the sea to 9280ft high, last erupted in 1995/6, very dramatic!

   Then the journey begins, a relief to get clear of inter-island effects, trade wind sailing, like being on holiday, only two ships in four days, but one would have been within a quarter of a mile if I hadn't called him up on VHF... Two days ahead of me is Bill in *British Tiger* (Contessa32), also sailing solo to Salvador...

...Some bl**dy shark ate my squid-with-a-hook-in-it yesterday, and 18' of line with it; hope it gives him bellyache for a while, as that would have caught my supper; maybe he ATE my supper?

Much, much more, but that's enough for now.
Take care!
Love to all,
Tuesday'n'me

TEXT MESSAGE 2/1/2004

Dropped anchor SALVADOR 1435 hrs, 2384NM non-stop solo in 23 days. All very well, now wiser, calmer (and younger) more news by email soon.
Love to all!!!

04/01/2004/ 02:16
Subject: Salvador, Bahia, Brazil.

Still can't face the thought of going ashore yet, and anyway there's no prospect of clearing in over the weekend (so I've been told by an Aussie in a rubber dinghy); probably explore the two marinas on Monday, in the morning before it gets windy, and only then face the natives.

No sign of Bill (and the cat Buddy) on *British Tiger*. I'll wait a few days, but it may well be that he got pushed too far to the west and ended up in Recife (or worse), but there's no answer to my email to him two weeks ago so I presume he's still at sea.

And poor Matti (the reindeer-singer) got caught by violent weather at five degrees north (roughly where my "brick wall" was), smashed a hand (which repaired itself, damaged his leg, wrecked both sets of his self-steering gears, and lost a stanchion wire; so he turned right, and is now in Barbados safely, having given up the idea of Brazil... *Forever* had a nasty rough first half to their crossing as well, and, sadly *Mad River* was put ashore by a vicious storm in Barbados. I was distraught until it was confirmed that Dick and Pat had escaped OK but I understand that although the ship has been recovered, there are considerable repairs to be done. It all makes you ponder a bit doesn't it? There but for the Grace of God.

Fresh fruit and veg lasted quite well really, without refrigeration.... Apart from the fruit and veg, I've now been living on ship's stores for the past six weeks, keeping a record of what needs replacing... water is pumped into 2 litre containers when needed, so I can accurately monitor what's happening... More details to follow. Take good care of yourselves! And All the Best for 2004!

(Received) Fri 02/01/2004/ 23:05
Subject: Joy and Disbelief

David, It is unbelievable that you and your own boat have got all the way to Brazil. I bet when you first put the canoes in the river at Wickham Market you never thought you would one day, all alone, sail across the world to South America. We are bursting with admiration for you and I only wish my parents were still alive today, they would be absolutely thrilled to think their grandson had achieved so much. A doctor in practice for many years, trained at a top world-famous hospital, a qualified micro-light pilot; a qualified yachtmaster; and a lone sail boat sailor crossing the South Atlantic to Brazil!!!! I can't get over it. And a damn fast swimmer too! COO! Haven't your children something to crow about! It is a great relief to know that you are safely tied up to a bit of real land instead of having many miles under you.
Heaps and heaps of love. **Mother.**

Text message sent (on a damaged mobile phone) at 1815 hrs 13th January 2004
"5 mins ago ship struck by lightning. All electrics u/s but ship and crew intact. Strong smell of burning but luckily no fire now. Will need a few days to sort out. Love"
and later.
"two electrical fires in cabin had self-extinguished. All electronics burnt out. Muscles ache 'cos I got hit too. Feel shaky but OK. Love"

Fri 16/01/2004 10:58
Subject: Nasty Whizzbang

Some of you know already but three days ago, while at anchor tucked tight in a bay under the hills of 'Cow Island', in another afternoon rainstorm, there was a colossal 'CRACK!', so loud it blew your senses, with extreme bright light both in and outside the cabin; it is impossible in words to describe how unspeakably VIOLENT it was... Immediately noticed the strong smell of burning in the cabin, smoke detector screaming at me, and grasped that we'd had a direct hit by lightning.

Interesting how logical one can be even when you're very scared. I remember clearly my first thought was "am I all right?" (answer, "I think, therefore I must be"); next, "forget the smoke, is the ship intact"?, so ripped up the floor boards where the transducers are, to find we are not going to sink immediately (I was going to ram her up the beach if we had been), then, "kill all the electrics, to stop the fire", so threw the two master switches to isolate the batteries, and disabled the bl**dy smoke detector.... "Ah, that's better, less smoke already, I can see roughly where it's coming from, wiring locker under the companionway, have a look, good, no flames now at least".

"Now what do I do?, "let them know you're safe", so quickly texted family... "what do I do now?", as it is obvious the ship has been very badly hurt; then I noticed the cuts on my feet from walking around in all the bits of glass and plastic from burnt fuses etc., picked pieces out of them, and cleaned the floor a bit; but still the foul stink of burnt plastic and rubber insulation material.

I could feel, very close to me, this black well of deep, deep despair, which I knew would disable me unless I was very careful indeed... but it's remarkable how all those years of Onsite Trauma Care experience surface when you need them; go back to basics... you can't do everything, so do what you think you can. And I realised that I'd already bought myself TIME, so that I could begin to plan logically.

So, to cut a very long story short, by assuming EVERYTHING was wrecked, anything that worked was a bonus to smile on; first found that batteries were still alive (though all voltmeters/ammeters were blown)... "Ah, now we are getting somewhere, we have an intact hull, a mast, sails, an engine and (amazingly) two means of producing electricity. Now put some food inside yourself even though you feel so desperately sick, and you're going to have to make yourself rest soon, and keep planning the next stages, to ward off that awful, incapacitating, frightening, terrible black hole of despair just behind your shoulder".

Sun 18/01/2004/ 01:48
Subject: Tough Old Bird

Blimey, but *Tuesday*'s a tough old bird! For the first time since the Nasties happened I've stopped to stand and have a good look at her from ashore. I'm amazed that after only four days of intensive work, this vessel is virtually legally seaworthy and functional again, and she did it all from her own stores and spares! How many modern "plastic fantastic" boats could do that after a direct hit from lightning?...

... And me? Well, I'm getting bits of memory back which I now realise had been missing. Today is the first time I know I'm really 'me' again. I was sure I was OK, but I was wrong, got a few new problems spelling, right letters, wrong order (Spell Check is a wonderful thing), and I keep forgetting where I put things down, but how bad was I before anyway? And my internal clock is completely up the spout, but I think that's hereditary; still can't cope with too many things at once but tomorrow I'm going to see if I can work out a sextant sight or two, without losing patience, that should be a good test.

Hey-Ho, it's supper-time, so I'd better get out the screwdrivers and spanners again to eat it!

Two months later:
Sat 03/04/2004 03:48 Subject:
Start of 2nd Transatlantic

We're ready to go again (at last!)

It's going to be a l-o-n-g but steady trip, "comfort" is the watchword for this next leg of '*Tuesday's Travels*', no drama if I can help it, no records to try to beat, nothing to prove.

The actual course will be dictated by the winds, so the little dots on Shiptrack may meander about a bit, looking for the EASY route, lighter winds if I can.

Don't know the total distance it will be yet, depends on how far south I have to go to find the winds I need, but approx 3000 miles to St Helena, so possibly around 4-6 weeks (but be prepared for a lot longer, if necessary). She's loaded like a ruddy fruit and veg ship again, food and water for six months if I'm careful with it....

Not really looking forward to the first two to three days, to be honest, what with re-finding my sea legs, avoiding other shipping and having to be close-hauled to get offshore, but once well offshore the risk of encountering other ships should be much less and by then I should be settling into "sea-mode"; there should be a nice moon for first few nights as well....

I'll keep in touch as best I can, but remember, NO NEWS IS STILL GOOD NEWS!

Fri 16/04/2004 22:25
Subject: South, out of the Tropics now.

Greetings from the Southern Ocean! It's already a lot colder at night, but what beautiful night skies! Southern Cross high in the sky, the Clouds of Magellan, and can still just see part of the upside down Plough on the northern horizon.

Still pounding/plodding close-hauled southwards, at present under double-reefed mainsail and stay-sail only, trying find the balance between reasonable progress to windward against the Tradewind and comfort, hoping to get a decent slant at St Helena... A bit limited at times by a re-sprain of the right elbow, was literally single-handed for a day or two, it is improving slowly I think.

How many lunatics do you know who have crossed the Tropic of Capricorn at sea THREE times in one day? My excuse is that it was due to tacking to work the wind shifts on 14/4/04...

...There are a lot of single-handers down here in the South, I've met nine of them, two by radio only, all of them seemed very sane indeed to me, which is a bit worrying, maybe I'm not fit to judge. (Ah! Except two French sailors, who were definitely 'peculiar')...

Had one or two fights on board here, one time *Tuesday* wouldn't let me get the mainsail down to reef, but I did it eventually after a very personal battle. The problem is alloy sail slides in an alloy track, only the top two, but they jammed very firmly; they're smothered in grease now, until the next time.

Meantime the ship is heading resolutely straight at the Antarctic until we can get a favourable wind.

Fri 07/05/2004 22:55
Subject: St Helena

Wow! What lovely people here! Lovely warm welcome from the Port Authority on the VHF, but assistant harbourmaster Bryan suggests not to swim today as a large shark was seen yesterday in Rupert's Bay (about 400 yards away), said to be a bit unusual on this side of the island...

...I LIKE this place, no "fifty quid" birds but wild Minah birds strolling around mimicking everything.

But first a bit of a recap... after the rough stuff it calmed down a lot and settled to a very pleasant swinging ride at 5-7 knots, in comfort and peace, still 2-3 metre seas, but kinder. The stunning view of the eclipse of the new moon when it reddened and dimmed, allowing the myriads of stars of the southern sky to come out in their full glory, on a cloudless, crystal clear night... that's something I could never forget.

Then as the sun set on Wednesday night 5/5/04, just managed to see (at 30 miles) the mountains of St Helena, so hove to at about 1 knot overnight to make sure of approaching in daylight...

...Nearly overshot the anchorage here, bowling along at 6-7 knots, I didn't realise how much ground we were covering and how tiny the island is, and Jamestown is so much smaller and hidden away than I expected. Hove to again to sort ourselves out, then tacked in very slowly under mainsail only, to anchor (under advice from Bryan by radio) in 19 metres (62ft) of amazingly clear water, 200 yards off the rocks at 1430 hrs, 6/5/04, that's 60 metres of chain to get back on board again next week sometime...3137 miles in 33 days, although not quick, was mostly comfortable, in spite of over 90% of it being close-hauled. One other yacht here, a charming American/Canadian couple, been here two weeks, and love it too much to leave!

And the rocks of the headland themselves are sighing and whistling every 10-12 seconds, like a sleeping giant, as the mighty ocean breathes in and out; it's due to a small 'blow-hole' in the rocks here, where the air gets trapped and compressed with each swell to make a noise like a vast flute, fascinating to listen to, as it seems to dream IN ITS SLEEP!

Going ashore at the landing-place is fun, have to time it well, with the swells, get it right and it's easy and elegant, get it wrong and you're going to break something and get VERY wet!

And the Royal Mail Ship *St Helena* came in this morning, everything (except the passengers of course, who do it by motor boat) comes ashore by lighter, using the ship's derricks, and you should see the skill of the crane operators ashore, plucking large containers out of the lighters at the peak of each wave, very professional indeed! There's so much more, but enough for now!

Sun 20/06/2004 03:07
Subject: 36th day at sea (and 3700 miles) since St Helena
Low battery voltage again, and virtually no wind, means having to run the engine again unfortunately, but at least it means I can play on this laptop while the batteries are being re-charged.
Still mile after mile of Portuguese Men-of War, every 100 yards or so, I had absolutely no idea there could possibly be so many of them!...

...I realised the other day that I have spent the last Christmas Day, New Year's Day, Easter, my wedding anniversary, and now my birthday, actually AT SEA in these last few months, not sure what you can read into that, but it's another Useless Fact!

I had hoped for a gentle wafting breeze from a favourable direction on my birthday, and the forecast was for 15 knots from the port quarter. Yippee! I thought, trouble is it all arrived in one lump...a full-blooded force 6+ for several hours, which was uncomfortable as I was carrying a little too much sail, and getting thrown around fairly, before the seas sorted themselves out a bit, but we covered 35 miles in 5 hours, so I can't really complain. One benefit of that wind is that it has retaught me the definition of the time you finally decide to reef – it's invariably 15 minutes BEFORE the time the wind drops again, having proved its point and got its way.

So we're now 400 miles from the Azores, in light winds still (but that should change in the next 48 hours), we've got through into the westerly air stream for the moment at least...

Not sure which island we're going to at first as it depends on how the weather looks, but hoping to settle for a short holiday in Horta by the end of this month, several bits of maintenance to do, and I want a good look at that lower rudder bearing before pressing on to England, looks like a good excuse for diving, if the Portuguese Men-of War will allow! Meantime, take good care of yourselves too,

Fri 25/06/2004 01:48
Dropped anchor inside HORTA harbour, FAIAL Island, AZORES, at 1410 GMT Wednesday, June 23rd, 4092 miles in 40 days, which includes crossing the Doldrums and cutting through the Horse Latitudes, and the ship and I are still on speaking terms too.

Mind you we've been very lucky with the weather, considerable help from both the Transatlantic and the Italian Maritime Mobile networks finding our way round adverse or light winds as every opportunity presented itself. It wasn't all sweetness and light though.

First there was a worry with the fresh water quality, a nasty sludge appearing in it... But I found that if it was given a chance, the sludge could be made to precipitate out if the water kept still enough... as usual, the simplest answer was best... Certain small bottles of fizzy drinks have a sort of a valve on them, instead of a cap... so cut a whole in in the bottom of a suitably fitted bottle... up-end it, fill it through the new hole and hang it upside down in the cockpit for 24 hours, in a place where it's free to swing, then briefly open the valve at the lower screw-cap end and all the gunk falls out onto the cockpit floor, leaving beautifully clear water fit for drinking, still in the bottle, ready for draining, and that's the stuff I've been living on for the last 5+ weeks...

...The second problem was a worry that really ate into me, and disrupted sleep, even made me collect all the film I've been making of this trip and add it into a waterproof container in the Panic Grab Bag (for the sudden sinkings). A gradually increasing 'clunk' had become more and more obvious...seemed to be in the very tail-end of the ship somewhere, and eventually it revealed itself to be coming from the lower rudder bearing at the bottom of the skeg, about five feet under the water surface, no possibility of inspecting it (and consider all those millions of Portuguese Men-of-War in the sea) even if I had felt that adventurous.

Had to nurse the ship carefully over the next ten days... the worry was that if it failed, the whole rudder would be wrung off sideways, with a distinct possibility of taking part of the hull with it, certainly concentrates the mind a bit... so, regretfully, decided to give Flores a miss and diverted 130 miles more downwind to Horta, to ease the strain on the rudder, a foul night in 25 knot winds, grey drizzle, then heavy rain blinding the radar, visibility less than 1 mile, awkward, steep, uncomfortable 3 metre waves, and a dramatic temperature drop, all caused a miserable few hours while approaching the island...

...But things improved just before dawn, and the final landfall was sunny and clear, and what a dramatic landfall it was too! The first sight was the top of the volcano of Pico appearing ABOVE the clouds ahead.

Couldn't face the thought of marinas etc., so anchored in the old traditional place in the harbour itself, near a thin scattering of other foreign yachts. Local official in a powerful rubber boat politely said that I shouldn't really anchor out there...but when I said I'd come a long way and was feeling somewhat tired and I didn't want to make any mistakes now, he agreed (only slightly reluctantly).

It's lucky I didn't have to explain how quickly I made a miraculous recovery in the next half hour and was able to spend nearly an hour and a half swimming in the cold water, scrubbing the topsides and knocking seven bells out of that rudder bearing to try to reproduce that 'clunk' again (bruised my foot as I karate kicked the rudder, and on one dive stayed down a bit too long... banged my head on the propeller in the rapid ascent, that's one stupid mistake I won't make again). I'd got too cold too, like a fool.

The hot cup of soup afterwards tasted wonderful! Only got moderate sleep in a rising wind, with the anchor chain grinding away on the rocky bottom, not used to the gentler motion too.

And so today we up-anchored and came in to clear Customs etc. (very friendly and pleasant officials here) but because it's so crowded at present... we're rafted up with other boats against the marina wall, nice neighbours, very friendly and quiet, Americans and English, good atmosphere though it's been cold, grey, rainy, and blowing hard.

Ship's water tanks now emptied and flushed through and refilled, took a long time, minor maintenance and cleaning since. Even though it feels so COLD I'll sleep well tonight!

Wed 21/07/2004 22.57
Subject Leaving Horta soon?

Sadly Fin had to fly home yesterday to work (otherwise she can't afford me). Once again the ship felt empty and cold for the first 24 hours but now I'm busy preparing to set sail again it's not quite so hard.

I've had a wonderful time here, and I'd like to return some time to explore some more of this group of nine islands. One thing I've enjoyed on this trip so far is comparing and contrasting all the islands: Culatra (Portugal), Porto Santo, Madeira, Graciosa, Lanzarote, Sao Vincenti (Cap Verdes), Itaparica, St. Helena, and now Faial (Azores).

Although on paper it may seem a simple journey back to England from here, I have the usual pre-voyage concerns and worries, but they're much more in perspective these days. I still think the optimum time to spend in one place is about one week, then you never get out of sea-going mode.

I'll not sail tonight, but I am considering possibly doing so tomorrow. The ship is all set, checks/repairs /improvements done, fresh fruit 'n' veg stowed, fresh-water tanks full (with CLEAN this time)...

...Anticipating 1300-1400 miles to Plymouth, depending on the wind direction and strength, so expecting about 2-3 weeks, hopefully less, we'll see.

Sat 07/08/2004 11:33
Subject: Plymouth

Exactly one year, one month, and one day from leaving here, we're back again. 14600 miles have passed the keel between times, but it's a well-known fact that The Almighty does not count those days actually spent at sea, so I myself am only about five months older.

The last night (5-6/8/04) at sea (as expected) was murder, with ships, fishing boats, invisible yachts, and vaguely determined tidal currents leaving no room for sleep; none at all, and then it started to drizzle in the cold wind, with rotten visibility for a few hours as a small front went through, thank heaven for cups of tea and bars of chocolate (a LOT of chocolate!).

England showed up where I last left it, Lands End and the Lizard lighthouse, a strangely moving and emotional moment. I wondered how I would react and now I know.

Dawdled for a few hours with a backed stay-sail to slow her down a bit and make an easy approach to Plymouth in the clearer air behind the drizzly weather-front. 1415 miles from Horta in 12 days.

Nice cheery welcome on the fuel pontoon (my first stop, as it's an easier berth to come alongside when I'm a bit out of practice at the close-in stuff), equally pleasant Dockmaster, not in the least bit fazed by my mentioning that for the same cost as one day here I had a WEEK in Horta and more than a MONTH in Brazil, with the same facilities; chuckles all round.

The Customs said to the Dockmaster over the radio. "Does he look British?" "OK then, just see his passport is reasonable, and that'll do." The Dockmaster says that's the very the first time he's ever been asked to be a deputy Customs and Immigrations Officer. He enjoyed it!...

...Lounging on the deck chatting in the evening sunshine. WONDERFUL tasting fish 'n' chips in the dark, sitting on the seawall by the Mayflower Steps, just where I'd eaten The Last Supper a year last July. And everyone speaks ENGLISH!...

...Still another 500 miles or so to do before we're home, but absolutely no rush now. Stay well and prepare yourselves for the most boring home-video you could imagine ("that's a wave; ooh look, there's another one"), 18 hours of it. I recommend you go into hiding, or leave the country now.

Tue 24/08/2004
Subject: Finally home at Orford
Dear Everybodies

Three days of gentle unwinding at anchor in the River Orwell in thundery showers and gusts of up to 40 knots, but we were in sheltered waters now, and felt safe and secure enough to enjoy it; still had to move anchorages twice to stay in the lee of the land more effectively though.

Lovely warm sunny force 4 to sail round along the coast to the (potentially) dangerous River Ore entrance, in close company with Chris and Gill on *Lady of Deben*. I had forgotten what an exceptionally beautiful coastline this area is, wide range of birdlife etc. All this part of the world needs to be PERFECT, is clean, transparent seawater instead of the 'soup' we float our boats in here, plus the climate of Itaparica. (Oh, and the price structure of Bahia, Brazil).

A very special moment when I dropped anchor in Abraham's Bosom, behind Havergate Island, 14 months and 14960 miles since leaving the same spot last year. It's so peaceful here, flat water, high cloud, birdsong, and distant views of Orford castle and the lighthouse on Orfordness; a quiet night and a good sleep.

Finally the last three miles up to Orford itself: to be waylaid by a veritable armada of other local yachts, all dressed overall with flags, and sounding their hooters and sirens as they fell into formation astern to welcome dear old *Tuesday* home; the rows of happy faces on the quay, waving flags and shouting greetings to us. Anglia Television was there too. I confess it brought a tear to my eyes for a moment, as it was all so overwhelming.

Interview with the TV people, speech and presentation at the Clubhouse, when I gave the remains of *Tuesday's* old burgee to the club (who want to frame it!) And in return I was given a new one to replace it...

... And I'm feeling a fraud because I met several other people on my adventure who would think nothing of the trip I've just completed, and would be surprised to find such a fuss being made of yet another safe voyage, but it wasn't my idea to have such a welcome, and it makes me feel proud and tall to accept it from my friends...

...And the main thing I've learnt from *Tuesday's* Atlantic Wanderings, quite simply the immense value of one's own family (which includes those very special friends I count as being part of my family); the support and reassurance from them felt like a physical prop, carrying me through some nasty times, helping me to make the right decisions at the right times; it was a sensation I had not expected, but was so very glad of when I needed it...

Thanks for all your help, each one of you, in different ways, over the past few years, but now, sadly, this series of 'Dear Everybodies' must come to a. (full stop)

Please keep in touch! Grateful Thanks and lots of love, from,
Tuesday'n'me.

At the end of his story David asks the question: "would I do it again?" And answers. "Yes, if I didn't wish to stay in the UK with my family. The rules out there are completely honest and fair, but totally binding. I'm still just as timorous as I was when I started out, but I'm a bit wiser now about how to cope with it."

He then adds some 'Relevant sayings', which 'seemed to help at times.' These include:

'Never doubt your motives if they lead you to something you really want to do...

...You may question the results, you may not succeed, you may even give it up, but at least try as hard as you can to make it work first. You'll regret it for the rest of your days otherwise.

In the future you'll be more disappointed by the things you didn't do, than by the things you did.

Decide what you really want to do, then decide what you are willing to risk

or to lose to achieve it, then (hardest of all) actually get up and go and do it.
A mountain is only as high as the person who is climbing it.
Courage isn't about not being afraid. It's about understanding that something else is more important than being afraid.
The greatest fear is due to Fear itself, not due to the reality of the situation.'

And finally, written on a wash-room wall in the Canaries, from an ancient comment, (possibly with the single-hander in mind?) he found this:

> "Happy is the Man, and happy he alone
> He who can call this day his own.
> He, who secure within, can say
> "Tomorrow do thy worst,
> For I have LIVED today!"

19. The Generation Game

Ever since my own childhood, indeed before that distant era, successive generations of young people have learned to sail on our river. They may have been taught by their parents or older siblings, listened to the wisdom of one of the Brinkleys, or benefited from the more systematic training programmes introduced by Ray Maunder and built upon by Liz Feibusch and others. For many of them it has made a mark on their lives and has prompted wider experiences and adventures at sea.

The stories that follow illustrate that influence over a period of more than 25 years from 1992 onwards. All these people have been involved in one way or another, often significantly, with OSC training courses during that time.

Fiona Cox (Fiona Hitchcock as she was then, or 'Fone' to many) did a sailing course with Ray Maunder in about 1984. She remembers Stephen Johnston as responsible for getting her 'single-handedly through the test', describing herself as 'clueless', which is emphatically not how I remember her, either as an instructor, later, with Liz Feibusch, or as a dangerous competitor in single-handed Mirror races for the Quantz Cup, or as the girl who went overboard with a sheath knife to clear a fouled mooring line from my propeller. In 1990 Fiona was aboard the *Malcolm Miller* for a Tall Ships Race which whetted her appetite for big ships and proper voyages.

So when it came to a Gap Year she knew she wanted to sail somewhere. Her father had an acquaintance in Gibraltar who knew a yacht skipper who was looking for crew so off she went, more or less into the unknown, getting a one-way ticket to Naples.

'In 1992 I took part in the Grand Columbus Regatta – a race involving a myriad of different boats from the largest tall ships to modern racing yachts. My vessel was unusual in its historical design – a 55ft lateen-rigged felucca with bowsprit, owned and skippered by an Italian who had previously taken her to the Antarctic in 1970. Her name was *San Giuseppe Due*, Italian-built but registered in the UK and sailing under the British flag. She was fitted with an icebreaker bow which increased her weight to 40 tonnes so we were very slow. At first, while in dry dock, the crew consisted of myself, the skipper Giovanni and his wife Esme, who was English. We were joined for the Atlantic crossing by her daughter Francesca, who was in her early twenties and doing research on ancient maritime instruments.

Giovanni was a stickler for maintaining the history of the boat and to that end we had limited modern equipment – a fridge, a radar, an echo sounder and a radio. It is a testament to his immense navigational skills that we sighted the expected landfall within a couple of miles after a transatlantic voyage from the Canaries to Puerto Rico using nothing but a sextant, compass and a chart, echoing the true spirit of Columbus. Because Francesca was researching ancient instruments alongside the daily sextant readings we were also using quadrants and a kamal, an ancient Arabian instrument. They were surprisingly accurate!

With three more Italian men on board we were a crew of seven for the Trans-Atlantic voyage working a strict watch system of four hours on, eight hours off, which we would continue for the 30 days at sea. The days were broken up by a small beer on a Sunday and champagne every 1000 miles. Otherwise we concentrated on trying to catch fish (flying fish would often helpfully land on deck) and watching the pilot fish who thought our dark hull was a whale and stayed with us just off the stern for about two weeks. Our efforts were concentrated on food most of the time, trying to make each day's menu different from the one before whilst eking out our fresh meat, fruit and vegetables for as long as possible. Bread we made daily, and it fell to me – a task that I soon began to enjoy. Water was also an issue as the tanks were old neoprene, so we sterilised with a splash of whisky, some more than others, but it was revolting if not flavoured a bit. Showers were on the deck with a bucket of sea water – a not entirely satisfactory wash but better than nothing.

The working language on the boat was Italian, but Francesca and her mother spoke to me in English when required. My watch companion was a lovely man called Giovanni (known as Giovannini – or little Giovanni – since he was much shorter than the skipper). He spoke virtually no English so we used a mix of French, Spanish and Italian to get by and became good friends by the end. He was a sweet, gentle man from Sorrento and looked rather like Manuel from Fawlty Towers! There were many exciting moments in the trip and equally many long dull days. The work on the boat was physically demanding – to change or trim a sail the yard had to be brought down to the deck. At 18 I could lower a one tonne yard alone by the end of the trip using simple pulleys and effort.

Our journey started in Italy near Naples, fitting out for the trip in dry dock. We were there seven weeks where I quickly tried to learn some Italian as this was our main language on board. We then sailed to Corsica and Sardinia preparing for the voyage before making our way to Cadiz for the start of the regatta. From there we went to the Canaries for last minute preparations. The main voyage was from Canaries to Puerto Rico, where we were so late we only had a few days to recover before the next leg. Crew changed here; we lost some really experienced people and their replacements proved to be woefully useless, so our new crew of eight was really four active members. There was now one other girl but she and her companions were so sea-sick that they didn't contribute at all.

From Puerto Rico we went to Bermuda, where, on June 21st, we experienced a mini hurricane whilst in port. It hit at 0230 and we were all out in driving rain in our pyjamas doubling up all our mooring lines and springs. We still managed to mangle the wind vane of the vessel in front of us – an ice breaker bow makes short work of things in that kind of wind. However, there was no damage to us and we were ready to do the next leg – to New York. Dad had managed to perfectly time a business trip so I had a lovely reunion with them in a very smart Manhattan apartment – the doorman was horrified at how filthy I was on arrival but my first power shower for months proved effective! On July 4th we had a grand parade of sail which was chaotic. Our skipper was nearly hysterical having to go full astern several times to avoid other ships in the fog.

We then changed crew again and sailed up to Boston before leaving the regatta and going on to St John's Newfoundland. Here we met a lot of fog and I learnt how to creep into a port in thick fog using nothing but a chart and an echo sounder and some very alert crew. During this time the skipper became increasingly anxious about the return leg and there were constant delays to our departure; sadly I didn't bring the boat home to Liverpool, the intended end of the voyage, but instead jumped ship and flew home. I had been away for about six months. As a parent now myself, I find it hard to imagine launching any of my own children off into the unknown without at least having met who they were going with, and I am all the more grateful to them for the encouragement.

It was an extraordinary experience throughout. A journey of self-discovery, resilience and patience. Living in a very small space with people that you don't know is a skill; you can't afford to fall out, and there is no space to be on your own. Every landfall was a source of immense relief, just to blow off some steam and get away from the boat and its crew for a little while.

I look back on the voyage, however, with great pride that I managed to cope with it all, even speaking a foreign language very badly. I learnt most of it by chatting to the night watchman at the yard in Torre Del Greco – almost definitely of Mafia descent – so I developed a very curious accent, or so I was told. Above all I learnt a great deal about the beauty of the open ocean, thousands of miles from the light pollution of land.'

Dan Spinney was 19 when he took part in the 1999 TransARC, sailing from Antigua to Bermuda, then to the Azores, and back to Plymouth during the summer of his Gap year before University. Eight years earlier he had gained his National Certificate at the end of the OSC Training Course led by Ray Maunder. There is also photographic evidence that he assisted Liz Feibusch as a junior instructor towards the end of his time at school. When he was

16, and still at Oundle, he sailed in the Tall Ships event from Rostock to St Petersburg aboard *Excelsior*, a restored Lowestoft sailing smack. Sailing, it seems, had cast its spell on Dan from an early age.

After some months of work experience in the City and a spell in a Swiss Ski resort, he found a berth on *Ocean Venture*, a schooner-rigged Ocean 60, and flew in to Antigua early on May 5th, much impressed by his first sight of the island and its surrounding reefs as the aircraft came in to land. The heat that night as he lay in a cramped bunk was less enjoyable and he was impatient to be at sea. His three fellow crew members, Charles, Pete and Roger, and the professional charter skipper, Ken, were older by 15 or 20 years, but Dan apparently had no trouble being part of the team, finding Pete, a Welsh fire-fighter, the most compatible.

They were under way for Bermuda the next day, a five-day voyage, sometimes tedious in calm weather, dogged at times by signs of oil-leaks and other minor problems but at least free of sea-sickness, which Dan never mentions again. The realisation that there were a full seven kilometres of ocean depth under the keel suddenly struck home. Sometimes the wind did blow and the angle of heel was a threat to the bolognese sauce Dan was striving to make with the stove at 45 degrees to the cabin floor. He actually enjoyed the ship's rolling motion with twin headsails set, especially when she reached a top speed of nine knots, averaging six or seven. Bermuda seemed even more attractive than Antigua during a six-day stay before the official start of the event. 'When I retire, I'm living here', he wrote in his journal. He enjoyed the friendliness of the local people, and the cuisine ashore but he was also keen to get out 'into the real Atlantic'. With repairs to several deficiencies they were ready for the noon Start on May 19th.

The 12-day passage to the Azores was either too busy, or too monotonous to warrant comment, apart from the sight of dolphins on the second day and some miserable weather with very poor visibility further on. He was hoping for whales – but they came later. One poor flying fish, having landed on deck, was eaten for lunch but judged plain and lacking taste. Sailing through three time zones they sighted the south shore of Faial in the very early dawn of May 31st – 'lovely to set eyes on land again.' The volcanic cones of the Azores, Pico in particular, disappearing into the clouds made an even greater impression than the Bermuda landfall.

They were in Horta or visiting Pico for the best part of a week. The sailing world often provides unexpected encounters and Dan was not the only young Orford sailor to have sailed the Atlantic that summer. Walking down the street he was hailed by Polly Bielecka who had 'come straight from Antigua' and was 'off to Antibes tomorrow – beautiful boat she's on, 80 foot schooner, really nice.'

Dan had more time to spare and was entrusted with painting his boat's pictures to join the many others along the harbour side.

Short passages followed to other island ports, Madelena, on Pico, Vela on Sao Jorge, Angre do Heroisme on Terceira and Ponta Delgado on Sao Miguel. From this point the last leg of the race was due to start on June 19th. Soon after arrival and not for the first or last time, Dan 'was up the mast again – nothing to it. A good 60ft up that rear mast.' Rather him than me. Four more crew joined the boat, including one – Ann, who knew Orford's Liz Feibusch.

Dan still has his plots of the last leg home, neatly marked, as befits an engineer, on graph paper. He shows the courses of the remaining, only five, entrants, to the north of the Great Circular Course; *Ocean Wave* taking the outer curve 'to catch westerlies after roughly 350 miles' then straight to Plymouth. Winds were elusive, and engine use was apparently permitted and used by all from time to time. On the second afternoon out, however – something special happened.

'WHALES!! The experience of a lifetime, really exhilarating. We think they were Fin whales, not seen a huge amount in the Azores, 40-50ft long, absolutely beautiful! They must have been just a few metres from me, and they stuck around for half an hour or so. Got loads of photos, after some great shots of dolphins this morning. This will always stay with me. It is the most amazing feeling. Fins are the second largest animal species in the world (after Blue whales) and I could have touched them with the boat-hook!!'

Two days later there were further sightings, one quite close, probably a sperm whale, and others further off jumping clear of the water. Dan wished he had been 'closer, but not too close.' By contrast somewhere south of Lands End they were in 'typically British Summer Weather, rain pelting down'. *Ocean Wave* crossed the line off Plymouth breakwater at 0920 BST on June 29th, which was also the Skipper's birthday. He was serenaded, twice, with everyone in 'high spirits.' Finally, without waiting for the official Party on the next evening, they set off with a reduced crew for a 24-hour sail to St Peter Port, Guernsey and a last passage back to the Hamble. Dan relished the speed through the Alderney Race, 13 knots over the ground, with seven knots of tidal current. Into the bargain he had achieved his Competent Crew's certificate and was hauled to the masthead yet again to retrieve the 'yellow duster', which someone, allegedly Ann, had managed to get lodged up there. Reading between the lines of his journal, Dan had certainly had an experience which would stay with him for ever.

Of course this has not been the end of Dan's sailing. I personally owe him a great debt for the crucial help he gave me and *Quantz* from Helsingborg to Karlskrona, round the south of Sweden in 2003. After University, he and Tom Scorer, an OSC contemporary, raced regularly in the Solent with *Born Slippy* a Prime 38. A young family and career demands may have cut down activity for the time being, but, as with his sister Hatty's children, there are plenty of signs that they will continue into another generation of more than 'competent' crews.

Florence Barrow, like Fiona Hitchcock and Dan Spinney, has been both pupil and instructor on the Training Courses at OSC. In her case the spirit of adventure did not take her across the Atlantic but involved an exceptional Cross Channel voyage and fund-raising effort. This is her story:

'I have only sailed a Laser One dinghy at Orford apart from one occasion when a friend and I strayed to France. In the summer of 2006, when we were 16, we set our sights on bigger seas and decided that the English Channel, from Dover to Calais, would make a good adventure in aid of the charity RYA Sailability.

Having not sailed a Laser at sea before (except on a lovely training day out to Orford Haven Buoy, where we were becalmed) this was an unexpectedly strenuous challenge. On the morning of the sail there was a force 5-6 blowing and even launching the dinghies in a heavy swell nearly overwhelmed us. I had naively imagined that Dover would offer an equivalent of Orford's gentle slipway; we would simply launch and be on our way. It took us ages to get the boats off their trolleys and I was ashamed at how unprofessional we seemed to the rescue crew we had persuaded to look after us. I imagined the mutterings of: "can they actually sail?", as I tried to hook the out-haul onto the boom with the boat trying to career away from me. Later, my mother disclosed that she did not even think we would set off.

Luckily, once under sail, I felt more in control of my craft and the Dover cliffs were soon behind us. I am a passionate rather than a technical sailor; the boat nosed through enormous waves, battering my face and rendering my glasses useless – contact lenses are now a must, lesson learned – but I knew we were going to make it. Container ships loomed large, and it was up to our rescue boat to keep up with us and point us away from the shipping channels.

We made it across in three hours 20 minutes. Once we were out of Dover Harbour we were on a single broad reach, a Laser's favourite stretch. With the dagger-board lifted, the bow climbed out of the water and the whole boat hummed on the plane the whole way across.

Approaching the beach at Calais, we were met by French security patrol boats who demanded to know from where we had come. We pointed at Dover behind us, which they refused to believe until we presented our passports. It was a brilliant sail and we celebrated in a local restaurant before making the journey back.

Since then, I do have something to confess. Unlike the impressive adventurers, I only really want to sail at Orford now. It is a magic combination of the club's amateurish charm, the muddy estuary and the memories of an idyllic childhood learning to sail or instructing the next generation. It manages to entice me back year after year – like the swallows returning to the same place – there's nowhere else I would rather be on the water – and off the slipway!'

This 'confession' does not tell the whole truth about 'Flo' Barrow's appetite for adventure. When she left university in 2012 she was not impressed by the graduate opportunities on offer and applied for a job as Postmistress with the Antarctic Heritage Trust, which looks after British historical sites in Antarctica. With three others she spent the 'summer' season, presumably our winter months, at Port Lockroy, a sheltered harbour on the west coast of the Antarctic Peninsula. Since 1990 it has been maintained as a museum full of Antarctic treasures as well as an official post office visited by cruise ships. It was, she says: 'an utterly beautiful place to live and work – four people and over 2000 penguins on a small island. The only frustration was that we were not given a boat.' But I dare say it was not a bad addition to her CV.

When it comes to 'instructing the next generation' the author of the next story in this series, Suzy Cooper, is not only a product of OSC's training course and a past assistant instructor, but has achieved all the qualifications enabling her to take on the responsibility of Chief Instructor herself while still at the undergraduate stage in her University studies. The young people who have been lucky enough to attend one of her courses, and her assistants, will testify to the combination of expertise, quiet confidence and enthusiasm she has brought to the job. I suspect that the experience related below has played its part in her development. It is also a salutary reminder of how easily and quickly things can go wrong at sea even when a fine sailing ship is in charge of a very experienced skipper.

TS *Astrid* July 14th – July 24th 2013

'Greenwich Borough was due to host the Tall Ships Regatta for the first time in 2014. As a part of this, there were 30 spaces on board one of the participating ships to be given to young people from the host borough, as trainees for the voyage. A year prior to this, the local council were looking for two people to go aboard a different ship, with the intention of them coming back and going into schools and youth clubs to encourage people to sign up to these 30 spaces. I was one of these two people as a volunteer at a nearby sailing charity (the AHOY centre) and a resident in Greenwich.

So, a couple weeks after turning 15, I boarded the *TS Astrid* in Southampton for a two-week trip to Cherbourg via Kinsale along with 25 other young people from Spain, France, Ireland, Belgium and the Netherlands. We spent ten days learning how the ship worked – climbing the rigging, plotting course, navigation, cooking, cleaning. We slowly made our way along the South Coast, and then made the crossing to Cork and down to Kinsale.

Here we were joining a flotilla of boats as part of a festival they were hosting before making the final leg of our journey to Cherbourg. On the morning of July 24th, with the wind picking up, we began to motor out of Oysterhaven Bay. As we reached the narrowest point of water, the engine cut out and we were left completely under the control of the elements.

The scramble to try and release and set sails to regain control and steering of the boat lasted less than ten minutes before we were instructed to get life jackets on and head to the poop deck at the back of the ship. Our captain knew exactly when it became too late, and we heard the Mayday call go out. We were told to sit together on the deck, and brace ourselves. The ship hit the rocks towards the bow on its starboard side. We jolted, hard, and the noise ran through us.

This is where we stayed, holding onto fixed parts of the boat, and onto each other as we rocked. One way and water would come spraying over the side, and the other we would tense as we grounded further. It's a funny thing – you would expect us to be shouting and screaming, especially as we were so young, but in fact the opposite was true. We were all completely silent, communicating only through scared but hopeful glances and reassuring hand squeezes. In some ways this uncertain time before the rescue services arrived felt like hours, but in other ways I had barely processed what was going on before it was already over.

A RNLI rib was able to make it to the side of the ship. The boat would be level with us and then suddenly metres below from the rocking of the ship and the building waves. A crew member, Uldrich, and a member of the rescue team stood on either side of us and threw us into the lifeboat. They managed to get 12 of us off the sinking ship before the rib was dragged away again. The remaining 18 had to jump into a life-raft that was then picked up by the rescue teams. Our captain, Peter, was the last off and as the rest of the crew sat huddled in the life-raft, he kept his head out and watched as 'his second wife' went down.

We were passed to a yacht, appropriately named *The Spirit of Oysterhaven*, where mild hypothermia and shock set in, as I threw up everything in my stomach and was wrapped in sleeping bags and foil blankets. We were told the incident had gone out over radio and that we needed to inform loved ones that we were all okay. We took turns sharing the one surviving phone as we approached Kinsale Yacht Club.

By the time we arrived the kitchen had been opened and hot food and drinks were waiting for us, the nearby hotel had bought clean blankets and towels, local people were turning up with bags of clothes, toothbrushes, underwear, offering up beds and sofas for us to stay on. Things I wouldn't have even considered us needing, but suddenly became vital, were provided en masse by people I had never met before. I've never seen a more concrete example of selfless, genuine, human kindness and compassion.

We stayed with local people that night, and in a hostel in Dublin the next night, after visiting our various embassies to get emergency passports. We had a session of group counselling, had takeaway pizza, and flew home the next day.

It was later found that, on a previous voyage, one of the fuel tanks had been accidentally filled with water by a trainee. Although the tank had been pumped out, the incident was never logged properly and obviously some water had remained. It would be easy to be angry about this, but the person one could blame was the person most affected by our sinking. Overall, the whole thing just taught me that mistakes are made and people are kind.'

Joe Iliff is yet another who like Fiona, Dan and Suzy, gained inspiration from a Tall Ships experience. In 2010, just before starting his medical studies at UCL he sailed on the Jubilee Sailing Trust's *Lord Nelson* from Hartlepool to Zeebrugge and back to London, assisting and instructing disabled crew members, for whom the ship is specially designed and equipped. Hoisting wheelchairs to the masthead was a recognised operation!

Clearly the taste for sailing adventure and the training of successive generations is the theme of this chapter. Until quite recently responsibility for the organisation of OSC training courses was held by Sheena Barrow, the mother of Florence, whose story was told above. But adventure appeals to all generations as Sheena's own special voyage also shows.

'In 1967 I first crossed the Atlantic in order to arrive at the British Virgin Islands where I lived for several years working on a hydroponics farm. After a missed opportunity to sail back to the UK, I had a persistent dream to one day join a boat and race across.

Mark Twain advised that it is always best to try to realise these dreams and not let regret overtake you. Armed with this advice, and fast approaching my 70th birthday, I signed up as a crew member aboard *Challenger 1*, a 70 foot steel boat ruggedly designed for world circumnavigation. Along with 12 other volunteers from all walks of life, *Challenger 1* was entered to race the

ARC from the Canaries to St Lucia.

St Lucia is the birthplace of Derek Walcott, one of my favourite Caribbean writers, and I set my sights on returning to this beautiful part of the world under sail, and before I was too old to qualify!

We formed three watches, and led by a professional skipper and mate we were rapidly transformed into a hard-working, efficient crew. *Challenger 1* offered few comforts or modern systems. We physically steered every nautical mile, all sails were hoisted manually and we slept in very cramped quarters in hard hammocks. Our 20-day crossing was apparently slow but saw us experience the extremes of a force 10 gale, also some very light, frustrating conditions.

There were many wonderful moments: sighting porpoises, catching fish, sailing in the moonlight. Baking bread and cakes. Listening to music and reading. Best of all surfing foaming waves under a bright blue spinnaker on a sunny day. For me the lowest moments were the dreadful force of the storm with all hands on deck battling to reduce sail and being hurled around mercilessly below.

The sweet taste of success was our landfall and crossing the finishing line at night in a dramatic squall. Imagine our delight to find a small steel band welcoming us along with all those cold Piton beers.'

To come right up to date James Finney has just sailed out of London aboard the Clipper 70 yacht *Zhuhai* to race Round the World. "All being well", as Ralph Brinkley so often used to say, he will return next year with the distinction of being Orford's first circumnavigator under sail – at least so far as I know. His father, Mike Finney, has supplied the background story.

'James began sailing with his parents at the age of one, and as he grew older became less and less impressed by the sedate speed of the family boats. He completed the RYA dinghy course at Orford in 2004, although it was only when the traditional force 7 hit the course on Day Three that he really began to get the buzz from sailing. Subsequent high performance dinghies, not entirely suited to this river perhaps, followed alongside his qualification as a dinghy instructor at OSC. It was this qualification that also got him a job instructing at Melbourne Yacht Club during his gap year travels in Australia.

James qualified as an Ocean Yachtmaster in 2014-5 and started work as a Flotilla Skipper for a holiday company in Greece. He did this for two years, earning further qualifications as a Day Skipper instructor and examiner. In the holiday off-season he built up the sea-miles delivering yachts.

Early in 2019 James applied successfully to be a Mate on a Clipper 70 in the Round the World Race in 11 identical 70ft yachts, originally inspired by Robin Knox-Johnston. He and the skipper of *Zhuhai* are the only professionally qualified members of the crew; the others all amateurs paying for the experience. Having set off from London in August 2019, the race takes in South America, South Africa, Australia, China, North America, the Panama Canal, Bermuda, Northern Ireland, and back to London in August 2020: six continents and five oceans. Quite an experience for a young man of 24!'

Like Jamie's family, members of OSC, especially his contemporaries, will follow the race with keen interest and best wishes for a good result and, above all, a safe return.

Amongst those near contemporaries is Harry Hitchcock, who has already made his mark as skipper of his own cruising yacht and was selected by the Royal Cruising Club in 2019, in a strong field of candidates, as a Cadet member. He too belongs to a generation of young sailing instructors developed by the OSC training programme and encouraged by mentors like James Robinson.

20. *Katrina* to St Petersburg

Like most of us Charles Iliff had a cherished goal to reach.

'I had long wanted to cruise the Baltic, and in particular had an ambition to sail my own boat into St Petersburg. There was one particular reason for this. For me sailing/cruising and St Petersburg come together in the life of Arthur Ransome, author of *Swallows and Amazons*. He spent the First World War as a war correspondent in the then imperial Petrograd, where he got to know well the Bolshevik leaders including Lenin (with whom he often played chess) and his Minister for War, Leon Trotsky, to the point where Ransome formed an attachment with Trotsky's secretary.

It sounds dangerous, chasing Trotsky's secretary in the middle of the Bolshevik revolution. But Eugenia responded, she became his mistress, and when he returned to Britain she went with him and they then married, settling down in the Lake District. John, Susan, Titty and Roger seem improbably removed from typing out death warrants in Trotsky's armoured train.

So in July 2013, when I read in Yachting Monthly of a proposed first trial Baltic ARC, to include St Petersburg as well as Estonia, Helsinki and Stockholm, all over six weeks, I leapt at the opportunity, and immediately registered. Mo and I asked James Robinson, with whom I have sailed very many miles over 30 years to join us. He accepted with the kind comment that *Katrina* could have been designed for the Baltic ARC.

Katrina is a 37ft deck-saloon cruiser, very comfortable; the contrast with the tiny, 20ft Orford cruisers of the late 1970s and early 1980s could not be greater. She was built in 2007 by Regina on the island of Orust just off Gothenburg and bears the latest in a line of family boat names at Orford going back to the 1930s, thus *Catharine – Cat – Kit – Kitten – Kit Kat – Katrina*.

There were 200 applications for 25 places and to our amazement we were accepted. Mo and I spent the winter making numerous alterations to *Katrina*. Principally we installed an AIS (Automatic Identification System) and rented a fully compliant offshore life-raft. Peter Norris fitted a wonderful three-bladed Gori folding propeller with overdrive, which gave extra range, speed and economy – important in the Baltic with light winds and much motor-sailing.

Then in March there was a setback. I found myself on a hospital bed with a blood problem and tubes coming out of me, wondering how I would ever get launched, let alone to the Baltic. But it sorted itself out.

We were in the water by mid-May and on June 2nd Mo and I left for Cuxhaven with Richard Waite and my nephew Richard Saul. Our crossing was fairly uneventful, 280 miles in 44 hours. Off Texel a flight of beautifully-handled Dutch F16s decided to use us as a target for anti-shipping strike practice and for 20 minutes we were at the centre of our own private air show.

Into the Kiel Canal – I make no secret of my weakness for the great inland waterways of Europe and it is certainly one of those. Operated with a light touch (but someone on board must have passed their CEVNI), we shared a lock with a 10,000 ton ship which came towering in behind and then above us, applying the handbrake just at the last moment. Halfway along, we passed the canal-side cafe that plays the national anthem of every non-German vessel – and we got our few bars of God Save the Queen.

Mo and I, this time with James Robinson, returned on July 2nd to *Katrina* at Wendhof Yacht Harbour just outside Kielerfjord, in a lagoon that was a pleasant mix of yachts and reeded wild-life sanctuary; all very helpful, reasonable charges and an excellent marine electrician who fixed the autohelm. We spent a couple of days making good and preparing, then crossed the mouth of the fjord to Schilksee.

Mo sent James and me off to the launderette. On returning there we found a well-spoken English lady folding our damp clothes. James and I are still pondering the correct etiquette in such a situation. Briefings were given, followed by dinner at the Kieler Yacht Club. First stop Bornholm, a small Danish island off the south-eastern corner of Sweden 180 miles from Kiel. The forecast was for 36 hours of settled weather and then a low. So we set off straight after dinner.

Through the night we went, past Fehman and Gedser; the dark plays tricks; I was spooked for a while by a starboard light that was keeping station abeam with our port light. Then I realised that it was another yacht on a parallel course about a mile away.

The following day we passed Arkona in light gentle weather; clicking sounds in the waves indicated tiny and very rare Baltic dolphins playing in our wake. Finally as the light went (and without having seen the island as we approached) we found the deep-water mark for Ronne harbour and entered the south basin. Then the wind came. A tour of the island, included Hammershus Castle. We used the fisherman's co-operative shower block, which also provided facilities for fisherwomen. Gradually the wind abated.

Next came the 190 miles to Visby on Gotland. There was still some wind – up to 32 knots but from the stern quarter crossing to Kalmar Sound, and we decided to go inside Oland to give ready access to shelter. The wind dropped, and going through the rocky Kalmar channel at night we took action to avoid one rock at the last moment and suffered only a glancing blow. A Rustler 42 hit a rock badly; we heard her Mayday, she was stuck fast. The lifeboat came out and she spent some time in Kalmar for checks. The crossing to Gotland from the north tip of Oland had poor visibility but was gentle. Mo's mobile went off; it was Jamie and Jane Wilson waiting on the quayside. They embedded in the stern cabin, with James saloon-surfing. There were more quayside barbecues, and sightseeing round the massive walls of Visby which had been a Hanseatic League stronghold.

There followed a day-sail north along the Gotland coast and the 20 miles across to Gotska Sandon, a forested sand-dune, unusual in the rocky Baltic, three miles by five with no harbour. We stopped briefly and went ashore to visit the chapel and museum, anchoring on the leeward side. After supper at anchor we left for Estonia.

A gentle 30 hours' motoring/sailing took us to Tallin, where the heatwave that was to last for four weeks now set in. There was momentary tension over a change of watch – *Katrina* was on Estonian time but some of the crew were still on Swedish time. Finally entering Pirata marina after midnight, Jane was on the helm following a series of leading lights and earned the title of "leading-light Jane".

Tallinn was a favourite; a tiny historic centre that speaks of a troubled and difficult past. But now we sensed huge optimism, everywhere hard-working young people rushing around – and, it seemed, wedding parties. We had a very special meal at Restaurant Leib, sited against the massive mediaeval curtain walls of the old town. I can still taste the soup of watercress and smoked trout.

Then the news began to filter through. St Petersburg was next – but an airliner had been shot down over the Ukraine, it was assumed by a Russian missile. Most of the passengers were Dutch; one family killed was known to a Dutch yacht in the harbour. Suddenly the small NATO squadron in Estonia of a British, a Dutch, a Danish and a Norwegian frigate seemed very relevant. Only briefly, we considered avoiding Russia. You clear out of the EU in Tallinn and Estonian border control officials came to the boat to take a crew-list and stamp another to hand in St Petersburg. They clearly thought that we were crazy to be going.

As you pass into Russian territorial waters (clearly marked by a line of buoys, and on the charts) you are required to call up Russian border control on channel 16. You are then moved to channel 10 or 12. James and I had arranged for us both to be on watch at that point in case a patrol boat with searchlights and Kalashnikovs came rushing up. For us this was just after midnight in the half-light of what the Russians call the white-night, a bit surreal, and I wondered how sensible we were being as I walked forward to the VHF set. I gave the boat's name and position, number of people and ports from and to. This they could correlate with the AIS signal and we were not investigated, although others were. Best to make the call straight away. Oh and log it properly – I forgot.

Not a patrol boat in sight, but another yacht saw one nudge over the border into Finnish waters. A Finnish frigate suddenly appeared and positioned itself in front of the patrol boat, training its gun, and the patrol boat backed off; we had been told that the Finns are "very clever" – the experience of 1939/40 is not forgotten.

That morning we were engulfed by an intense bowl of light that continued throughout our visit; a continuous heatwave at 30°C (but only 250 miles from the Arctic Circle). You are required to keep to the shipping lanes, which goes against the grain for those used to the southern North Sea. We proceeded along the edges, from buoy to buoy, joining up the dots as we put it.

St Petersburg was built by forced labour on the orders of Peter the Great starting in 1703, on a marshy delta, and the old centre is nowhere more than 15 feet above sea level. The large lagoon 25 miles across, which the city is at the head of, is now enclosed, and the seawall incorporates the old naval base island of Kronstadt, where there is a controlled entrance for shipping.

We came through the entrance on the starboard side of the channel, but the customs quay was to port, and we needed to cross the channel just as a convoy of ships came through from behind. As a huge ship towered past we throttled back, and as the ship's stern came abeam, I swung *Katrina* round and across the wake. Then came clearance by customs and border control, where we were assisted by the ever helpful Vladimir Ivankiff, who is strongly recommended by the Baltic Pilot. The boat was searched by a couple of nice lads. Twenty miles along one of the lanes of the lagoon, the light combined with the reflected water and the low horizon to create a shimmering effect that I had only seen before in Venice. But this is a place with a violent and cruel history, the waters metaphorically soaked with blood.

Once into the old imperial yacht harbour, now run by the River Island Yacht Club, we celebrated with a bottle of champagne presented to us before leaving on the OSC pontoon by James and carried all the way. And we marvelled at Ray and Margo Glaister's ventures. For us this was a destination achieved. For them it had been just the beginning.

There was a neglected 1960s clubhouse on several storeys, with the use of a shower room. On the top floors old ladies were living in cupboards. All swelteringly hot there, but that heat would probably be welcome in January. The hinterland was semi-derelict dockland, with the immediate area full of competing hospitality venues that pulsated with noise and music through the night until breakfast; everywhere partying girls and wedding groups, and a small helicopter pad.

Laundry was taken away by a babushka with an old tractor pulling a trailer, and a huge dog walking 20 yards in front, who always seemed to know where to go. The washing came back next day clean but damp. In a traffic jam the tractor confronted a supercar and forced it to back off. We heard of guns being pulled, a mafia turf war. Models wearing very little draped themselves over the yachts for a photo-shoot in the heatwave. About the only normal facility in the area was a simple restaurant in a nice green setting; the rally dinner was held there and we were all offered a samovar to smoke. The only yacht to accept was *Katrina*, and James and I puffed away.

Several excursions were made into the city including the Hermitage – there is nothing new about Russian bling. There was an extraordinary collection of portraits of the Tsar's generals in 1815, by an English artist, conveying the characters of each without being a cartoon. We also visited the *Aurora*, the cruiser that fired the first shot in the Russian Revolution, and, very special, Dostoyevski's flat, where *Crime and Punishment* was written. Such a feeling of history was reflected in that flat – and at the end the lady curator whispered "do not judge us by Putin". Plus ça change – the hairs went up at the back of my head!

Jamie and Jane had bought tickets for us all to see *Giselle* at the Marinski. Afterwards back on a trolley bus, where the conductor was worried for us apparently heading for a dubious dock area. Someone else explained that we were getting back to the yacht harbour.

Jamie and Jane left to fly to Boston, and Mo, James and I left in *Katrina* on July 27th. Still the heatwave and shimmering light persisted as we cleared out of Kronstadt. The yacht in front of us insisted on keeping in the narrow shipping channel; the oncoming ship informed him by VHF "you must be crazy" in a thick Russian accent.

The border in the sea is marked by a series of buoys and is close to the first Finnish islands. Through the day we had heard on the VHF the Russians searching for a yacht – clearly not us – the co-ordinates given were quite different. But with the boundary buoys in sight we saw a Russian patrol boat racing towards us. At the last moment it sheared away. The mid-evening arrival at Haapasaari, 15 miles off the mainland, was in many ways a relief from St Petersburg.

Round the back of the tiny island we went, to access the customs post quay; on a mound above it was a large grey building from which the Finns monitor border activity. The friendly young customs official breathalysed James – they automatically do this to the person on the helm on arrival – and said he could clear us quickly before the arrival of a motor yacht from Russia, aboard which they had instructions to carry out a deep search. Scrutiny of the modest alcohol on board – and his review of his preferred brands of Finnish lager sufficed for us. Our crew list was stamped, handed back and placed with the ships papers, proof that we had cleared back properly into the EU.

Katrina was then able to enter the tiny lagoon that almost bisects the island, entrance just a few yards wide. With her 1.6m draft, designed for archipelago cruising, she could access many places that others could not. We were just able to berth at the end of the tiny ferry jetty. In the morning young children from small family cruisers came to practise their English; there were children everywhere, enjoying cruising and the heatwave, unlike Russia where we saw hardly any.

We headed north-west to Loviso on the mainland, our first introduction to archipelago cruising with its unforgiving focus on position, markers, clearing lines and leading marks. One wrong turning took us down what looked like a narrow passage between two islands – only to come up against a low bridge between them; then up a broad inlet to Loviso, past a fort that had held the Royal Navy off during the Crimean War. The final approach had a depth of 1.8m, just enough; we stayed at a harbour in a glorious setting and went into the town, a Finnish Woodbridge, very Russian in style as if from Dr Zhivago, and Sibelius' favourite retreat.

There followed two days of cruising through the islands to Helsinki – very warm water, regular swimming even for me. The approach to Helsinki is studded with islands covered with defensive forts. We stayed at the Nylandska Jaktklubbe on tiny Blekholmen Island in the middle of Helsinki harbour. It has a grand and splendid clubhouse with a wonderful first-floor ballroom and banqueting hall – built in 1863, again Russian-looking. It has survived so much, 1905, 1916/18, 1939/40 and 1944. In the berth next to us was an elderly Finn flying the White Ensign instead of the Finnish flag – Royal Yacht Squadron, whose few foreign members are the only non-British allowed to fly a British ensign. I wish I had learned his full story.

These were special surroundings and it was the hottest day in Helsinki for 51 years. Richard and Sue Waite came aboard – James again graciously gave up the stern cabin, and we joined a parade of sail around the harbour.

Then we sailed westward, keeping as far inshore as we could because we wanted to see the country. Near disaster threatened in a busy, narrow channel – as we passed another yacht starboard to starboard a large motor yacht roared between the two at perhaps 20 knots. Moments before she appeared to be on a collision course, and with restricted visibility. Another Finnish alcohol problem I think.

After a night at anchor in the lagoon of a small island, on we went into the Aland Islands, westward from Hanko on the south western corner of the mainland. Still the heatwave continued. Then across 30 miles to Kokar, perhaps the most perfect day of the whole six weeks. Tiny islands of the Aland archipelago all around, but at a distance, much more open, seascape rather than landscape – all under a terrific bowl of light. Every discipline of archipelago pilotage was needed and the last couple of miles into Sandvick on Kokar required the co-ordinated input of all five of us.

We moored up to a small visitors' pontoon, the characteristic smoothed granite slabs all around. In the heat of the late afternoon (water very warm) Mo put on her swimming costume. James looked over the side and said "there is a big eel down here". It was a huge grass snake, swimming in this inlet of the sea, on a tiny island far from the mainland, serpentine head just above the surface, swirls from its coils behind. It swam round the boat, and then out towards an anchored yacht. Several smaller snakes then swam by.

On to Mariehamm, through the narrow channel between Sommaro, Degero and Foglo. The holding tank was blocked; we anchored by a huge reed bed, Richard very nobly went overboard and pushed a broom handle up the skin fitting – problem solved. We spent three days in Mariehamm – Finnish but Swedish speaking. We had a tour around the four-mast grain ship *Pommern*, built in Glasgow in 1861. All agreed that it is to Finland that we would most like to return.

It was 20 miles across to the Stockholm archipelago and then a long run through the islands that started between Yxlan and Bilidosund. We spent the night in the pool of a tiny island that had been recommended; pleasant enough, but shared with what appeared to be every second yacht from Stockholm. The following day we entered Stockholm harbour, to reach the grandeur of the Royal Swedish Sailing Club at Saltsjobaden. The 19th century developer had built a railway direct from the yacht club quayside (and a very grand hotel) to the Parliament building in central Stockholm, 20 miles away. We visited the remarkably preserved *Vasa*.

Finally back out to sea to Arkosund – not yet mid-August and the Swedish sailing season starting to wind down. Two more days of gentle cruising for us through the Blue Coast Archipelago, thence to Kalmar. It is a nice town with a great visitors' harbour in the old ferry basin, right by the train station, with direct trains to Copenhagen airport. We left *Katrina* there; we were running out of time and Hurricane Bertha was raging between Sweden and Orford.'

By way of Postscript Charles gave a talk at the OSC Laying Up Supper which offered useful tips on the demands of Baltic archipelago cruising:

'It is possible to get almost the whole way from south-east Sweden to the Finnish/Russian border sailing in and amongst little islands. Obtain a full set of locally produced paper charts beforehand. Do not rely on stocking up on arrival, the local chandlery/bookshop may have run out, and you may have already lost your keel.

Keep to the marked recommended tracks but even these are not guaranteed rock-free. Remember that the deeper water represented by the tracks can be very narrow. Use your GPS/chart-plotter to check and confirm your position, but use your paper charts to plan, identify marks, work clearing lines and follow leading marks.

One crew member, not the helm, should be appointed to co-ordinate the process. The moment you are unsure, slow right down, it is better to hit that granite reef at half a knot. It is a tiring process, so stop and rest, there are natural harbours everywhere.

N.B. It is essential to encourage everyone to sit down. A Baltic yacht we knew hit a rock, one person was on the foredeck at the time, she was thrown forward by the impact and hit her head on the pulpit. An ambulance boat was sent out and she spent ten days in A & E.'

Those of us who have been fortunate enough to sail among these islands on the Blue Coast would endorse his warnings but never forget its beauty. As the next chapter shows, experience of these waters is not confined to Orford sailors with cabins in which to shelter from weather or mosquitoes.

Sailing Course Picnic

Popeye fully loaded for cruise

Rocky harbour in the Baltic (John Colvin)

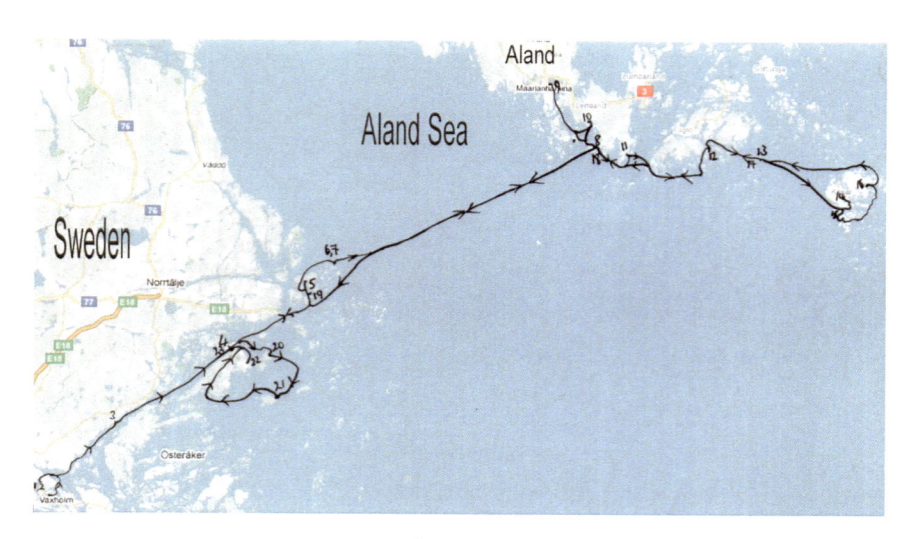

Route to Aland (John Colvin)

Sea Urchin safely moored

Talisker 1 off Orkney (James Tomlinson)

Azores Landfall (James Tomlinson)

Talisker 1 in charge (James Tomlinson)

Aboard *Aimée* 2005 Keble to the fore

Sunrise over Lindisfarne seen from *Cornelia* (Chris Gill)

Dolphins at play in Bristol Channel round *Cornelia's* bow (Chris Gill)

Cornelia enters Whiteshill (Harbourmaster)

Molly Cox in Feva with Thomas, aged 3 (Claire Davidson)

Annabel Cox in Optimist with Jessica, aged 4 (Claire Davidson)

21. Dinghy Cruising

There is one category of cruising sailor whom I greatly admire but have never wished to emulate – those who voyage in half-decked or open boats and are prepared to sleep in those cramped, unforgiving conditions. Like the crews of Viking longships or the ancient Greeks they bed down on bottom boards, crawl under thwarts to lie alongside centreboards. They do so without the protection from flying spray or breaking waves, which cabin tops and sprayhoods offer even on smaller yachts. At night they rig a tent over the boom and hope that will keep the rain out. If the cruise extends for any length of time or distance, the stowage of food and water, spare clothes, sails and outboard fuel, stove and much other equipment all has to be fitted in somewhere, somehow. Perhaps even more than ocean sailors they need to be aware of weather patterns, tidal streams and the dangers of a lee shore.

In an earlier chapter the exploits of John Sherwill and Ben Johnston in *Cockleshell*, John Seymour and his crewman in *Willynilly*, Charles Iliff in the family Squib and the Glaisters in their Wayfarer, pre-figured such voyages. Most of these, unlike me, used these experiences as apprenticeship for longer voyages in larger boats, as did Richard Waite with nights aboard *Hebe*, their Bombay Tomtit. Many of us, less bold or hardy, have planned and executed day cruises in small boats, Mirrors or Ten Footers for instance, which still require tidal planning and sensible forethought on equipment, clothing and supplies.

Every summer generations of younger OSC sailors have been given the freedom to camp overnight down river on the Ness, to sleep, or not to sleep, on the shingle, to look at the stars, swim in the sea and cook their evening meal and breakfast. If they forgot to take the tent pegs or a frying pan they learned a valuable lesson. One memorable time our own sons, with Ginny Iliff, embarked on a Swallows and Amazons venture upriver to camp overnight on the beach at Little Japan beyond Aldeburgh. When the irate estate gamekeeper told them they were trespassing they pointed out that it was now low tide; they had no means of departure. They received a grudging permission to remain, with the firm instruction not to try it again.

In 1992 Michael Collins, who enjoyed sailing his Mirror *One Day*, presented the 'Day Trophy' to be awarded to the best account of a daytime dinghy cruise submitted each season. This has been won on 15 occasions since then by 12 different people in varying types of craft including Wayfarer, Wandererer, Laser Stratos, Hawk 20, Mirror and Ten Footer. Ten years later John Colvin, who was a keen dinghy cruiser himself, added the 'Colvin Chalice', beautifully carved by him from hardwood, as a further challenge to OSC dinghy sailors with the same enthusiasm. This has been won 15 times since and some of these cruises have ranged much further afield, in Scandinavia and the Hebrides, or in East Anglian coastal waters. (Lists of winners of both trophies will be found in the appendix).

To reflect this activity I have selected just four of these winners and some extracts from the logs submitted. Liz and Johnny Feibusch had been cruising Wayfarers regularly for 20 years almost every summer before they came to Orford. While Liz has always been a keen and very successful racing competitor, Johnny much preferred cruising and this was their normal summer holiday focus. "What else would you want to do?" as Liz put it. The Western Isles of Scotland, Cornwall and the South Coast of England were as familiar to them as the Suffolk estuaries which they explored from their caravan base near Waldringfield. The earlier voyages, before they joined OSC, are beyond the scope of this book but in 1996 the Day Trophy was won by Liz and Johnny in *Wansfell* on very local water. These extracts from her log will resonate with all who know our river well and also illustrate some differences between dinghy and yacht cruising.

'Occasionally one experiences a perfect day. October 1st 1996 was just that. The diary was free of engagements, the forecast was for sou'westerly winds force 3 to 4, dry, sunny and warm for the time of year. The tides also co-operated with High Water at Orford Quay near enough 1600. Ideal.

The last time Johnny and I had sailed together in W3277 *Wansfell,* our 24-year old cruising Wayfarer, was in the 1995 Club Cruise to Snape, so this little outing was long overdue. We surprised ourselves how easy it was to rig and launch a boat which was in the dinghy park more or less ready to sail. It was a rare treat as most of our trips in the past involved early starts, long drives and rigging – from stepping the mast onwards. Then the loading would commence – all the equipment for a week or week-end of living on board! My 'just in case' bag on this occasion was a mere token. (It still contained, towel, warm top, binoculars, camera, chart of the Alde and Ore, a hand-bearing compass, sun-tan lotion, sunglasses, bird-book, VHF radio, dinghy spares, bit of cash, insect repellent).

So with minimum fuss we were soon under way, sailing easily against the tide not having even to think about the best way to beat or go faster. Johnny helmed as I have more opportunities than he does. I was content to crew and fly the kite a bit and simply soak up the whole scenario. We sailed on, leaving Chantry buoy to starboard and entrance to Stoney Ditch to port. Close reaching on the Havergate Island side of the Narrows, we marvelled at the rate we were going and enjoyed the waders, Curlew and Dunlin (I think) among them, busy foraging on the glistening mud. We were ahead of our schedule, so decided to extend our cruise to North Weir Point.

There was an autumnal crispness in the air which made me reach for my woolly hat for a while as we headed towards the open sea. We passed the entrance to Barthorp's Creek with its very own mini shingle bar still exposed and providing a platform for some birds. There, for a few moments we held still and made nothing over the ground, allowing time for us to wonder who Barthorp was and to note that it would probably never be possible to explore his creek in a Wayfarer even though we claim they can reach the waters that other cruisers never can! The breeze then obligingly picked up as the strength of the tide increased and as we approached what I consider to be the strangest river mouth on the east coast. I have sailed in and out of this river on several occasions, but always in the company of either cruising or racing Wayfarers, so there have been distractions, and yet I have always found there to be an eerie atmosphere. Today was no exception and the swirling pools, glassy patches and irregular ripples through which we slowly slid, made those last few minutes disturbing, unreal. What was under us causing the erratic writhing and seething of these waters?

Another yacht entered the river under genoa only. Who needs a mainsail in that tide? The motor vessel *Progress* overtook us and tempted us to venture further, after all *Wansfell* is on the Small Ships Register so the North Sea crossing was technically, legally... But no, it is not one of our ambitions and anyway, we had to return to feed the dog by late afternoon! Going-about in that tide was a peculiar sensation as we were swept along so fast sideways throughout the manoeuvre.

Soon we were back in the cosier reaches of the Ore with the smell of farming activities wafting past our noses. It was good that we had sailed down relatively slowly enabling us to enjoy the surroundings, because we really tore back, trying to estimate how many knots we were making. We rushed past brick huts, pill boxes, black sheds, upturned tenders and little inlets as if we were in a great hurry. Glancing back we saw the yacht we had overtaken, silhouetted in the strong sunlight and the surface of the river sparkled actively and brightly. No camera could have done it justice, so we looked back again and committed it to memory.

Then we were within sight of the entrance to Lower Gull and as we altered course we both looked over to the bank opposite Dove Point where we have enjoyed so many happy picnics during Club Training Courses; nothing marks the spot, except in our memories the buzz of children's excited voices as they arrive after what is, for them, nearly always a testing expedition. As we approached the entrance to the Butley River I prepared the anchor for immediate use as an alternative to coming alongside Old Boyton Dock, our planned picnic venue. However, as we beat in with the tide we decided to sail past the quay, then drop the main and come back to it under genoa.

"Aren't those seals?" I said. "Ready About!" came the reply. Johnny was concentrating, there was not much room at this state of the tide. "They are seals". "No, no they are just logs." "Well, if they aren't seals, they are moving logs!" "Lee-oh!" "Oh, you're right, they ARE seals; ready to get the main down?"

Once we were tied up I took a couple of snapshots before they sensed my presence and slipped into the water. They were definitely laughing as they played around in the tide. It was not 'quiet' tied up to the quay, but certainly peaceful, except when a fishing vessel came in at about 15 knots! The wake was wider than the river and washed along the banks. We fended our boat off the solid walls of the quay till it died down and I wondered whether we would ever buy fish again. Once relaxed we could hear the calls of the various birds, the less musical screeches of the gulls when they spotted the sandwiches, a droning aeroplane, too high above to see, the interruptive sound of a helicopter which, by contrast, was very low, and the sound of the water rushing in and lapping against the boat. It was unusual to be so still and hear the movement of the tide. The Butley River looked beautiful as the large cumulus clouds shifted aside for the sun to shine on it as it running inland towards the ferry crossing and the moored boats beyond.

The saying that time goes quickly when you are having fun is very true. We noticed that *Wansfell* had risen two rungs on the old iron steps since our arrival. Eventually we slipped silently away from the quay under genoa and once out into the Gull we hoisted the main and headed, somewhat reluctantly, homewards.

As we sailed on past the Club's racing marks, Long Gull and Short Gull, not needing to 'negotiate' them in any specific direction, we seemed to be participating in a different sport altogether, nevertheless one I realised I still enjoyed. Apart from the short beat into the Butley River the entire cruise had been on close, beam and broad reaches with the occasional goose-winged runs. These points of sailing favoured maximum observation time and a little further on we were able to watch a grey heron poised on the shore, no doubt looking for his next meal, not in the least ruffled by our close passage. He was seriously outnumbered by a gaggle of Canada geese on the salt marsh nearby, so it was to be hoped his diet was not in competition with theirs. Rounding Chantry Point the distinctive profiles of Quay House and Orford Sailing Club were highlighted by the sun and our conversation turned again to landing procedures. We both agreed that it was a pity that not everyone who had boats on all these moorings and in the Club dinghy park could take a day off and share those glorious sailing conditions. We were the lucky ones today.

Time for philosophising finally ran out as we landed, quite gracefully, right next to the tap and our trolley at the top of the slip, at the top of the tide, on top of the world.'

Simon Baker's story of his Wayfarer voyage in *Scatterling* from the Deben to the Ore requires a short prologue. Simon has sailed dinghies since boyhood, but in 1978, the year he first met his wife Ann, he had just been on a long summer cruise to St Katharine's Dock in London after finishing at university. Before this he had done a few short 'overnighters' with different crews. This time a whole month afloat had given him a fine tan, which, he suggests, had some effect. He and Ann married three years later but did not sail much together until about 2002. They started cruising in 2007. On the first occasion, in Butley Creek, the mooing of cows kept Ann awake for much of the night, but the experience did not prevent voyages to other east coast rivers, the Orwell, the Stour and Walton Backwaters. Simon salutes another of his wife's great attributes – 'she is a superb dinghy cook – one saucepan and one frying pan – nothing she can't sort out!' And by the sound of the account below she can cope with a dinghy pump too.

'It was a bit touch and go. The Deben entrance (or in this case exit), has its "issues". The tide runs fast especially the second half of the spring ebb. It was running very fast and we went like a rocket when we reached Felixstowe Ferry. The wind wasn't so strong, probably not even a force 4, and conditions were dry, forecast was good, and an ESE wind would suit us well up the coast and back to Orford.

It was when we had just passed the Horse Nº1 buoy I first began to be a little concerned, but my first thoughts were of the advantages of the weather and wind, the nice sail up the coast and the tides well-timed for once. Tides of course are vital to a cruising dinghy which carries no engine and is an absolute beast to row. While the shallow draft allows us to use the eddies, out on the sea and through the entrances, a favourable tide is nearly essential unless the wind is uncommonly kind. Which it often isn't. No turn of the key and "donk, donk, donk" to get through the entrance for this little beauty, and if it's a beat into the river entrance expect a wet and bumpy ride.

Nor is the tide schedule the same for us little estuary-hoppers as it is for the bigger keel boys. They are looking for plenty of water under the keel at the river mouth; the most important thing for us is a favourable tide getting into the next estuary. So today that meant getting over the bar at Orford, where we wanted the flood – but we also wanted the ebb out of the Deben and North up the coast. Having the turn of low tide as we approached Orford Bar seemed like good planning to me, so the new flood tide could welcome us back to the cosy warmth of our home waters and we could have the best of everything. But it did mean leaving the Deben about two hours before low water. I thought I had planned that quite well. Perhaps…

The next few minutes flashed by with four knots of tide added to five knots of boat speed, much faster than usual, despite a reefed main and partly rolled jib. It was only another minute or so before Ann, wife and crew, noticed something was wrong. She had gamely taken up sailing when she saw how much I loved it and somehow we ended up cruising the Wayfarer, sleeping on the bottom boards under a canvas tent at night and with all our gear on board. To this day I don't understand how, as a latecomer to this cold and uncomfortable sport, she had even encouraged me to get a tent and start cruising. She had not been sailing long but has a very practical wisdom. Whereas I had been sailing since I was about 11 but not found much wisdom yet!

Her: "There's no one else at the entrance". (pause)
Me: "Yes there is a motor cruiser there"
Her: "But he is bouncing up and down on the waves" (pause).
Me: "Yes dear, small motor cruisers are not really made for waves"
Her: "Looks very choppy out there, can we turn back?" (longer pause)
Me: "I don't think we could sail against this tide if we wanted to now."

By this time, we were passing the Felixstowe Ferry SC about a third of a mile from the bar; waves were building a little, not much yet, but we were rushing forward. I noticed the motor cruiser did turn back. I said nothing. There were indeed certainly no other vessels large or small anywhere near the entrance. The waves were short and steep, about three waves to our boat length and half a metre high.

The bow began to slap on the waves, sending white spray which blew back at us with a cool wetting sting. As we neared the bar, they became very short and higher than ever. Now the bow dug right into the waves as it slapped down, and the sea-green water covered the bow for a moment or two until she heaved herself out. Some of the water was deflected by the washboard on the bow but a worrying amount found its way over the top and down into the boat. The cockpit was beginning to fill and the bow dug deeper into each wave as it did so. By this time both of us were alarmed but I managed to pretend to keep a clear head. I slid aft to raise the bow if possible and asked Ann in the least panicky voice I could muster to start using the hand pump. Ann proved very proficient at pumping! Meanwhile my mind was making all sorts of projections about how long we could continue to ship water at this rate and checking where the radio and flares were…

Once the bar was behind us, the waves settled as quickly as they had come and it wasn't long before we found ourselves on a reach heading for home with the northerly ebb tide under us. The water was soon cleared from the boat. A cup of tea from our flask revived our spirits and before we had time to think about it we passed over the relatively quiet bar to the Ore, wind and tide now in harmony with us and each other. We were more than grateful for the safety of home waters that time.

I wonder if there were a few folks at Felixstowe Ferry who looked out at us crossing the bar, closed their eyes and sent up a quick sailor's prayer for us that day!'

John and Polly Colvin are another couple who have carried out an impressive series of cruises in their Wayfarer *Sea Urchin*. Starting in 1998 they have explored more of the Swedish coastline and archipelagos than I ever managed, circumnavigated the Danish island of Funen and crossed the sea to Aland, which belongs to Finland. Nearer to home they have sailed from Orford to Brightlingsea and from Walton to the Medway. I have chosen the log entries on just one day from their 2008 voyage to stand for many others.

'It is Day Eight, July 27th, wind light SW. Distance 30 miles.

We awake at 0400 to the radio alarm. We are going to cross the Åland Sea. The forecast is good. A slow dawn is breaking over the north-eastern sea, and as we pack up the bedding, stow it and organise breakfast the sun rises through layers of delicately coloured cloud.

A light following wind is forecast (and indeed arrives) so for once we not only shake out our familiar reefs but hoist the genoa instead of the working jib – and thereby re-discover the taped-up crack in the genoa window which needed a proper repair during the winter, but got overlooked. Drat!

At 0615 up come both the anchors. We use two, linked in series, on the advice of a fisherman friend. The first holds down the second, so they can be relied upon to dig in, even in light, shell-covered bottoms, or among slippery weed-blanketed rocks. We normally travel with them clipped to the floorboards under the thwart, but this morning I simply lodge them on the foredeck to begin with, while we perform the crucial manoeuvre, in restricted space, of sailing *Sea Urchin* over the deepest part of the rocky sill at the entrance of our little harbour. Once safely out, I stow them properly, and we set sail on a compass-bearing out to sea.

We pass the last navigational markers, leaving Tjärven behind, and head out into open water as the sun rises and the day gets properly under way. Early on, we notice what appears to be a positive fleet of yachts hull-down on the horizon ahead, but although they gradually become more clearly visible they don't seem to be approaching us themselves. At length it is apparent that they aren't masts but the turbines of a wind-farm, and finally we discover that they're built on the coastal islets of our Åland destination – they form a sea-mark, had we but known.

A shipping lane runs NW/SE up through the Åland Sea, and we avoid a freighter making its way along it. We also change course in the middle of the day to stay away from one of the Viking ferries plying back and forth between Stockholm and Mariehamn. As we begin to enter the Åland archipelago we have a rather more alarming moment when a Silja-line ferry/booze-cruise ship slithers out unexpectedly from behind a headland, turns and makes straight for us like a tank. With no debate we abruptly swerve and head for the edge of the deep-water channel and from there safely watch it go by.

Otherwise, the wind remains behind us, the sun sparkles on the waves and we skim along quietly often goose-winged, mainly entirely alone, while the hourly readings on the GPS comfortably confirm what our eyes tell us: the landmarks of the Swedish islands are falling away behind, and the lighthouses on the outer Finnish skerries are gradually coming into view.

The sun shines, the waves gurgle and we sail on. A few yachts and motor cruisers are using the same route, but none comes particularly near. Cruise ships, ferries and freighters ply to and fro, and the remnants of their wake travelling across the open sea create a reasonably mild criss-cross swell for us to contend with. It's John in the main who helms, with some breaks. I take two delightful snoozes: what bliss to lie under a blue sky, the gentle curve of the sail reaching up overhead, the sound of the waves bustling past one centimetre of plywood away under my ear. Who would have guessed that to lie bundled up in my buoyancy-aid, wedged under the foredeck and the thwart, squashed between centreboard, bucket, and anchor-warp drum, could be so much more comfortable – and comforting – than being in my bed last night? For both of us, in different ways, this sail is bringing us contentment: I, because of that heady mixture of freedom and safety that comes with bobbing happily along so far from shore, and John, because *Sea Urchin* is sailing so well.

But as we approach the Finnish islands, John becomes more uneasy. The tower on the Nyhamn island, though very conspicuous, does not look to the naked eye like a navigational marker at all, which makes us doubtful. It's unmistakably a water-tower, not a lighthouse. (Later on we discover that the Finns use all sorts of towers and constructions as lighthouses). And of the other myriad cardinal markers that dot the approaches to Åland, scarcely any can be seen until we are almost upon them – little painted mudsticks they seem to us, and very hard to identify. So we have quite a job figuring out where we are and where we should go, and a change in scale onto the Finnish charts doesn't help. And the Silja-line ship buzzes us at this point.

At length we successfully locate Rödhamn and its leading markers, and sail around a green headland through a narrow cleft into its yacht harbour. It turns out not to be a settlement like Furusund, which is what we were more-or-less expecting, but simply a little sailing club among trees with some visitors' berths clinging to the side of the big whale-backed rock that forms the otherwise uninhabited island. The sailing club pontoon says sternly 'Members Only' in English on its signboard; the rest of the berths are nose-on moorings onto a high rock-hugging walkway, occupied by a whole row of glossy white yachts strung between it and the buoys at their sterns. Above on the shore we see a club-house and a couple of other buildings, but no shop, no harbourmaster and no suitable place for a small sea-going dinghy to tie up. We make a couple of passes back and forth along the row of yachts to examine the situation, then without much debate decide together simply to move on.

Round another couple of headlands we surge in with a distinctly fresher wind, and drop anchor in the 'vik', or bay, formed by U-shaped Granö. The enclosing rocks are too low to shield us much from the wind, but the water is calm. We both are really tired after about nine hours sailing – so even though it's mid-afternoon we put up the tent to shelter us from the blustery wind. We even pull down the window-blinds of the tent so that the bright sun shining in doesn't bother us as *Sea Urchin* swings on her anchor-line. Then we simply stretch out on the floor and sleep.

We awaken to cook supper and organise ourselves for the night – and listen to the forecast – but that's all. We feel happy after today's sail, and somewhat excited: we're in Finland at last.'

In 2018 *Sea Urchin* passed to another generation. Polly now sails a Cornish Shrimper and John plays table tennis. He is happy to say that they never capsized *Sea Urchin* and never had an engine.

The name of Chris Best and his Laser Stratos, *Popeye,* appears more than any others on the list of OSC Dinghy Cruise trophy winners. Starting in 2003, he cruised for a week or more every year until 2017. These voyages became more adventurous as he gained experience, and the last few years involved cruises off the north-west coast of Scotland with his friend Bridget Chadwick, also a member of OSC at the time. His most arduous hours were spent off Cornwall, clawing his way past the Manacles, against the tide, one very windy afternoon and evening, until he and his 70 year-old crewman, finally reached Falmouth.

The six-day circumnavigation of Skye he counts among his top achievements although the June temperature during that trip never exceeded ten degrees. Ranked with this, in much warmer weather, he places his 2016 cruise in the

Outer Hebrides, which won the UK Dinghy Cruising Association's trophy for that year. But every voyage had its special moments, like the thrill of rowing into Fingal's Cave, where the swell was a serious challenge in a rubber dinghy, or the stunning beauty of the Treshnish Isles with their teeming bird life. These extracts from the 2016 log must stand for much more:

'**Monday June 6th.** Sunny all day. Variable 0-3. Woken early by a very noisy Arctic Tern which had landed on *Popeye*! Left our delightful anchorage at 0915 and part sailed/part drifted into the Sound of Taransay. At the entrance to the bay we passed what looked like two habitable buildings possibly used by the Castaway 2000 group who lived on the Island, self-sufficient for the year. We had a close encounter with the sandy beach that extended a remarkably long way into the Sound.

Beating our way up the East coast Bridget spotted an otter which proved very camera shy. The wind died as we were crossing West Loch Tarbert so we had lunch. When the wind returned we beat towards Hushinish Point where we saw a dolphin. Once round the Point we entered Caolas Scarp, a blue lagoon-like stretch of water between Lewis and the Island of Scarp. The crystal clear shallow waters and extensive sandy beach with a stunning backdrop of the mountains on Lewis made a very tempting anchorage.

However, the tide seemed rather strong and we therefore decided to look for somewhere more protected. We found an inlet on the north extremity of Scarp where we dropped anchor at 1900. (25 miles, max speed 6.9 mph.)

Wednesday June 8th. Very misty start then cloudy, turning sunny mid-afternoon onwards. Wind W 0-3. Awoke to a blanket of mist such that we could barely see the other yacht at our anchorage so we took our time prior to departing at 1100, when the mist had lifted sufficiently that it was safe to sail. Given so little wind again we had decided to take the opportunity to explore the usually inaccessible and very dangerous West coastline of North Uist. We motored the seven-mile stretch to the Sound of Harris which we eventually crossed in a force 2 with the gennaker up. While sailing across we were accompanied by some dolphins and managed to photograph some gannets. There was also the sound of seals singing again as there tends to be most days. We passed slowly through the Sound of Pabbay which was very shallow, down to a metre in places, and arrived at our destination of Boreray at 1530 just as the sun came out and the wind kicked in! We enjoyed a walk to the high point of the island which afforded panoramic views of the surrounding islands and their numerous white, sandy beaches.

After having a cup of tea on the beach we were greeted by the sole resident, Gerry, who kindly offered to fill our water container. We anchored off the beach and had our supper and then moved the two miles to a more sheltered anchorage behind the island of Lingay where we dropped the anchor at 2015.

Thursday June 9th. Sunny all day, wind variable, 0-4. After finding that the forecast had changed overnight we had to be prepared to return to Lochmaddy tomorrow. We therefore decided to explore more of the many islands in and around the Sound of Harris and set off at 1030 towards Berneray, travelling along the four-mile west coast of endless sand dunes. We had the fastest sail of the trip so far with the gennaker up. Off the NW coast of Bernaray we entered the notoriously dangerous Cope Passage, which frequently consists of heavy breakers and shifting sand banks, but was today in benign mood. We crossed the Passage to Killegray where we had lunch on the island and climbed to the cairn at its peak, which gave spectacular panoramic views over the whole of the Sound.

As the tide was dropping we were keen to get round the west coast of the island before that route dried. This took us into Caolas Skaari between Killegray and Ensay which has 5-knot streams at springs and is strewn with rocks and changes in both course and depth. We concentrated very hard throughout this 4-mile passage until we arrived at the anchorage of Groay. Here we relaxed with a cup of tea next to a fish farm but were soaked by the waves created by a rib with workers leaving the farm and giving us a friendly wave! We then headed south in the Sound to the Hermetray group of islands where we eventually found a delightful anchorage in the very peaceful Calm Bay in the NE tip of North Uist at 1800.

Sunday June 12th. Cloudy with rare sunny intervals, wind E 0-3. We left Lochmaddy at 1040 and as we were head to wind coming out of the bay we decided to motor into the Minch. Given that our wish was to get to at least East Loch Tarbert 30 miles away, we decided to continue motoring for about the first third of the trip to make the most of the tide. However, the wind gradually died and we found ourselves motoring for the rest of the day. We then realised we had an opportunity to visit the Shiants and, although this would make it a long day, as it has been a long-held ambition to go – often prevented by the dangers of the Minch, we finally made it. The Shiants are a stunningly majestic group of islands with basalt rock formations which are also found on Staffa and the Giant's Causeway in Northern Ireland.

Neither of us had ever seen such a mass of bird life such that the sky and sea were full of them as well as the cliffs and rockfalls. We also saw an eagle being chased off the north cliffs. We left the Shiants at about 1730 and continued motoring to East Loch Tarbert where we found a snug little anchorage in Plocrapool Bay at 1930. (55 miles).

Monday June 13th. Rain then cloud then sun, wind SW 0-2. Rain until mid-morning meant we took our time over breakfast and getting ready to sail, and we eventually left our anchorage under sail at 1100. We sailed round

Gloraig Dubh into Braigh Mor and headed out into the Minch. East Loch Tarbert is very big and it would have been nice to explore it but with very light winds and at least 25 miles ahead of us we couldn't spare the time. Once in the Minch we found our progress dropped away completely and we had to continue under motor. After five miles we were opposite Loch Stockinish and were able to sail for a few more miles until the wind died again. On attempting to drop the mainsail we had great difficulty because it had slightly come out of the track and was resisting our efforts to pull it down! We motored gently down to the Sound of Harris deliberating the forecast as strong winds were due in about 24 hours. We decided to spend one last night afloat and returned to Calm Bay back on North Uist, arriving at 1815. (25.4 miles).

Returning to the harbour where we were going to get *Popeye* out of the water we had a last fling around the bay enjoying the best wind of our trip!'

22. Pearly Miss to Westerly Typhoon

As with David Foreman's account of his voyage to Brazil and back, it was a privilege for me to read the story of James Tomlinson's apprenticeship and developing confidence as a single-handed sailor. For James, as for many of us, this dated back to childhood.

'It is July 8th 2018. As we sail slowly north in a light easterly breeze I look back over the starboard quarter at the beautiful island of Santa Maria. Her peaks are cloud-covered, much as they were a few days ago when we approached the island from the east. After a few days alone in the ocean, landfall was becoming an interesting experience for me and my sail-boat *Talisker 1*. We are clearing the west side of the island. Santa Maria is the most easterly one in the beautiful Azores chain. Sixty nautical miles to the north lies San Miguel. Later today we will pass the eastern side of San Miguel. We will then be clear of land and traffic and have the Atlantic Ocean much to ourselves. Lands End is 1,150NM to the north-east, Cabo da Roca, the most westerly point of Europe, 750NM to the east. I am hoping the easterly winds that are promised for a day or two will get us well to the north.

The breeze is more consistent out of the lee of Santa Maria. We are romping along at seven knots through the water with 15 knots of wind over the deck. It's overcast and warm. The depth sounder is no longer working. A few minutes ago it registered 110 metres. The descent to the ocean bed is steep here. Shortly we will have 2,000 metres below our keel that will soon descend further to unimaginable depths. A double check of our course confirms what I already know. We are going to clear the uninhabited Formigas Bank, well to the east. You can never be too careful. There is no traffic showing on radar and AIS.

I am expecting very variable winds in the next 10 days or so. With the jet stream so high, we should not have heavy weather. Even so my anxiety is palpable and I feel queasy with the underlying fear of what is ahead. This feeling normally calms down quickly and is always at its worst before casting off. I usually settle down pretty quickly once under way; 24 to 36 hours from now I'll be into a routine and starting to feel comfortable.

The furthest I've sailed alone non-stop is 800 nautical miles. Managing myself is crucial. An incapacitated sailor means the boat is disabled. I do not want to let *Talisker 1* down but I am the weakest link. I think this voyage could take as long as 14 days. The boat is well balanced and sailing well. It is time for a cup of tea.

So, where did it all begin?

I was born in June, 1956. My actor father, David, was informed of my arrival whilst swimming in the Thames. Dad was filming *Three Men in a Boat*. My interest in water might have had early beginnings due to that! Although our home in the Vale of Aylesbury could not have been further from the sea, I'm pretty sure boating is in the genes. Indeed my Tomlinson ancestors were bargemen who came to London from Yorkshire.

My great-great-grandfather, William John Tomlinson, was born in 1810. His father George was a Thames Waterman, the equivalent of the London cabby today, the watermen rowed clients across the river. William won the prestigious Doggett's Coat & Badge Race, the annual race for Watermen, from London Bridge to Chelsea. The winner was entitled to wear an orange-coloured Livery with Badge. The Morning Chronicle of August 8th 1834 reports:

"The annual contest for the Coat and Badge bequeathed by Doggett, the comedian, took place on Friday. The contest lay between six young Watermen just out of their time, three from above the bridge and three from below the bridge. The six started about an hour and a half before flood, and after labour against tide, which it is even painful to witness for such an extraordinary distance, Tomlinson was declared the winner, the second man being a few lengths astern."

William realised, with the steady increase in the number of bridges, that the days of the Watermen were numbered. There is evidence that he had a boat building business but he made his fortune in property.

As for me, my first ocean voyage was from Southampton to Cape Town. I have no recollection of this. I was hardly six months old; but my first memory of boats is of the small child's inflatable kind, afloat in a calm sea off Sandgate. I do remember not thinking much of the murky grey water, preferring instead to be dry, inside the vessel. Later there was a clinker-built pram dinghy with a seagull outboard.

Then came the 1961 Boat Show at Earl's Court. My Dad bought a Pearly Miss speed boat with a 25 HP Gale engine, built at Wroxham. It was very 1960s style, with an aluminium hull, a sky-blue deck, and red and white-striped seats. I have no memory of a capsize off Folkestone but, soon after, the boat was towed to the south of France, where it was to remain for 18 years. The Pearly Miss survived many scary moments. The infamous Mistral wind powers down the Rhône Valley and into the Mediterranean, but our family holidays were made for me by that little speed boat.

From the moment I was able to pull the engine starter cord I was allowed to go water skiing alone with my big brother, who had accomplished the starting test long before me. That also made us the crew to take Dad water skiing. I remember my brother David being 13 and me 11. Dad had bought a wet suit. In those days they were very heavy duty and seemed to be about an inch thick. Dad went over the side and I started to pay out the ski line with David Junior at the helm.

There were two control levers for the driver. A short lever with a black knob operated forward, neutral and reverse. Just above that lever was a totally separate one with a red knob that operated the throttle. Both worked independently! Frankly – incredibly dangerous! No thought had been given to a kill cord.

"FORWARD!" came the command from the water "DON'T GET THE SKI LINE CAUGHT IN THE PROPELLER!" Something along those lines anyway.

I heard the engine roar but there was no propulsion. Without idling the throttle my brother accidentally thrust the lower lever into forward gear and the boat, throttle fully open, leapt forward, the ski line tangled and was ripped from Dad's hands. By the time the boat was brought under control father was bobbing in our wake some 100 metres astern. The air was hot with invective. My father could have been heard in Monte Carlo.

"You could have taken my so and so hand off!"

We had no intention of going anywhere near him. We felt fairly safe with him in the water so far away, and the ski line was terribly tangled! I fumbled away trying to untangle it while David looked anxiously over my shoulder at our distant father. Neither of us realised that Dad was extremely buoyant in his wet suit. After what seemed like a good hour – probably five minutes – the line was half untangled. The air was very tense. Brother David nudged me

"I think he's going to go under," were his immortal words.

Today the Pearly Miss lives snugly in my garage, fully restored. She's occasionally launched at Orford where she is very popular with young Orford SC member Freddy Cox and his sisters!

Still in France, I loved the sound of the rhythmic chug of the small fishing boats as they put to sea at first light. We stayed in Jules Verne's beautiful villa, then a small hotel 'Le Nautilus'. Paradise! Throwing open the shutters there was always a mirror calm and an azure blue sky, as the heat of the Mediterranean day began. With little brother Henry, and long before breakfast, we would be up and across the road and into the harbour.

What really delighted me was watching the fishermen repairing their wooden boats on the hard. There always seemed to be about a dozen in various stages of repair. By the late 1960s the boats would have already been a great age. I was fascinated by the meticulous way the fishermen slowly brought the boats back to life, carpentry, caulking and painting in a variety of colours – maroon below the waterline and shining white top sides. The shear-strakes, rubbingstrakes, toe-rails, decks and hatches in dazzling blues, yellows, greens and reds and all applied with such artistry. Their masts were rarely stepped even in the 1960s – no sign of sails. I knew the names of most of the men working in the harbour. One of them, a Monsieur Jacquet, gave me an oil painting of Le Mourillon Harbour that hangs in my office today.

I was always utterly depressed when the car pulled away from the sea. I hated leaving the Mediterranean to turn inland and head north. My parents also rented a coastguard cottage on the beach in Sandgate, Kent. It did not matter if it was the dull waters of the Channel or the azure blues of the Mediterranean I still loved the sea and hated my last glimpse as we drove away at the end of a holiday. I might have to wait a whole year or more before returning to the salt!

I can't imagine not living by the sea today. I feel quite peculiar when I'm inland. During my early working and married life my boating did not progress, but I loved getting on the water when I could. Living in Wimbledon and knowing my interest in the sea, my first wife enrolled me in a shore-based Day Skipper course in Raynes Park, south west London!

In the early 1990s we moved to Woodbridge and I started a business that was to consume me for the next 20 years. The Pearly Miss was now in Suffolk and I had started to explore some of Suffolk's estuaries in a somewhat clueless way. In 1998 I was single again. I had been craving to be a big boat owner for far too long. *Rosie J*, a Westerly Centaur, was for sale at Woolverstone Marina. I was given the keys and went on board. My rash offer was immediately accepted! Having rarely 'sailed', this might have seemed an odd thing to do!

I had a berth booked in the Tidemill Yacht Harbour on the River Deben close to my work but *Rosie J* was in the Orwell. How do I move her? How does the engine start? What do the sails do? What are all those ropes for? A marine engineer at Woolverstone had serviced the engine. He was slightly surprised to be asked by her new owner how to start the darn thing. I certainly knew nothing about the sea-cocks. Thank goodness he pointed out the valve for the raw water intake!

With *Rosie J* now ready to go, I sat on board, tried not to look foolish and fooled nobody. I need to OBSERVE MORE!!! But how do I move the boat? Is there a book I can buy?

I then remembered that my brother Henry had been sailing in the Mediterranean with the actor, James Wilby, and had even reached Corsica from the mainland. Henry had mentioned his host's incompetence over (was it 'topping lifts'?) and how lucky it was that Henry was there to avert the catastrophe of a bump on his beautiful girl-friend's head. I telephoned Henry, who was very happy to help and would also bring Toby, a sailing friend.

It was an interesting cruise to Woodbridge and when I think of the care I take now in the Orwell and the approaches to the Port of Felixstowe, not to mention the Deben river bar; we did get away with it, but *Rosie J* and I had completed our first short cruise. The late Rufus Plummer was a very experienced sailor, Delivery Skipper and RYA Instructor. I asked Rufus to accompany me on my first sea passage to Osea Island. Rufus brought his stepson, Simon, fresh out of Plymouth University. At 22 Simon was already an East Coast veteran with numerous North Sea crossings, Transatlantics and plenty of sailing while at university. So, while I was taking my first small steps learning to handle my boat, Rufus and Simon were very relaxed, and like all people who are extremely good, they made sailing look easy.

I've been fortunate to know some very capable sailors in the last 20 years. Several have helped me enormously to achieve goals that would have been impossible without their encouragement. Incredibly, most weekends for two solid summers, Simon was available to go sailing with me and my daughter Hannah. Hannah invariably brought a friend to share the fore-peak with her. I was given a flying start; and what a fabulous patient teacher Simon was! So much so that by the end of the first summer I'd clocked enough miles to complete the practical side of my Day Skipper course with Philippe Taylor, and I met the incomparable James Robinson for the first time.

It was late in 1999 and bitterly cold when an unusually grumpy Simon joined me for a sail to the Orwell. Out of the Deben we were making slow progress.

"It's a bloody bath tub with a pole in it!" Simon growled at me.

"What is?" I asked searching the horizon.

"This boat" Simon replied. "It's a hideous sailing boat. Time for a new boat, mate!"

I've made some good decisions in my sailing life and *Rosie J* was just the sort of sea-kindly, forgiving vessel to have got me started. I bought a Westerly Consort and in 2001 took a mooring for the first time at Orford. *Kyle* continued to teach me all manner of things including nearly wrecking her on the Orford Bar.

By this time James Robinson was not only the very best instructor but also a terrific friend. James happily told me that he'd done the same thing himself! "You won't do that again, will you!" The novice was learning the ways of the sea despite enjoying the busiest time at work. My wonderful Sally was working with me too and was happy to bear the brunt of Saturdays at work to allow me to get away and go boating for the whole weekend, often not returning until Monday night.

At this point I should say that without Sally I would not have the sailing knowledge I have today. It was Sally who packed my sailing bag, provided the food and sent me off to my ships. My thousands of nautical miles were clocked up because I was never pressured to be at home or work. As much as I liked going sailing I also loved coming home to Sally. I look back today as if in a dream as to how little I knew then, how far I've managed to sail since, and how much more I have to learn. Often there was no one to go sailing with, so I boated alone. For a social animal on land I started to prefer my own company on a boat. I have rarely sailed with others since 2005 and I like it that way. *Kyle* lasted just two years. Then I bought *Wahine*, a Holman 26, which sailed very well.

I spread my wings when I bought a Sadler 32 in 2006. Over the next eight years *Samingo II* and I clocked up North Sea miles and I became proficient enough to do professional boat deliveries further afield. I was invited to the Mediterranean to deliver a classic yacht and I looked after the Philip Rhodes *Undina* for a couple of years in home waters.

David Foreman and *Tuesday* were on the mooring next to mine. The input of 'Doc' into my sailing has been equal to that of James Robinson. I've ruthlessly exploited their knowledge, which both have generously shared over the years.

I knew I wanted to sail further. Quite how far I did not know! I felt I'd prepared pretty well. *Samingo II* and I had sailed across the North Sea at least three times a year since 2007. We'd been caught in a Southern North Sea gale. I'd been appallingly sea-sick and cold 40 miles from land. I would, and will be sea-sick again, but I never want to be so cold. I sailed back from Ostend on one of the coldest winter days on record. The sheets and decks were crisp with ice. The strong wind backed north-west earlier than expected and we had a long beat to reach Long Sand Head. Only my nose got cold! I'd sorted the warmth issue!

I had sailed plenty of miles but James and Doc left me in no doubt that if I was to sail further, I had to do longer cruises offshore to find out how I would really feel deep in the ocean. By this time they'd persuaded me to buy a Westerly Typhoon.

After two years of painstaking preparation on *Talisker 1*, I was ready to do a shake-down cruise in 2016. *Talisker 1* and I headed north and life at sea changed. Fair Isle was an amazing experience and I met some long distance cruising boats. The sail to Shetland in beautiful weather was unforgettable. Was I really this far from home and 60° north? Sailing from Shetland to Norway seemed like a very long way in 2016. I was exhilarated to make landfall in Norway. The 2016 cruise took 12 weeks and we sailed home via the Skagerrak, Kattegat and the Kiel Canal.

I'd fallen in love with the north and in 2017 sailed again to Scotland and on to Orkney, this time sailing through Scapa Flo to Stromness. It was a privilege to sail in Scapa Flo and the history of the place was palpable. The weather gods had other ideas about my plans to sail to Faroe and possibly Iceland. Instead, after two weeks sheltering from the weather in Stromness with new friends, David and Candy from US SV *Endeavor,* both boats sailed to Fair Isle and on to Shetland.

The weather was fair for a return to Norway. *Endeavor* sailed north-east to Floro while *Talisker 1* sailed east to Bergen. The crossing to Norway was testing. *Endeavor* took longer and reported rough seas. For *Talisker 1* and me it was a good rehearsal of our abilities to cope together at sea.

My longest solo sail to date was the return from Stavanger to Peterhead, Scotland. I was becoming used to not thinking about arrival. I'd become extremely aware of the importance of 'finals' – those last few hours when concentration should be at its peak. Now I'm never relaxed until I'm moored up or the anchor is down and holding. My boat and I were beginning to feel like a fairly well-oiled team; I felt we were ready to sail much further.

2018 dawned with several cruising plans. It would depend on which way the wind was blowing on departure day. South-westerly winds would mean heading north again. I did not want to be away for more than three months. I also wanted to return with my boat. One ocean cruise I'd thought about was an Atlantic circuit to Madeira, the Azores and then home.

At the beginning of June 2018 a week of easterly winds were forecast. *Talisker 1* sailed from Orford on the June 1st to L'Aber-Wrac'h on the north-west tip of France, with stops in the Orwell, Ramsgate, Eastbourne, the Solent and Cherbourg. We crossed Biscay (my first Biscay alone) and made landfall in beautiful Cedeira, just east of La Coruna.

The next passage was 800NM non-stop to Porto Santo, Madeira. We experienced the Portuguese trades and for much of the five days it blew a fairly constant force 6 to 7, but never less than 5. For some of the passage the mainsail was triple-reefed on a preventer with a handkerchief of genoa poled out. I was hypnotised by a big spectacular sea, a beautiful blue in sunlight and a dull forbidding slate grey when overcast. Waves marched up like an army behind us and *Talisker 1* just flew, hardly taking a drop of water in the cockpit. Our 24 hour runs averaged 180 nautical miles plus. I had nothing to do but set her up, admire the ocean and let my ship run.

Porto Santo appeared on the horizon. I was astonished to have sailed so far and overjoyed to round the south-east tip of the island and sail in the lee of the island. I wanted to cherish the moment and took an age preparing *Talisker 1* for a safe arrival. It was a huge moment for my ship and me. I'd listened in hushed awe to Doc for years as he described his landfall in Porto Santo. I was so proud to know now what Doc had felt.

The sail home from Madeira was upwind, the first 550NM to the Azores.

I could not believe that we'd made it to these famous islands. It was another windward passage to Falmouth from the Azores. Out of 1,400 miles eventually sailed on this leg, 1,000 were close hauled under stay-sail and double-reefed, sometimes triple-reefed main. I took satisfaction that I'd managed myself very well. I'd learnt to get enough sleep, which is a vital ingredient and the greatest danger, together with avoiding injury, in sailing alone. Very occasionally I'd had to remind myself to eat. I realised that a little sea-sickness one evening was caused by not eating. A bowl of cereal with banana, honey, raisins and milk followed by several of my Mum's crystallized stem ginger cubes was a perfect remedy. I felt tip top after that.

I broke the voyage down into sections. Based on my 'grib' maps (weather maps down-loaded from satellite) I was looking seven days ahead but trusting the information for four to five days. The wind shifts all arrived as forecast and having sailed north from the Azores we tacked and were close-hauled on port for many days. On day two out from the Azores I wrote:

"The expected wind shift is due tomorrow. The wind will back to the north and then we will tack and head east, sailing as high as we can until the predicted westerly and south-westerly winds arrive sometime around Saturday".

The penultimate tack, 130NM from Finisterre, took us 60 miles back out into the Atlantic where we finally tacked back on to port, the wind backed, as predicted and we then laid a course directly for the western approaches well outside Biscay. The whole voyage had been about decision making. When to tack? Today? Tomorrow? Perhaps at 0100 or leave it until 0700? I felt my decision-making had been all right.

I also tried to have the weather for each leg in our favour for departure. The first 36 to 48 hours are always the hardest, so having a good easy start was always going to be a bonus and allow me to get in to sea mode. There was very little traffic. But after a solitary ship on Day Three there was an unsettling experience that evening.

A small vessel that had been steadily approaching from our port quarter, MMSI 204211000 eventually passed half a mile in front of *Talisker 1*. Watching the ship get nearer had me feeling vulnerable and scared. There was no response on VHF and my binoculars confirmed there was no-one on the bridge. I later identified the name of the vessel heading off to the east as the FV *Mar Portugues*. Mid-ocean – who cares? The crew were probably playing Monopoly!

With the sun out the deck was hot on Day Four. I could have burnt the soles of my feet. There was early morning dew for the first time and it was very slightly colder but I was still living in pyjamas to keep cool. My AIS alarm sounded. CS *Pacific Reefer* was bearing down on us from the N at 17 knots. "Have you seen us?"

From the sleepy reply – obviously not! The ship turned to starboard. We wished each other a good watch. I could set an audible guard alarm around both AIS and Radar but plenty of squalls set the radar alarm off – often. One of the features of the sail from Madeira to the Azores and from the Azores to Falmouth was the frequent squalls.

On Day Five, bound for Falmouth, I wrote:

"Clouds have to be watched but resting down below I'm pretty quick to get up on deck to reef. A squall, bringing 45 knot gusts, is disappearing behind us. Our gray forbidding visitor is fleeing south, her skirts right down on the waves. Behind her, blue skies, a breath of breeze and a wind shift. NNW would you believe. The wind veers north again. We could set the genoa and shake out the reef but there is more cloud heading this way. With the wind freshened we are making six knots plus through the water with stay-sail and reefed main".

The ocean is certainly punishing on a boat. Days and days of non-stop wear and tear. Every time I was tempted to fly full sail I decided not to. Being slightly underpowered and nursing the boat was key. I searched for weakness on my daily deck and rig checks.

Tomatoes were over-ripening so I had to eat the whole supply quickly. Green bananas ripened as fast as the yellow ones. The delicious Santa Maria small melons went too soon. But I had enough food on board to last several weeks including loads of dried fruit. I was able to send emails daily and I felt, with satellite communication, I was cheating compared with sailors of the past.

On Day Five I sent this email: "Subject: Weather Brains:

Uncomfortable night bashing into northerlies close hauled. Lumpy seas. But she does not get stopped. I'm at 42 21 N 18 23 W. I continue like this until Saturday morning by which time we should be 43 30 N 13 25 W. Tack and head NNW until wind backs and we resume course for the English Channel. Winds increase a bit. Have I missed anything?"

Simon Abley replied: "No it's about all you can do to play the angles and get set for the new breeze". Since first teaching me in 1998/99 Simon has added numerous further transatlantic crossings, Fastnets and the Sydney Hobart race to his sailing CV.

John Pennington replied: "You're doing all the right things; just got to keep

plugging away until Saturday's switch. It's a marathon – not a sprint – as there's a fair wind on the way and nothing scary on the forecast – so don't forget to look after yourself too. A few hours hove to for a comfortable meal, a cup of tea that won't slosh out, and a longer stretch in the bunk always does wonders for me when it all just seems like too much work! We're in Bantry Bay doing some shopping and watching the weather for Biscay crossing. Mostly light winds forecast, so we've got out the full-size spinnaker and are trying to figure out which end is up – doih! Stay safe, Love,
John, Kara and Dean."

John and Kara Pennington have sailed one and a half times round the world in a very small boat, *Orca*. Their new bigger boat is *Sentijn*, which they bought in Holland and restored in Ipswich. As of June 2019 they (with baby Dean) arrived on the eastern seaboard of the USA via Scotland, Ireland, the Canaries and Caribbean.

 I never slept for more than 30 minutes in one go. Each time I set a wake-up alarm it was rare that a wind shift would not wake me first and have me up to reef, re-check the horizon, AIS and Radar, before resetting the alarm for another 30 minutes. I continued this routine day and night. I averaged about six to seven hours of sleep in 24 hours. I never felt deeply asleep. If I was not working the boat, drinking, eating, enjoying the scene around us, I was resting. At the end of day five out from the Azores my diary continues:

 "Last night, close-hauled, in variable wind strengths we ended up at midnight with a couple of reefs in the main and flying the stay-sail. The sea was sloppy and uncomfortable as *Talisker 1* smashed her way to windward. I have to catch up on some sleep. I'd triple-reefed for one squall and with darkness approaching: I left the deep third reef in and we fore-reached slowly, but comfortably, into a messy sea state. This is okay! Forward momentum. Control. No stress. Into my pilot berth 2230, out at midnight, a check around, set the alarm on radar and AIS and then set a wake-up alarm for 30 minutes. We still made 29NM in the six hours. I've just slept six hours, but broken! Now that's better"!

The following day I had a golden ocean encounter as I watched a vessel approaching from astern on AIS. The CPA (closest point of approach) was showing half a mile! Was it going to be a repeat encounter like the *Mar Portugues*?

 I got an immediate response on VHF. "Don't worry, we see you … we are deciding which side to pass you". And then: "Can I help you with anything? Do you need a weather update? Where are you heading?" *Lutador* was returning to Vigo having fished the Grand Banks. Her skipper Alfredo had sailed dinghies including Lasers. He raced a Dufour 44 in Portugal.

"Can I call family to give them your position?" I told Alfredo we had satellite communication. I felt really chuffed with human nature. I had met a really kind professional sailor that day. It got quite windy after *Lutador* disappeared over the horizon and *Talisker 1* bashed her way, close-hauled, under triple-reefed main and stay-sail. Friday July 13th was an interesting day!

A couple of days later I noted that: *'Talisker 1* is still cutting a path towards the English Channel. Nothing stops this boat'. Many boats are stopped by waves, particularly to windward. Not mine. Days of sailing to windward, smashing through the Atlantic caused a minor weep from the small hatch just forward of the mast. I meant to remove the hatch and re-bed the frame when I repaired the large fore-hatch but you never get everything done.

As the Western Approaches got closer traffic would increase and there would be less time to sleep. On July 17th we were finally on to the continental shelf. The winds were light but we were still sailing. As I've written before, concentration is very important on 'finals'. It's easy to drop your guard. It's easy to think you've arrived! We arrive WHEN we arrive and this is the time to be extra careful. I felt well rested but I also knew I had to try and get more sleep as traffic would build over the final 24 hours.

There had been a huge contrast between the downwind ocean passages from L'Aber-Wrac'h to Cedeira (350 NM) Cedeira to Madeira (800 NM) and the upwind passages from Madeira to the Azores (550 NM) and now the current one from the Azores to the UK. I felt the ocean gave us our sail south to Madeira. However windy and rough, it was never taxing downwind. From Madeira to the U.K. via the Azores the ocean made us work hard for every mile. I enjoyed the challenges and the lessons learned. Now my boat and I had nearly completed what I'd wanted and prepared to do for so long. A small voyage in the ocean. It was a completely humbling experience. I now have an inkling of what some very special friends do all the time.

I was delighted to be still sailing on Day 11 as my 'grib' maps had predicted less wind. The engine hours on the whole voyage had almost been completely used for battery charging. The one disappointment of the voyage was battery management. But we did carry loads of fuel.

The lights of the Scilly Isles were finally visible at 0200 on July 18th. Later the same day we anchored in St Mawes after 11 days and 1,400 nautical miles non-stop from the Azores. I had only three more days of tea bags. I'd cut that fine. It was a lovely place to prepare for heading up Channel.

On July 31st *Talisker 1* and I returned to our home port of Orford, Suffolk, having sailed 4,000 nautical miles in two months. I am grateful to my friends James Robinson and David 'Doc' Foreman for pointing me in the direction of a Typhoon as the right boat for ME. *Talisker 1* handled everything thrown at her. If I had been sailing my choice of boat I would still be far from home. In lighter airs we simply would not have made progress.

In March 2019 I sailed across the Atlantic Ocean with my great friend James Robinson. We joined David Frost and Kris Adams on their Kaufman 49 *Taipan* from Lanzarote to Grenada, via Gran Canaria, Martinique, St Lucia and Bequia. James Robinson was a tower of strength and did not allow the morale of the single-hander to drop. Sailing with James is always a joy. But the voyage confirmed to me that I will not agree to sail far again offshore unless I am alone.'

23. Time Past and Time Future

Early in the morning of July 7th 2010 *Quantz* left Pyefleet Creek and sailed south to the Wallet Spitway. At 0800, near the South Buxey buoy and heading for Burnham-on-Crouch with the freshening wind now dead ahead, I decided to lower the main and continue under engine. The tide was with me but the waves were short and choppy. One hour further on the red warning light on the engine panel glowed, and steam rose from engine casing. This was an unwelcome recurrence of a symptom the day before, entering the Colne. It was supposed to have been cured following a call to James Robinson, who advised me to check the coolant reservoir and top up if necessary, which I had done.

Conditions did not favour raising the mainsail again and reefing, with no engine to maintain steerage in a relatively narrow channel between the sandbanks of the outer estuary. I might even have to cut my losses and head back towards the Colne. For a quarter of an hour I tacked back and forth with the genoa, making little progress. The realisation was beginning to dawn on me that sailing single-handed, this far from home, at the age of 78, might be tempting fate. Then I was hailed by a man at the helm of *White Magic*, a smart-looking yacht, about 30ft I guessed, which had motored past me five minutes before. He must have turned back. "Are you OK?" he shouted.
"Well, not really. Engine's packed up. Not getting anywhere."
"Stand by! I'll take you in tow."

Just at the right moment, as I furled the jib, he ranged alongside, a foot clear, and passed a line across, waiting long enough for me to make it fast on the foredeck, with a turn round the mast as insurance. Then with perfect judgement and expertise, he edged forward to take up the slack and the weight before settling down to a steady tow – impressive seamanship on his part. So far as I knew he was alone. Only about an hour later, approaching the actual river entrance, did a female head appear in the hatch-way, probably surprised by the sight of the boat in tow astern. Finally, at 1100, after I heard him radio ahead to Burnham Yacht Harbour, he cast me adrift just off their outer pontoon where a reception committee waited to take my lines.

I managed to persuade Duncan and Pat, the owners of *White Magic,* to pause long enough for a quick drink in the Marina bar, before they pressed on to their mooring up river with the last of the tide. Duncan, I gathered, had served as a sailing instructor for the Services, before joining the police. To my great regret I never asked his surname or address. They mentioned an ambition to find a larger ocean-going boat and sail across the world. Did this come to pass, I still wonder? I should love to know, and remain most grateful for that prompt and efficient help.

Engineers diagnosed corrosion in the exhaust elbow of the heat exchanger, which would have to be replaced at some expense. I returned to Burnham a week later with our son Don, who was on holiday by then in Orford, and we sailed happily home together.

This was the furthest point south and west which I had reached since my return from the Baltic six years before. Visits to West Mersea and up the Blackwater to Heybridge Basin had also given me great satisfaction and enjoyment. But, over the years since then, my range and stamina have gradually diminished. The Walton Backwaters, Hamford Water, Stone Point and Titmarsh Marina were re-visited once more in 2012. Thereafter I was content with the Orwell and the Stour or the Deben as destinations beyond our own estuary, which still had much to offer. Wrabness, opposite Holbrook, was a favourite anchorage, so long as the wind blew somewhere south of west or east. Halfpenny Pier in Harwich always felt like a proper harbour, although Shotley Marina offered better shelter and the luxury of a proper full-length bath. It was there, in 2013, that I met *Dutch Dream* and *Sanderling* on their return from Holland or Ostend, the occasion of a happy evening in the Hitchcocks' saloon cabin with Barry, Sheila and James Robinson, all the more precious since the loss of Barry.

This was a 15-day cruise for me and *Quantz*, including some time on the Deben and nights at Pin Mill, Royal Harwich, Titmarsh, Wrabness and Levington. In a concluding log entry I summarised it as: 'a very satisfying mini-cruise with some good sails as well – proved to myself I could still do it.' I might have added 'in my 80th year'.

A year later I managed nine days, mainly on the Orwell, and in 2016 I was content with a short trip to Harwich early in September – 'pleased to have done it but needed a day or more to recover.' Finally, in 2017, I was in Shotley once more, meeting by chance *Sanderling*, *Caveat* and *Throstle*, who had been on a club cruise together across to Holland and back. Such joint ventures were now regular events in the club calendar with other destinations up and down the coast or up the Thames to St Katharine's Dock, a measure of the development of this activity over the decades. On return my assessment in the log suggested that I was – 'satisfied to have done trip, in easy conditions, but now demanding if single-handed'.

This recognition of physical limitations made me wonder whether I could justify launching *Quantz* in 2018 or whether I should really be looking for a buyer. In the event I was glad to have her afloat. Jamie accompanied me from the Deben to Orford that May and I took her back myself. During the summer I did not leave the river but enjoyed several days using *Quantz* as a floating base for my ten-footer, northwards to Mansion Reach near Iken, south to North Weir Point and back into Butley Creek. I had hoped to sail the dinghy up to Snape but a fickle wind and less than ideal tidal timing frustrated that ambition. I did however take her from Boyton Dock well up into the head waters near Butley Mill. At least this gave me the satisfaction of planning and partially carrying out a mini-venture.

Often, when returning towards Orford Quay from the south, I have admired the lines of *Aimee,* moored near Chantry point. She is a Robb Class 38 centre-board yawl owned by Tom Griffin and Jenny since 1998. She was purchased in a rather run-down state at a yard in Burnham-on-Crouch with many hours since spent on bringing her to her present fine state. Brian Upson at Slaughden relaid the deck with some magnificent Burma oak out of science laboratories. Since then Tom and Jenny have enjoyed many happy days, cruising on the East Coast rivers whenever they had the time.

One of their highlights was the trip to the south, in 2005, with the late Keble Paterson, to participate in the 200th anniversary celebration of the Battle of Trafalgar, which evoked memories of past Spithead Reviews. Mike and Suki Pearce were also there in *Naivasha,* their 36ft Hallberg Rassey, which they cruised for ten years from 1996 ranging from the Friesian islands to the West Country and Brittany. They went aboard *Aimee,* thus enabling her to fly the OSC Commodore's flag at the mast-head in the 'Gold Box' of vessels chosen to sail past Her Majesty the Queen on a truly memorable day. (See photograph page 303)

The ship's records show that at some stage *Aimee* was sailed in the Mediterranean, since the radio was serviced in Malta. This has been confirmed by Mary Goldin, née Webb, who is well-acquainted with the daughter of the then owner, and once enjoyed a day's sail in *Aimee* from Lymington in the mid-70s.

In 2018, over towards the shore opposite the Griffin's mooring lay *SV Endeavor.* The American spelling is correct; she flies the Stars and Stripes and her port of origin is Seattle. This beautiful steel yawl with her low-slung ocean-going lines has been mentioned already by James Tomlinson, who met her and her owners, David and Candy Masters, in Stromness, Orkney, and sailed with them to Shetland before crossing to Norway. Like David Foreman, James has found one of the most rewarding aspects of his sailing experience to be the encounters and developing friendships with members of that select ocean-sailing fraternity who have sailed all over, and often round the world.

The summary which Candy has provided of her great adventure with David and *Endeavor* is characteristic in that she says much more about other people than themselves. Sitting in the cabin with her one day I looked at photographs of the 15-year period when they devoted almost all their free time to a virtual re-build of the boat from the inside outwards. I learned just a little of the patience and determination with which they waited for the right weather in the Southern Hemisphere and, later, battled towards South Georgia before wisely easing the sheets to make for Tristan da Cunha. It is in itself a great tribute to David who died suddenly not long after their return to the USA in 2017, leaving *Endeavor* in the UK with other voyages in mind. Orford and OSC have been proud to have her based here since.

'David and I departed Seattle July 2005 and cruised in the Pacific and Atlantic for 12 years. In 2017 we visited Orford before sailing on to St Katherine Docks in London.

The question I am asked most often by far is. "What was your MOST favourite part?" That's a huge question because it is just vague enough to include it all, not just the sailing, not just the culture or the animals, and not merely my favourite place; so it's a very good question. My answer is usually the inverse to my LEAST favourite part, that is to say: the hardest thing I found while cruising was always saying good-bye to my new friends.

David and I never set out to sail 'around' the world; we set out deliberately to sail 'about' the world, trying not to rush over much or abide by anyone else's schedule. We wanted to see new places but also to enjoy the journey. We wanted to see stuff and scuba-dive, we wanted to photograph unusual birds and fish. We wanted to hike and eat picnics in wonderful new places and we wanted to make new friends. Our route wouldn't be following the route everyone else was taking, we were sailing 'about' after all. We'd go south, way south, through Mexico, the Galapagos, then visit Ecuador and beyond. We practised our Spanish, we prepared for high latitudes, we talked about Shackleton's *Endurance* and Antarctica, but I baulked, and suggested South Georgia instead.

We pressed on into the southern summer arriving at the peak of the cherry season at Valdivia in Chile's 'fruit basket' at Christmas time. Pot-luck parties were organized and before you knew it, a whole new group of friends was formed only to drift apart a few days or a week later. Hurried hugs, an exchange of emails and promises made to keep in touch. Thanks to the miracle of the Internet, keeping in touch, like many things, is easier than it used to be.

We include in our wider circle of friends, a few dozen of the thousands of members of the Seven Seas Cruising Association or SSCA. We joined, like most people after speaking to some nice folks at a Boat Show in about 1988. Once on the mailing list we were hooked, the SSCA Commodore's Bulletin has stories of real sailors that we wanted to emulate; Cruisers in Patagonia, the Black Sea, New England, Europe, the Far East, Alaska and other enchanting places. We worked hard on our goals and departed Seattle in 2005.

For 12 years, cruising became our way of life and making and parting from friends just one of the hazards of that lifestyle. To cut a long story short, last year our friends in the club selected us for an award given especially for "not doing stupid stuff"! It's called the Seven Seas Award and is given to sailors who demonstrate a commitment to good seamanship and an understanding of their ship and the environment. It was a great honor just to be nominated but to win was an incredible acknowledgement of my husband David's energy, skills and dedication, our boat's sea-kindly ability and strength, and my inspiration, patience and very good fortune!

In 2017 while cruising in Northern Europe, it was also a stroke of good fortune to meet four members of the Orford Sailing Club or OSC. *Endeavor* was tied-up alongside in a marina in Stromness, Orkney waiting for weather in June of 2017. David and I had just done an "overnighter" from Stornaway on the Isle of Lewis when a single-hander happened to approach, well-fendered and skilfully reversing into the slip opposite. David hopped up to catch a line and in that small moment fast friends were made yet again. This was how we came to meet James T on *Talisker 1*. This was to be a fortuitous friendship as we later came to draw on James' experience for lots of first-hand information about Norway (our next destination after Lerwick) and bits about the Kiel Canal, the Netherlands and the Thames Estuary also on our summer agenda.

Also on hand were the crew of *Cornelia II* – Chris and Caroline Gill and Frances Barnwell, on a summer cruise of their own. A supper party, a bottle of wine, a nutritious meal, a scrummy salad, a tasty dessert, "bring and share" might be the motto of cruisers everywhere.

Friends – they come in all shapes and sizes, they help us develop an understanding for our future endeavors and they buoy us up when we need rescue. In addition to other benefits, cruising is a great way to gain new and like-minded friends.'

Just as North Sea crossings have become almost routine, if never to be under-estimated, Round Britain sailing or cruises to the Northern Isles have been more frequent for OSC cruising members. As Candy recalled the Gills were in Orkney in 2017. I have taken the liberty of summarising their circumnavigation that year from the excellent account provided by Chris.

He and Caroline left Orford in May, taking the classic clockwise route. After Ramsgate and Brighton they went outside the Isle of Wight to Dartmouth, Falmouth and Newlyn, the all-tide harbour here being a better point of departure for rounding Land's End than Penzance. They faced a long day to Padstow but the Bristol Channel crossing from there to Milford

Haven was enriched by porpoises playing in the bow wave. Leaving Milford Haven for Fishguard, the area known as the 'washing-machine' lived up to its name. A highlight of the Welsh coast stages was the beautiful bay of Dillean (pronounced Dinthlean) where they spent a second day. Strong winds between Holyhead and Peel on the Isle of Man made that harbour even more attractive but in Bangor, Northern Ireland, poor visibility and rain kept them there an extra day.

On leaving the Irish coast for the Isle of Islay strong tides and overfalls were a feature but opposite Port Ellen's small marina there lies another pretty bay. They were also grateful for the sheltered Crinan Basin, where strong winds and rain kept them for three days, compensated by showers, Wifi and a coffee shop. The small islands in the Sound of Luing towards Oban required careful pilotage, followed by a scenic trip up the Sound of Mull to Tobermory. Two more days of rain were spent in soggy Mallaig before reaching the village harbours of Plockton and Badachro. I am envious of their visit to the Summer Isles, if only because of the name. They anchored overnight in Kyle Rintoul, an inlet on the mainland shore opposite.

From this point they intended to reach Kinlochbervie, 15 miles from Cape Wrath, but decided to press on so as to arrive at Stromness in time for the first of the flood tide in the Sound of Hoy. After they rounded that angry landmark at the north-west corner of mainland Scotland the wind kept rising, force 6 or 7. Rather than risk arrival on the ebb in heavy overfalls they wisely altered course for Scrabster to make port at 2330 still in twilight! They then crossed to Stromness and were able to visit the main archaeological sites of Orkney, Skara Brae and the Stone Ring of Brodgar as well as the Italian Chapel and St Magnus Cathedral. It was during this time in Orkney that the meeting with David and Candy Masters forged important links between *Endeavor* and Orford.

Cornelia was now homeward bound, south to Wick and by stages down the East Coast. Passing inside the Farne Islands to Sunderland, Whitby and Scarborough, they opted for the 100-mile stretch to Wells-next-the-Sea. After the final challenge of beating into a south-westerly from Lowestoft they were back in Orford. It was now July and they felt a mixture of sadness that it was all over and gladness to be home for a spell ashore.

One year later *Cornelia* headed for northern waters yet again, as she has done in 2019. Happily Chris appears to have recovered well from his efforts as a human fender on a windy night in Peterhead.

Mike Redmond describes his 2018 voyage in *Martiena Due* as one item off his bucket list.

'The plan was simple; out of the river, turn right, cross from the Scilly Isles to Southern Ireland, up the east coast of Ireland, over to Scotland, up the Caledonian Canal, and back down the East Coast. With lots of stops on the way, and clearly a good deal more planning than this summary suggests. And cheating a bit by leaving out NW Scotland, thus a 'sort of' circumnavigation.'

Amongst all that planning, this cruise, lasting from May 20th to July 5th, involved more frequent changes of crew than those on *Cornelia*. They included Mike's wife Kate, two sons and a son-in-law, OSC members Ben Johnston and David Pannell, at least nine different people for different stages, only the skipper himself aboard throughout. There were some lessons, Mike suggests:

'Firstly, 45 days for the trip, which included eight in various ports, was far too short a time to get full enjoyment. For instance, we arrived in the Scilly Isles in fog, the next day was raining, so we decided to push on to Kinsale overnight, where there was good weather. With more time it would have been better to hang round the Scillies for the weather to improve, and then explore them.

The second lesson is linked – with several crew changes involving flights we had to press on to meet those flying in. Either we needed a looser time-frame or a lesser dependence on crew needing to fly in. The other drawback I could do nothing about – the wind. For most of the time it was either very light or on the nose, or both.

Having said all that, the trip was very enjoyable; the stretches from Kinsale to Inverness involved some beautiful areas and interesting planning issues, which were very satisfying. There was only one stormy day, and we were tucked up in Bangor, outside Belfast. This gave us the opportunity to visit the Titanic museum, which was extremely well curated, when in Belfast, something to be recommended. On Islay the Ardbeg distillery proved a welcome diversion.

It was personally very rewarding to have a range of family and friends with me. Ben had been on the boat before, when he came with me to Itchenor to pick her up after purchase. On the homeward leg I noted that, between Ben, Roger, a friend from Bury, and me – we had about 180 years of sailing behind us!'

By contrast my own horizons have had to close in. Soon after *Quantz* returned to her Orford mooring in 2019 I became increasingly aware that the equation between enjoyment and exhaustion was no longer in balance. Even short trips downriver required at least 24 hours of recovery ashore and the one night I spent afloat in Butley Creek, despite the magic of sunset and dawn, was less restful than ever before. I knew the time had come to make the decision to put her up for sale. Two family excursions at the end of July, one to the beach at Dove Point and the other to the Crouch landing, almost made me hesitate. A photograph taken by Don's friend, Sean MacBride-Stewart, of *Quantz* at anchor off Dove Point actually proved instrumental in attracting her new owner, George Freeman, with whom, thanks also to the persuasive influence of James Robinson, the sale was speedily concluded. It may be the end of an era for me, but happily not for *Quantz* or her connection with this river.

Past, Present and Future: the last of these is the one that counts. On a fine Friday morning towards the end of August I launched my 10ft dinghy *Ariel II* to catch the last of the ebb tide and then sail round Havergate Island. One circumnavigation is as good as another at my age. Preceding me was Josh, the nine-year-old grandson of Michael and Suki Pearce, on his Topper, responding to his grandfather's challenge. "Sail round the Island non-stop and without assistance." He was out of sight well before I reached Chantry and back home with hours to spare.

Unlike Josh, I did stop for lunch at Dove Point, where I found three generations of Hitchcock, Robinson, Cox and Cornford connections. There were Toppers, a Mirror and Optimists drawn up along the beach, and Freddie Cox was demonstrating his expertise near the south mark buoy, under the watchful eye of 'Mads' Cooper. I can be confident that they and their descendants, with those of many other Orford families, will be gaining these skills and enjoying these delights in the decades to come. Who knows, there might be an Iliff, a Roberts or a Waite among them.

LAST WORD
From Hebe to *Tahira*

This is given, deliberately, to the contribution provided by Richard Waite. His name has been mentioned at several points in the course of this story – sailing with Charles Iliff on short rations across the North Sea, or again with Jamie Roberts on *Sea Swallow's* last sea voyage under our ownership. More importantly he has managed to encapsulate in a few hundred words the development from keen embryo sailor to one who takes his own vessel far beyond home waters.

'I am writing this at home in midwinter. 'Home' is *Tahira*, a 42ft double-ended cutter, built in Taiwan in 1987, which at the moment is securely tied to the dock in Cartagena, south-east Spain. It is neither simple nor easy to cut loose from house, work, supportive neighbours and accumulated stuff – in fact the drive to do so has to run pretty deep if it's to happen at all. That drive has its origins in Orford and her waters.

Ten footer racing in *Poppet* from the old bathing-place ensured an early dose of mud in the veins and led to a Mirror dinghy (*Apple*) in the early 70s. This was also the time when my parents became the proud owners of *Hebe*, Bombay Tomtit number 5, bought from Neil and Ann Iliff in, I think, 1971. Funny what one remembers and how early adult remarks have an impact. We were 'test-sailing' *Hebe* with Neil, who asked me to tie his tender onto the mooring-strop. Worried by such a responsibility, I tied enough knots to secure a liner, with both Neil and my father John saying as much – one of those early lessons – the right knot is the one you can untie quickly. Another memory from that time – receiving Ralph Brinkley's appreciation for helping him dig the mud out of his mooring-barge after she sank in a storm – Ralph's approval meant a lot to me.

Hebe, all 18ft of her with spitfire-wing centreboard and a foredeck you could stand on without capsizing, was a proper ship, and it did not take long to realise she could go places and I could sleep under the mainsail. It took longer to realise that sails were not waterproof. A night in Butley Creek aged 12 (1973) was followed the same year by the first voyage to the Deben and within a couple of years *Hebe* and I had got as far as the Blackwater. I devoured and made sense of books on navigation and voyaging – unsuccessful in every way at school I had found something that I could do – (knowing how important this had been to me was a motivation for setting up an outdoor centre for children in my late twenties).

Some memories of that early voyaging on *Hebe* stand out: cooking at anchor on the foredeck as the sun set over marshes; getting drenched in a deluge under the sail and looking at the cosy cruiser with a proper cabin anchored next door in the Walton Backwaters (I started saving for one from that day); sailing against a flood tide and building north-east wind and sea off Southend, tying up to a buoy labelled "for distressed fishing vessels" off the beach, rowing ashore in search of a shear pin for the outboard and realising what a dangerous mistake I had made when I returned to find crashing waves, and my non-sailing friend bailing *Hebe* among a jumble of whitecaps; running back to West Mersea under storm jib for ignominious collection by car (after more lessons learned in one day than ever before or since). Then there was feeling vaguely sea-sick but determined to keep on smoking, while using the transistor radio to 'direction find' our way to 'the Ship that Rocked', Radio Caroline. I could not have had such formative early experiences if my parents, John and Julia Waite, had not trusted me with *Hebe* and contained worries they might have had; (until they told Alec Comins, demon helm and aficionado of all things Tomtit, that I was at sea somewhere off the Essex coast, who said: "get him home, those boats are not designed to be at sea in weather like this!").

Another Tomtit-related snippet comes to mind. I was in Bombay, aged 19, and cheekily went to the Royal Bombay Yacht Club – without a tie and in full backpacking garb – put my request to the steward and was ushered in front of the full Committee, who were kindness personified as they told me what they knew about the history of these craft in India. I was told that the first boats had come originally from the Humber and had been gaff-rigged, and that they had always been more popular in Karachi than Bombay, where there were none left at that stage (1981).

I never did make it across the North Sea in *Hebe*. My first sailing on a proper cruising boat was aged 16, crewing for Nick Oglethorpe, who at that stage kept his 32ft ketch in the Baltic near Stockholm (a wonderful cruising ground to which I returned, first in sea kayaks with my wife Sue and children, Lucy and Angus, in 2011 and then with Charles and Monica Iliff and James Robinson during their 2014 Baltic cruise in *Katrina*). Charles, in his 22ft Hunter Sonata *Kehaar* gave me my first taste of a North Sea crossing from Ijmuiden to Orford with Howard Nash, and the distance bug was well and truly embedded.

Like many at that time I cut my skippering teeth during the Orford cruiser events organised by Charles. The first event was especially memorable for me as Richard Roberts, having recently bought *Quantz*, had a 'spare' boat, the 22ft bilge-keeled *Sea Swallow*. Richard invited me to take her across to Flushing with his son Jamie, and we did so along with Ginny and Catherine Iliff, and with 'For Sale' painted on a sheet tied to the guardrails. Nervous about my ability to arrive in anything like the right place in Holland, I asked for a log, radio or radio direction finder to add to *Sea Swallow's* compass and Richard told me, ever so kindly, that I really did not need anything else. He was absolutely right of course as it threw me into navigating out of sight of land using all my senses – something that has always stood me in good stead.

Aged 21, I had my own boat, the 7 metre Hunter 701 *Icterus* which was a stretched Hunter 19 (itself a Squib with a lid) and joined the second Orford cruiser North Sea 'race' with a memorable inland trip through northern Belgium and southern Holland. *Icterus* went on to cruise the Channel coast as far as the Scillies and northern Brittany and in 1984 to the Hardanger Fjord on the west coast of Norway via the Kiel Canal and the Baltic. This was all seat of the pants sailing in a small boat with minimal gear, low budget and some difficulties because of illness which made me familiar with hospitals in interesting places. If *Icterus* had a base it was Orford until I moved to Scotland in 1988 and sailed her round to Oban. Then in 1991 I sailed *Icterus* to Falmouth where I passed her to a friend who I knew could use her properly (running an outdoor centre at that stage left little time for cruising).

Sailing and kayaking on the West Coast never quite stopped and Orford's pull as the family base never waned, so I took every opportunity to return with Sue and our children, Lucy and Angus. Plans to do something different with our lives led to buying *Tahira* (the Tayana 42) and, from our point of view, a boat/travel capsule to live on. She arrived on a truck from France to be parked at Larkmans, on the Deben, while Peter Norris (OSC) became engineer and project manager on three winters of restoration. Orford, then Scotland, became her testing ground and in 2017 Sue and I sailed *Tahira* to Norway for three months as a taster for living aboard. 2018 saw us moving out of our house and onto the boat. We'll be back in Orford with *Tahira* of course!'

On re-reading this modest account by Richard of his development as a cruising sailor I am sorry that I did not insist on extracting more from him. Most of all I would love to know more details of his adventures in *Icterus*. I hope he took little notice of my rash advice to rely almost solely on a compass and chart as navigational aids. Even I was very glad, in later years, to make increasing use of GPS, without ever regarding it as infallible. I also valued the reassurance of VHF radio and up to date marine weather information.

Richard has only hinted at the contribution which he has made to the lives of many younger people through adventure training given at Chapelhope in the Scottish Borders, and more widely through his later social work. It is good to know that it was, at least partly, inspired by his boyhood sailing on the Ore and round our coast.

Writing in September 2019 I can report that *Tahira* is about to set sail from

Sardinia to Sicily with a view to wintering there. It is entirely appropriate that this takes her, and us, to the heart of the Mediterranean, the ocean of Ulysses, wiliest and most persistent of sailors. The German poet Heine once hailed it as 'the eternal sea' and years ago I copied a passage from another poet, Cavafy, an Egyptian Greek, into my personal treasury of cherished quotations:

> 'Be sure you are quite old when you drop anchor in Ithaca.
> Rich with experience you have gained upon your voyage,
> do not expect the island to give you riches. Ithaca
> has given you your wonderful voyage.
> Without Ithaca you would never have started.'

For me and many others, including those whose stories you have just read, Orford is our Ithaca.

Appendix

OSC Dinghy Cruising Trophy winners

The Day Trophy

1992	*Wanda*	J & M Sculpher
1993	*Buttercup II*	M & H Andrews
1994	*Buttercup II*	M & H Andrews
1996	*Wansfell*	A & E Feibusch
1997	*Pussyfoot*	R Roberts
1998	*Hayfever*	H Goody
1999	*Wanuq of Lorne*	D Bridges
2000	*Sea Urchin*	J & P Colvin
2001	*Sea Urchin*	J & P Colvin
2002	*Knot Shore*	A Rogers
2009	*Sea Urchin*	J & P Colvin
2013	*Popeye*	C Best
2014	*Ariel II*	R Roberts
2015	*Mizpah*	D Owen
2016	*Harris*	R Nex

The Colvin Chalice

2002	*Ten Grand*	E Feibusch
2003	*More Please*	S Ball
2004	*Goldfinger*	M & E Parish
2005	*Knot Shore*	A Rogers
2006	*Gazelle*	B Logan
2007	*Scatterling*	S & A Baker
2008	*Sea Urchin*	J Colvin
2009	*More Please*	S Ball
2010	*Scatterling*	S & A Baker
2011	*Popeye*	C Best
2012	*Popeye*	C Best
2013	*Popeye*	C Best
2014	*Popeye*	C Best
2015	*Popeye*	C Best
2016	*Popeye*	C Best

Rules for Crew on *Babaji*

1. Harness clipped to jackstays must be worn when going forward under way, especially at night.

2. One hand to hold on, one to work with.

3. Men must not pee overboard; most MOB result from this practice.

4. Be familiar with Safety Equipment and "Understand" list.

5. No smoking except on foredeck or in cockpit if door already closed.

6. Drinks must never be placed on chart table.

7. Blue Ensign hoisted at 0800 and lowered at 2000 in harbour. Worn under way but furled after dark when it may obscure stern light.

8. Mains'l halyard falls to be secured in RYA-approved manner and not hanked.

9. Sail covers to be fitted after berthing, and anti-sheet slapping bungees fitted.

10. Please volunteer for about one hour's maintenance a day (e.g. whipping rope ends, polishing brass, cleaning GRP and windows, applying teak oil if necessary)

Ray Glaister
Skipper, *Babaji*
Issue 2, 14 May 1998

Index of Yachts

Name, Orford Owner, Type and LOA in feet (where known), Chapter(s)

Aimee Tom Griffin, Robb Class 38	C23
Akathisia David Foreman, Hunter 19	C4
Alruna II Michael Pearce, Rival 38	C4
Andrum T Glover, up to 5 tons TM	C1
Anne Marie Smy, Fishing boat up to 15 tons	C1
Athene Robin Guilleret, Victoria 30	C13 23
Babaji Ray Glaister, Colvic Sailor Ketch 31.5	C10 12 13 16 17
Bosham Dreamer Colin Barry, Sadler 32	C12
Caveat David Robinson, Moody 336	C23
Chaperone Daniel Craig, Converted lifeboat 35	C2 3
Ciovo Howard Nash, Maxi 84 28	C7 9
Cirrus Henry Baker, Catalac 26	C8
Cornelia Chris Gill, Hood 38	C23
Crossjack VI Philippe Taylor, Freedom 33	C14
Curlew V Graham Bush, Najad 331	C17
Dewdrop Sir Ernest Rowney, up to 5 tons TM	C1
Dolphin Geoffrey Smeed, Sabre 27	C8
Dona 5-7 tons TM	C1
Dura James Robinson and Peter Norris, Westerly Storm 33	C6 11
Dutch Dream Barry Hitchcock, Westerly Fulmar 33	C23
Elan John McCarthy, Vindo 32	Foreword
Endeavor Candy Masters, Henk Tingen Steel Yawl 46	C23
Esmeralda Hallam Roberts, Gaffer 20	C1
Flapper Barry Hitchcock, Seal 22	C12
Gemma B de Quincy, up to 5 tons TM	C1
Gracedew Neil Iliff, Squib 19	C4
Gudgeon Ralph Webb, Bermudan Yawl 42	C1 2
Hebe Sir John Waite, Bombay Tomtit 18	C21 Last word
Hermione of Burnham Clem Lister, Contest 33	C8 12
Hind Thomas Eve	C1
Hvar Ben Johnston, Maxi 84 28	C7 9 14
Icterus Richard Waite, Hunter 701 23	C8 Last word
Iolanthe Ray Glaister, Westerly Tiger 25	C10

Katrina Charles Iliff, Regina R35	C9 20 Last word
Kehaar Charles Iliff, Hunter Sonata 22	C6 7 8 Last word
Killean Daniel Craig, Classic Motor Cruiser 35	C3
Kyle James Tomlinson, Westerly Konsort 29	C22
La Cucuracha Daniel Craig, Roach Class 26	C3
Lady Dane Tony Carr, Great Dane 28	C14
Mako David Foreman, J24	C7
Maratu Chris Gill, Sparkman and Stevens 34	C8 12
Martiena Mike Redmond, Southerly 32	C23
Mary George Brinkley, fishing boat up to 15 tons	C1
Mary Alice John Fulford, Sloop 28	C12
Melody of Suffolk Jamie Webb, Contest 31	C4 6
Merlin Dewar Davidson, Bermudan sloop 21	C1
Moette Ray Glaister, Halcyon 23	C10
Naivasha Michael Pearce, Hallberg Rassy 36	C14 23
Narcissus Dr A Travers Kevern, up to 5 tons TM	C1
Nerita James Robinson and Peter Norris, Snapdragon 21	C6 11
Patience of Orford Gilbert Aikens, Pintail 27	C5
Paulina P Faraday up to 5 tons TM	C1
Petronella James Robinson and Peter Norris, Frances 26	C11 12
Popeye Chris Best, Laser Stratos 16	C21
Premuda Charles Iliff, Maxi 84 28	C7 9 11
Privateer Thomas Eve, Sailing smack	C1
Quantz Richard Roberts, Wing 25	C4 7 8 9 11 12 13 14 15 16 17 19 23 Last word
Quintet Michael Pearce, Sadler 32	C4
Rinjinn Paul Blaxill, Contessa 26	C6 12
Rosie J James Tomlinson, Westerly Centaur 26	C22
Sage Nicholas Oglethorpe, Contessa 26	C8
Samango II James Tomlinson, Sadler 32	C22
Samara of Ore Chris Gill, Samphire 26	C7
Sanderling Jonnie Howard, Westerly Fulmar 32	C23
Scatterling Simon Baker, Wayfarer 16	C21
Scylla Rowney, up to 5 tons TM	C1
Sea Swallow Richard Roberts, 4-21	C5 7 8 Last word
Sea Urchin John Colvin, Wayfarer16	C21
Semiranis 1 John Fulford, Jeanneau Attalia 32	C12

Semiranis 2 John Fulford, Jeanneau Voyage 36	C12
Semiranis 3 John Fulford, Beneteau 40	C12
Sensibility Nicholas Oglethorpe, Contessa 32	C8
Sensibility Nicholas Oglethorpe, Sovereign 35	C8
Shelanda Ben Johnston, Westerly Storm 33	C17
Silba Chris Tweed, Maxi 84 28	C11
Siwash Thomas Eve, pocket cruiser 20	C1
Susak David Foreman, Maxi 84 28	C7 9 12
Tahira Richard Waite, Tayana 42	Last word
Talisker I James Tomlinson, Westerly Typhoon 37.5	C22 23
Tarka I Roddy Webb and Michael Pearce, Hurley 22	C4
Tarka II Roddy Webb and Michael Pearce, Halcyon 27	C4
Te'Aroa Colin Barry, Sadler 34	C12
The Cockleshell John Sherwill, open Victory Class Bermudan sloop 17.5	C4 21
Throstle Guy Marshall, Westerly Konsort 29	C23
Tuesday David Forman, Rival 41	C18 22
Ultra Thomas Eve	C1
Vale Gilbert Aikens, Broads cruiser 21	C4
Wahine James Tomlinson, Holman 26	C22
Wansfell Johnny and Liz Feibusch, Wayfarer 16	C21
Wenonah Charlie Stoker, fishing boat up to 15 tons	C1
Wild Child Chris Tweed, Leisure 23	C6 8
Willynilly John Seymour, open coble 21	C4 14 15 16 21
Withy Henry Baker, Contessa 26	C8
Wombat Howard Nash, Hunter Europa 19	C7 8
Xara Robin More Ede, Kestrel 22	C4
Zut Chris Tweed, Maxi 84 28	C7 9 12